Shojo Beat

S•A
Special A

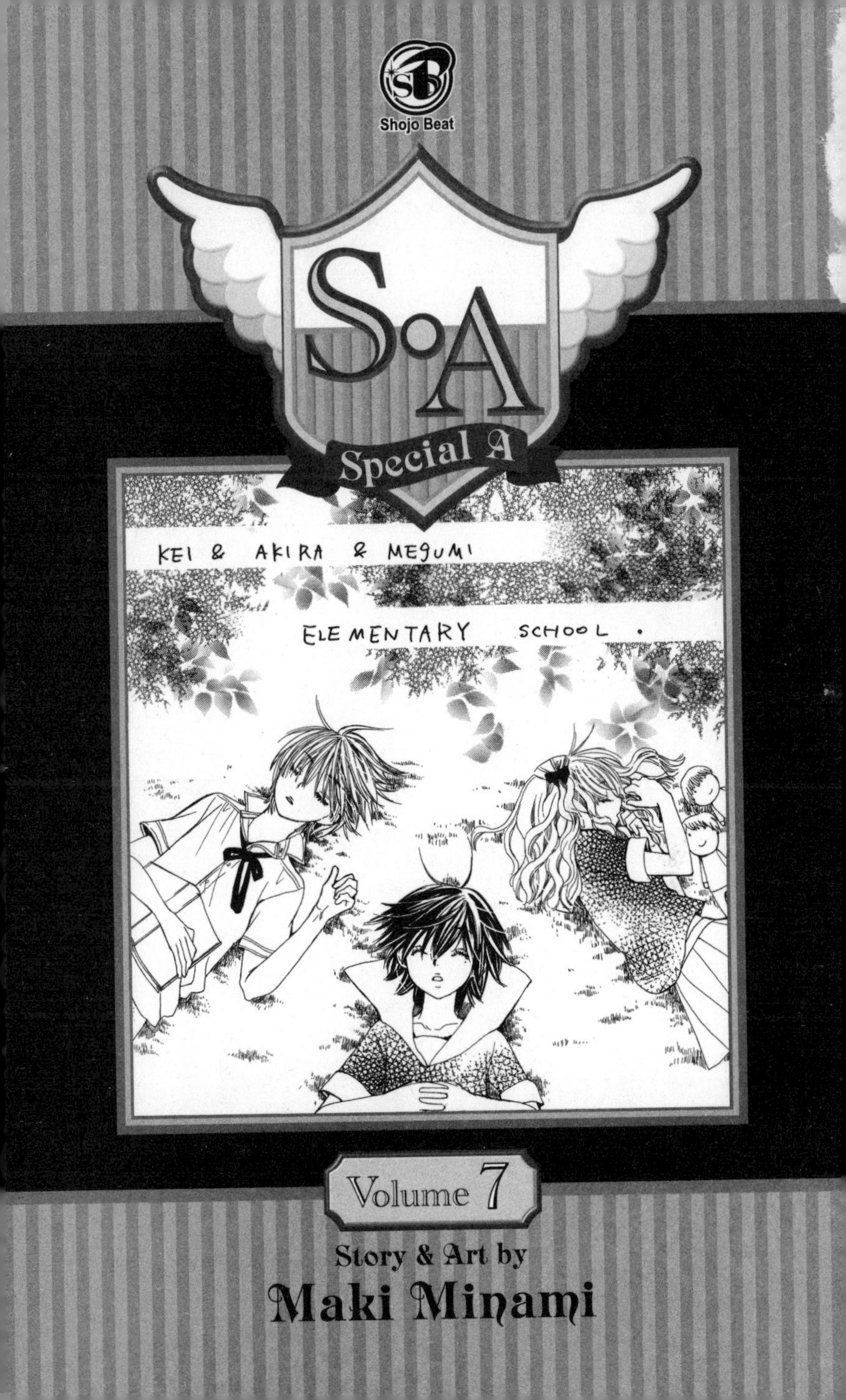
KEI & AKIRA & MEGUMI
ELEMENTARY SCHOOL.

Volume 7

Story & Art by

Maki Minami

STORY

★At the tender age of 6, carpenter's daughter Hikari Hanazono suffered her first loss to the wealthy Kei Takishima in a wrestling match. Now the hardworking Hikari has followed Kei to the most elite school for the rich just to beat him! I call this story "Overthrow Takishima! Rise Above Perpetual Second Place!!" It's the story of Hikari's sweat, tears and passion, with a little bit of love thrown in!

★Kei's grandfather sent his lackey Aoi to bring Kei to London. Kei refused, but Hikari developed an odd kinship with Aoi! Now Hikari is focused on the school athletic meet, but her grades are suffering...

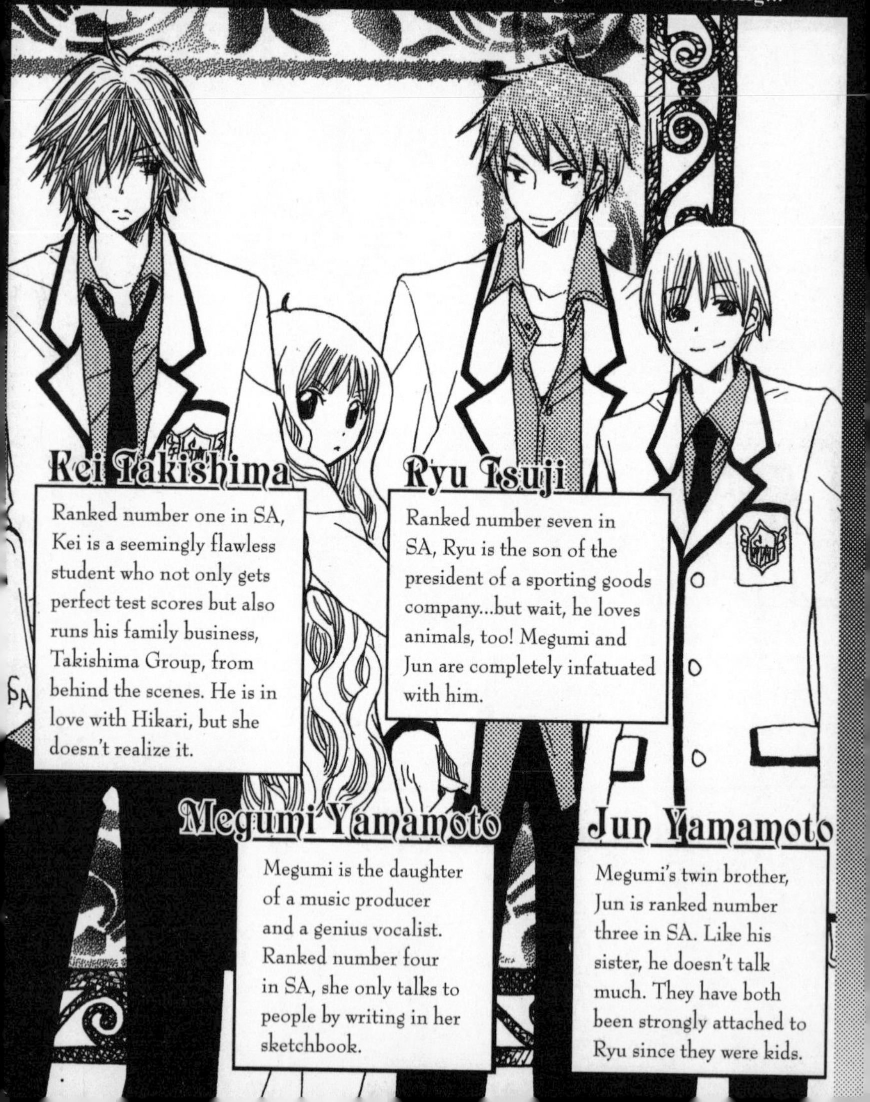

Kei Takishima

Ranked number one in SA, Kei is a seemingly flawless student who not only gets perfect test scores but also runs his family business, Takishima Group, from behind the scenes. He is in love with Hikari, but she doesn't realize it.

Ryu Tsuji

Ranked number seven in SA, Ryu is the son of the president of a sporting goods company...but wait, he loves animals, too! Megumi and Jun are completely infatuated with him.

Megumi Yamamoto

Megumi is the daughter of a music producer and a genius vocalist. Ranked number four in SA, she only talks to people by writing in her sketchbook.

Jun Yamamoto

Megumi's twin brother, Jun is ranked number three in SA. Like his sister, he doesn't talk much. They have both been strongly attached to Ryu since they were kids.

S·A CHARACTERS

Hikari goes to an elite school called Hakusenkan High School. This school divides each grade level into groups A through F, according to the students' test scores. Group A includes only the top seven students in each class. Then the top seven students from all grades' A-groups are put into a group called Special A, which is considered much higher than all others. Known as SA, they are "the elite among the elite."

What is "Special A"?

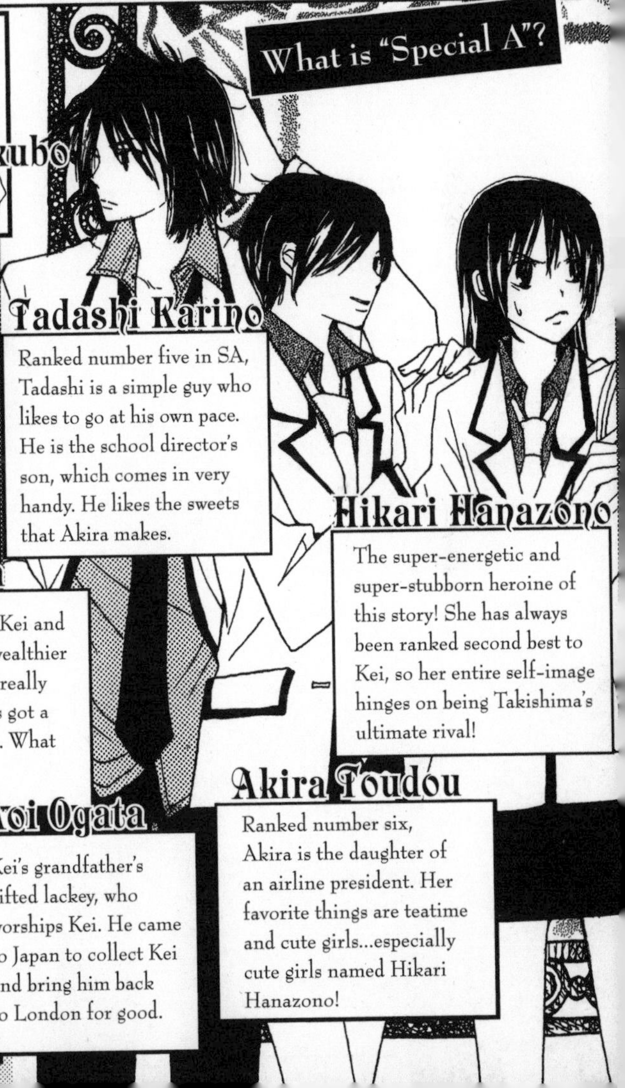

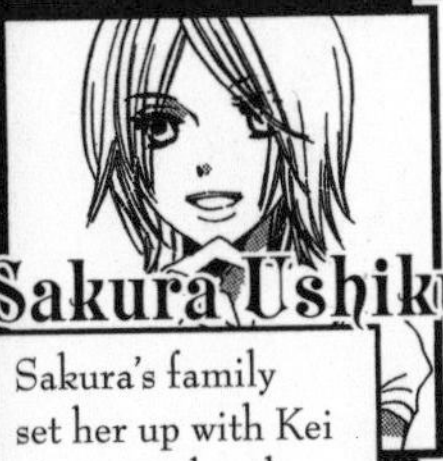

Sakura Ushikubo

Sakura's family set her up with Kei via a matchmaker. But if she married Kei, it would only be for her family's convenience. Right now she is head-over-heels for Jun.♥

Tadashi Karino

Ranked number five in SA, Tadashi is a simple guy who likes to go at his own pace. He is the school director's son, which comes in very handy. He likes the sweets that Akira makes.

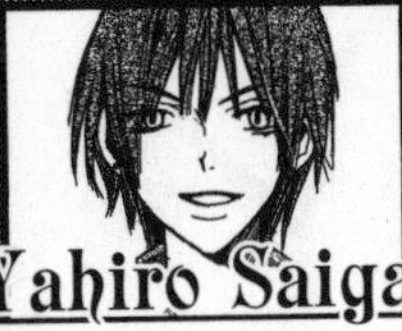

Yahiro Saiga

A childhood friend of Kei and Akira, Yahiro is even wealthier than Kei. He seems to really care for Akira, but he's got a mysterious side as well. What is his real objective?

Hikari Hanazono

The super-energetic and super-stubborn heroine of this story! She has always been ranked second best to Kei, so her entire self-image hinges on being Takishima's ultimate rival!

Aoi Ogata

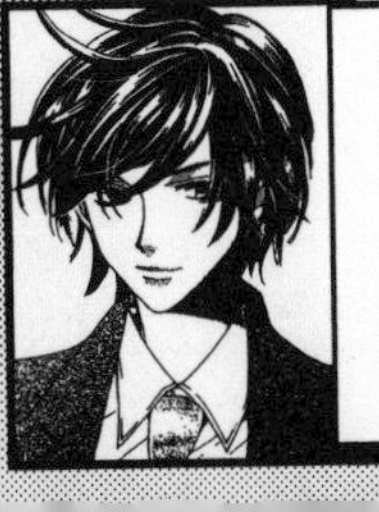

Kei's grandfather's gifted lackey, who worships Kei. He came to Japan to collect Kei and bring him back to London for good.

Akira Toudou

Ranked number six, Akira is the daughter of an airline president. Her favorite things are teatime and cute girls...especially cute girls named Hikari Hanazono!

Contents

Chapter 35...................... 5

Chapter 36................... 35

Chapter 37................... 65

Chapter 38................... 98

Chapter 39................. 131

Chapter 40................. 161

Bonus Pages 191

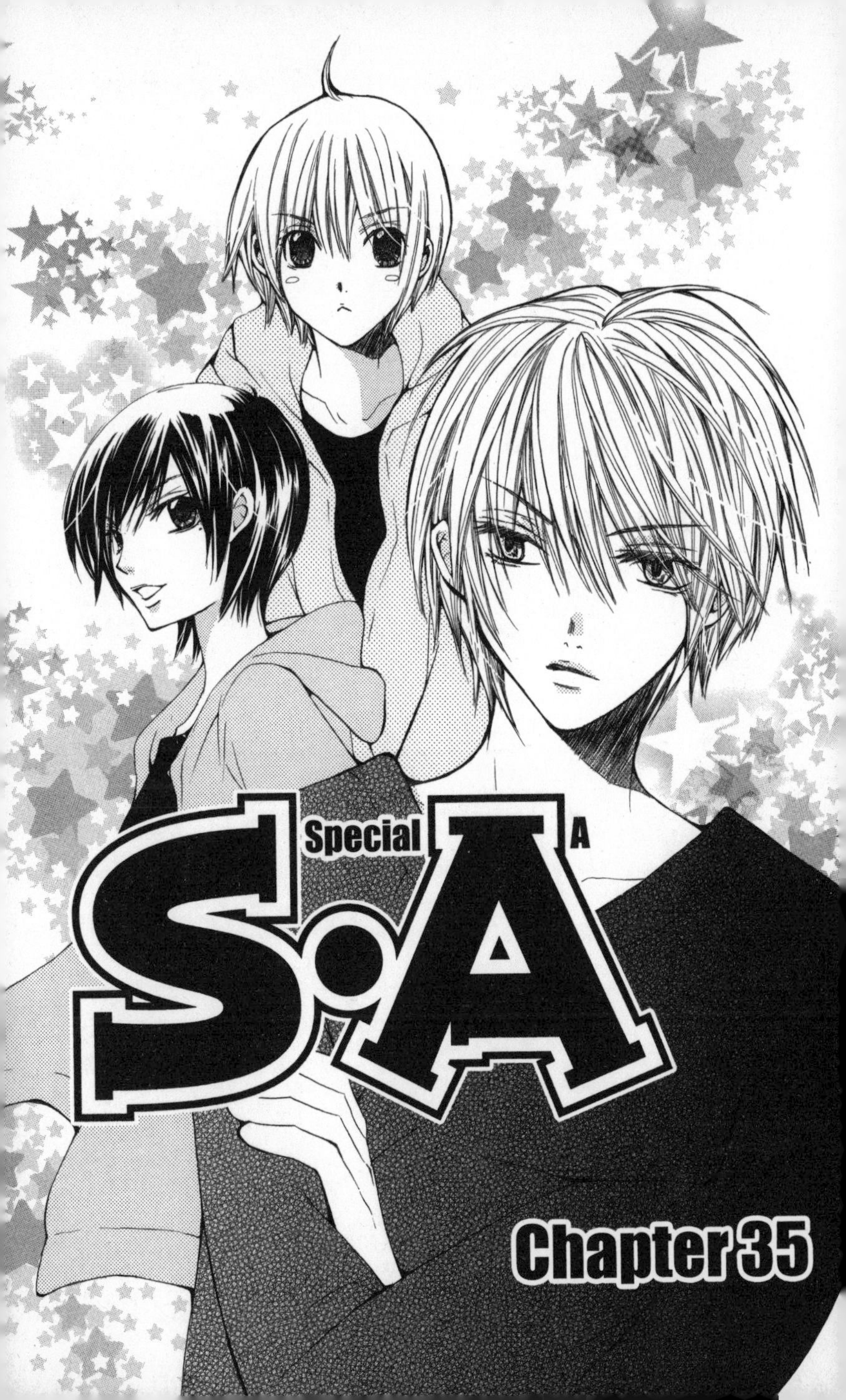
Special A
S·A
Chapter 35

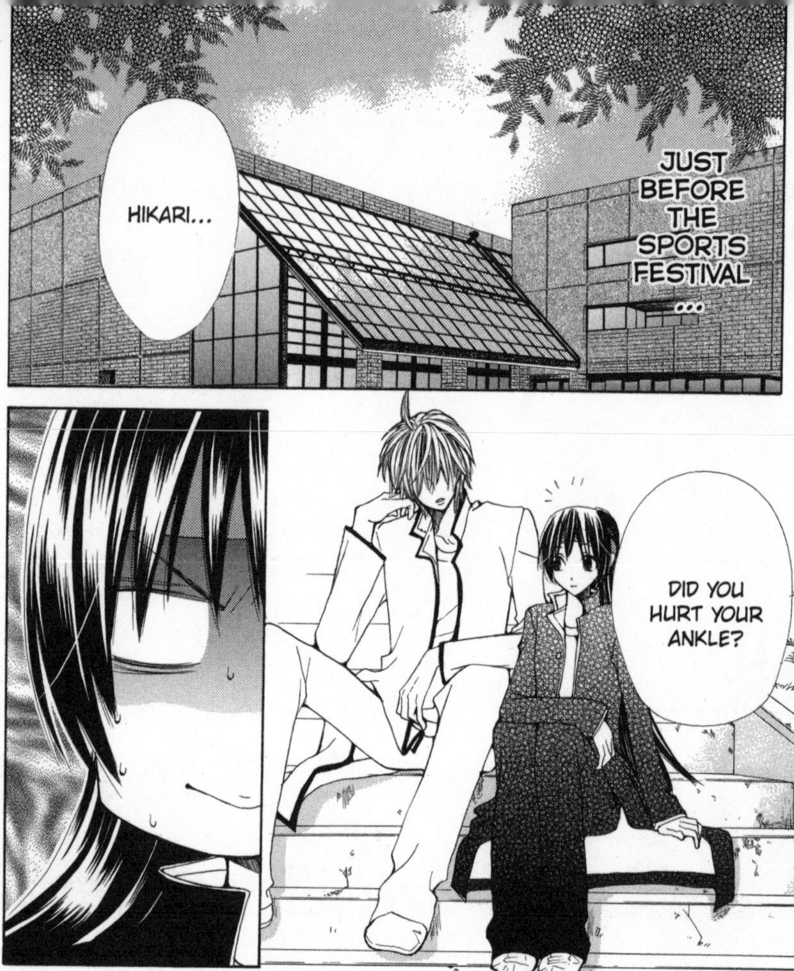
JUST BEFORE THE SPORTS FESTIVAL...
HIKARI...
DID YOU HURT YOUR ANKLE?

• CHAPTER 35 •

WHEN THE SPORTS FESTIVAL STORY WAS FIRST PUBLISHED, I HAD ALL OF THE TEAMS WEARING WRISTBANDS. BUT WE FOUND A TON OF MISTAKES, LIKE KEI WEARING THE BAND ON HIS RIGHT WRIST AND THEN SUDDENLY IT'S ON HIS LEFT. WE CORRECTED ALL OF THEM WHEN WE DID THE MANGA...

PLUS, THERE WAS A NIGHT SCENE WITH KEI THAT SUDDENLY TURNED INTO DAYTIME!

THERE WAS JUST SO MUCH TO CORRECT IN THIS CHAPTER!

THEY ARE ALL CORRECTED IN THIS VERSION, THOUGH...I THINK...M-MAYBE...

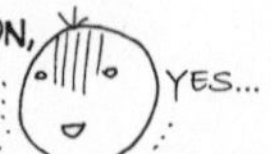
YES...
I'M AN IDIOT.

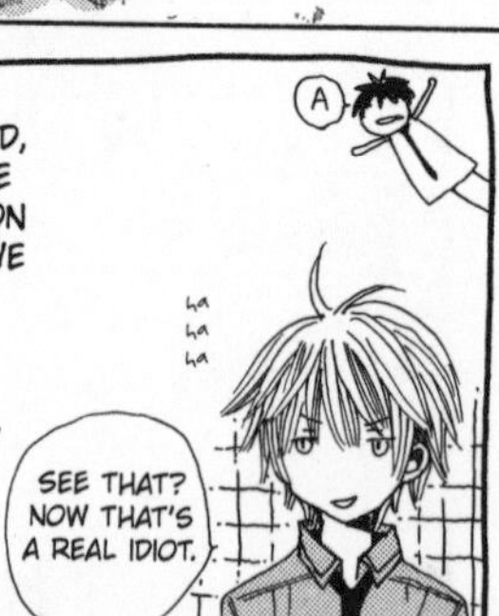
A
HA HA HA
SEE THAT? NOW THAT'S A REAL IDIOT.

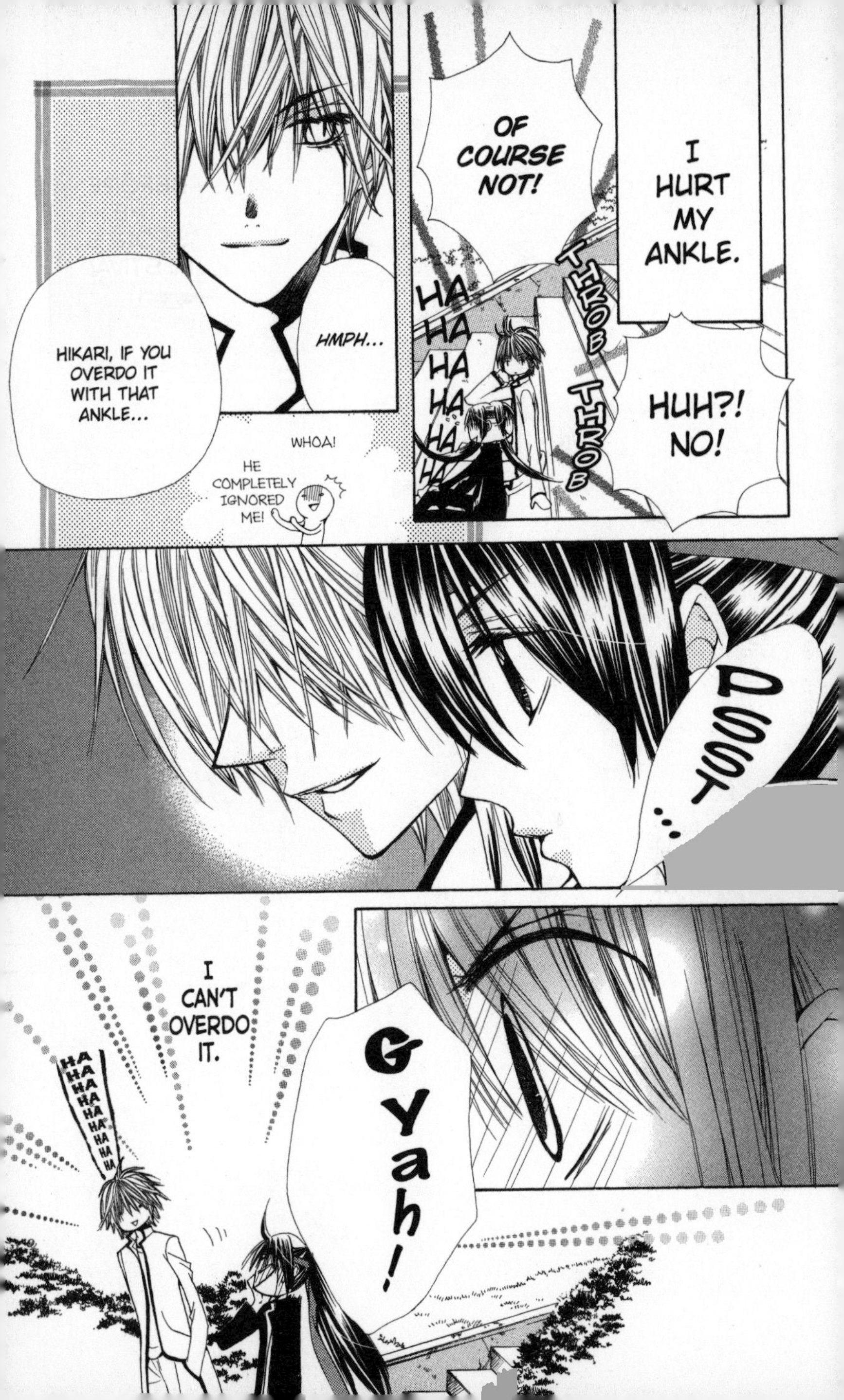
I HURT MY ANKLE.
HUH?! NO!
OF COURSE NOT!
THROB THROB THROB
HA HA HA HA HA HA
HMPH...
HIKARI, IF YOU OVERDO IT WITH THAT ANKLE...
WHOA!
HE COMPLETELY IGNORED ME!
PSST...
Gyah!
I CAN'T OVERDO IT.
HA HA HA HA HA HA HA HA HA

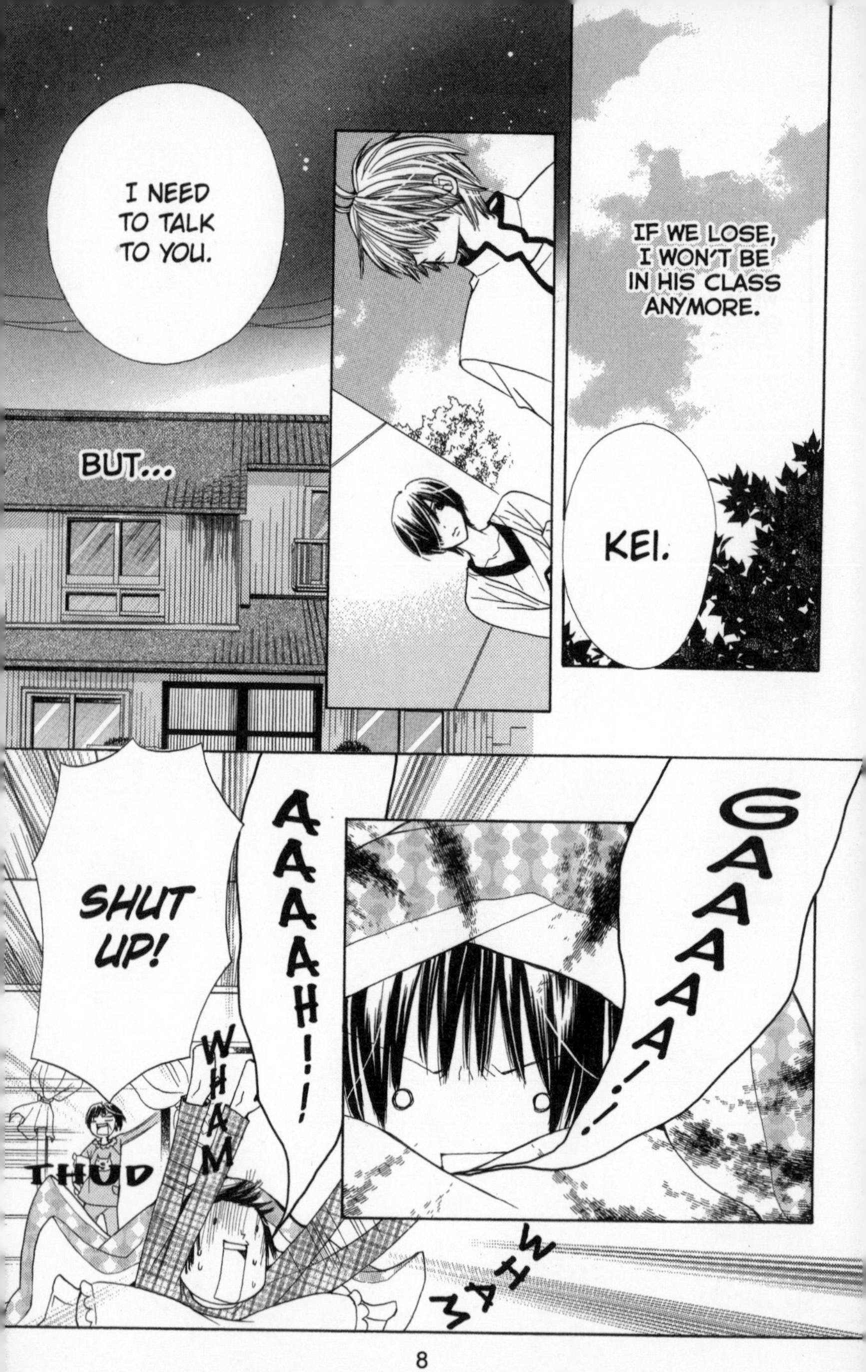

IF WE LOSE, I WON'T BE IN HIS CLASS ANYMORE.
KEI.
I NEED TO TALK TO YOU.
BUT...
GAAAAA--!!
AAAAH!!!
SHUT UP!
WHAM
THUD
WHAM

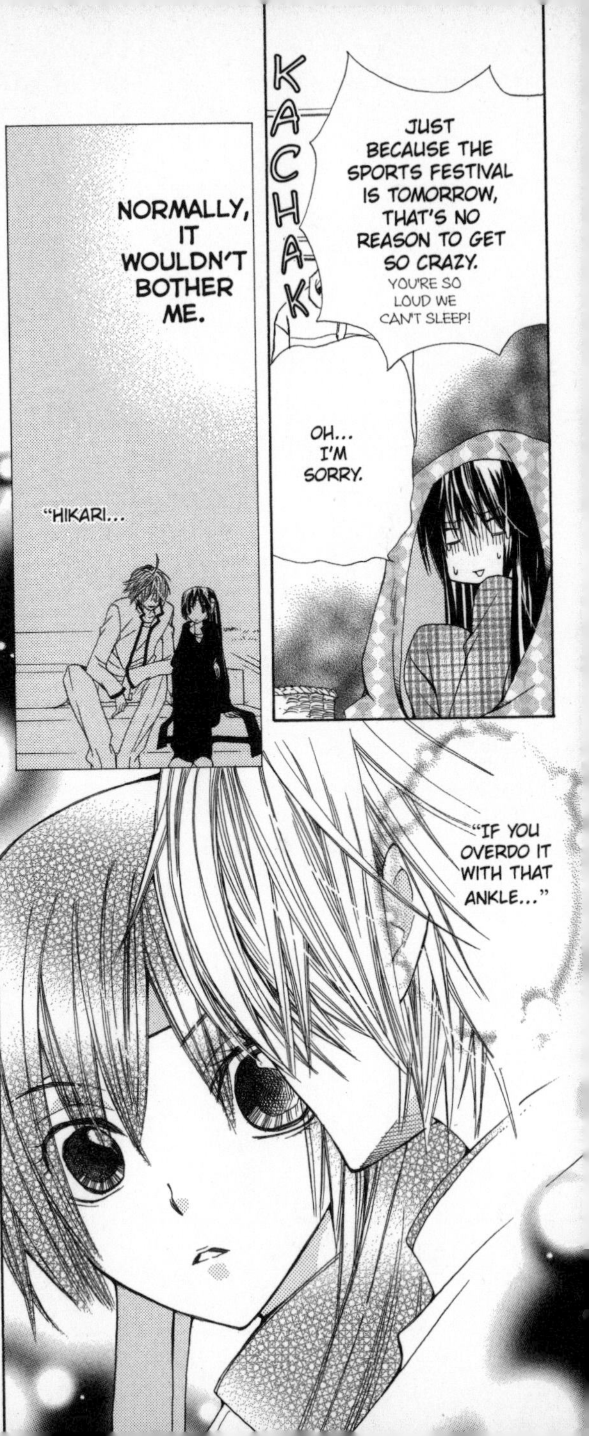
KACHAK
JUST BECAUSE THE SPORTS FESTIVAL IS TOMORROW, THAT'S NO REASON TO GET SO CRAZY.
YOU'RE SO LOUD WE CAN'T SLEEP!
OH... I'M SORRY.
NORMALLY, IT WOULDN'T BOTHER ME.
"HIKARI...
"IF YOU OVERDO IT WITH THAT ANKLE..."

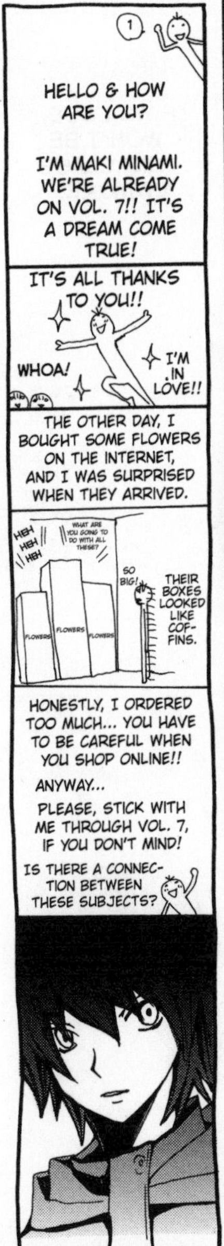
1
HELLO & HOW ARE YOU?
I'M MAKI MINAMI. WE'RE ALREADY ON VOL. 7!! IT'S A DREAM COME TRUE!
IT'S ALL THANKS TO YOU!!
WHOA!
I'M IN LOVE!!
THE OTHER DAY, I BOUGHT SOME FLOWERS ON THE INTERNET, AND I WAS SURPRISED WHEN THEY ARRIVED.
HEH HEH HEH
WHAT ARE YOU GOING TO DO WITH ALL THESE?
SO BIG!
THEIR BOXES LOOKED LIKE COFFINS.
FLOWERS
FLOWERS
FLOWERS
HONESTLY, I ORDERED TOO MUCH... YOU HAVE TO BE CAREFUL WHEN YOU SHOP ONLINE!!
ANYWAY...
PLEASE, STICK WITH ME THROUGH VOL. 7, IF YOU DON'T MIND!
IS THERE A CONNECTION BETWEEN THESE SUBJECTS?

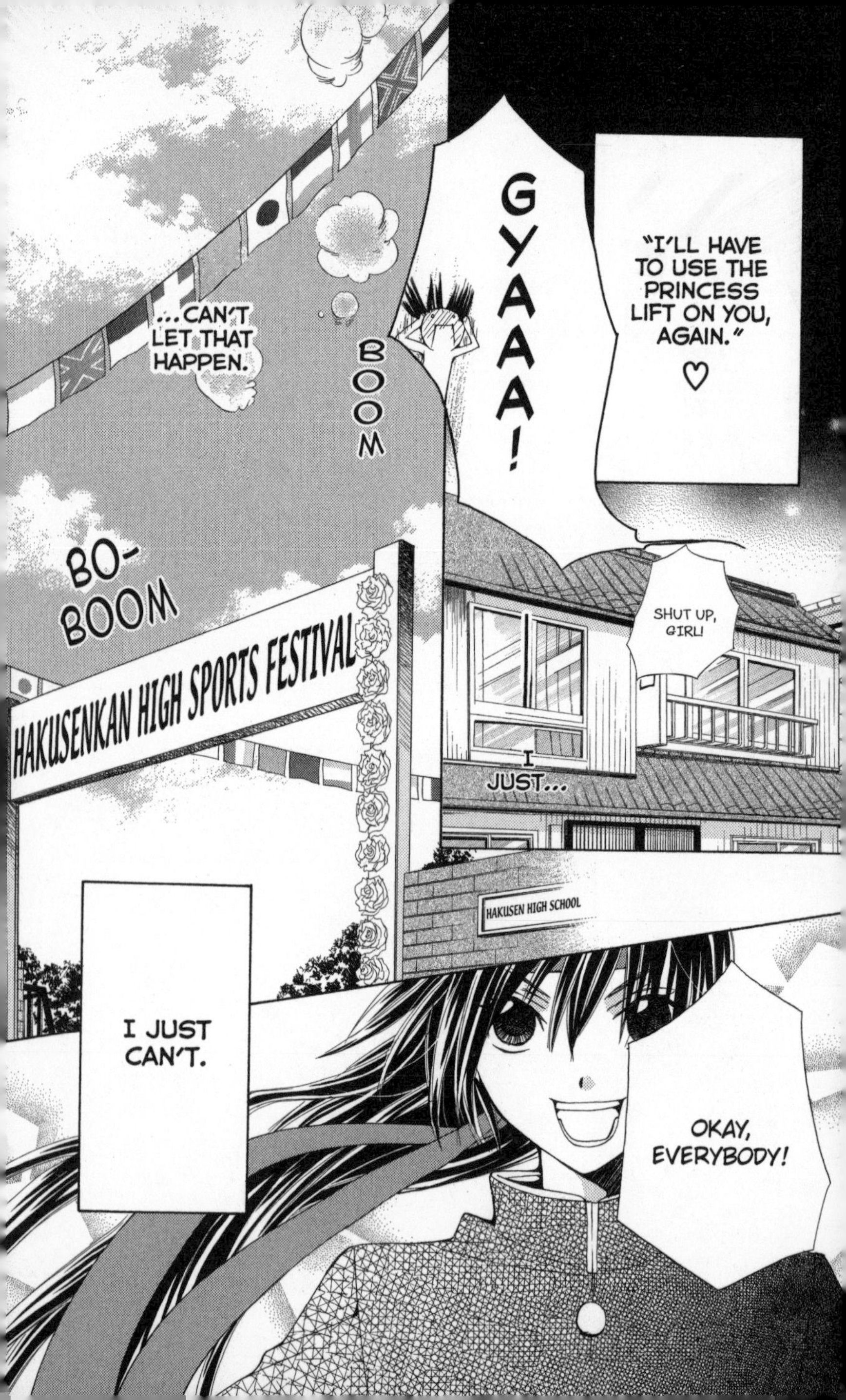
"I'LL HAVE TO USE THE PRINCESS LIFT ON YOU, AGAIN." ♡
GYAAA!
BOOM
...CAN'T LET THAT HAPPEN.
BO-BOOM
HAKUSENKAN HIGH SPORTS FESTIVAL
SHUT UP, GIRL!
I JUST...
HAKUSEN HIGH SCHOOL
OKAY, EVERYBODY!
I JUST CAN'T.

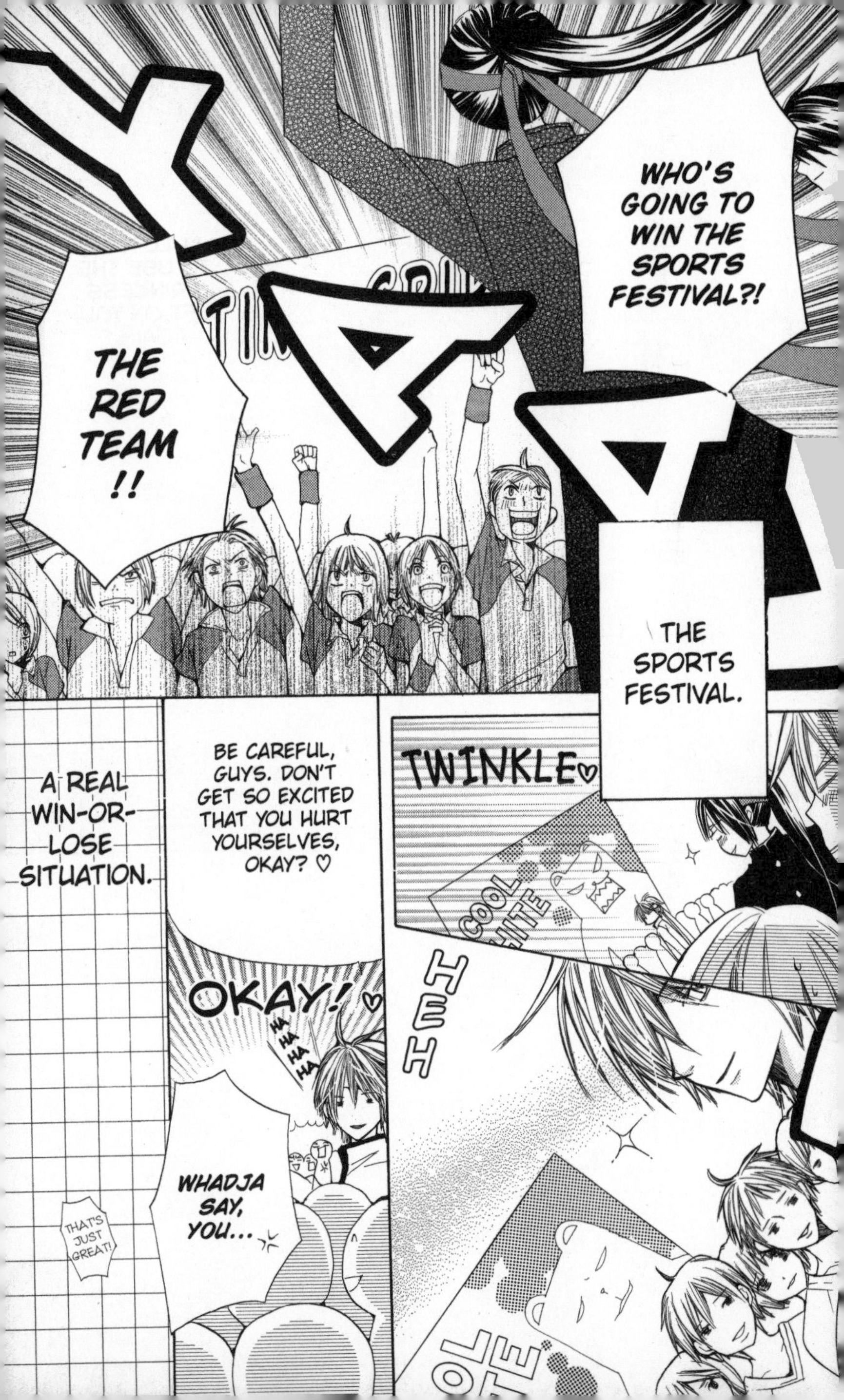
WHO'S GOING TO WIN THE SPORTS FESTIVAL?!
THE RED TEAM!!
THE SPORTS FESTIVAL.
TWINKLE♡
COOL
HEH
BE CAREFUL, GUYS. DON'T GET SO EXCITED THAT YOU HURT YOURSELVES, OKAY? ♡
OKAY! ♡
HA HA HA HA
WHADJA SAY, YOU...
THAT'S JUST GREAT!
A REAL WIN-OR-LOSE SITUATION.

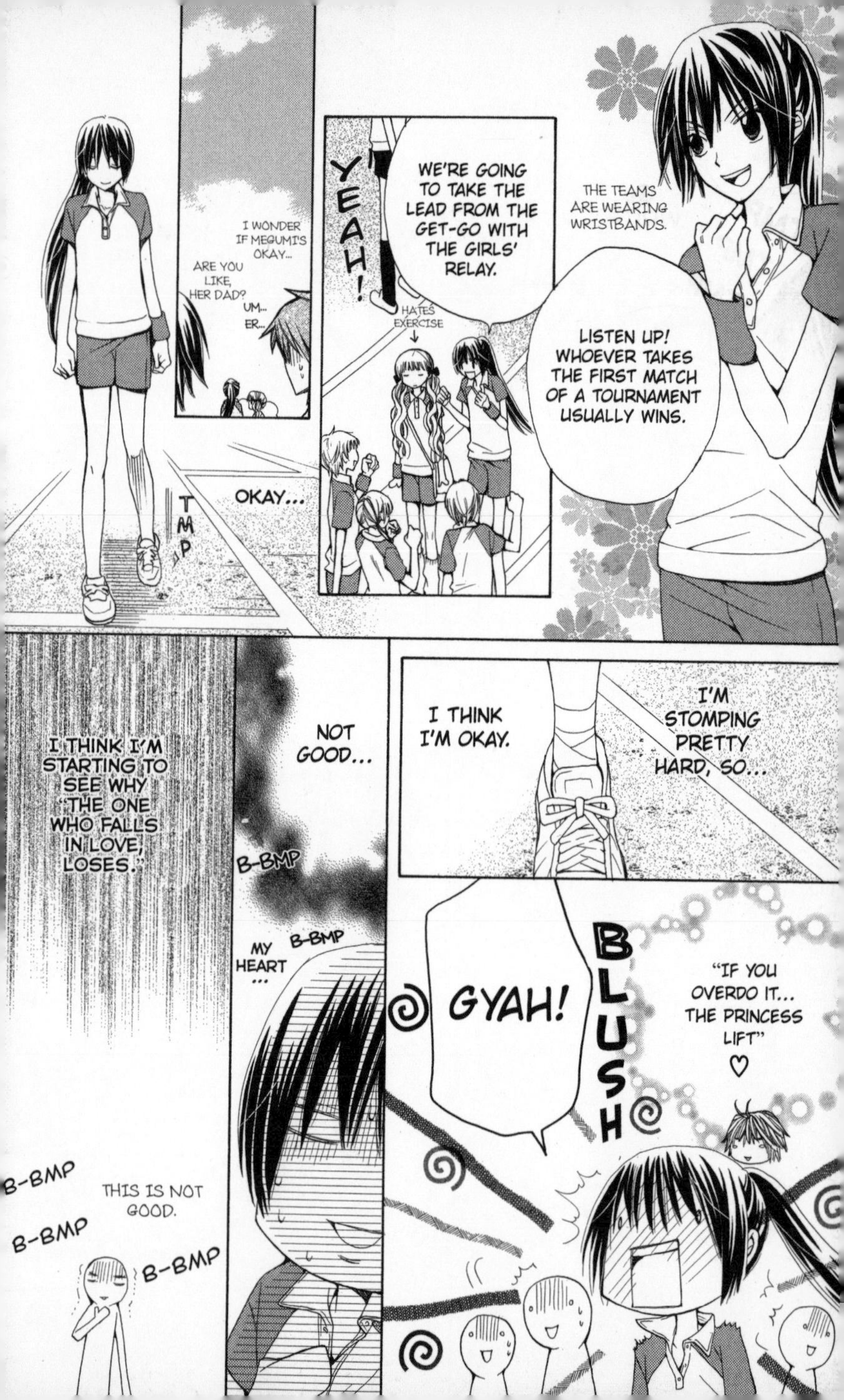
THE TEAMS ARE WEARING WRISTBANDS.
LISTEN UP! WHOEVER TAKES THE FIRST MATCH OF A TOURNAMENT USUALLY WINS.
WE'RE GOING TO TAKE THE LEAD FROM THE GET-GO WITH THE GIRLS' RELAY.
YEAH!
HATES EXERCISE
I WONDER IF MEGUMI'S OKAY...
ARE YOU LIKE, HER DAD?
UM... ER...
OKAY...
TMP
I'M STOMPING PRETTY HARD, SO...
I THINK I'M OKAY.
"IF YOU OVERDO IT... THE PRINCESS LIFT" ♡
BLUSH
GYAH!
NOT GOOD...
B-BMP
B-BMP
MY HEART...
I THINK I'M STARTING TO SEE WHY "THE ONE WHO FALLS IN LOVE, LOSES."
B-BMP
THIS IS NOT GOOD.
B-BMP
B-BMP

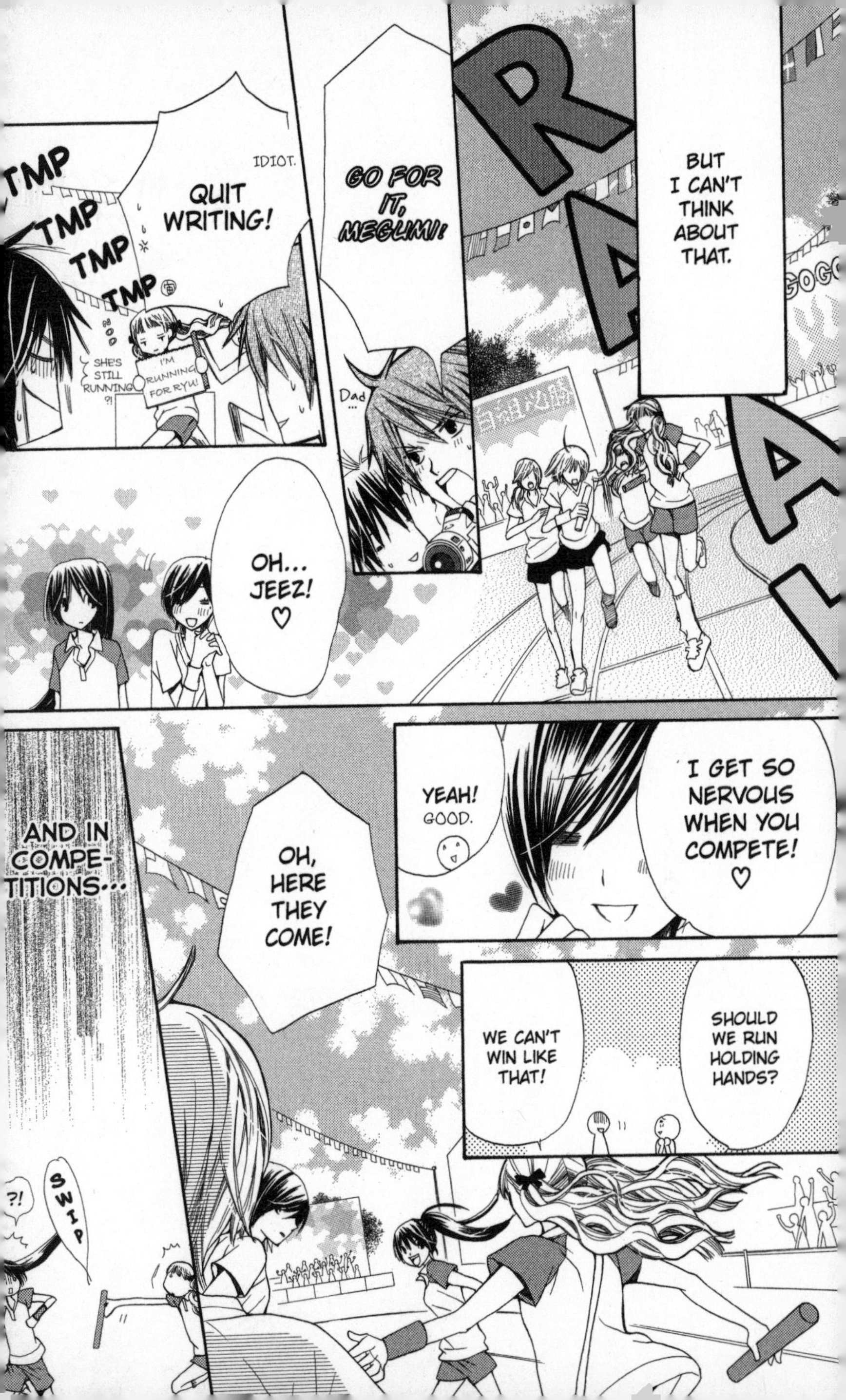

BUT I CAN'T THINK ABOUT THAT.
RAA
GO FOR IT, MEGUMI!
Dad...
QUIT WRITING!
IDIOT.
TMP
TMP
TMP
TMP
NOD
I'M RUNNING FOR RYU!
SHE'S STILL RUNNING?!
OH... JEEZ! ♡
I GET SO NERVOUS WHEN YOU COMPETE! ♡
YEAH!
GOOD.
SHOULD WE RUN HOLDING HANDS?
WE CAN'T WIN LIKE THAT!
OH, HERE THEY COME!
AND IN COMPETITIONS...
SWIP
?!

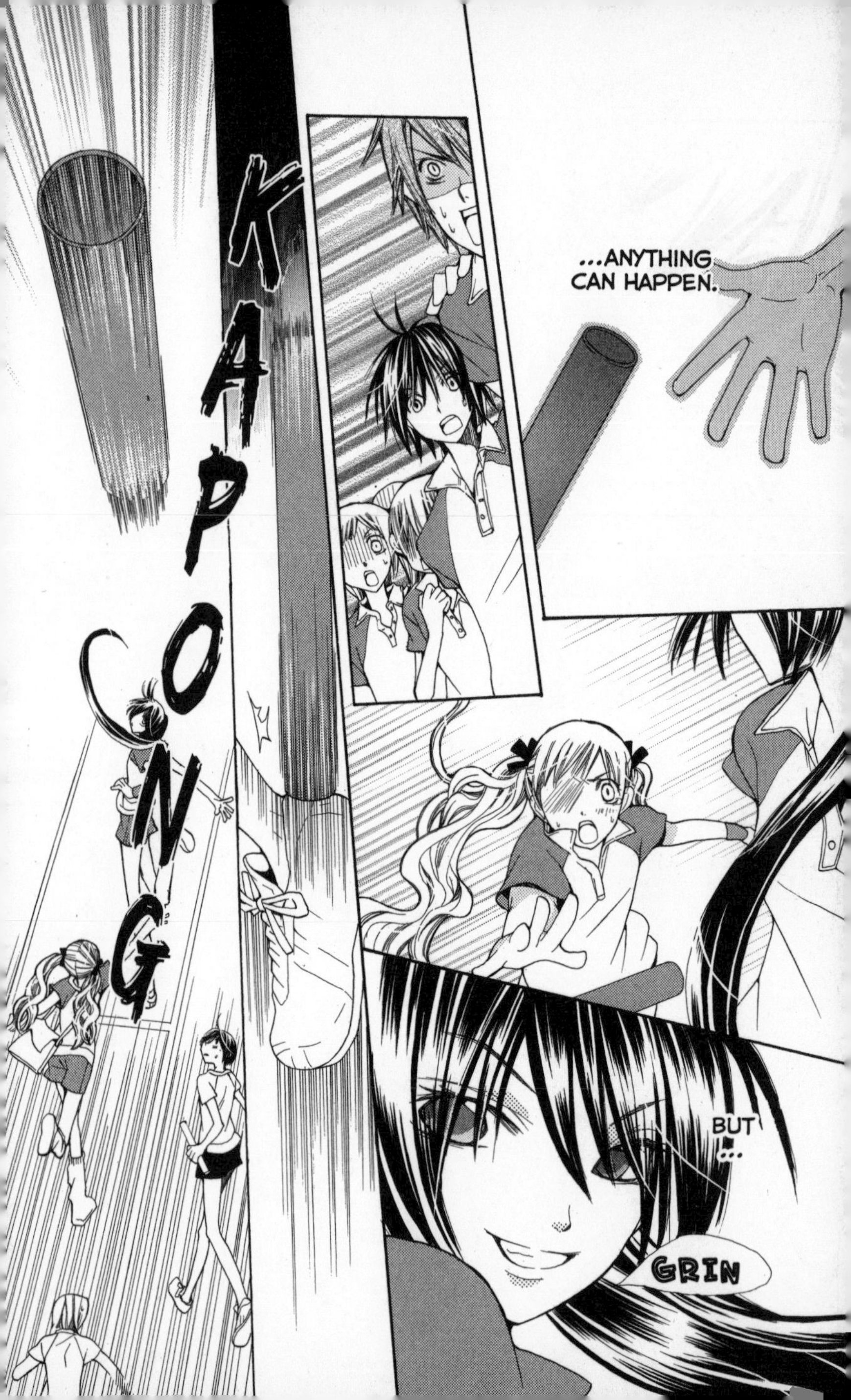
...ANYTHING CAN HAPPEN.
KAPONG
BUT ...
GRIN

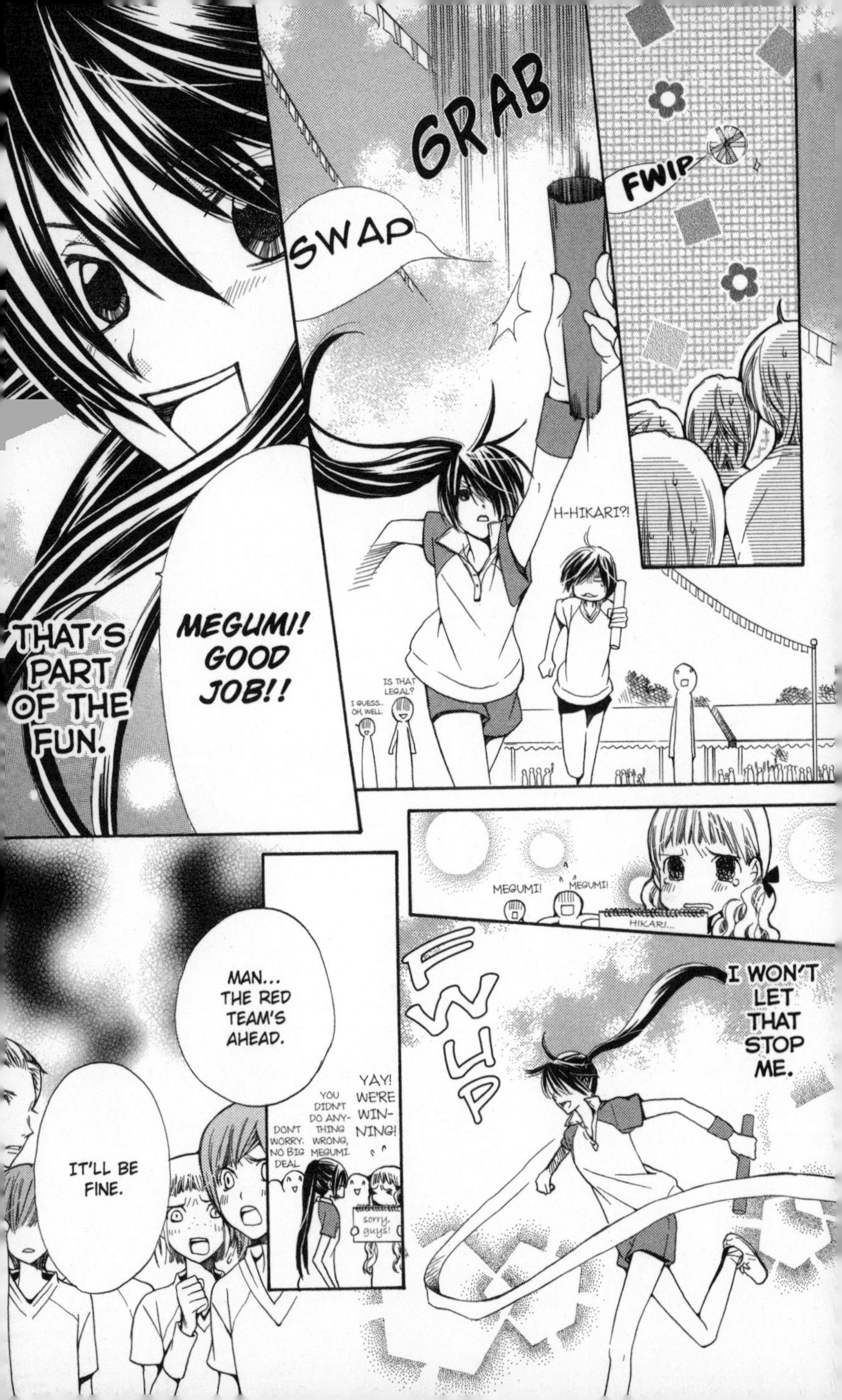
FWIP
GRAB
SWAP
H-HIKARI?!
IS THAT LEGAL?
I GUESS... OH, WELL.
MEGUMI! GOOD JOB!!
THAT'S PART OF THE FUN.
MEGUMI!
MEGUMI!
HIKARI...
I WON'T LET THAT STOP ME.
FWUP
YAY! WE'RE WIN-NING!
YOU DIDN'T DO ANY-THING WRONG, MEGUMI.
DON'T WORRY. NO BIG DEAL
sorry, guys!
MAN... THE RED TEAM'S AHEAD.
IT'LL BE FINE.

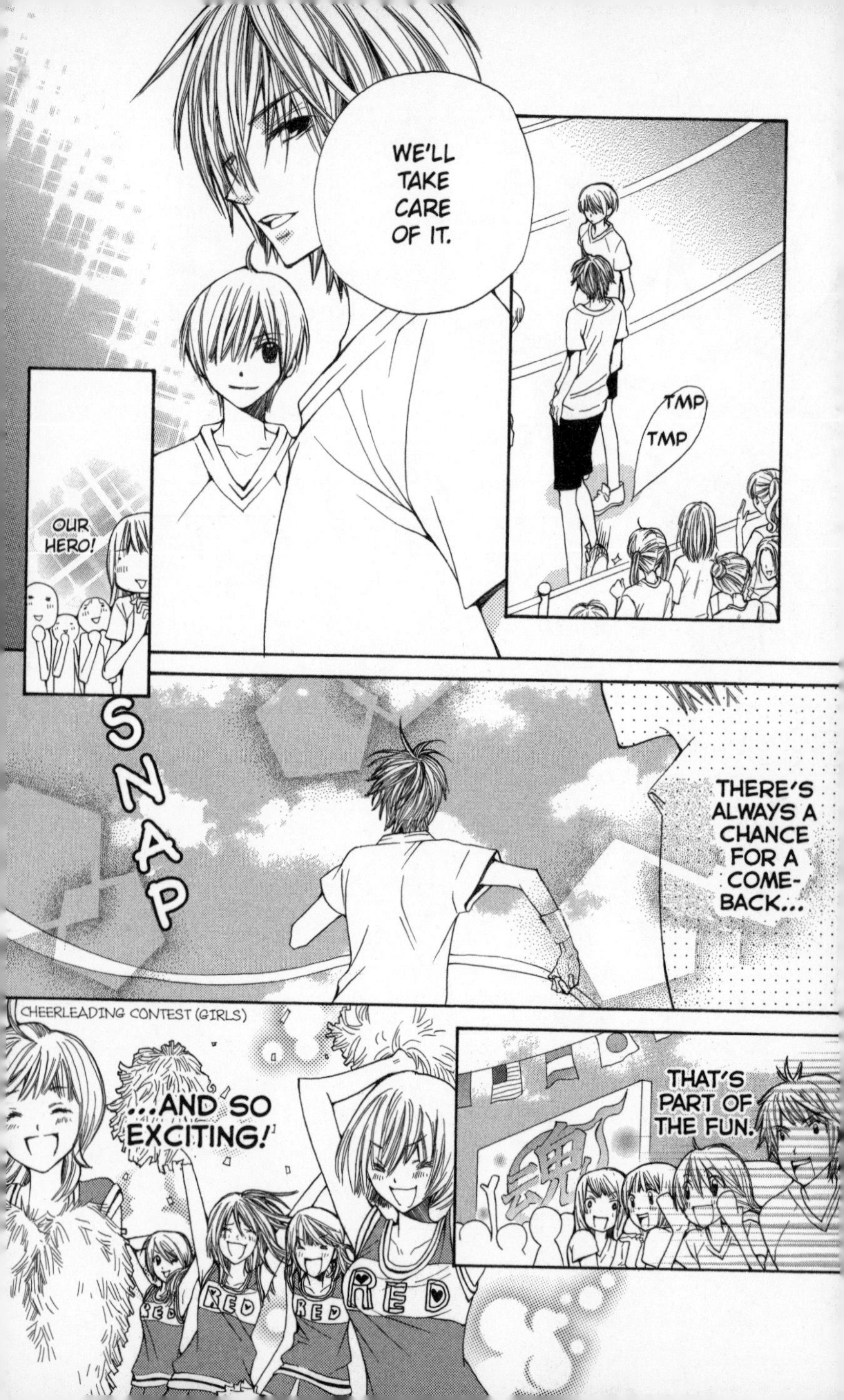
WE'LL TAKE CARE OF IT.
TMP
TMP
OUR HERO!
SNAP
THERE'S ALWAYS A CHANCE FOR A COME-BACK...
THAT'S PART OF THE FUN.
CHEERLEADING CONTEST (GIRLS)
...AND SO EXCITING!
RED
RED
RED
RED

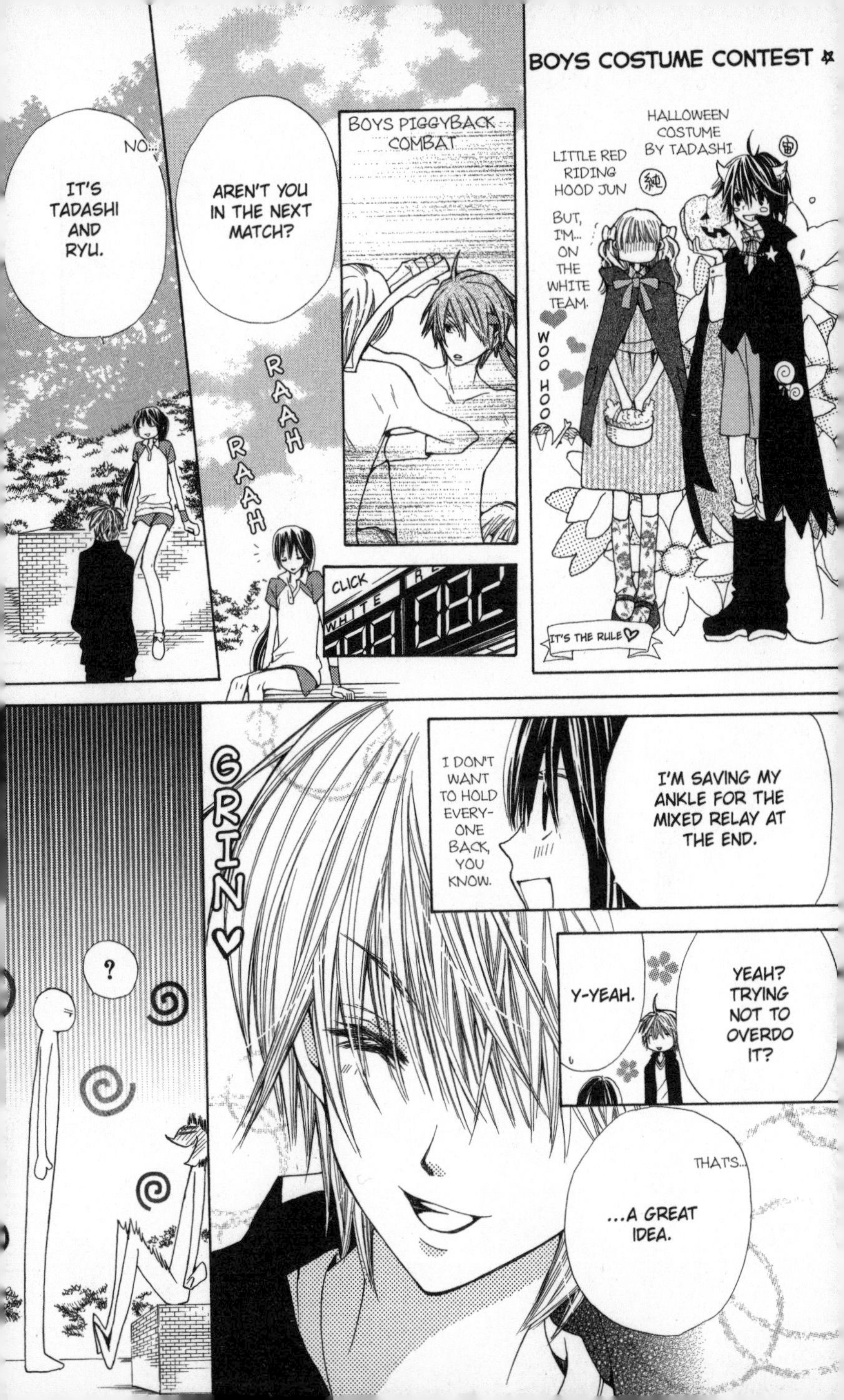
BOYS COSTUME CONTEST ☆
HALLOWEEN COSTUME BY TADASHI
LITTLE RED RIDING HOOD JUN
BUT, I'M... ON THE WHITE TEAM.
WOO HOO
IT'S THE RULE ♡
BOYS PIGGYBACK COMBAT
CLICK
WHITE
RAAH
RAAH
AREN'T YOU IN THE NEXT MATCH?
NO...
IT'S TADASHI AND RYU.
I'M SAVING MY ANKLE FOR THE MIXED RELAY AT THE END.
I DON'T WANT TO HOLD EVERY-ONE BACK, YOU KNOW.
YEAH? TRYING NOT TO OVERDO IT?
Y-YEAH.
THAT'S...
...A GREAT IDEA.
GRIN ♡
?

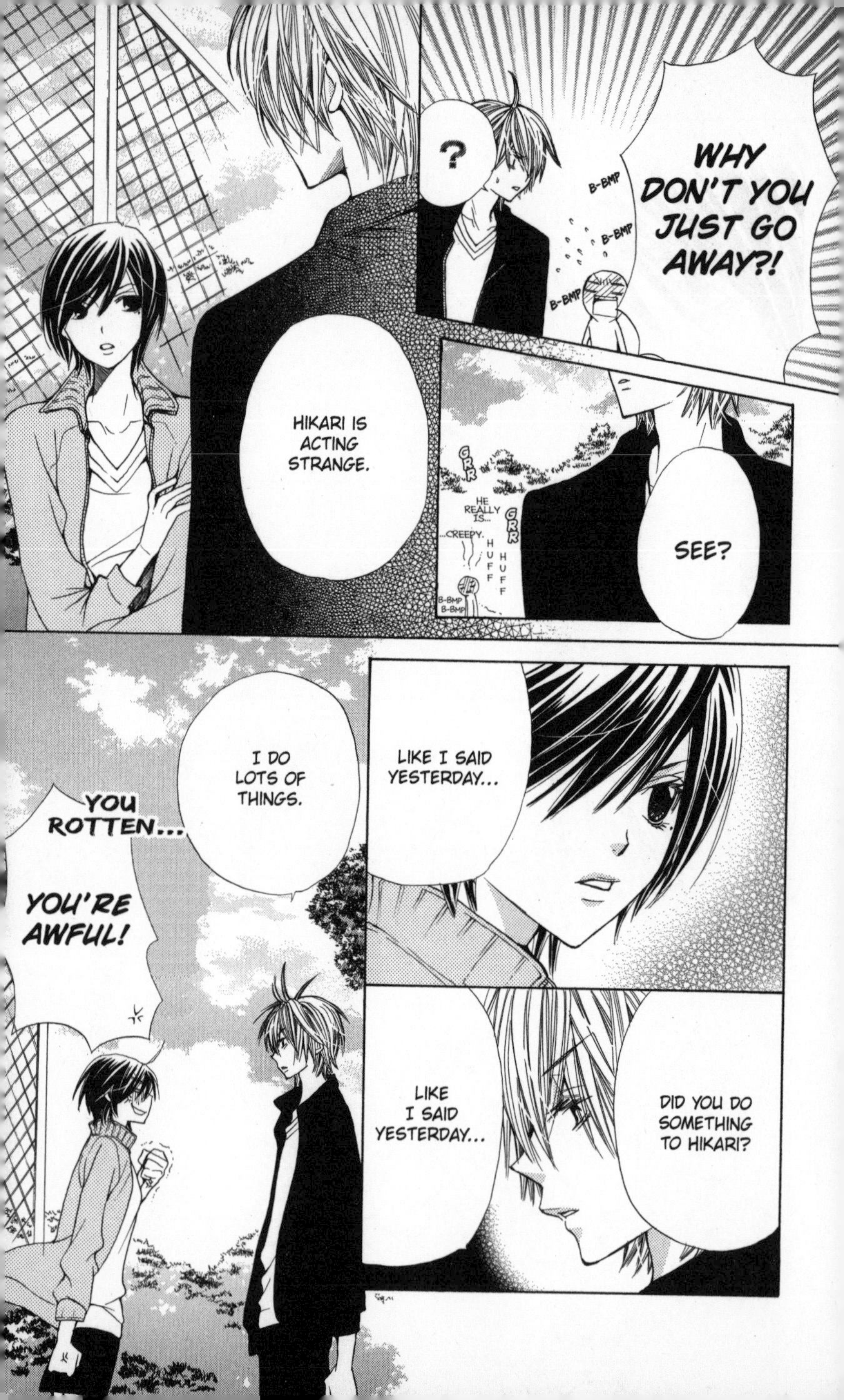
WHY DON'T YOU JUST GO AWAY?!
B-BMP
B-BMP
B-BMP
?
SEE?
GRR
GRR
HE REALLY IS... ...CREEPY.
HUFF HUFF
B-BMP B-BMP
HIKARI IS ACTING STRANGE.
LIKE I SAID YESTERDAY...
DID YOU DO SOMETHING TO HIKARI?
LIKE I SAID YESTERDAY...
I DO LOTS OF THINGS.
YOU ROTTEN...
YOU'RE AWFUL!

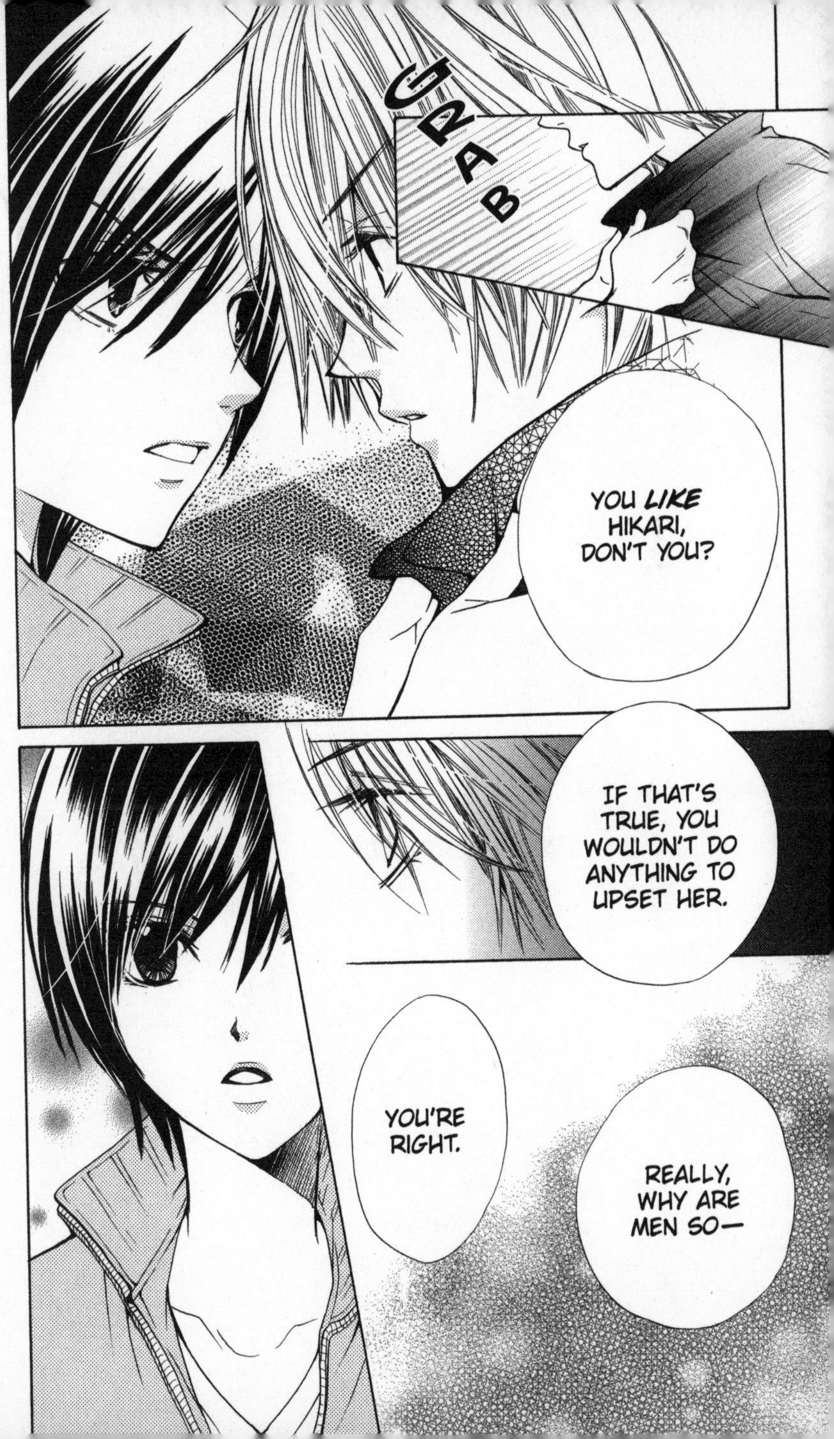
GRAB
YOU LIKE HIKARI, DON'T YOU?
IF THAT'S TRUE, YOU WOULDN'T DO ANYTHING TO UPSET HER.
REALLY, WHY ARE MEN SO—
YOU'RE RIGHT.

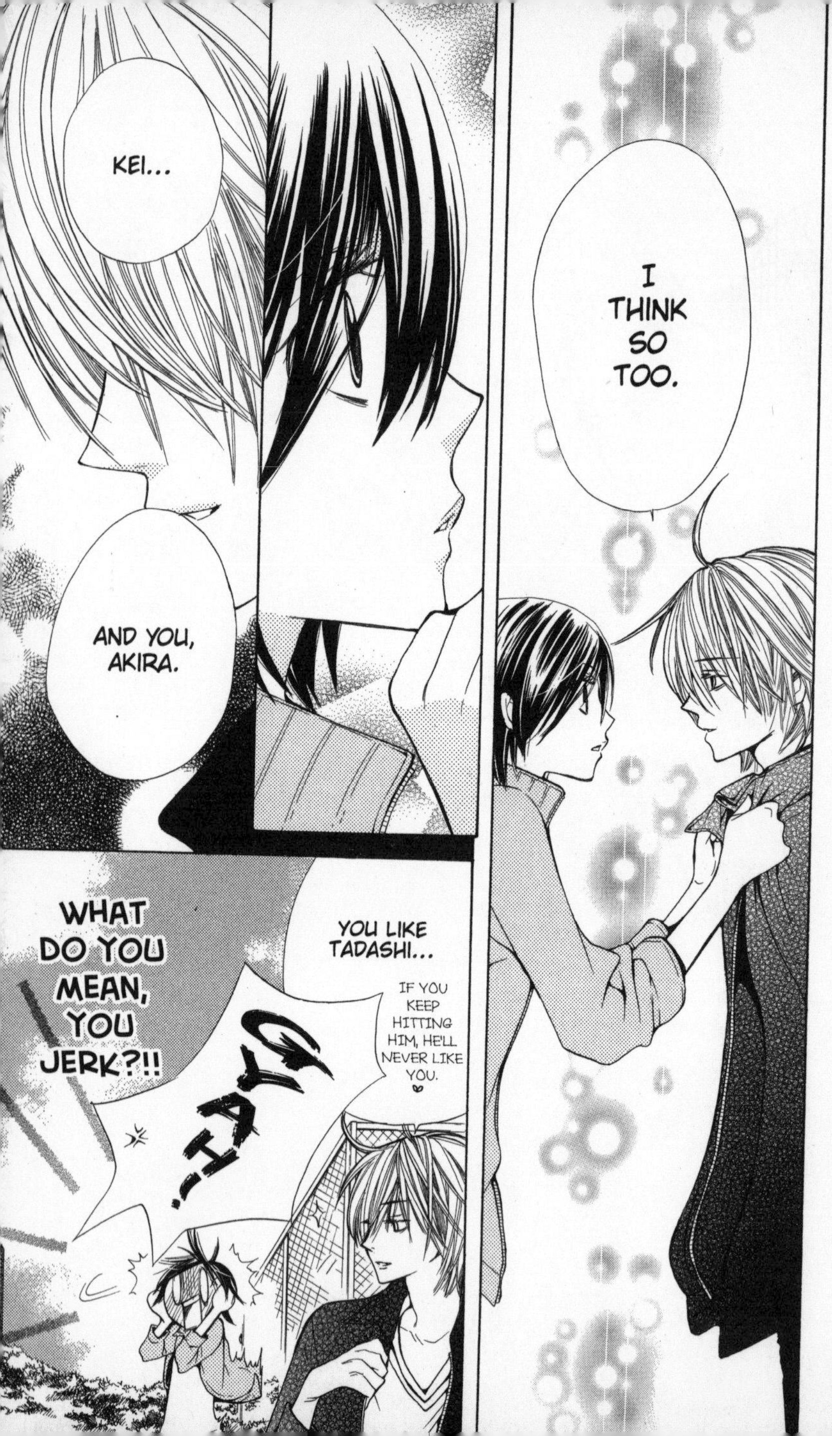
I THINK SO TOO.
KEI...
AND YOU, AKIRA.
YOU LIKE TADASHI...
IF YOU KEEP HITTING HIM, HE'LL NEVER LIKE YOU.
GYAH!
WHAT DO YOU MEAN, YOU JERK?!!

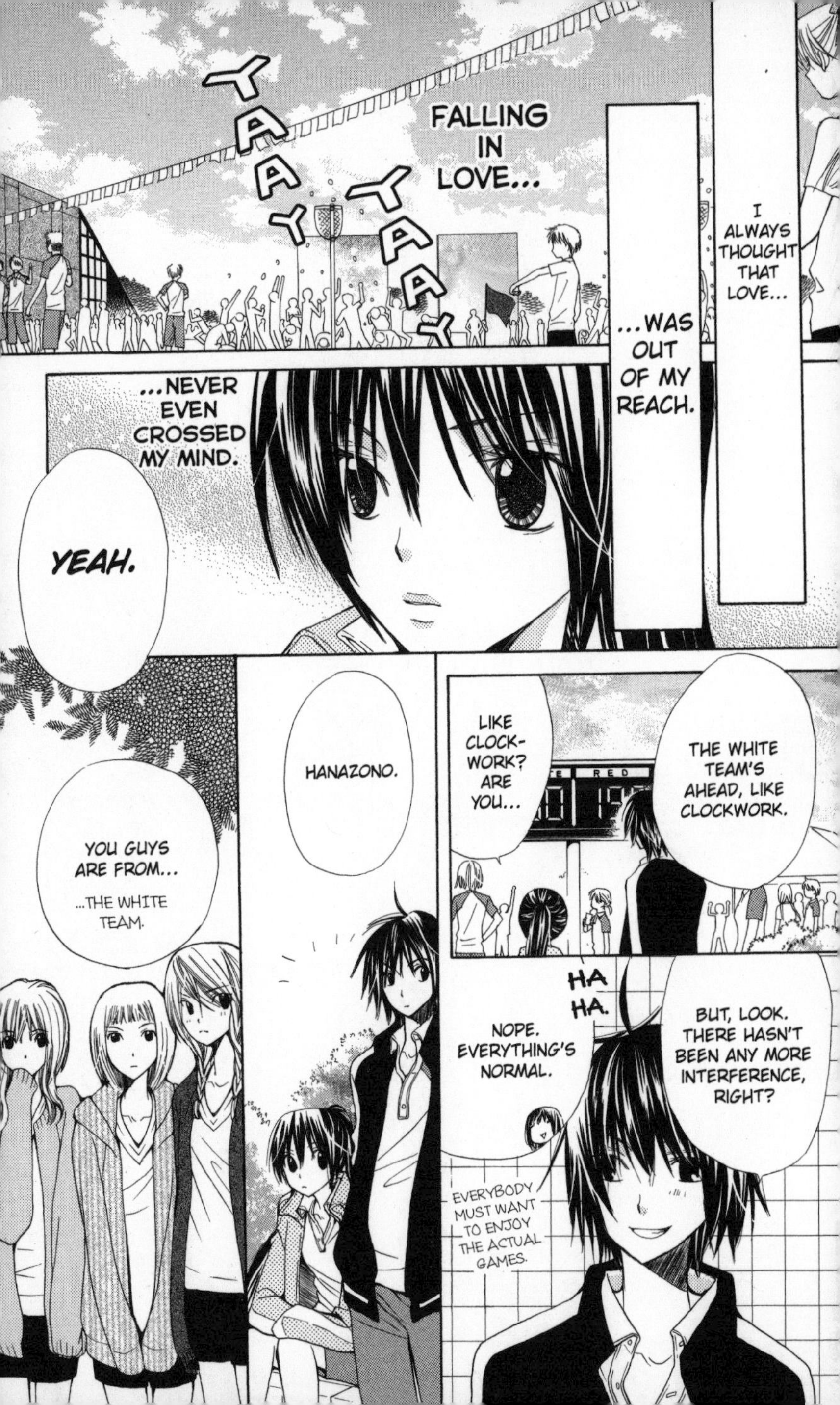

I ALWAYS THOUGHT THAT LOVE...
...WAS OUT OF MY REACH.
YAAY
YAAY
FALLING IN LOVE...
...NEVER EVEN CROSSED MY MIND.
YEAH.
THE WHITE TEAM'S AHEAD, LIKE CLOCKWORK.
LIKE CLOCKWORK? ARE YOU...
HA HA.
BUT, LOOK. THERE HASN'T BEEN ANY MORE INTERFERENCE, RIGHT?
NOPE. EVERYTHING'S NORMAL.
EVERYBODY MUST WANT TO ENJOY THE ACTUAL GAMES.
HANAZONO.
YOU GUYS ARE FROM...
...THE WHITE TEAM.

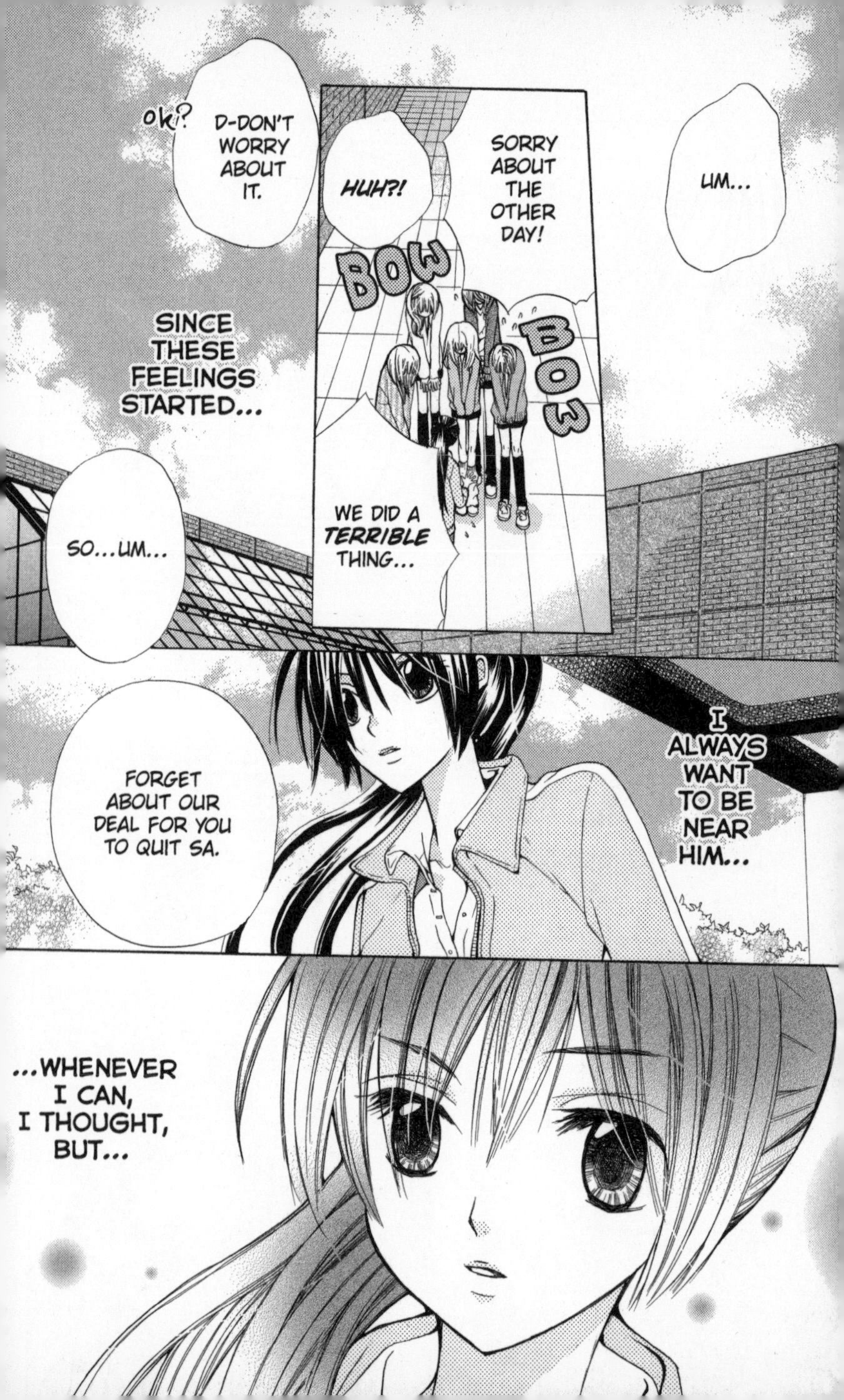
UM...
SORRY ABOUT THE OTHER DAY!
BOW
BOW
HUH?!
WE DID A *TERRIBLE* THING...
D-DON'T WORRY ABOUT IT.
ok?
SINCE THESE FEELINGS STARTED...
SO...UM...
I ALWAYS WANT TO BE NEAR HIM...
FORGET ABOUT OUR DEAL FOR YOU TO QUIT SA.
...WHENEVER I CAN, I THOUGHT, BUT...

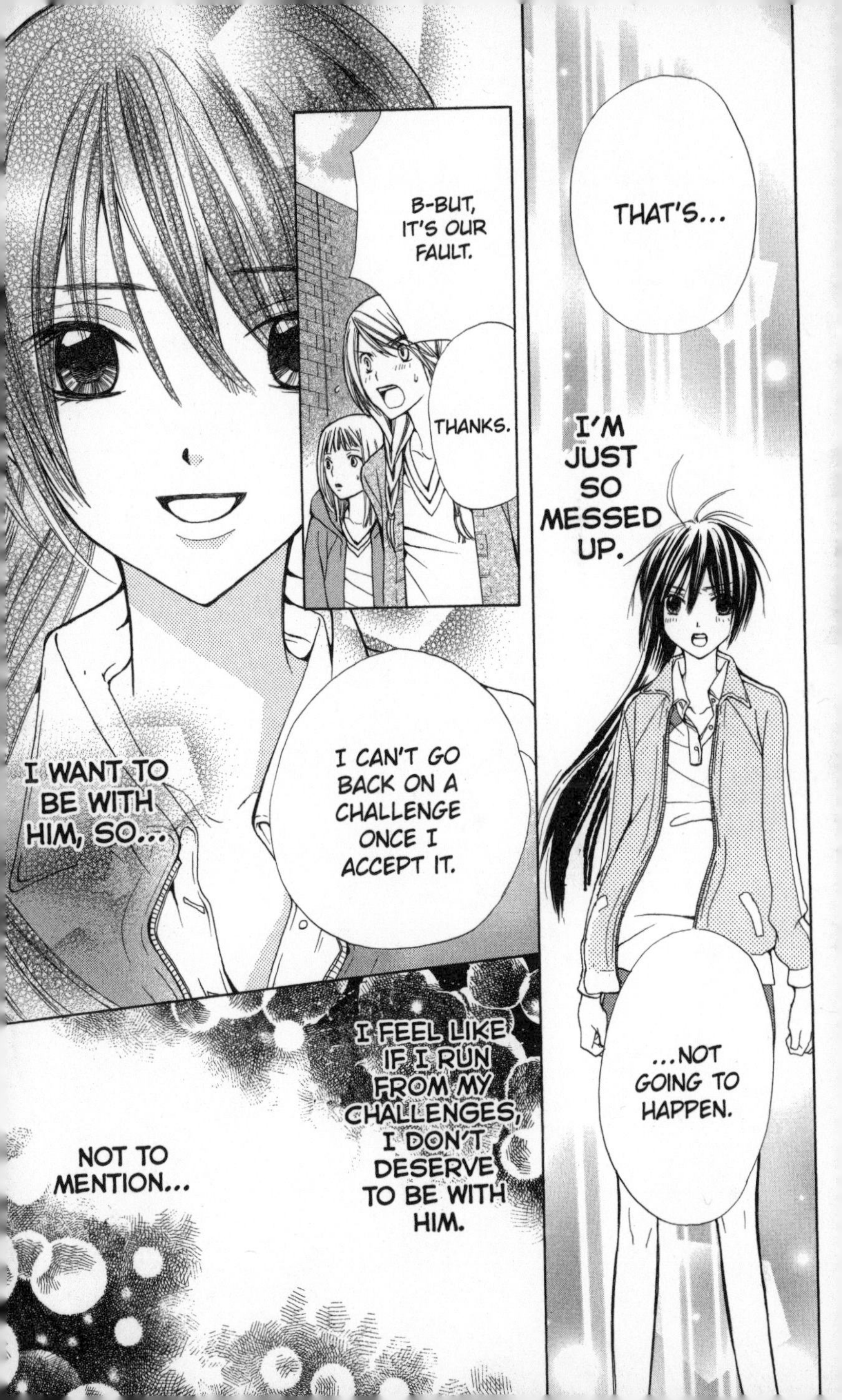
THAT'S...
I'M JUST SO MESSED UP.
...NOT GOING TO HAPPEN.
B-BUT, IT'S OUR FAULT.
THANKS.
I CAN'T GO BACK ON A CHALLENGE ONCE I ACCEPT IT.
I WANT TO BE WITH HIM, SO...
I FEEL LIKE IF I RUN FROM MY CHALLENGES, I DON'T DESERVE TO BE WITH HIM.
NOT TO MENTION...

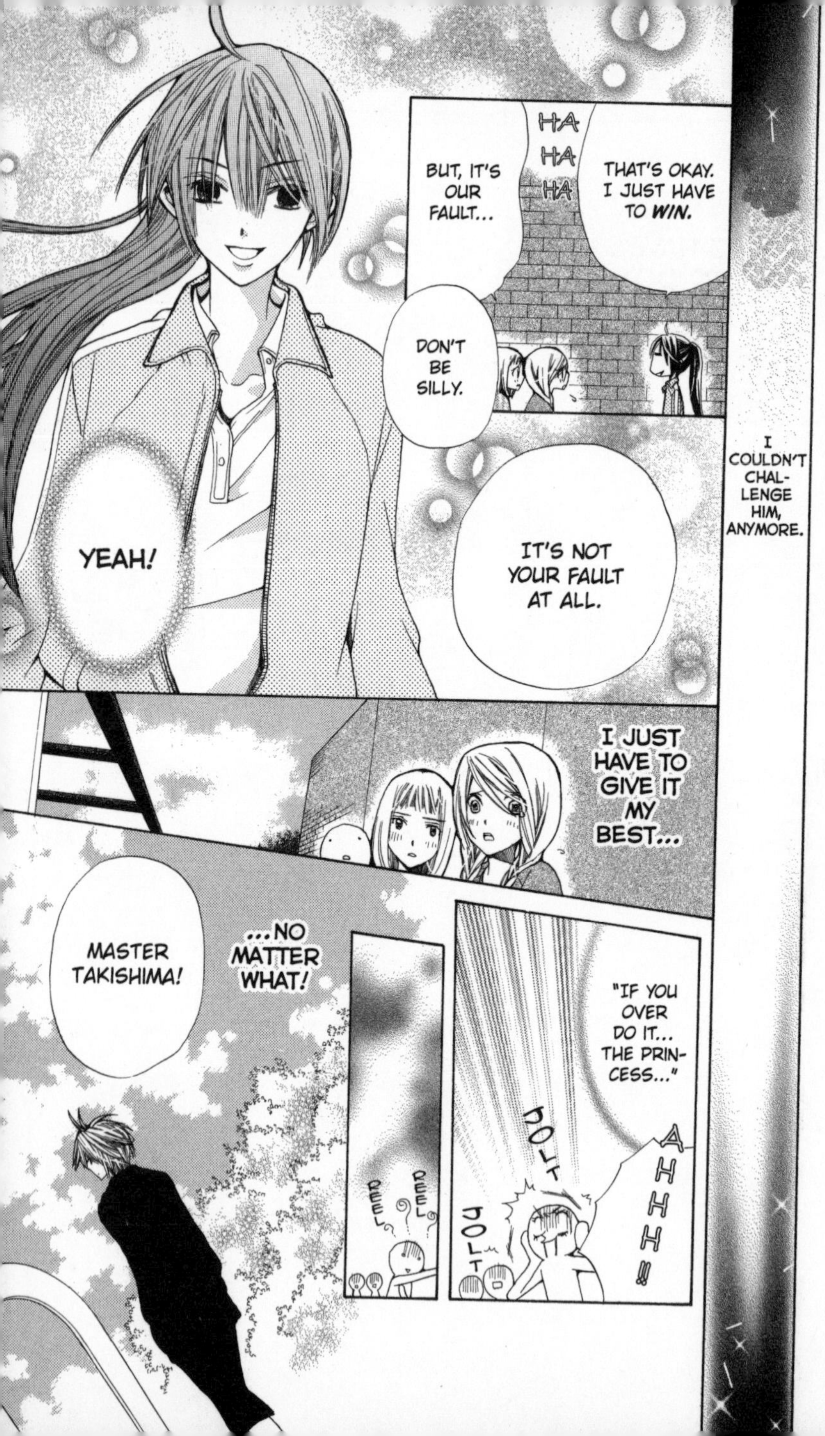
I COULDN'T CHAL-LENGE HIM, ANYMORE.
THAT'S OKAY. I JUST HAVE TO WIN.
HA HA HA
BUT, IT'S OUR FAULT...
DON'T BE SILLY.
IT'S NOT YOUR FAULT AT ALL.
YEAH!
I JUST HAVE TO GIVE IT MY BEST...
"IF YOU OVER DO IT... THE PRIN-CESS..."
AHHHH!!
JOLT
JOLT
REEL
REEL
...NO MATTER WHAT!
MASTER TAKISHIMA!

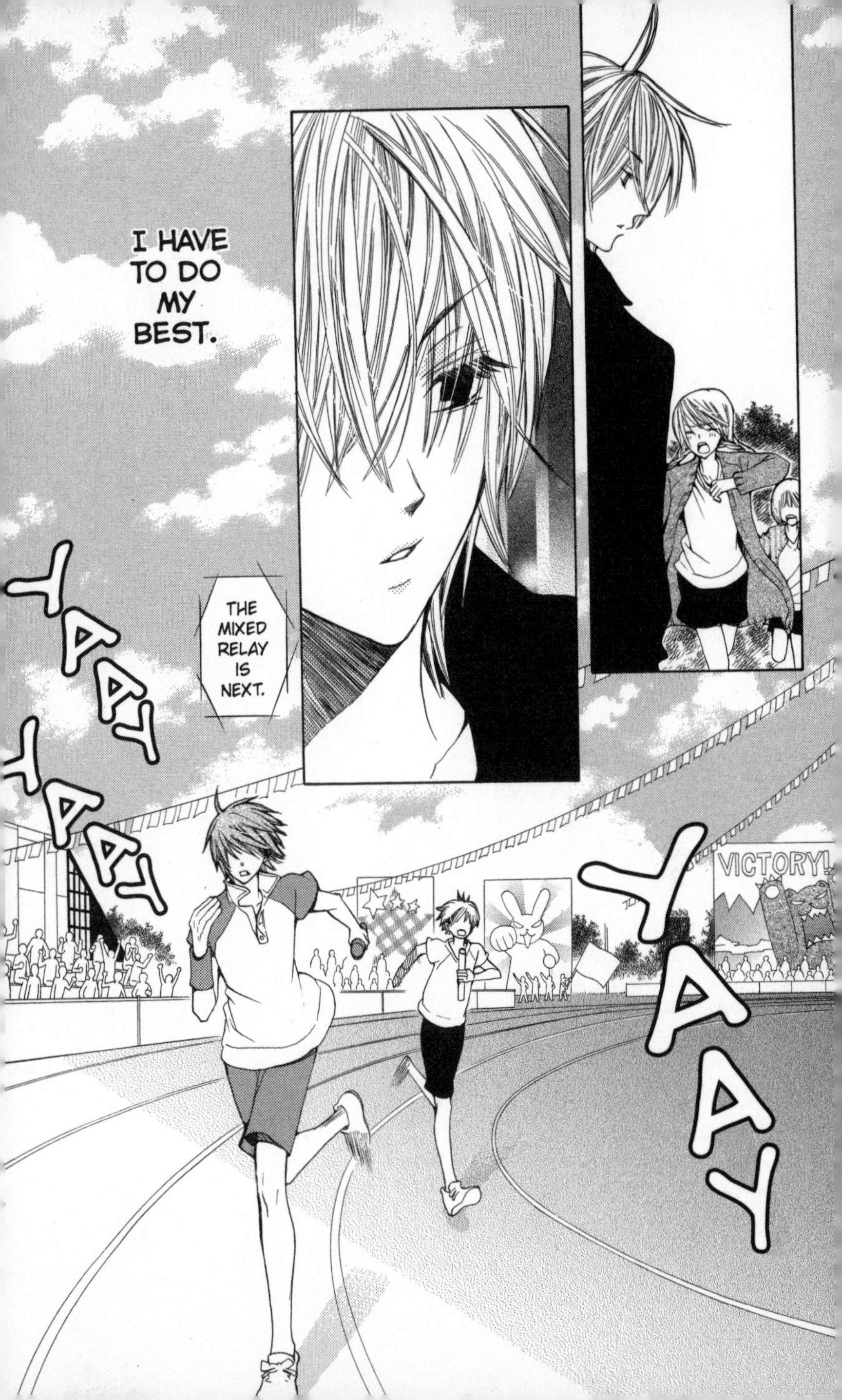
I HAVE TO DO MY BEST.
THE MIXED RELAY IS NEXT.
VICTORY!
YAAY
YAAY
YAAY

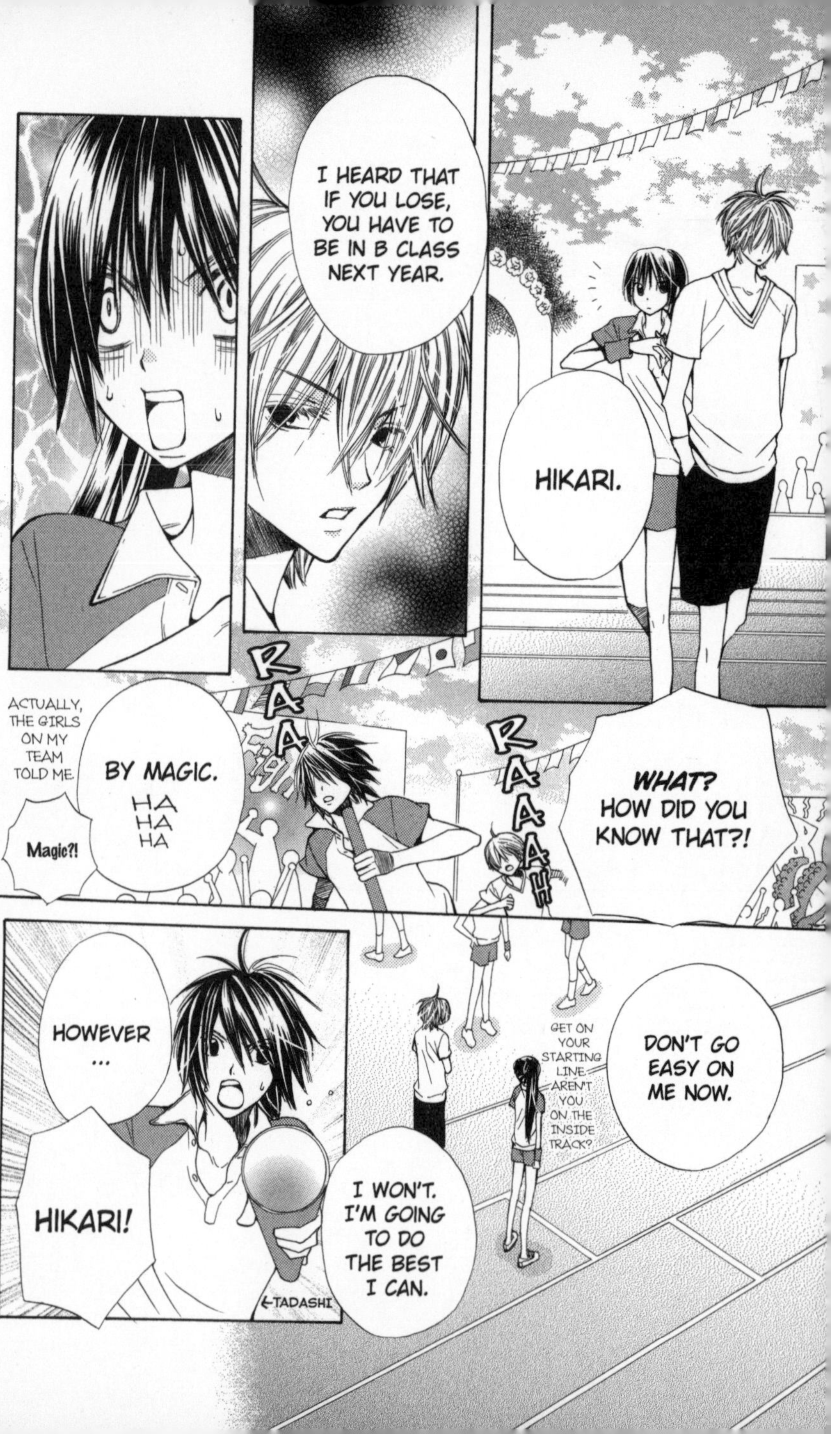
HIKARI.
I HEARD THAT IF YOU LOSE, YOU HAVE TO BE IN B CLASS NEXT YEAR.
WHAT? HOW DID YOU KNOW THAT?!
RAAAAH
RAA
BY MAGIC.
HA HA HA
ACTUALLY, THE GIRLS ON MY TEAM TOLD ME.
Magic?!
DON'T GO EASY ON ME NOW.
GET ON YOUR STARTING LINE. AREN'T YOU ON THE INSIDE TRACK?
I WON'T. I'M GOING TO DO THE BEST I CAN.
HOWEVER ...
HIKARI!
←TADASHI

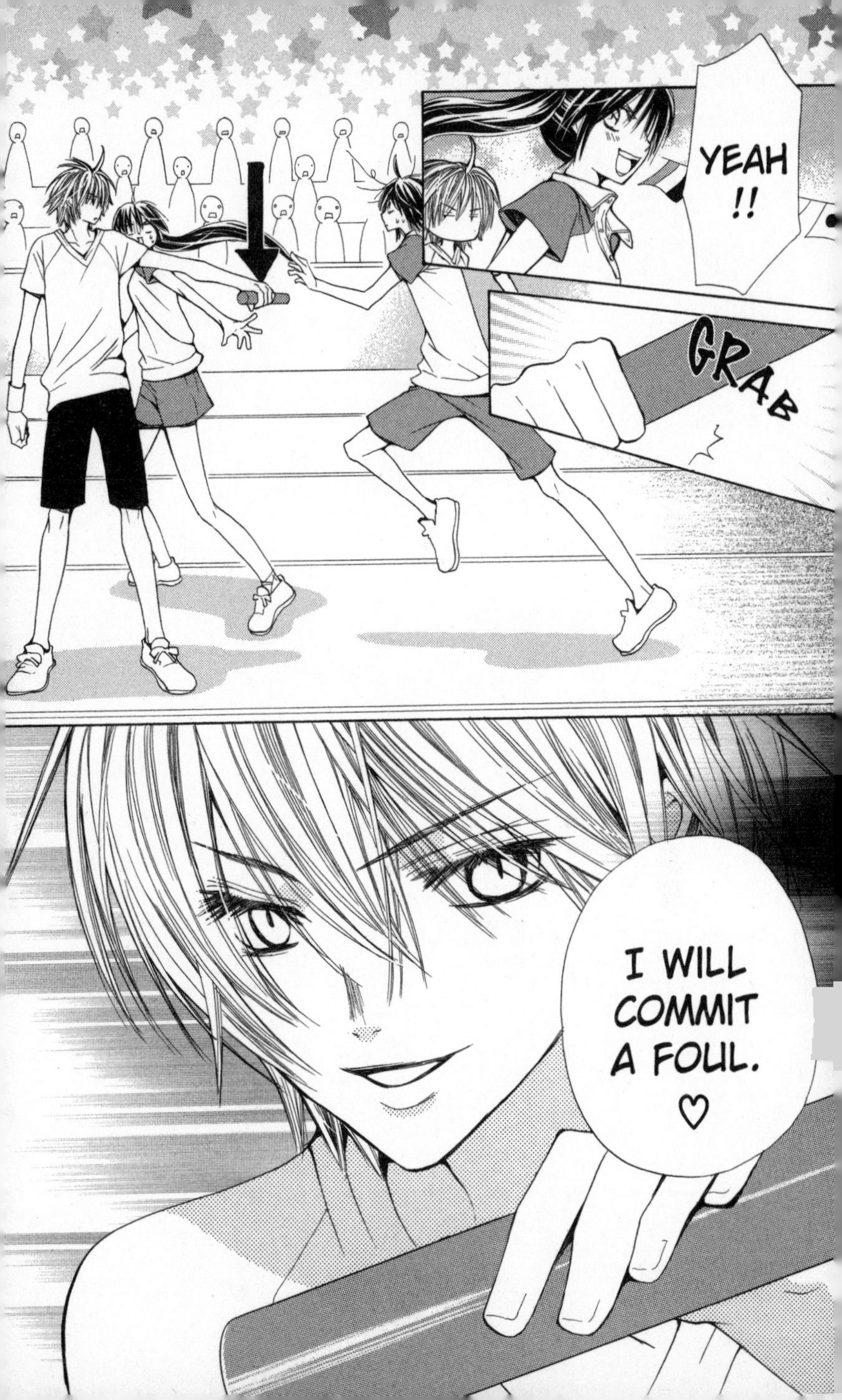
YEAH !!
GRAB
I WILL COMMIT A FOUL. ♡

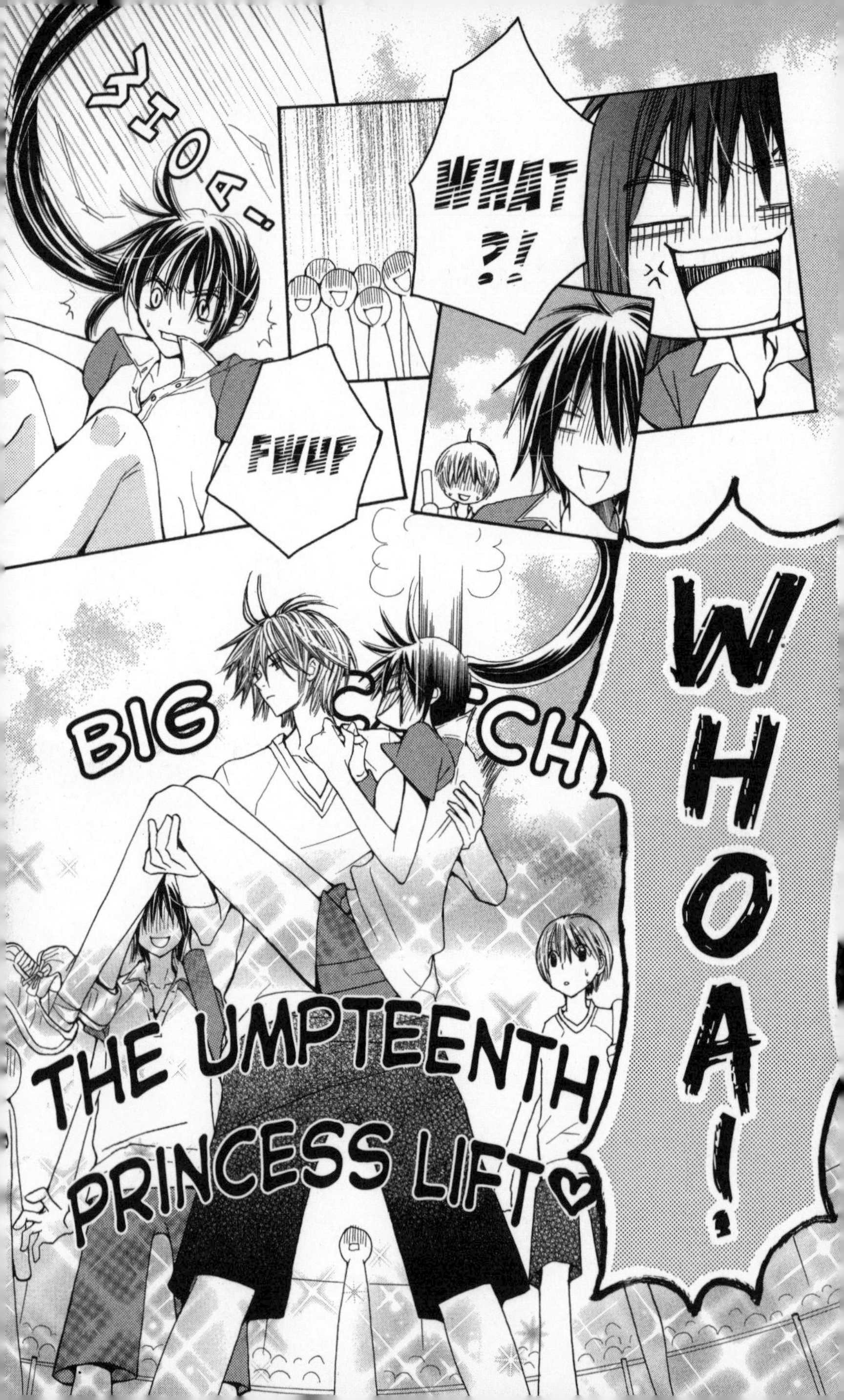
WHAT?!
WHOA!
FWUP
WHOA!
BIG CH
THE UMPTEENTH PRINCESS LIFT♥

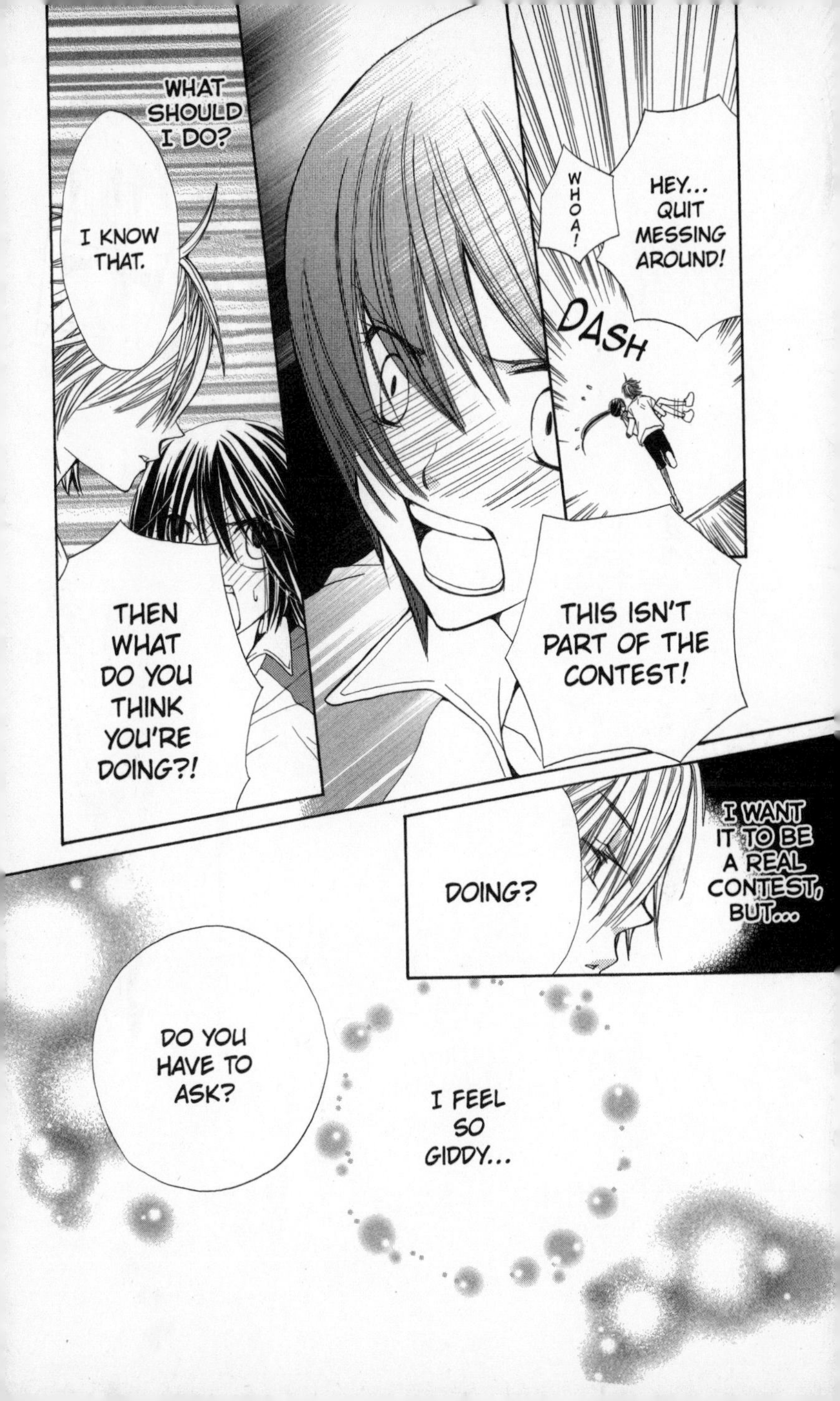
HEY... QUIT MESSING AROUND!
WHOA!
DASH
THIS ISN'T PART OF THE CONTEST!
WHAT SHOULD I DO?
I KNOW THAT.
THEN WHAT DO YOU THINK YOU'RE DOING?!
I WANT IT TO BE A REAL CONTEST, BUT...
DOING?
DO YOU HAVE TO ASK?
I FEEL SO GIDDY...

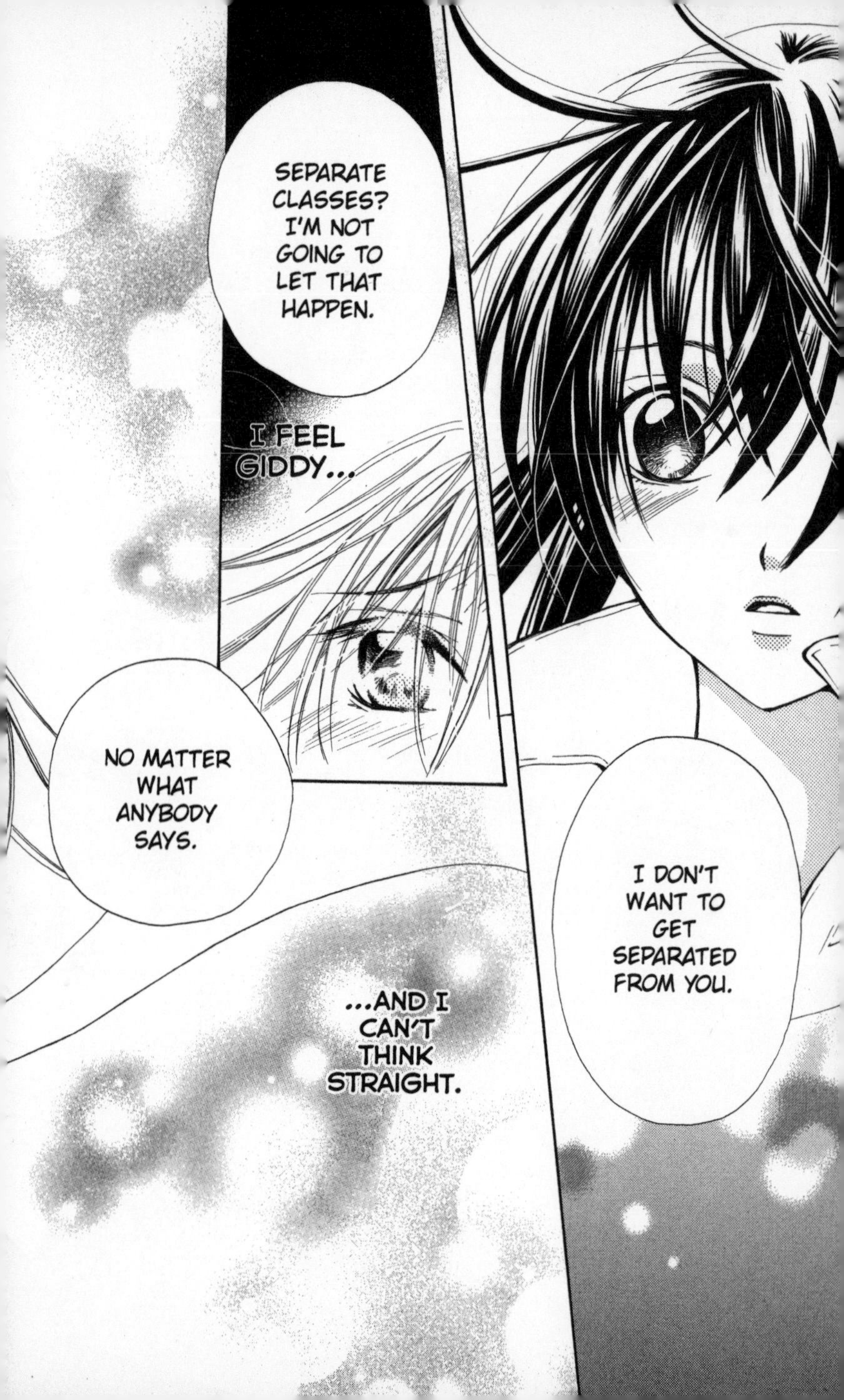
SEPARATE CLASSES? I'M NOT GOING TO LET THAT HAPPEN.
I FEEL GIDDY...
NO MATTER WHAT ANYBODY SAYS.
I DON'T WANT TO GET SEPARATED FROM YOU.
...AND I CAN'T THINK STRAIGHT.

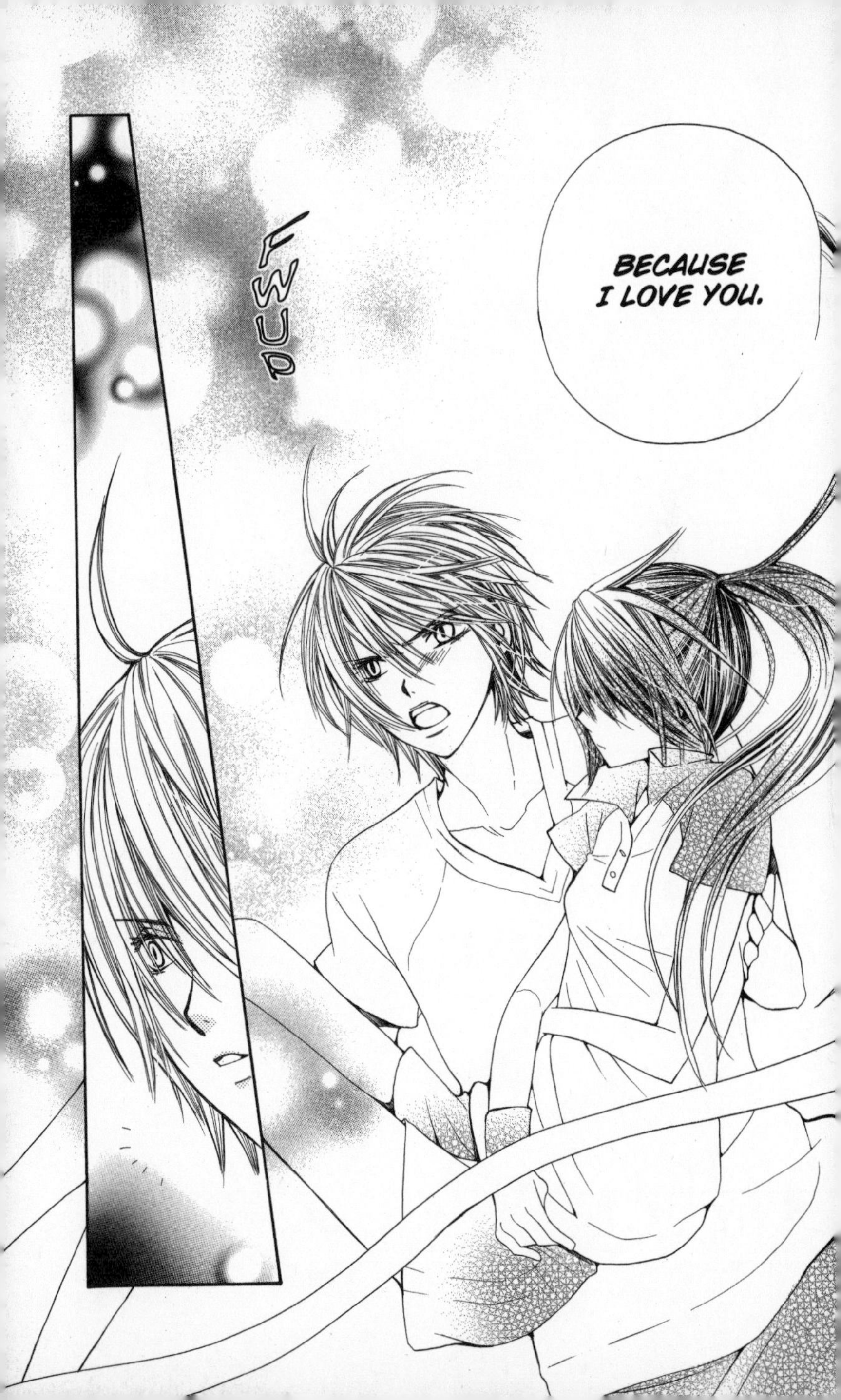
BECAUSE I LOVE YOU.
FWUP

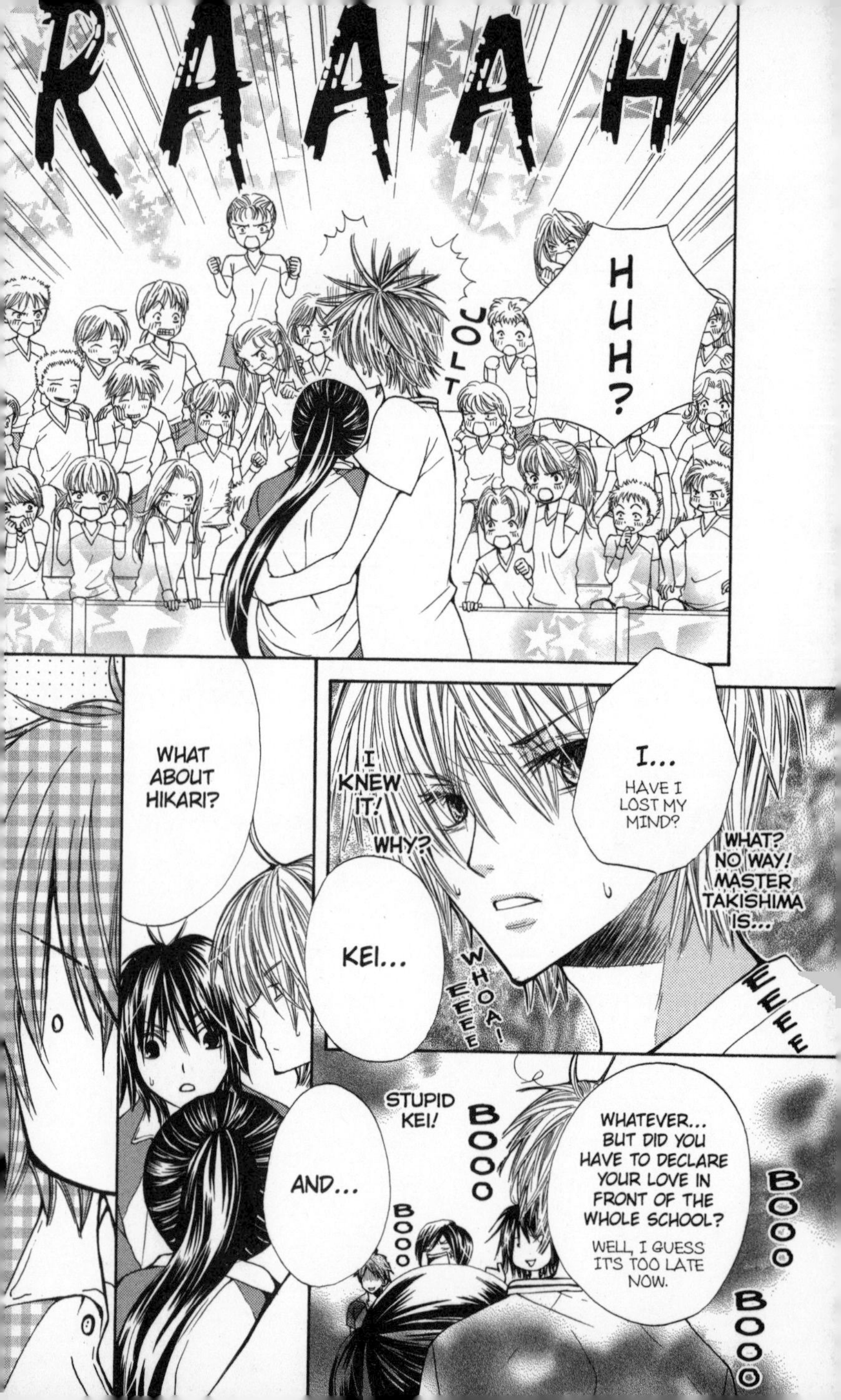
RAAAH
HUH?
JOLT
I...
HAVE I LOST MY MIND?
WHAT? NO WAY! MASTER TAKISHIMA IS...
EEEE
I KNEW IT!
WHY?
WHOA!
EEEE
WHATEVER... BUT DID YOU HAVE TO DECLARE YOUR LOVE IN FRONT OF THE WHOLE SCHOOL?
WELL, I GUESS IT'S TOO LATE NOW.
BOOO
BOOO
STUPID KEI!
BOOO
BOOO
WHAT ABOUT HIKARI?
KEI...
AND...

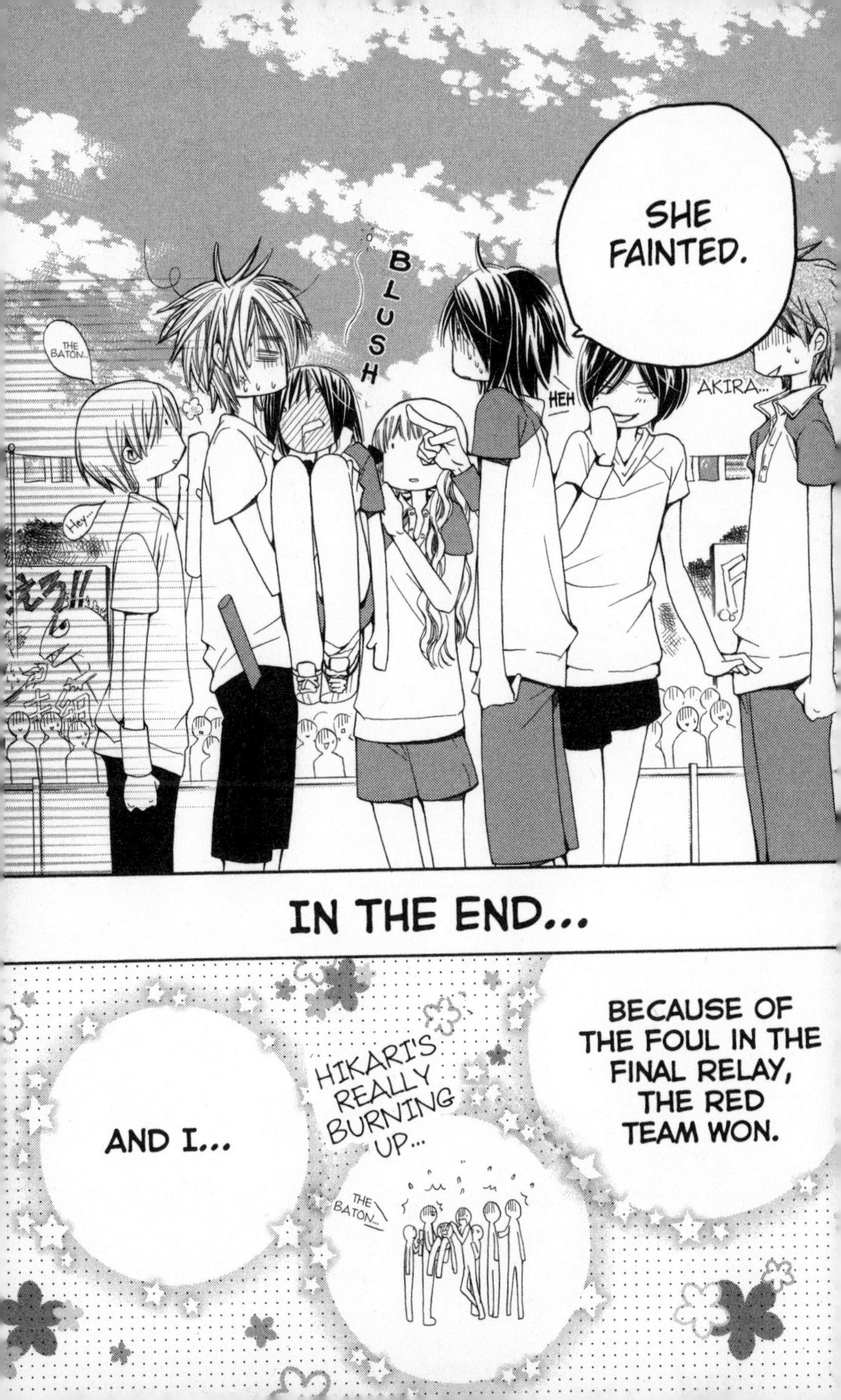
SHE FAINTED.
AKIRA...
HEH
BLUSH
THE BATON...
Hey...
IN THE END...
BECAUSE OF THE FOUL IN THE FINAL RELAY, THE RED TEAM WON.
HIKARI'S REALLY BURNING UP...
THE BATON...
AND I...

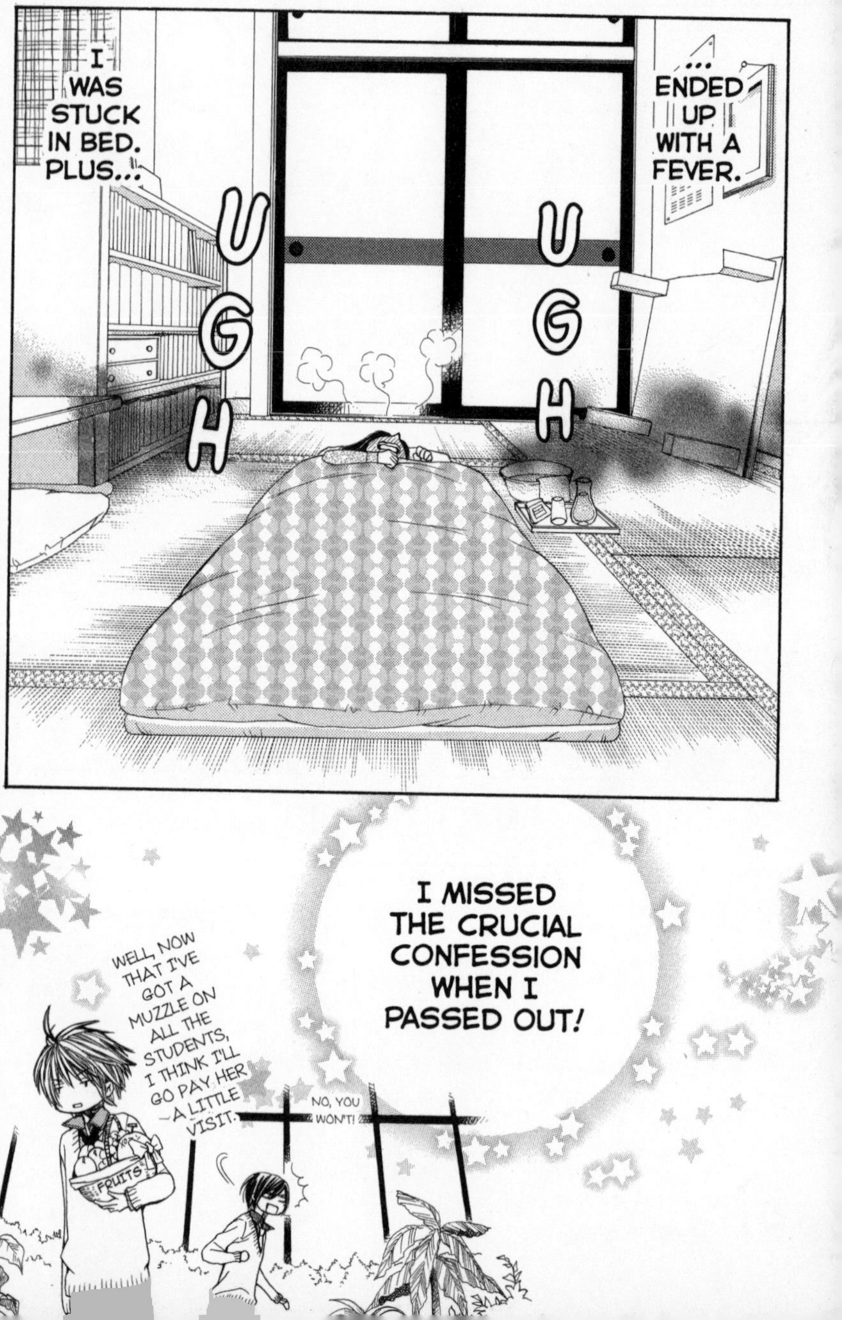
I WAS STUCK IN BED. PLUS...
...ENDED UP WITH A FEVER.
UGH
UGH
I MISSED THE CRUCIAL CONFESSION WHEN I PASSED OUT!
WELL, NOW THAT I'VE GOT A MUZZLE ON ALL THE STUDENTS, I THINK I'LL GO PAY HER A LITTLE VISIT.
FRUITS
NO, YOU WON'T!

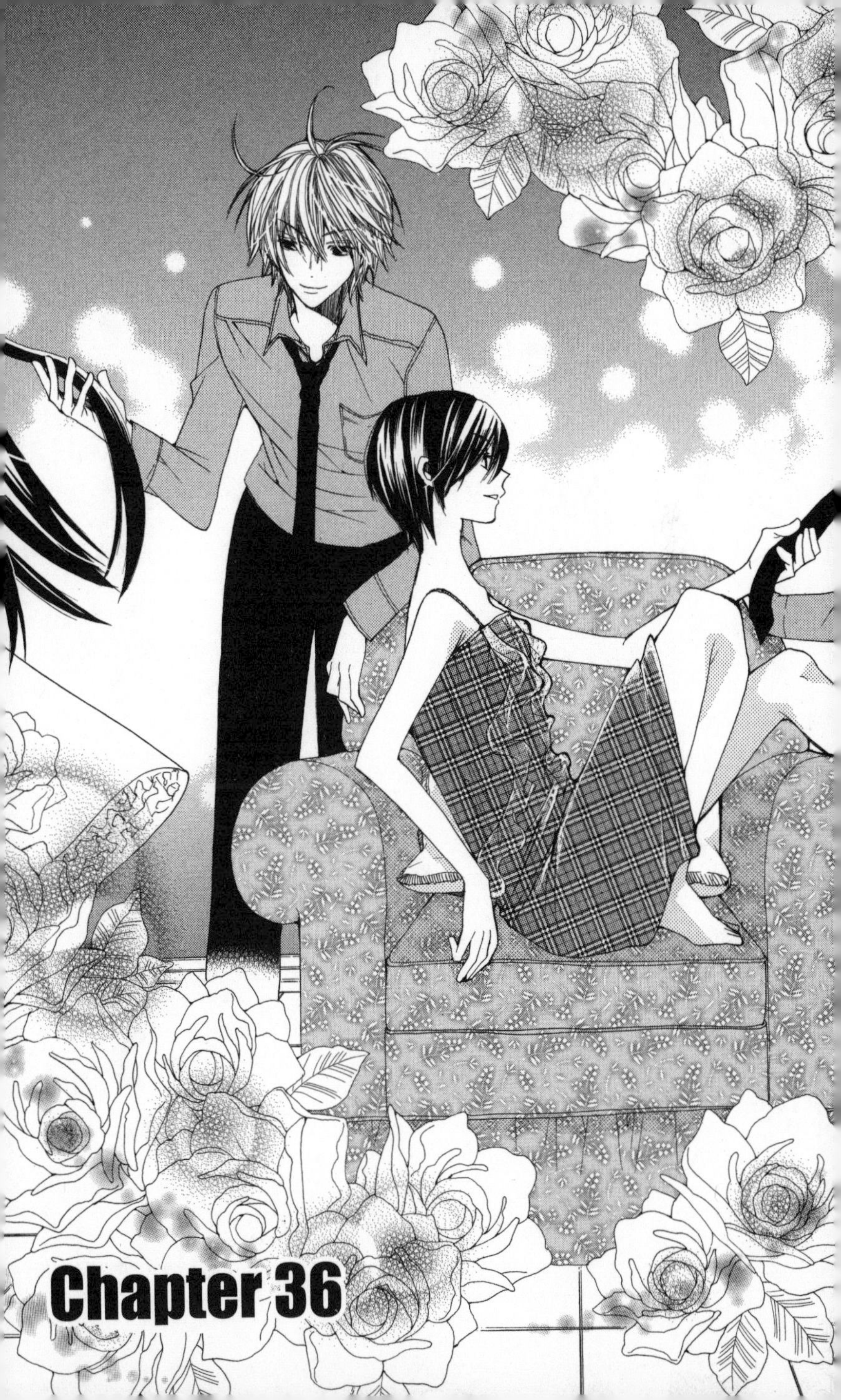
Chapter 36

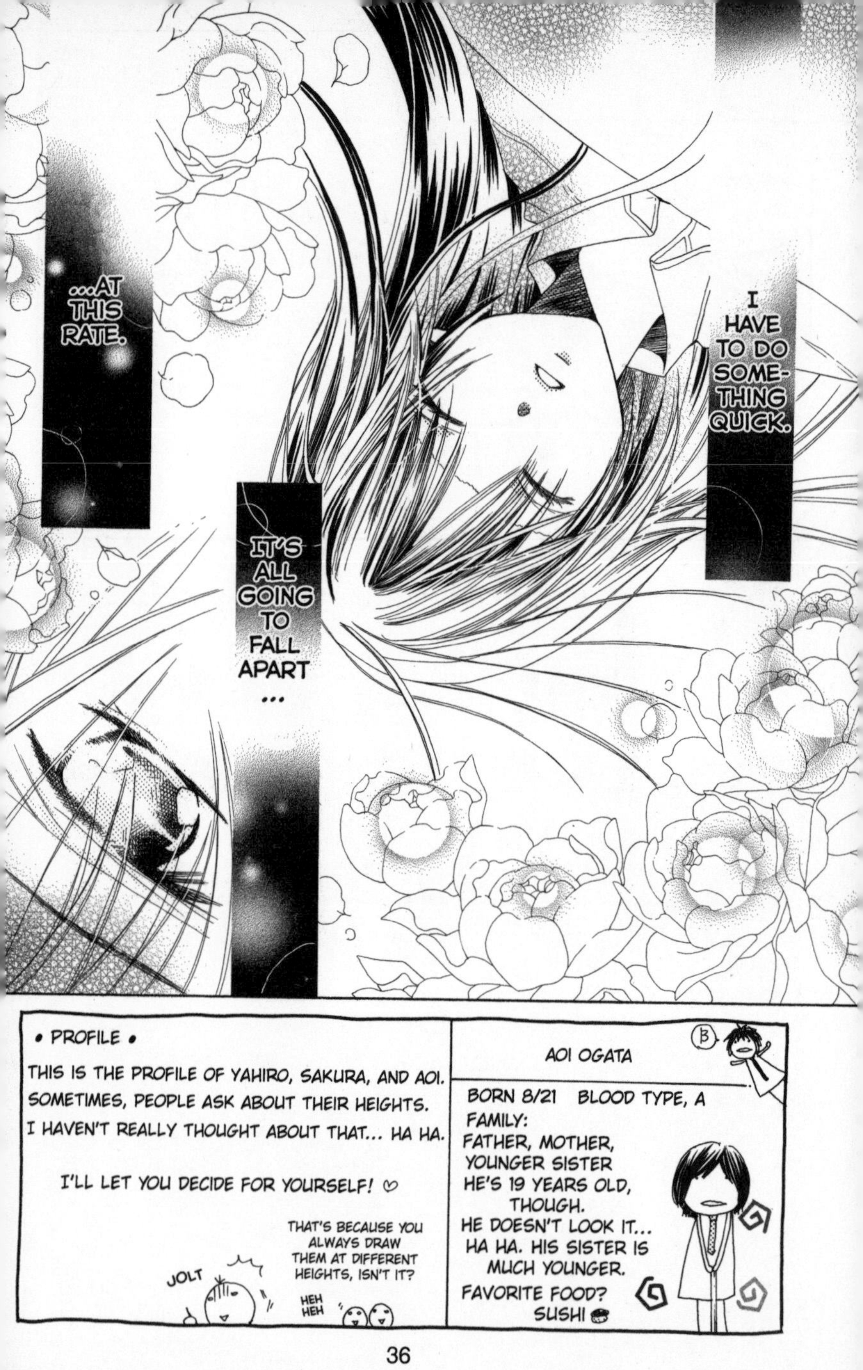
I HAVE TO DO SOME-THING QUICK.
IT'S ALL GOING TO FALL APART...
...AT THIS RATE.

• PROFILE •

THIS IS THE PROFILE OF YAHIRO, SAKURA, AND AOI. SOMETIMES, PEOPLE ASK ABOUT THEIR HEIGHTS. I HAVEN'T REALLY THOUGHT ABOUT THAT... HA HA.

I'LL LET YOU DECIDE FOR YOURSELF! ♡

JOLT

THAT'S BECAUSE YOU ALWAYS DRAW THEM AT DIFFERENT HEIGHTS, ISN'T IT?

HEH HEH

AOI OGATA

BORN 8/21 BLOOD TYPE, A

FAMILY:
FATHER, MOTHER, YOUNGER SISTER
HE'S 19 YEARS OLD, THOUGH.
HE DOESN'T LOOK IT... HA HA. HIS SISTER IS MUCH YOUNGER.
FAVORITE FOOD? SUSHI

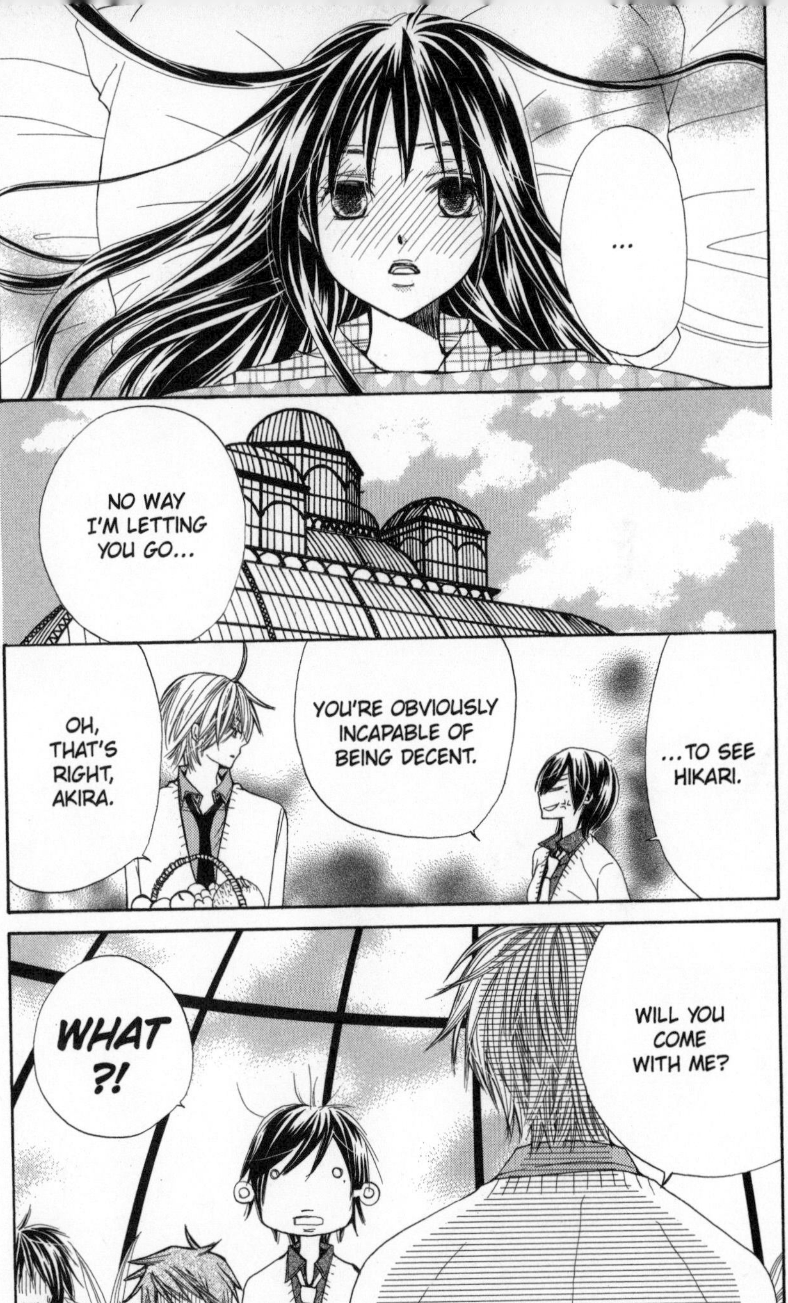
...
NO WAY I'M LETTING YOU GO...
...TO SEE HIKARI.
YOU'RE OBVIOUSLY INCAPABLE OF BEING DECENT.
OH, THAT'S RIGHT, AKIRA.
WILL YOU COME WITH ME?
WHAT?!

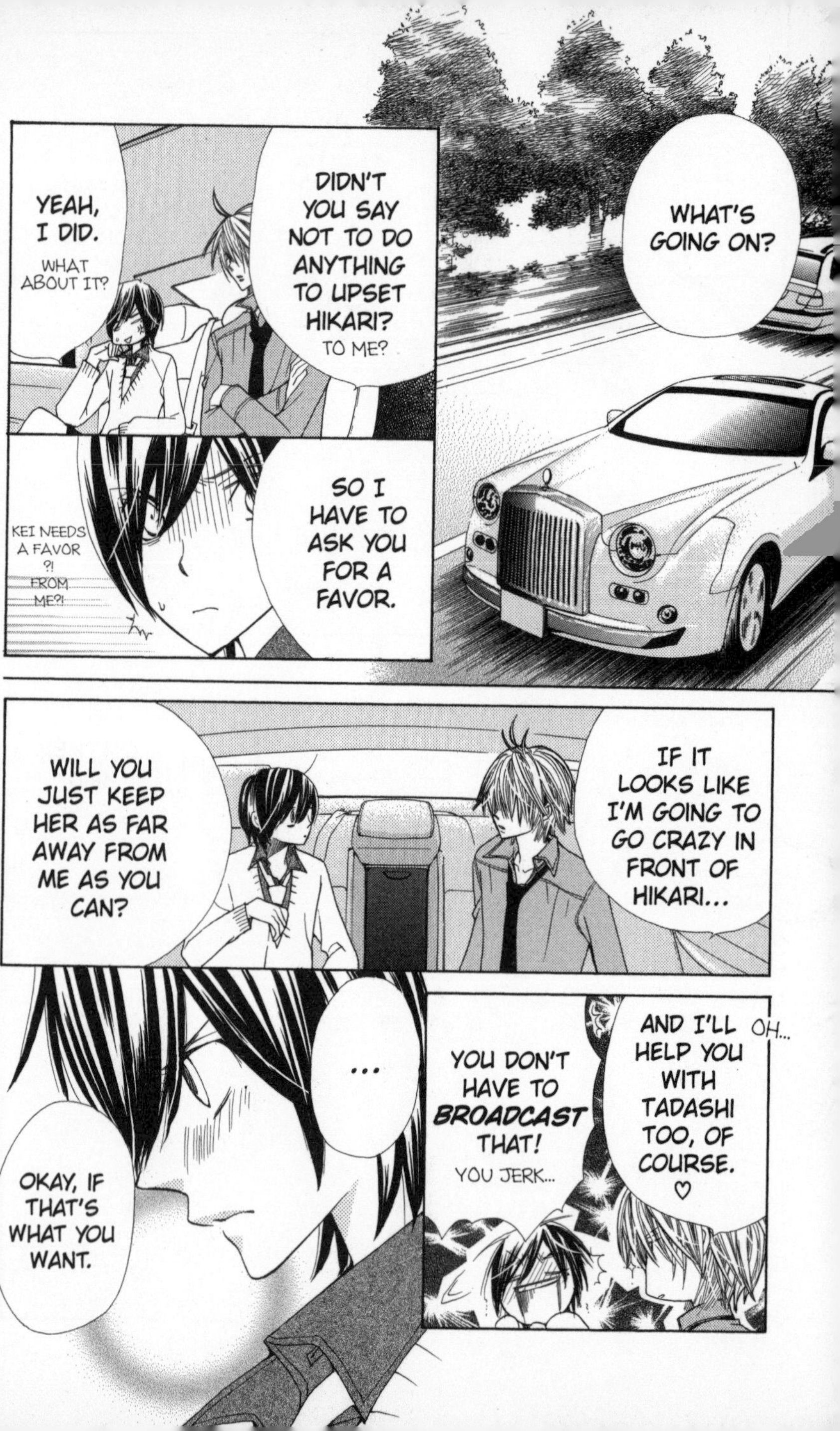
WHAT'S GOING ON?
DIDN'T YOU SAY NOT TO DO ANYTHING TO UPSET HIKARI? TO ME?
YEAH, I DID. WHAT ABOUT IT?
SO I HAVE TO ASK YOU FOR A FAVOR.
KEI NEEDS A FAVOR ?! FROM ME?!
IF IT LOOKS LIKE I'M GOING TO GO CRAZY IN FRONT OF HIKARI...
WILL YOU JUST KEEP HER AS FAR AWAY FROM ME AS YOU CAN?
AND I'LL HELP YOU WITH TADASHI TOO, OF COURSE. ♡
OH...
YOU DON'T HAVE TO *BROADCAST* THAT! YOU JERK...
...
OKAY, IF THAT'S WHAT YOU WANT.

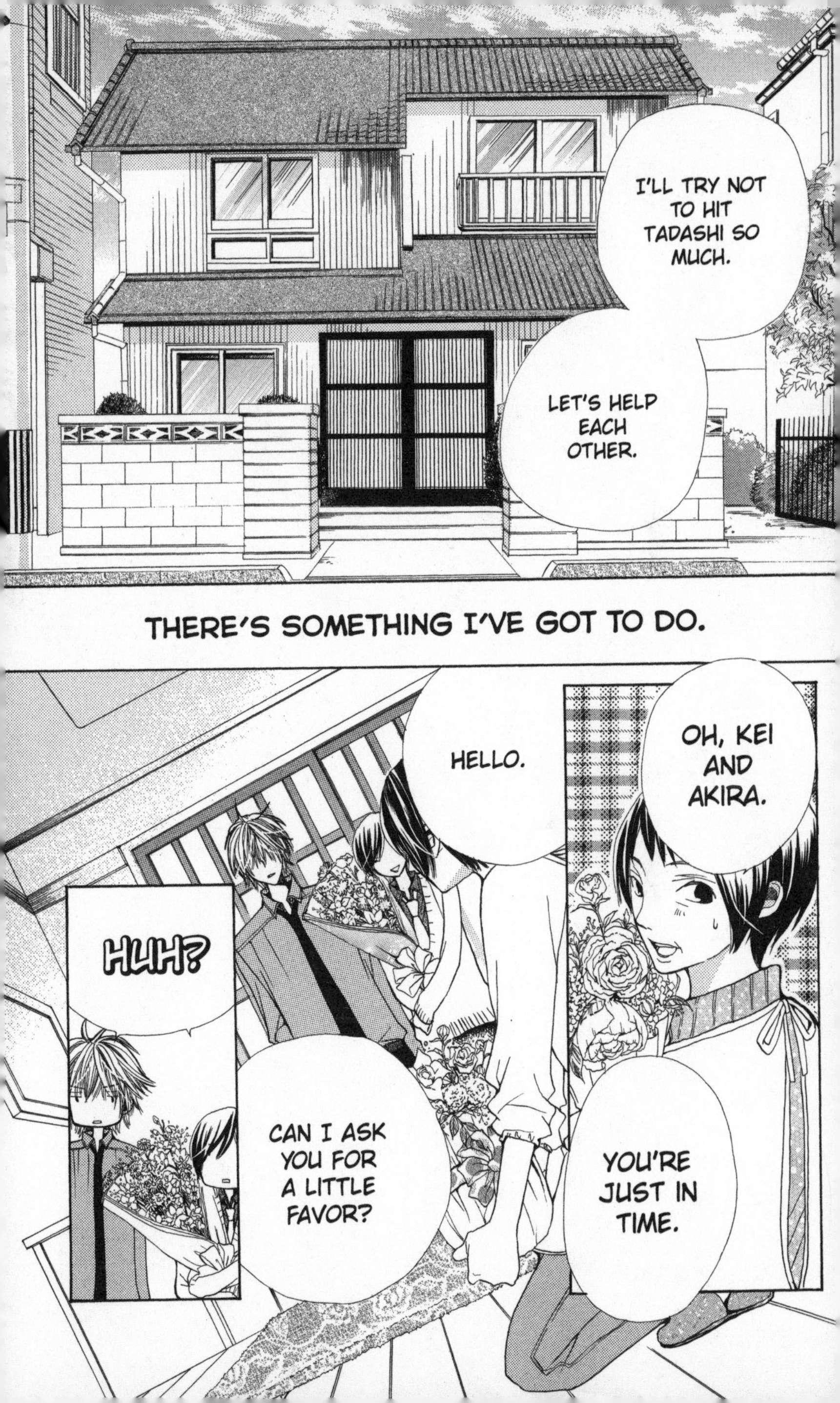
I'LL TRY NOT TO HIT TADASHI SO MUCH.
LET'S HELP EACH OTHER.
THERE'S SOMETHING I'VE GOT TO DO.
OH, KEI AND AKIRA.
YOU'RE JUST IN TIME.
HELLO.
CAN I ASK YOU FOR A LITTLE FAVOR?
HUH?

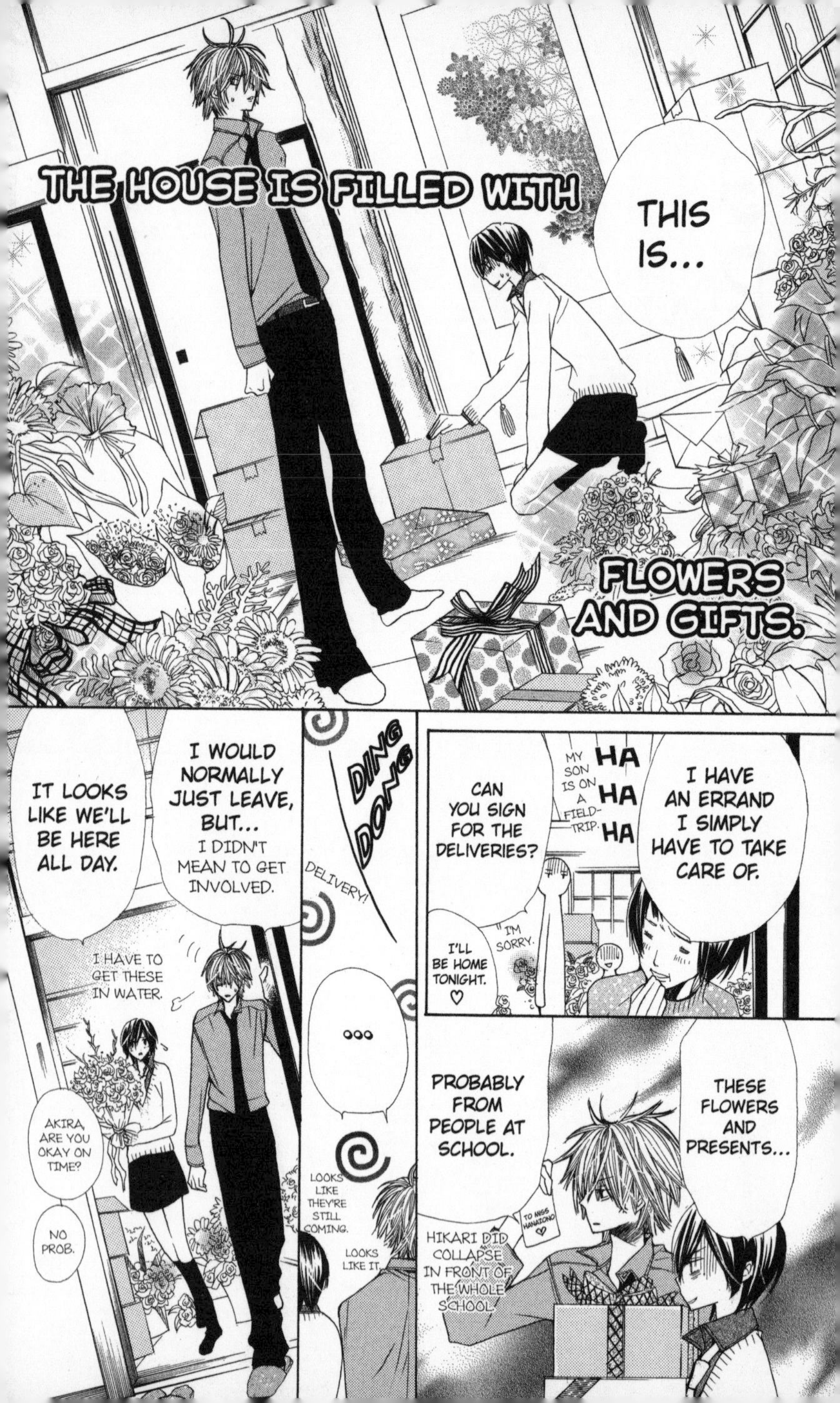
THIS IS...
THE HOUSE IS FILLED WITH
FLOWERS AND GIFTS.
I HAVE AN ERRAND I SIMPLY HAVE TO TAKE CARE OF.
HA HA HA
MY SON IS ON A FIELD-TRIP.
CAN YOU SIGN FOR THE DELIVERIES?
I'M SORRY.
I'LL BE HOME TONIGHT. ♡
THESE FLOWERS AND PRESENTS...
PROBABLY FROM PEOPLE AT SCHOOL.
TO MISS HANAZONO ♡
HIKARI DID COLLAPSE IN FRONT OF THE WHOLE SCHOOL.
DING DONG
DELIVERY!
...
LOOKS LIKE THEY'RE STILL COMING.
LOOKS LIKE IT.
I WOULD NORMALLY JUST LEAVE, BUT...
I DIDN'T MEAN TO GET INVOLVED.
IT LOOKS LIKE WE'LL BE HERE ALL DAY.
I HAVE TO GET THESE IN WATER.
AKIRA, ARE YOU OKAY ON TIME?
NO PROB.

THERE ARE TWO OF US, SO IT SHOULD BE FINE.
I'M WARNING YOU...
GRR
I'M COMING RIGHT BACK, AS SOON AS I'M FINISHED WITH MY APPOINTMENT!
IF YOU DO ANYTHING TO HIKARI, YOU'LL BE SORRY!
AND... I'll be back!
I CALLED TADASHI TO COME OVER!
I COULDN'T GET RYU OR JUN AND MEGUMI.
WHY...
YOU BETTER NOT GO INTO HIKARI'S ROOM. GOT IT?!
...IS THIS HAPPENING?
FROZEN
OH, WELL...
WHAT'S IMPORTANT IS THAT SHE'S ASLEEP IN HER ROOM...
OH.

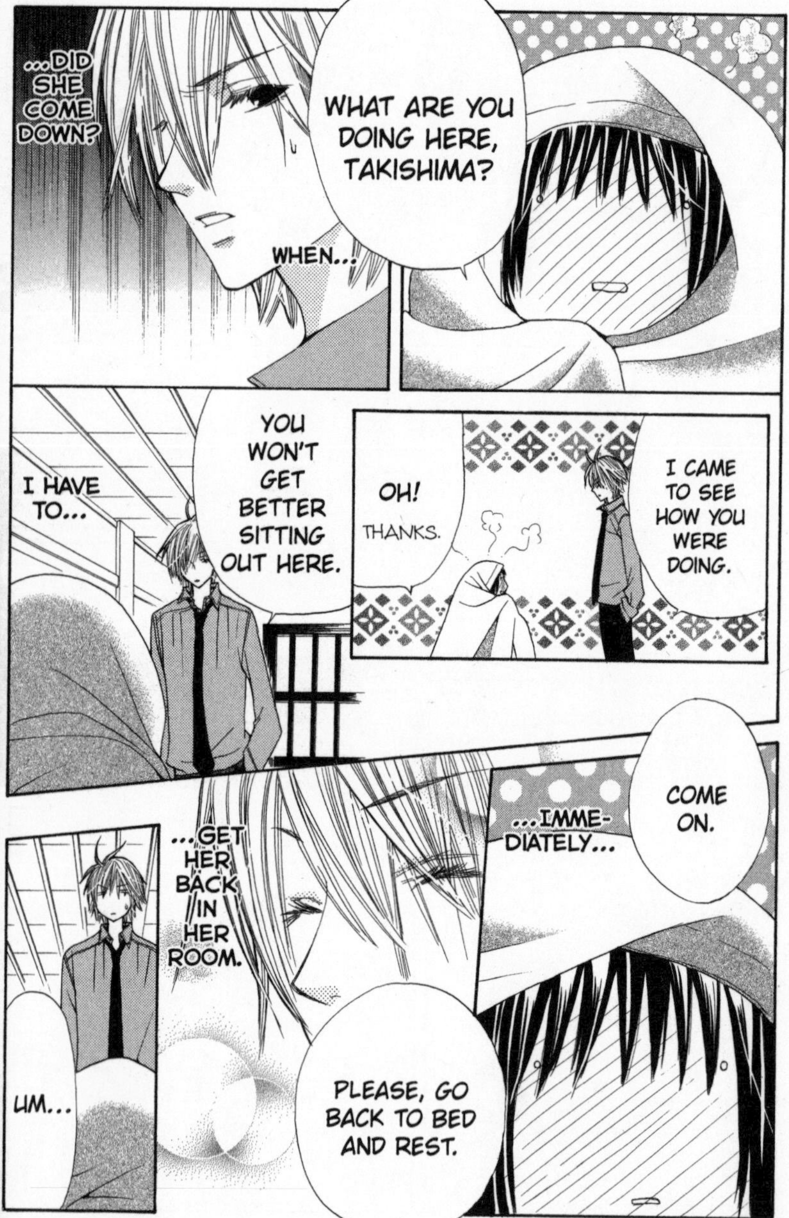
WHAT ARE YOU DOING HERE, TAKISHIMA?
WHEN...
...DID SHE COME DOWN?
I CAME TO SEE HOW YOU WERE DOING.
OH!
THANKS.
YOU WON'T GET BETTER SITTING OUT HERE.
I HAVE TO...
COME ON.
...IMME-DIATELY...
...GET HER BACK IN HER ROOM.
PLEASE, GO BACK TO BED AND REST.
UM...

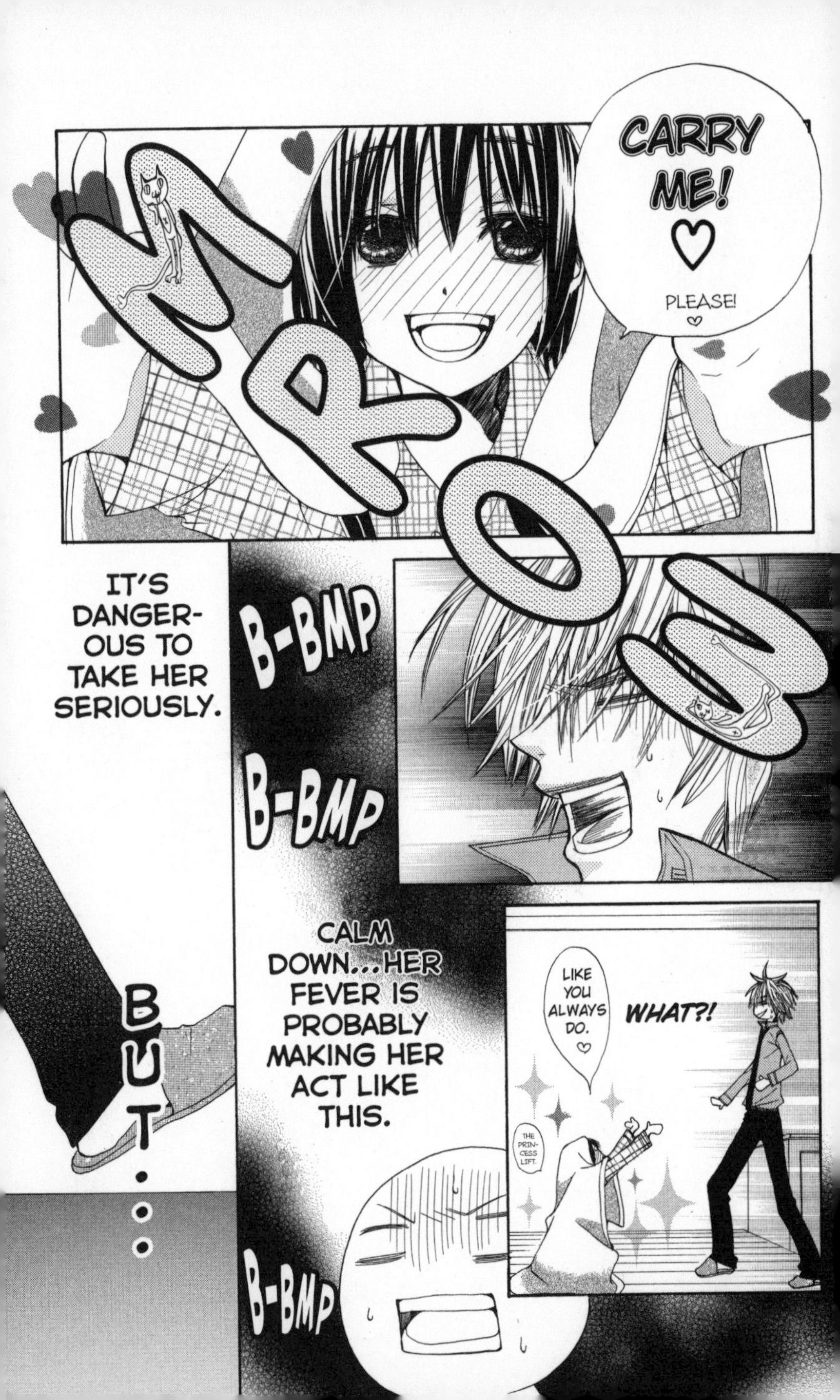
CARRY ME! ♡
PLEASE! ♡
MROW
B-BMP
B-BMP
IT'S DANGEROUS TO TAKE HER SERIOUSLY.
WHAT?!
LIKE YOU ALWAYS DO. ♡
THE PRINCESS LIFT.
CALM DOWN... HER FEVER IS PROBABLY MAKING HER ACT LIKE THIS.
B-BMP
BUT...

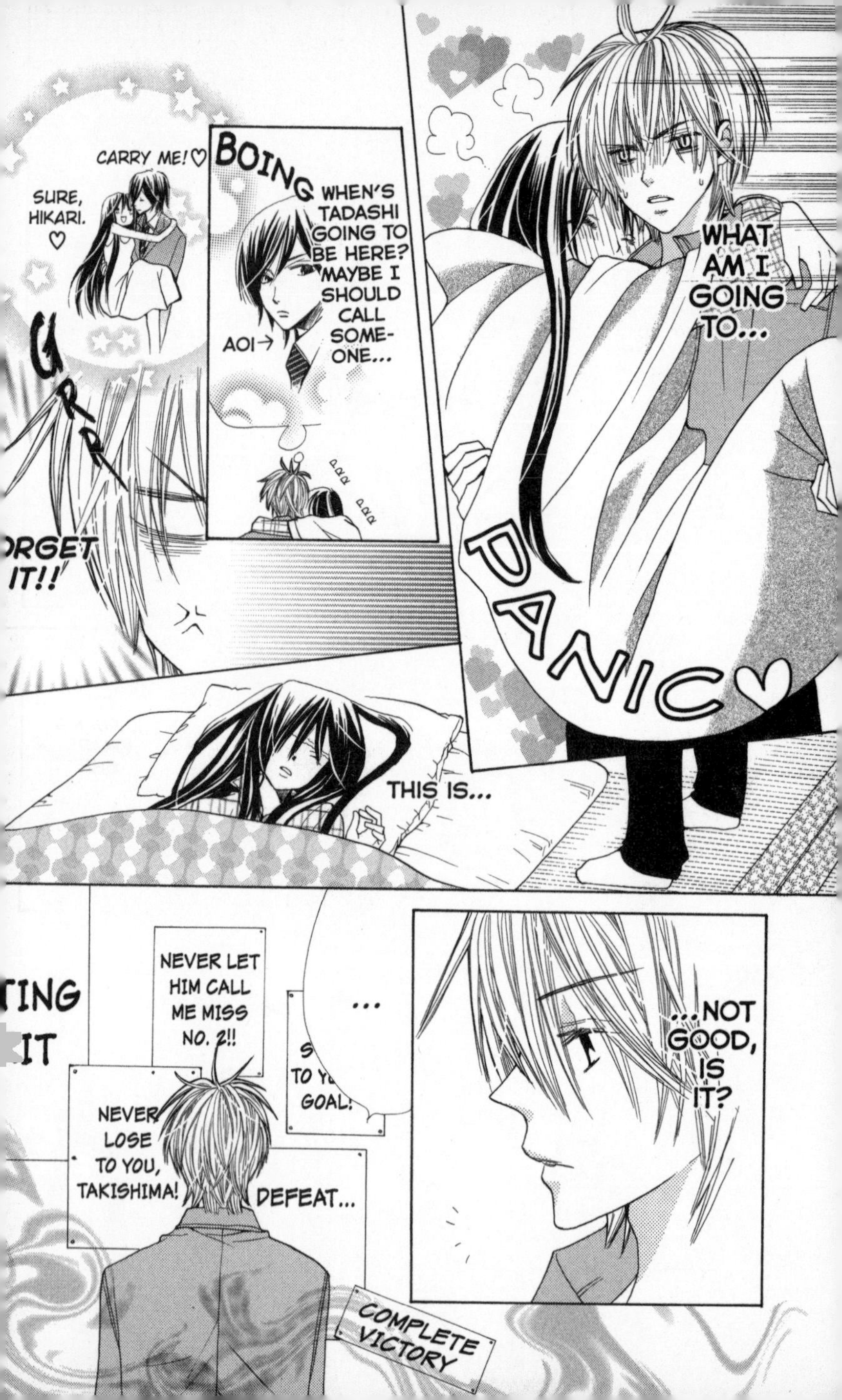
WHAT AM I GOING TO...
PANIC♡
BOING
WHEN'S TADASHI GOING TO BE HERE? MAYBE I SHOULD CALL SOME-ONE...
AOI→
CARRY ME! ♡
SURE, HIKARI. ♡
GRRR
RGET IT!!
THIS IS...
...NOT GOOD, IS IT?
...
NEVER LET HIM CALL ME MISS NO. 2!!
GOAL!
NEVER LOSE TO YOU, TAKISHIMA!
DEFEAT...
COMPLETE VICTORY
TING
IT

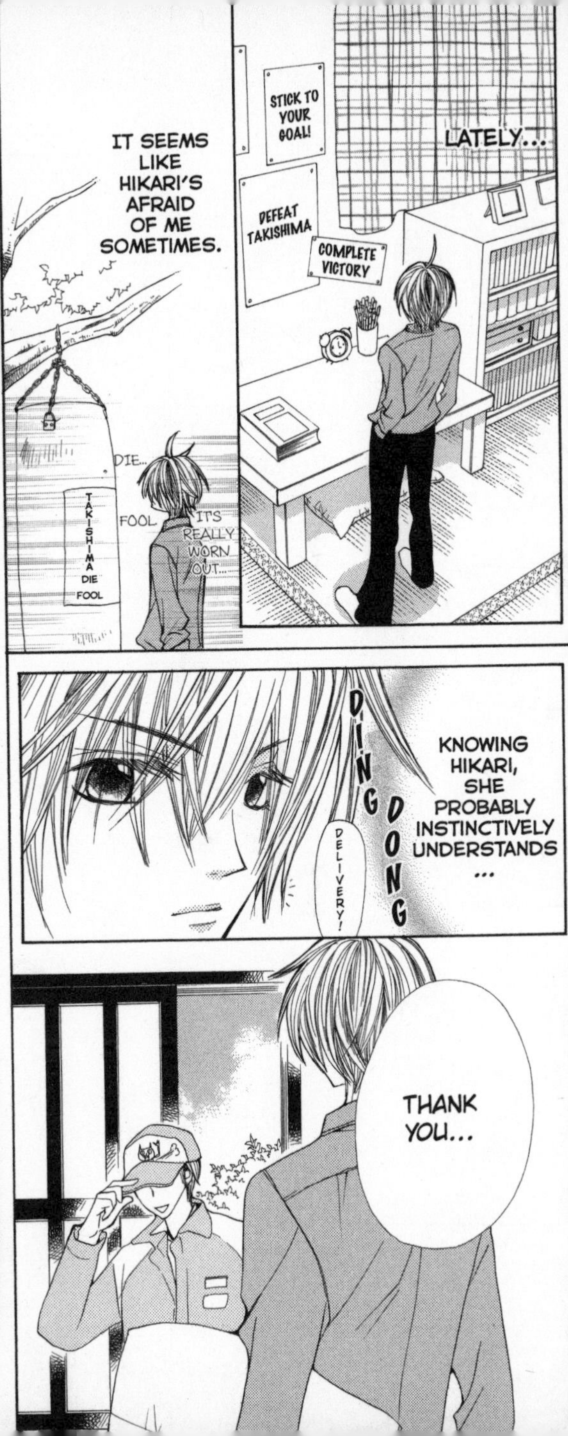
STICK TO YOUR GOAL!
DEFEAT TAKISHIMA
COMPLETE VICTORY
LATELY...
IT SEEMS LIKE HIKARI'S AFRAID OF ME SOMETIMES.
TAKISHIMA DIE FOOL
DIE...
FOOL
IT'S REALLY WORN OUT...
KNOWING HIKARI, SHE PROBABLY INSTINCTIVELY UNDERSTANDS...
DING DONG
DELIVERY!
THANK YOU...

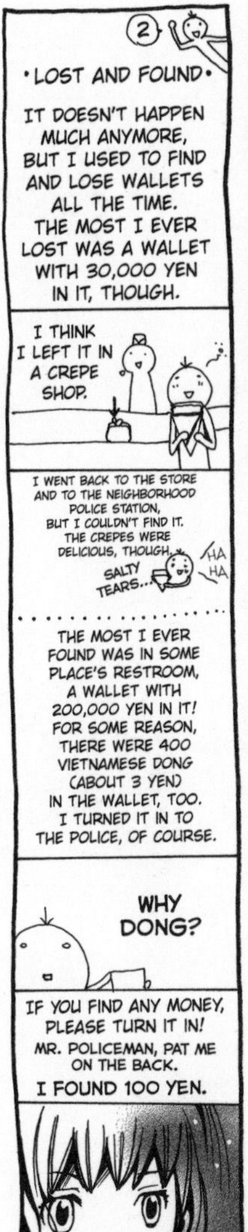
2
•LOST AND FOUND•
IT DOESN'T HAPPEN MUCH ANYMORE, BUT I USED TO FIND AND LOSE WALLETS ALL THE TIME. THE MOST I EVER LOST WAS A WALLET WITH 30,000 YEN IN IT, THOUGH.
I THINK I LEFT IT IN A CREPE SHOP.
I WENT BACK TO THE STORE AND TO THE NEIGHBORHOOD POLICE STATION, BUT I COULDN'T FIND IT. THE CREPES WERE DELICIOUS, THOUGH.
SALTY TEARS...
HA HA
THE MOST I EVER FOUND WAS IN SOME PLACE'S RESTROOM, A WALLET WITH 200,000 YEN IN IT! FOR SOME REASON, THERE WERE 400 VIETNAMESE DONG (ABOUT 3 YEN) IN THE WALLET, TOO. I TURNED IT IN TO THE POLICE, OF COURSE.
WHY DONG?
IF YOU FIND ANY MONEY, PLEASE TURN IT IN!
MR. POLICEMAN, PAT ME ON THE BACK.
I FOUND 100 YEN.

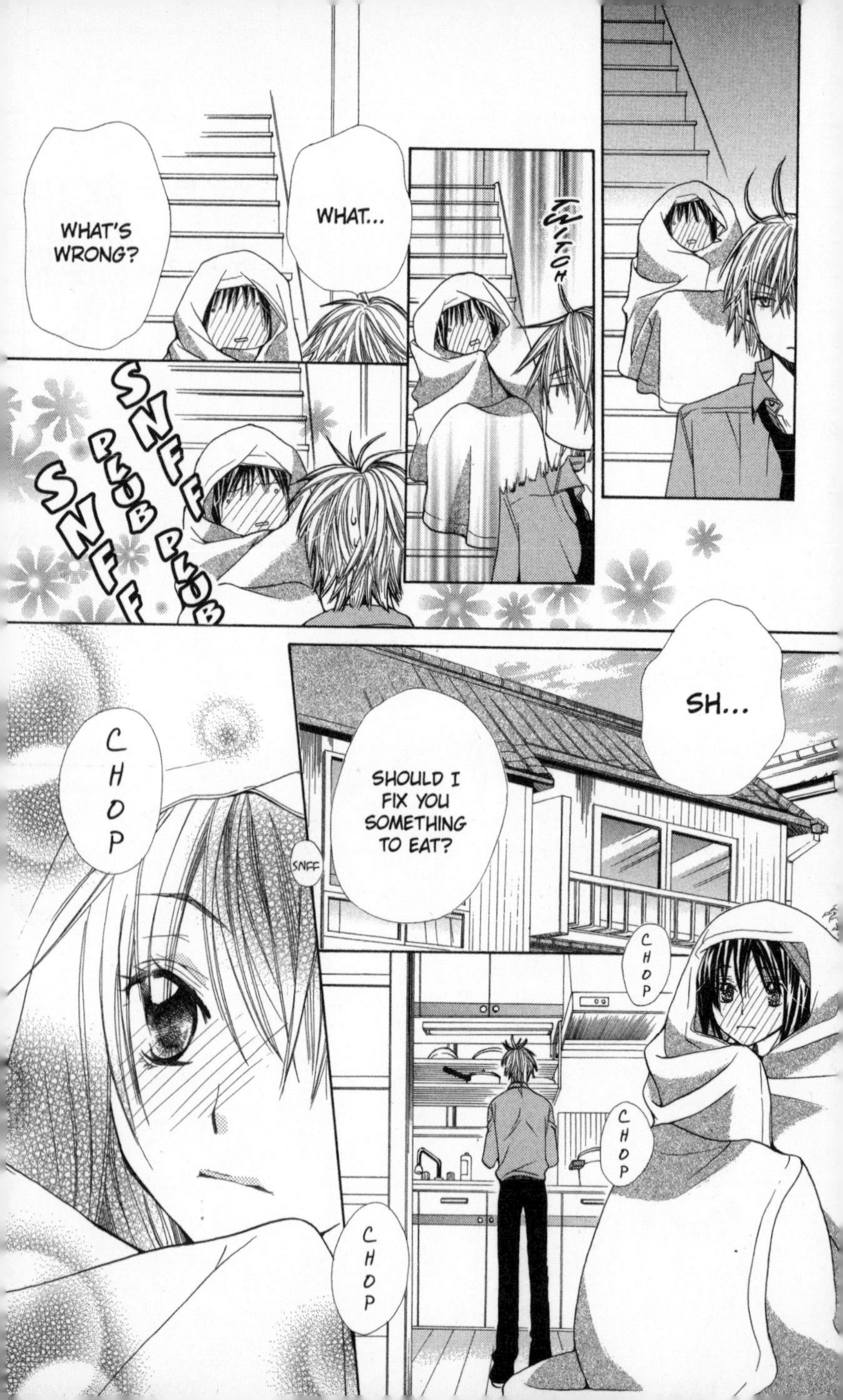
TWITCH
WHAT...
WHAT'S WRONG?
SNFF
PLUB
PLUB
SNFF
SH...
SHOULD I FIX YOU SOMETHING TO EAT?
SNFF
CHOP
CHOP
CHOP
CHOP

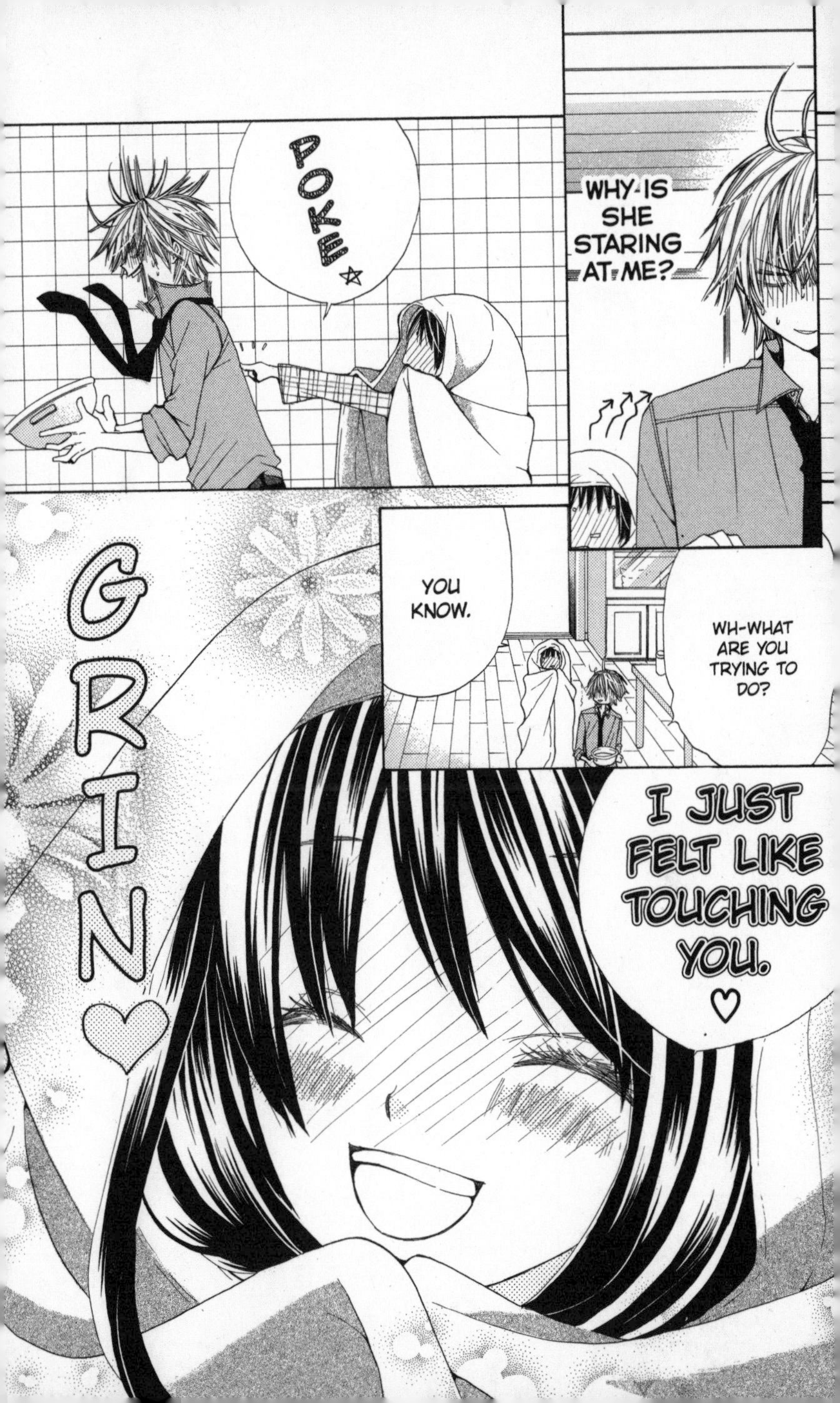
WHY IS SHE STARING AT ME?
POKE☆
WH-WHAT ARE YOU TRYING TO DO?
YOU KNOW.
I JUST FELT LIKE TOUCHING YOU. ♡
GRIN♡

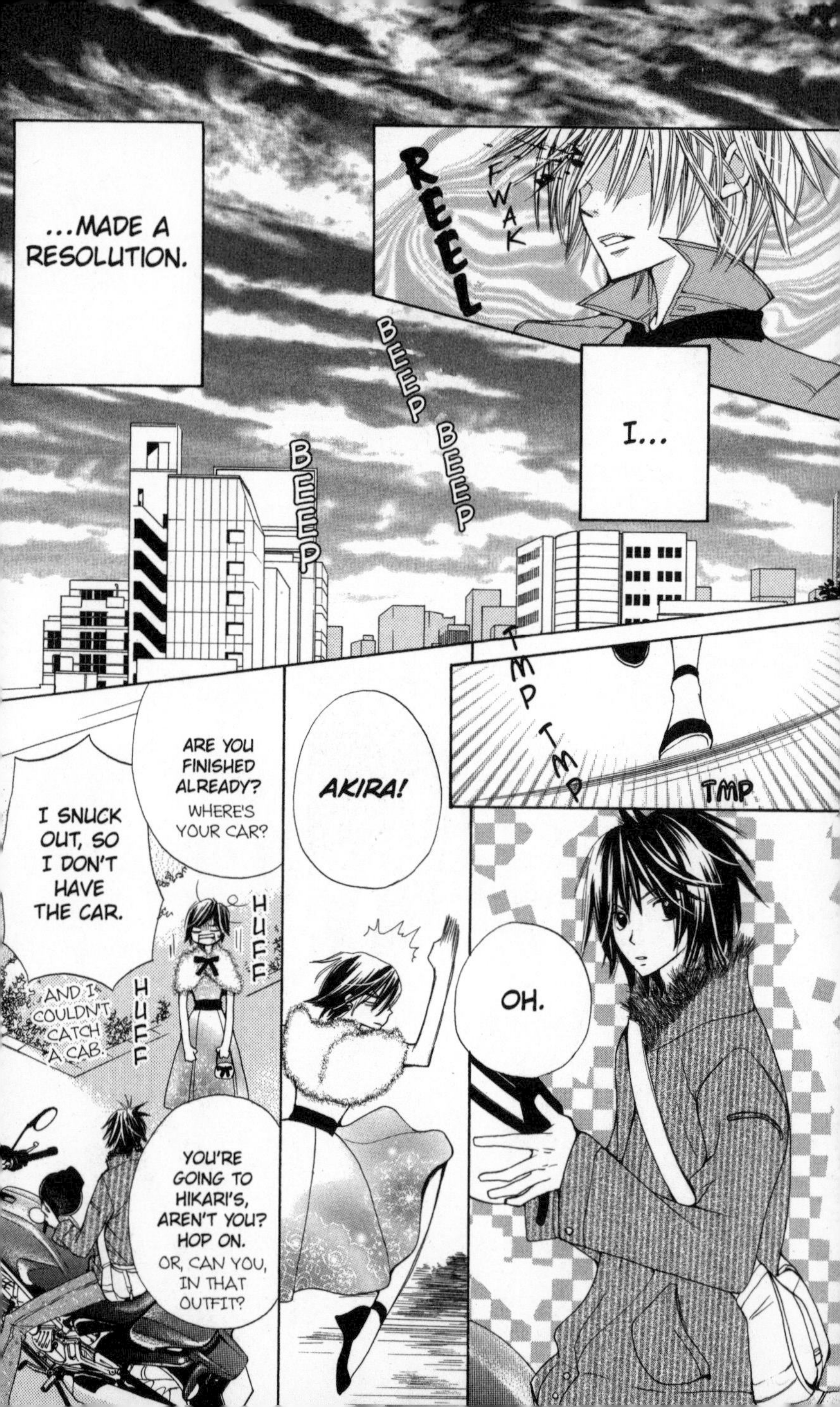
REEL
FWAK
I...
BEEP BEEP
BEEP
...MADE A RESOLUTION.
TMP TMP
TMP
AKIRA!
OH.
ARE YOU FINISHED ALREADY? WHERE'S YOUR CAR?
I SNUCK OUT, SO I DON'T HAVE THE CAR.
HUFF
HUFF
AND I COULDN'T CATCH A CAB.
YOU'RE GOING TO HIKARI'S, AREN'T YOU? HOP ON. OR, CAN YOU, IN THAT OUTFIT?

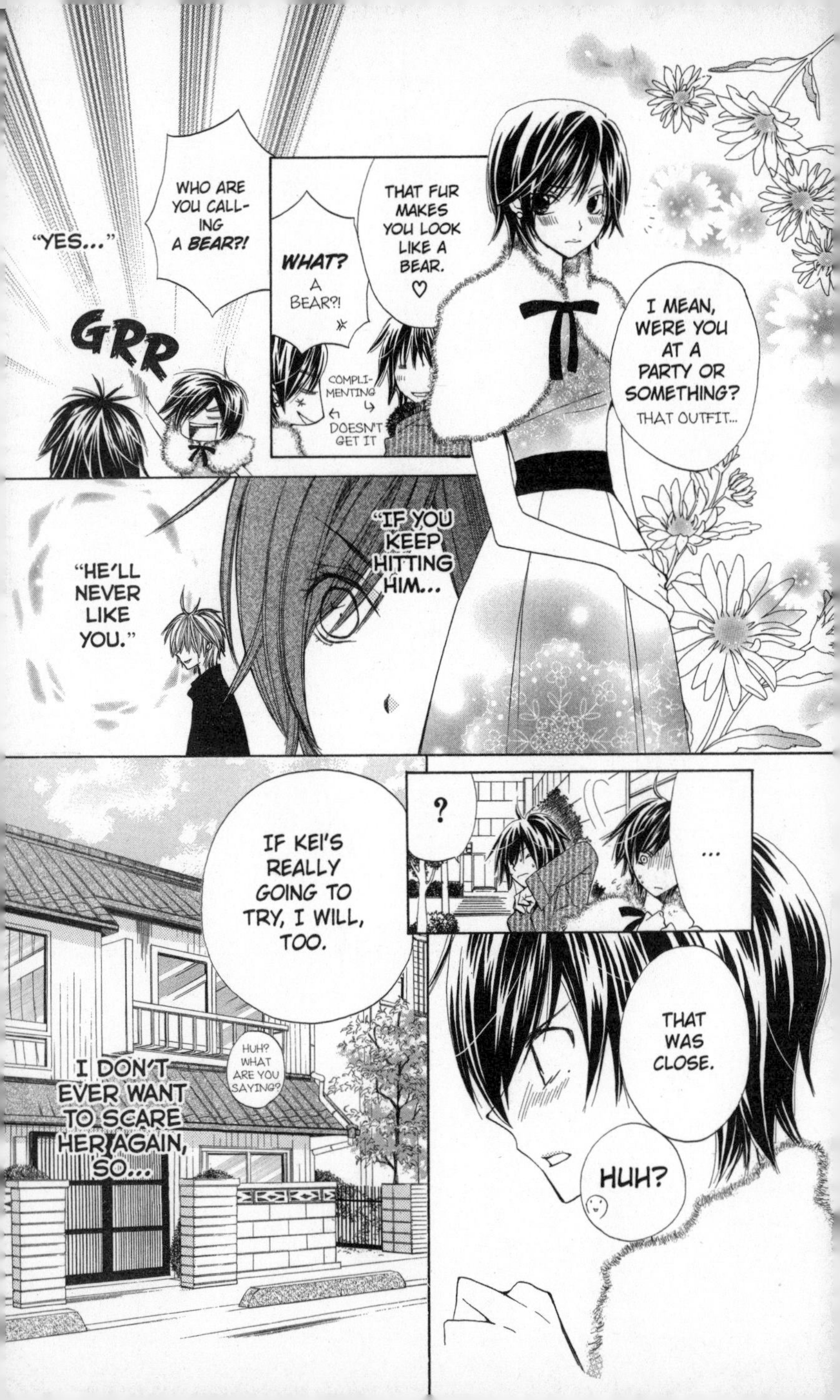
I MEAN, WERE YOU AT A PARTY OR SOMETHING?
THAT OUTFIT...
THAT FUR MAKES YOU LOOK LIKE A BEAR. ♡
WHAT? A BEAR?!
COMPLIMENTING
DOESN'T GET IT
WHO ARE YOU CALLING A BEAR?!
"YES..."
GRR
"IF YOU KEEP HITTING HIM...
"HE'LL NEVER LIKE YOU."
...
?
THAT WAS CLOSE.
HUH?
IF KEI'S REALLY GOING TO TRY, I WILL, TOO.
HUH? WHAT ARE YOU SAYING?
I DON'T EVER WANT TO SCARE HER AGAIN, SO...

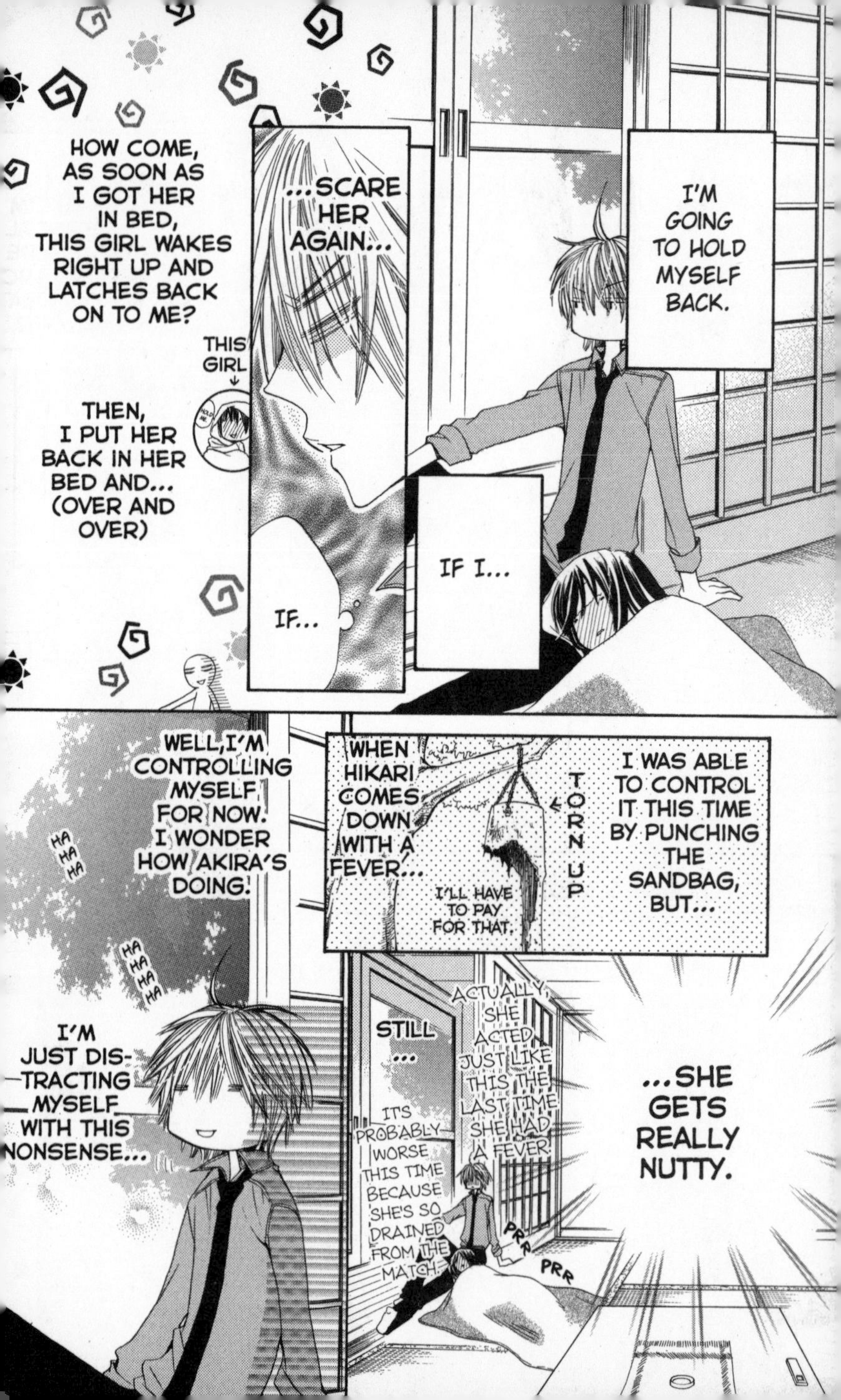

I'M GOING TO HOLD MYSELF BACK.
IF I...
IF...
...SCARE HER AGAIN...
HOW COME, AS SOON AS I GOT HER IN BED, THIS GIRL WAKES RIGHT UP AND LATCHES BACK ON TO ME?
THIS GIRL
THEN, I PUT HER BACK IN HER BED AND... (OVER AND OVER)
I WAS ABLE TO CONTROL IT THIS TIME BY PUNCHING THE SANDBAG, BUT...
TORN UP
I'LL HAVE TO PAY FOR THAT.
WHEN HIKARI COMES DOWN WITH A FEVER...
...SHE GETS REALLY NUTTY.
ACTUALLY, SHE ACTED JUST LIKE THIS THE LAST TIME SHE HAD A FEVER
STILL...
IT'S PROBABLY WORSE THIS TIME BECAUSE SHE'S SO DRAINED FROM THE MATCH.
PRR
PRR
WELL, I'M CONTROLLING MYSELF FOR NOW. I WONDER HOW AKIRA'S DOING.
HA HA HA
HA HA HA HA HA
I'M JUST DIS-TRACTING MYSELF WITH THIS NONSENSE...

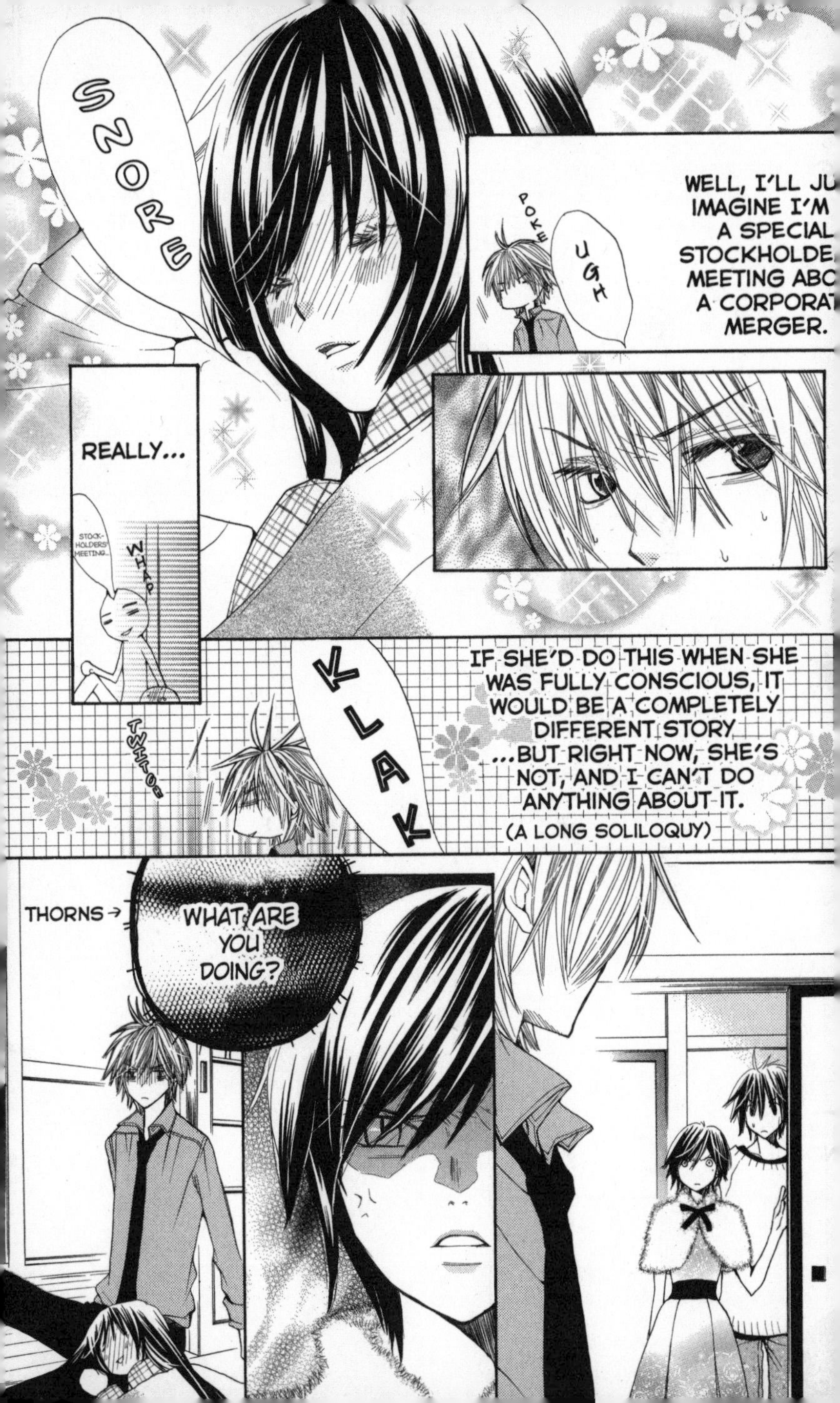

WELL, I'LL JU IMAGINE I'M A SPECIAL STOCKHOLDE MEETING ABO A CORPORAT MERGER.
POKE
UGH
SNORE
REALLY...
STOCK-HOLDERS' MEETING...
WHAP
IF SHE'D DO THIS WHEN SHE WAS FULLY CONSCIOUS, IT WOULD BE A COMPLETELY DIFFERENT STORY ...BUT RIGHT NOW, SHE'S NOT, AND I CAN'T DO ANYTHING ABOUT IT.
(A LONG SOLILOQUY)
KLAK
TWITCH
THORNS →
WHAT ARE YOU DOING?

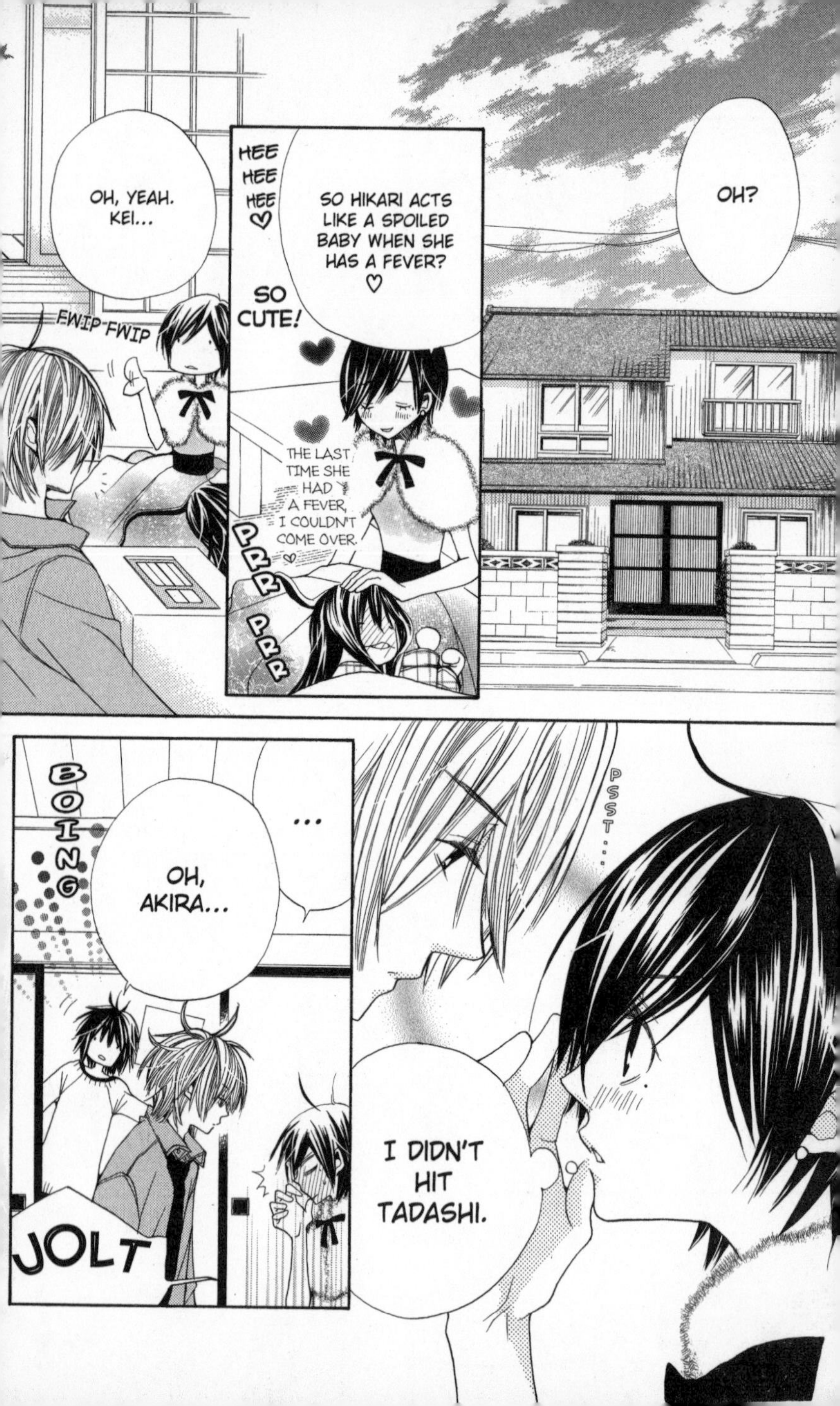
OH?
HEE HEE HEE ♡
SO HIKARI ACTS LIKE A SPOILED BABY WHEN SHE HAS A FEVER? ♡
SO CUTE!
THE LAST TIME SHE HAD A FEVER, I COULDN'T COME OVER. ♡
PRR PRR
FWIP FWIP
OH, YEAH. KEI...
PSST...
I DIDN'T HIT TADASHI.
...
OH, AKIRA...
BOING
JOLT

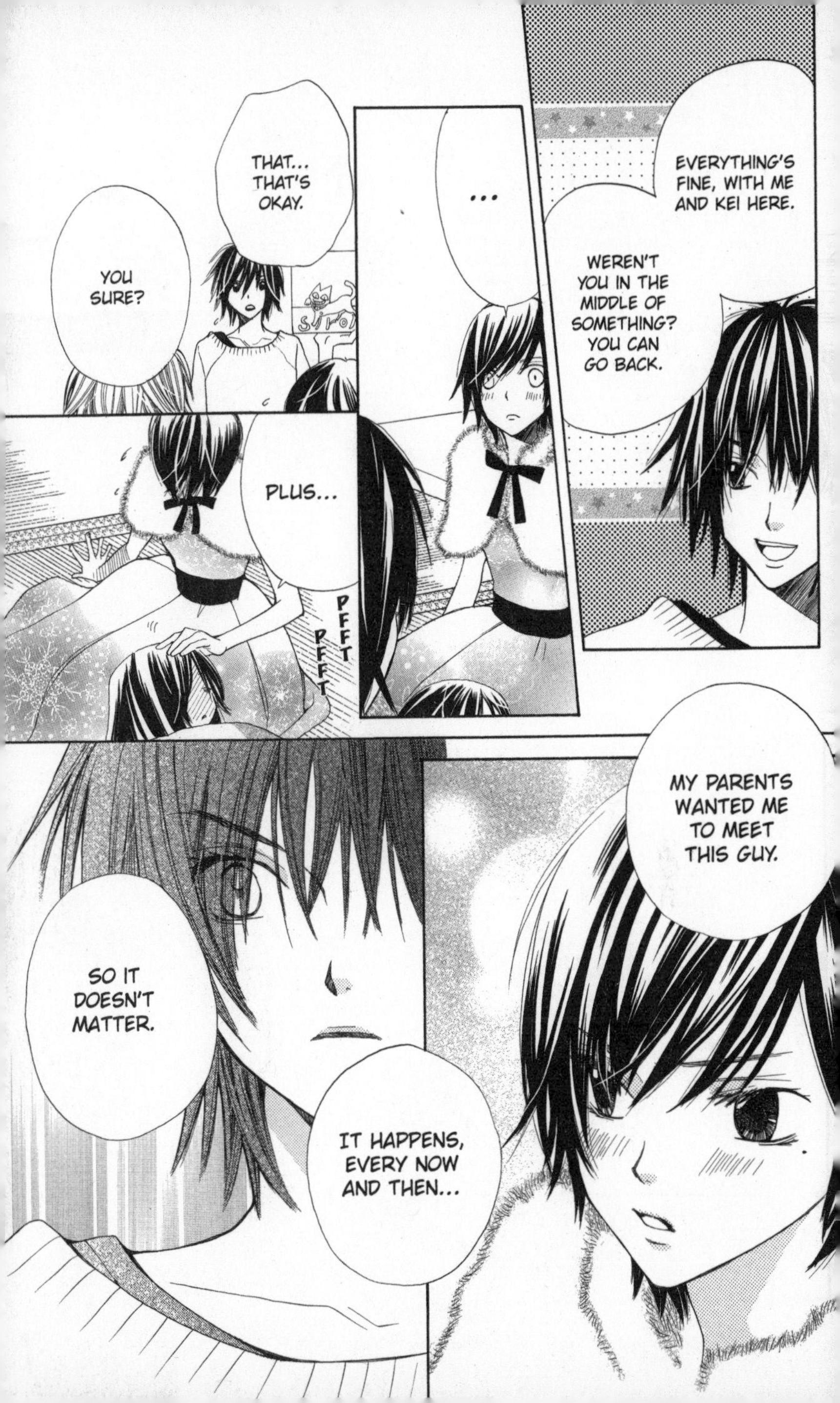
EVERYTHING'S FINE, WITH ME AND KEI HERE.
WEREN'T YOU IN THE MIDDLE OF SOMETHING? YOU CAN GO BACK.
...
THAT... THAT'S OKAY.
YOU SURE?
PLUS...
PFFT PFFT
MY PARENTS WANTED ME TO MEET THIS GUY.
IT HAPPENS, EVERY NOW AND THEN...
SO IT DOESN'T MATTER.

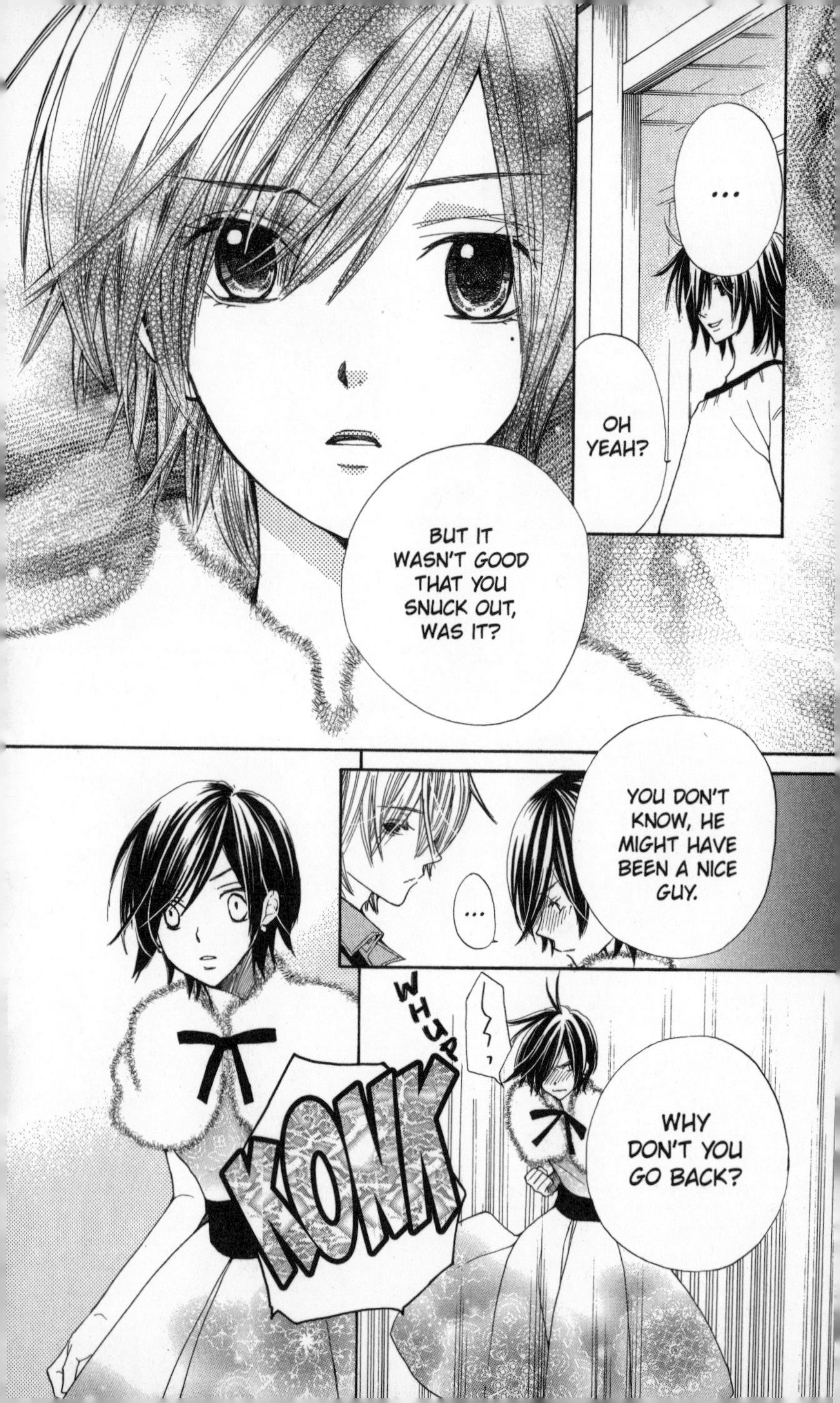
...
OH YEAH?
BUT IT WASN'T GOOD THAT YOU SNUCK OUT, WAS IT?
YOU DON'T KNOW, HE MIGHT HAVE BEEN A NICE GUY.
...
WHUP
KONK
WHY DON'T YOU GO BACK?

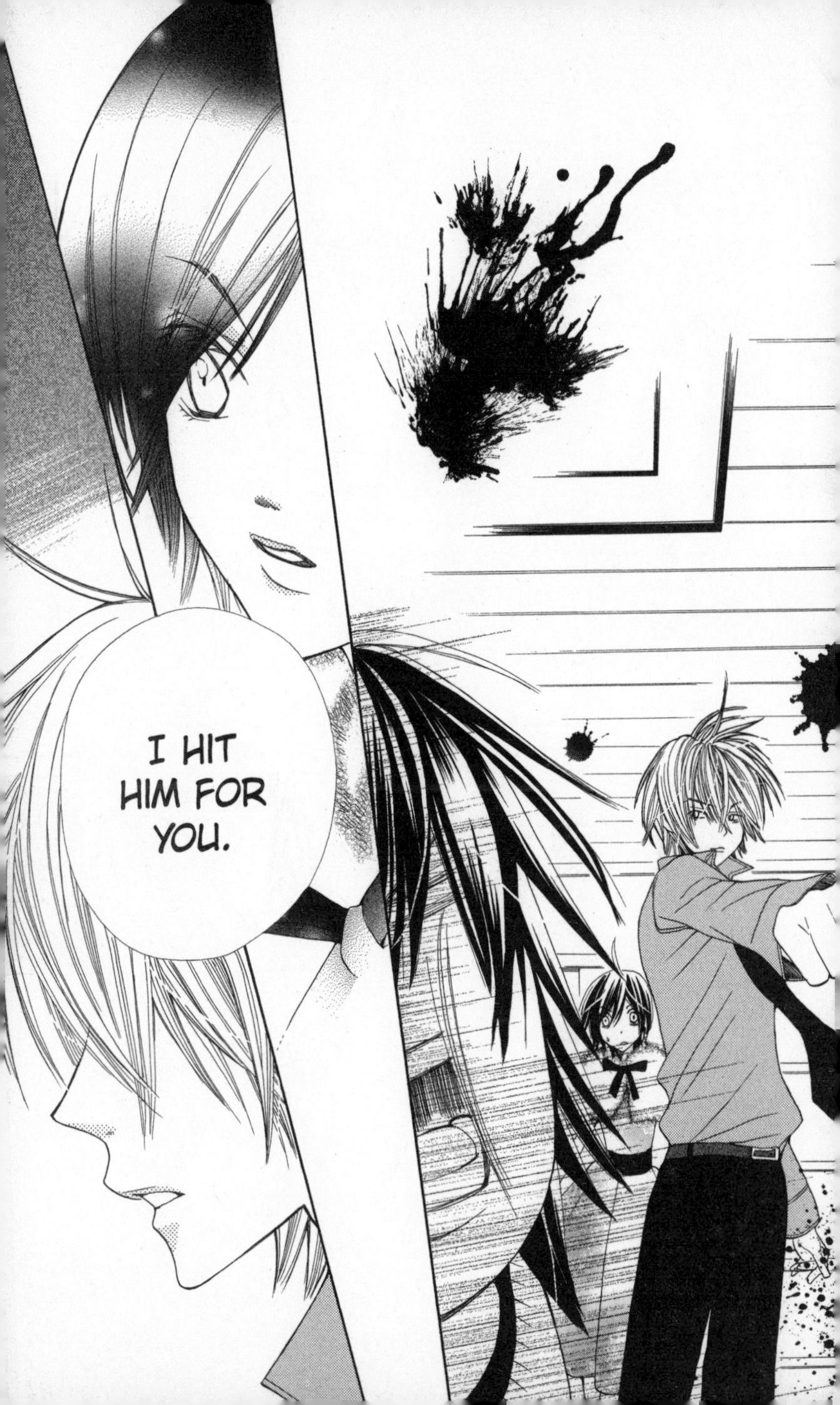
I HIT HIM FOR YOU.

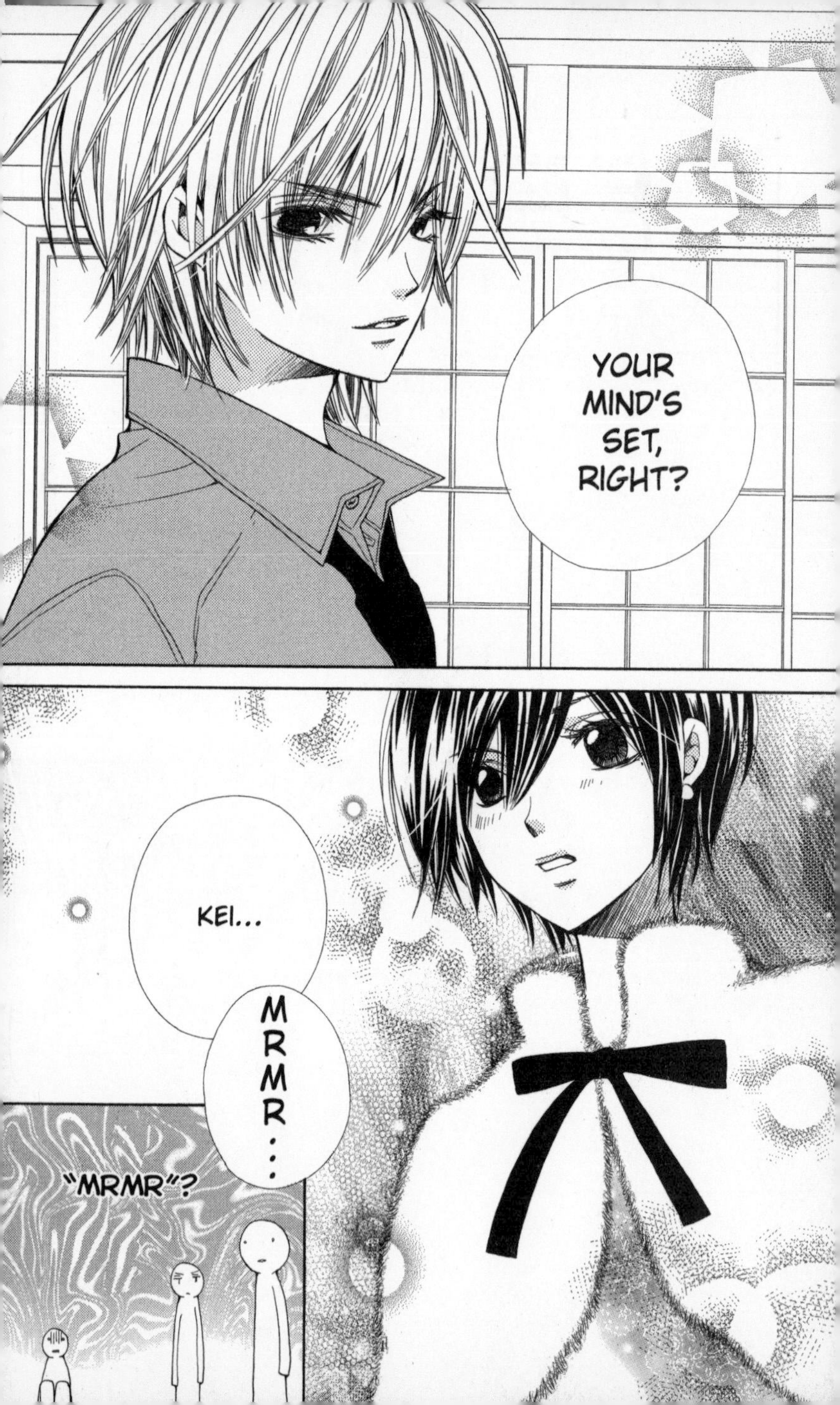
YOUR MIND'S SET, RIGHT?
KEI...
MRMR...
"MRMR"?

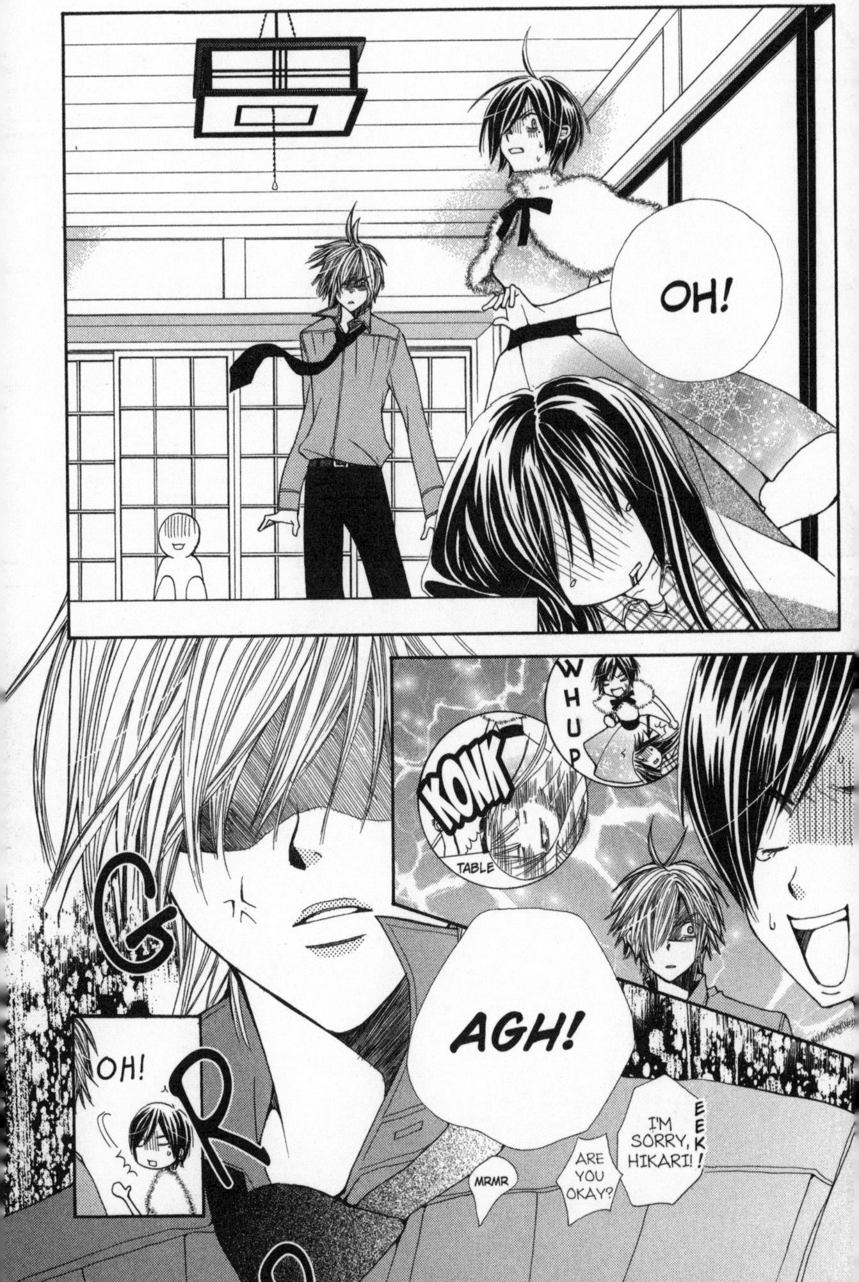
OH!
WHUP
KONK
TABLE
AGH!
GR
EEK!
I'M SORRY, HIKARI!
ARE YOU OKAY?
MRMR
OH!

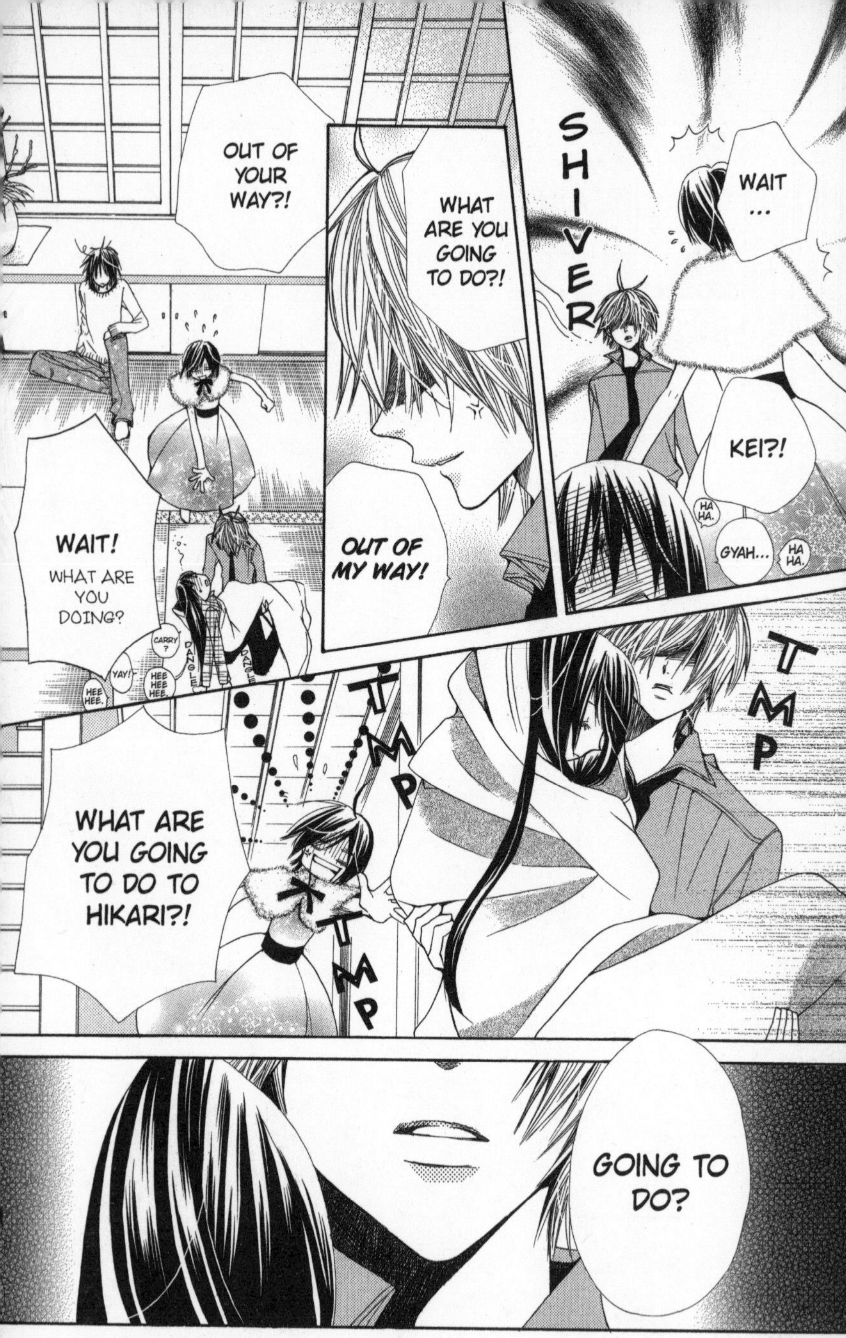
WAIT ...
SHIVER
KEI?!
HA HA.
GYAH...
HA HA.
WHAT ARE YOU GOING TO DO?!
OUT OF MY WAY!
OUT OF YOUR WAY?!
WAIT! WHAT ARE YOU DOING?
CARRY?
DANGLE
DANGLE
HEE HEE HEE.
YAY!
HEE HEE.
TMP
TMP
TMP
WHAT ARE YOU GOING TO DO TO HIKARI?!
TMP
GOING TO DO?

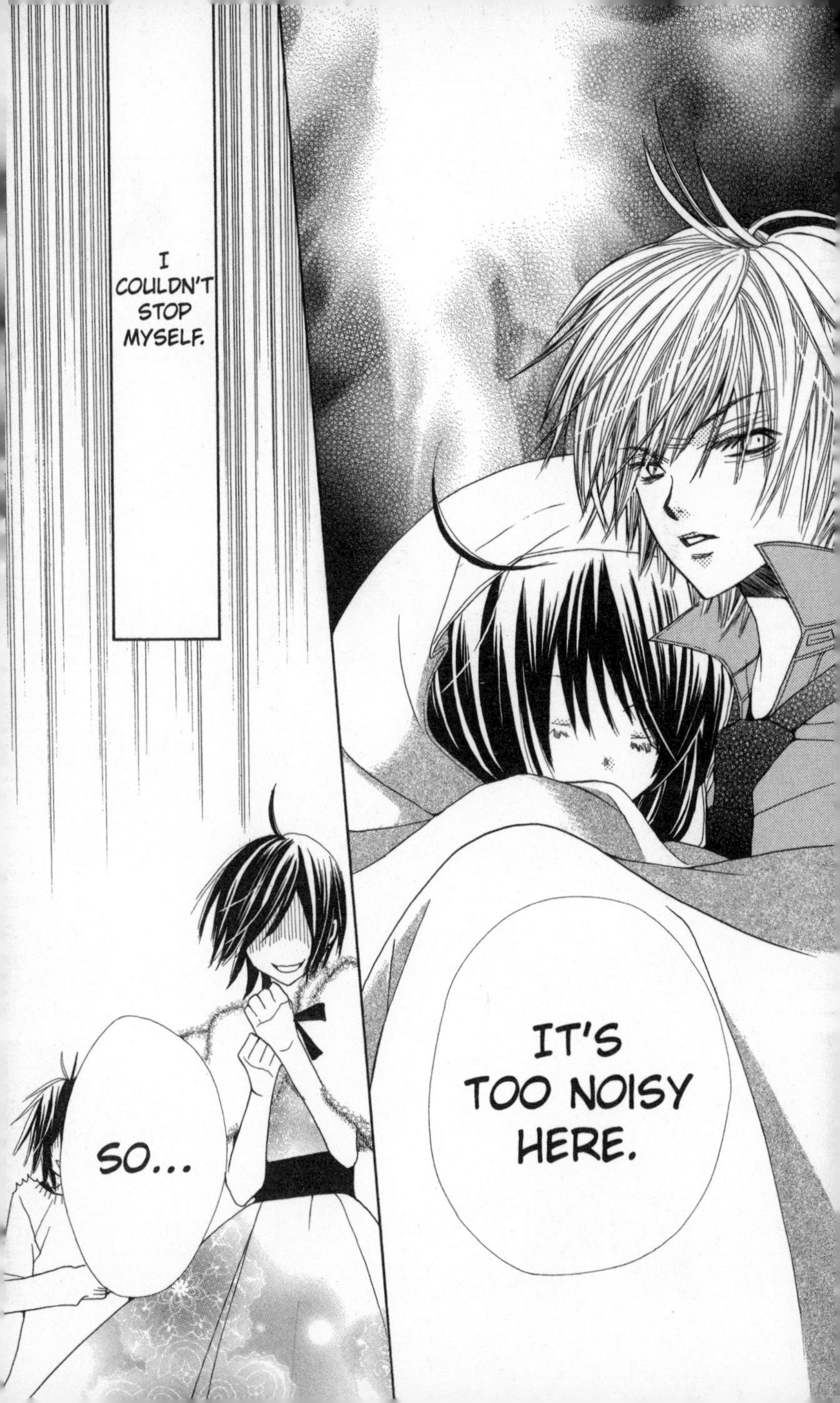
IT'S TOO NOISY HERE.
I COULDN'T STOP MYSELF.
SO...

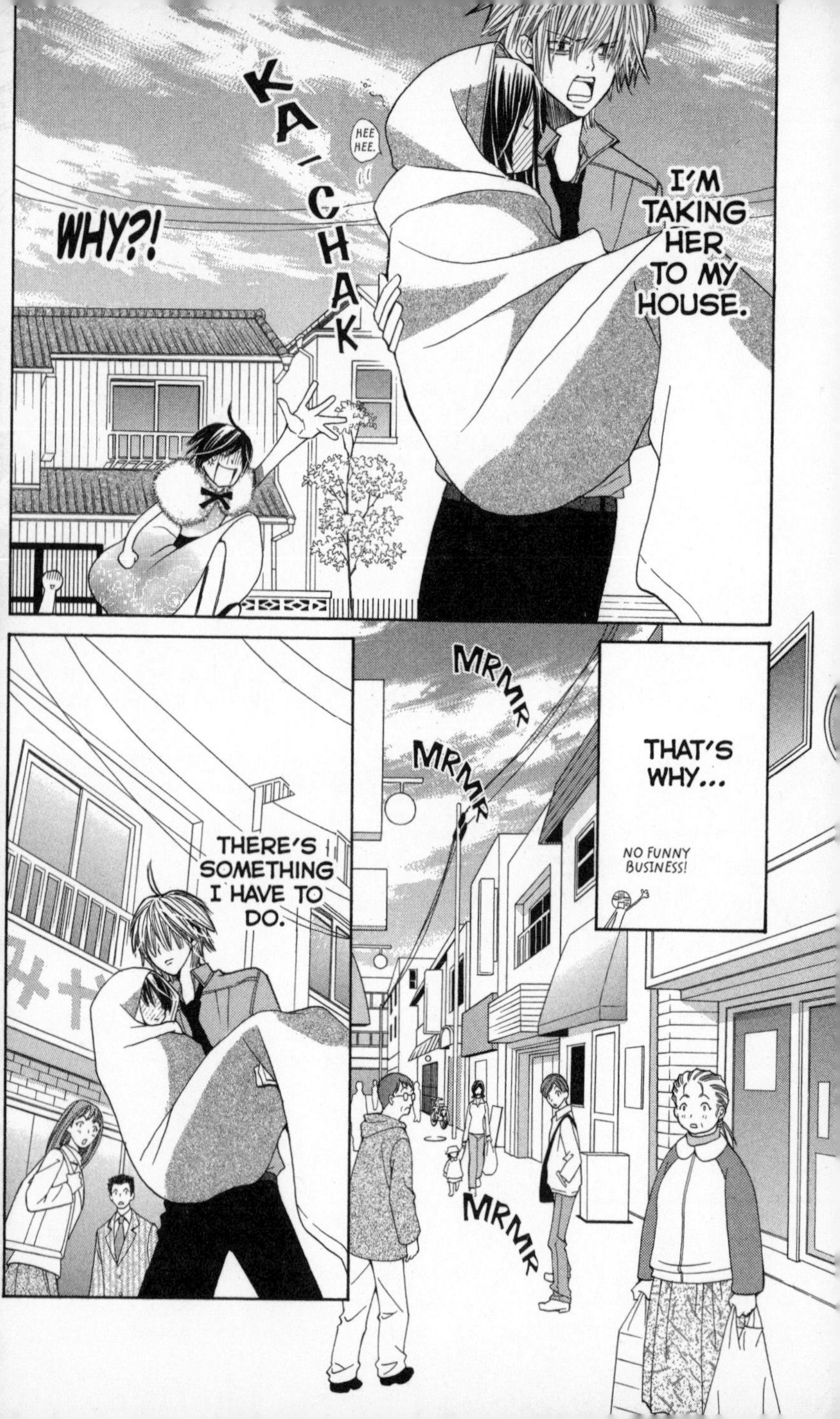
I'M TAKING HER TO MY HOUSE.
KA-CHAK
HEE HEE.
WHY?!
THAT'S WHY...
NO FUNNY BUSINESS!
MRMR
MRMR
MRMR
THERE'S SOMETHING I HAVE TO DO.

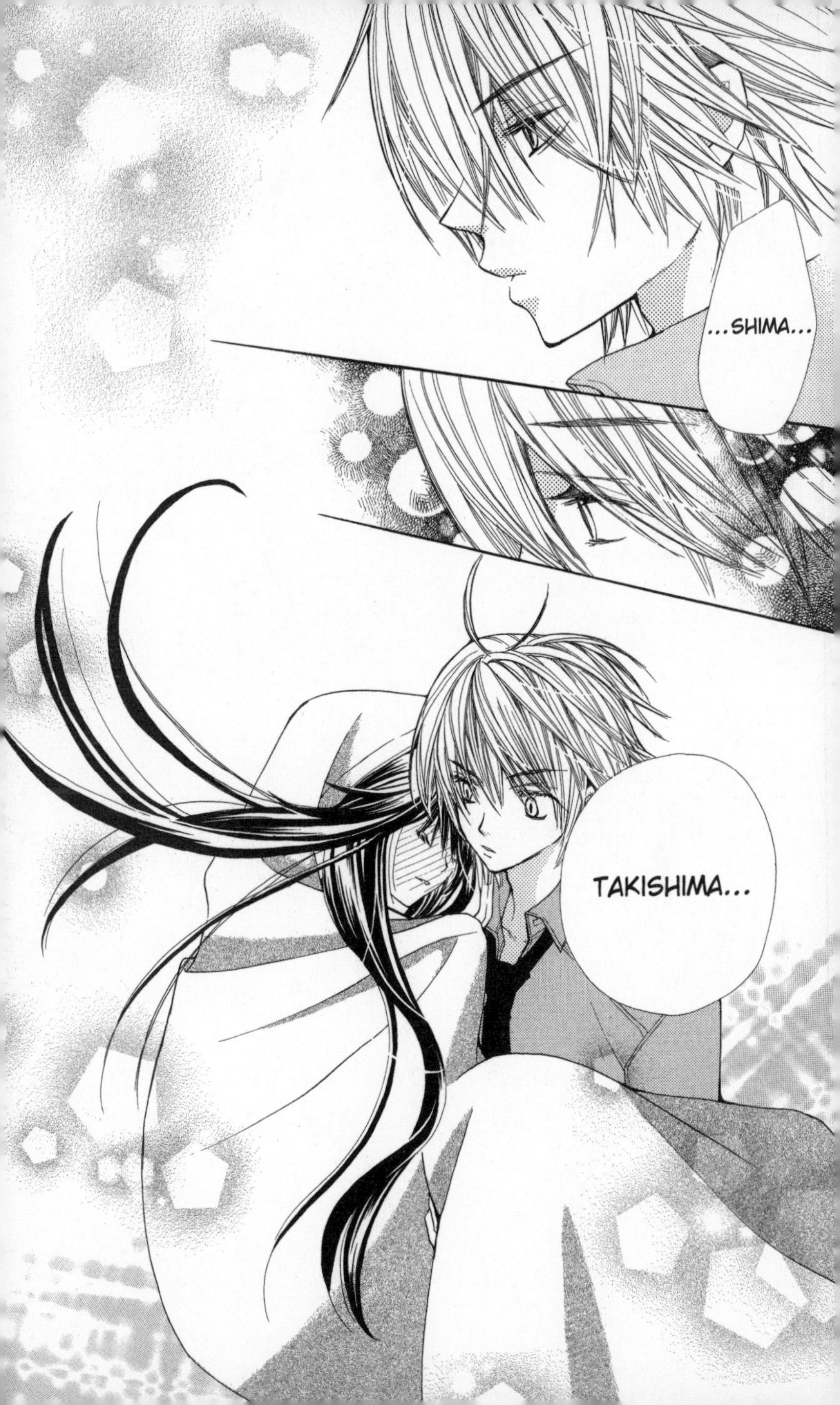
...SHIMA...
TAKISHIMA...

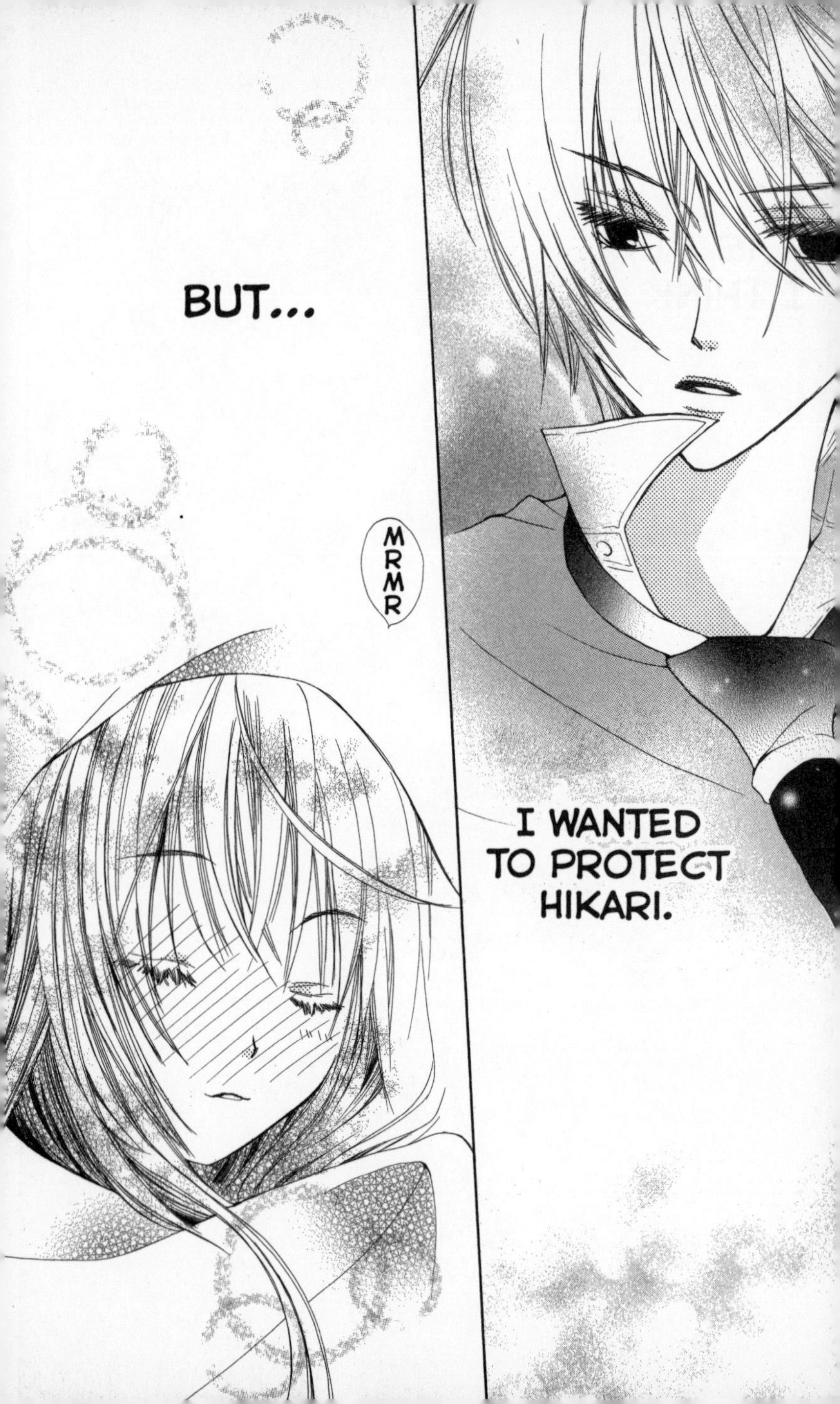
I WANTED TO PROTECT HIKARI.
BUT...
MRMR

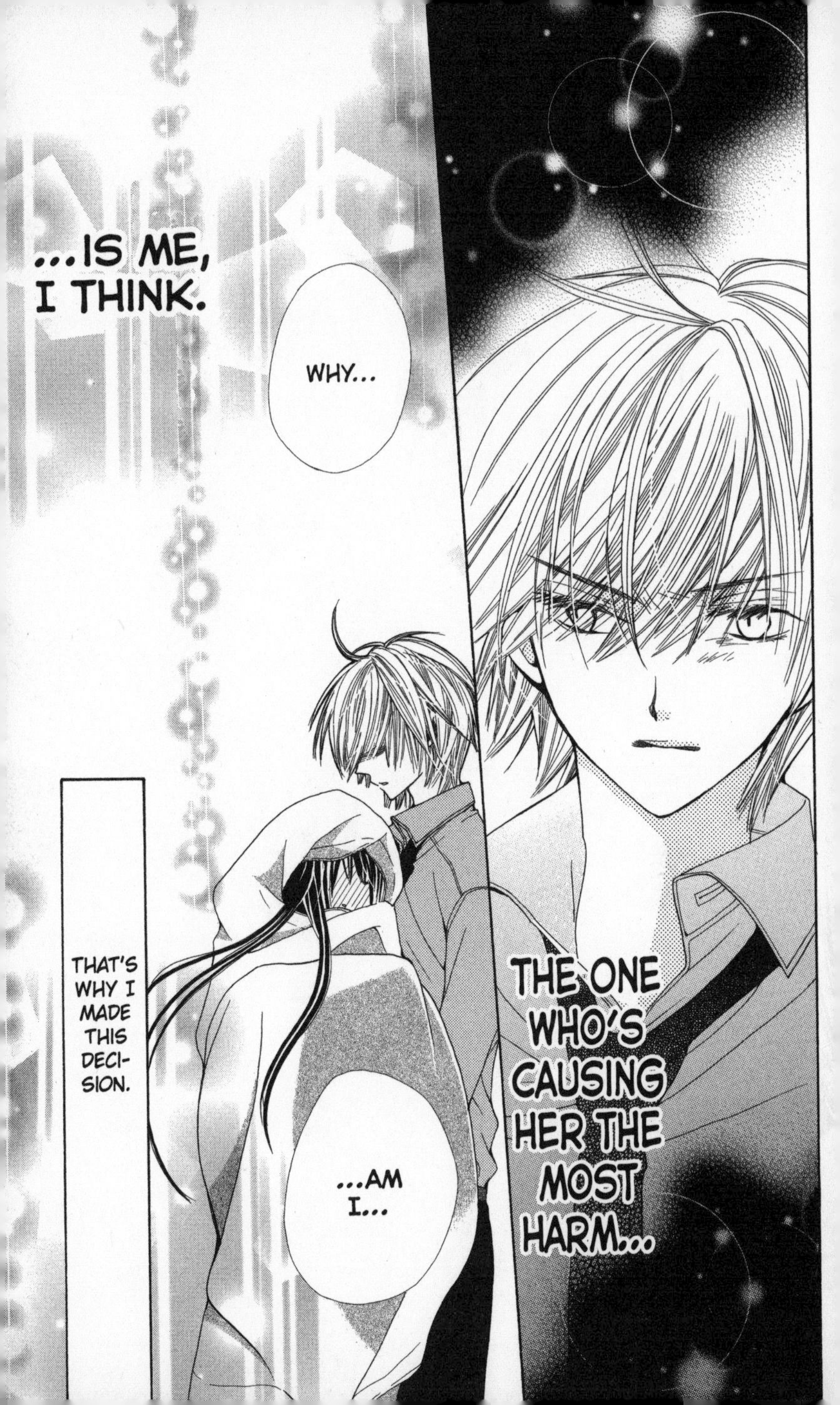
THE ONE WHO'S CAUSING HER THE MOST HARM...
...IS ME, I THINK.
WHY...
...AM I...
THAT'S WHY I MADE THIS DECISION.

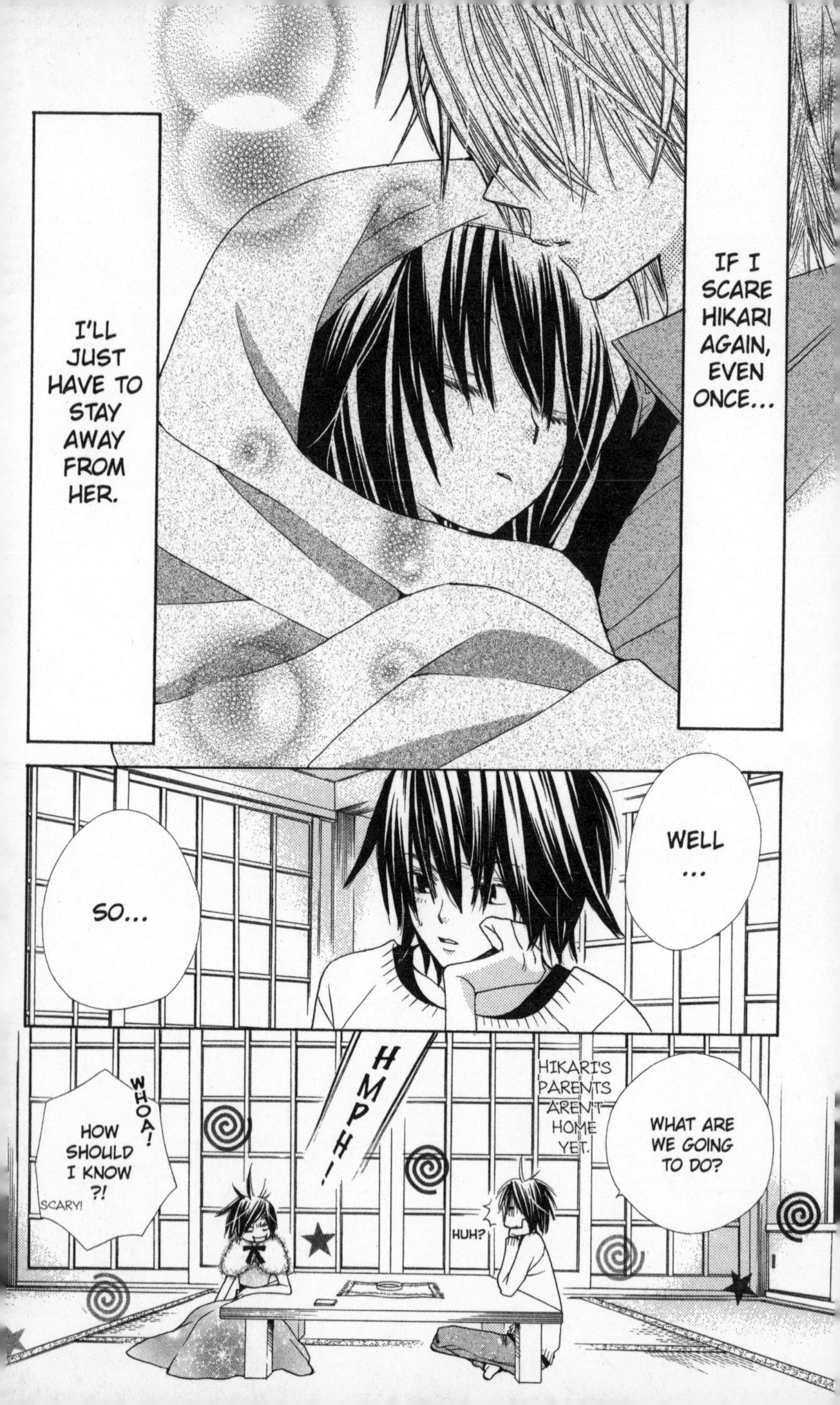
IF I SCARE HIKARI AGAIN, EVEN ONCE...
I'LL JUST HAVE TO STAY AWAY FROM HER.
WELL ...
SO...
WHAT ARE WE GOING TO DO?
HIKARI'S PARENTS AREN'T HOME YET.
HUH?
HMPH!
WHOA!
HOW SHOULD I KNOW ?!
SCARY!

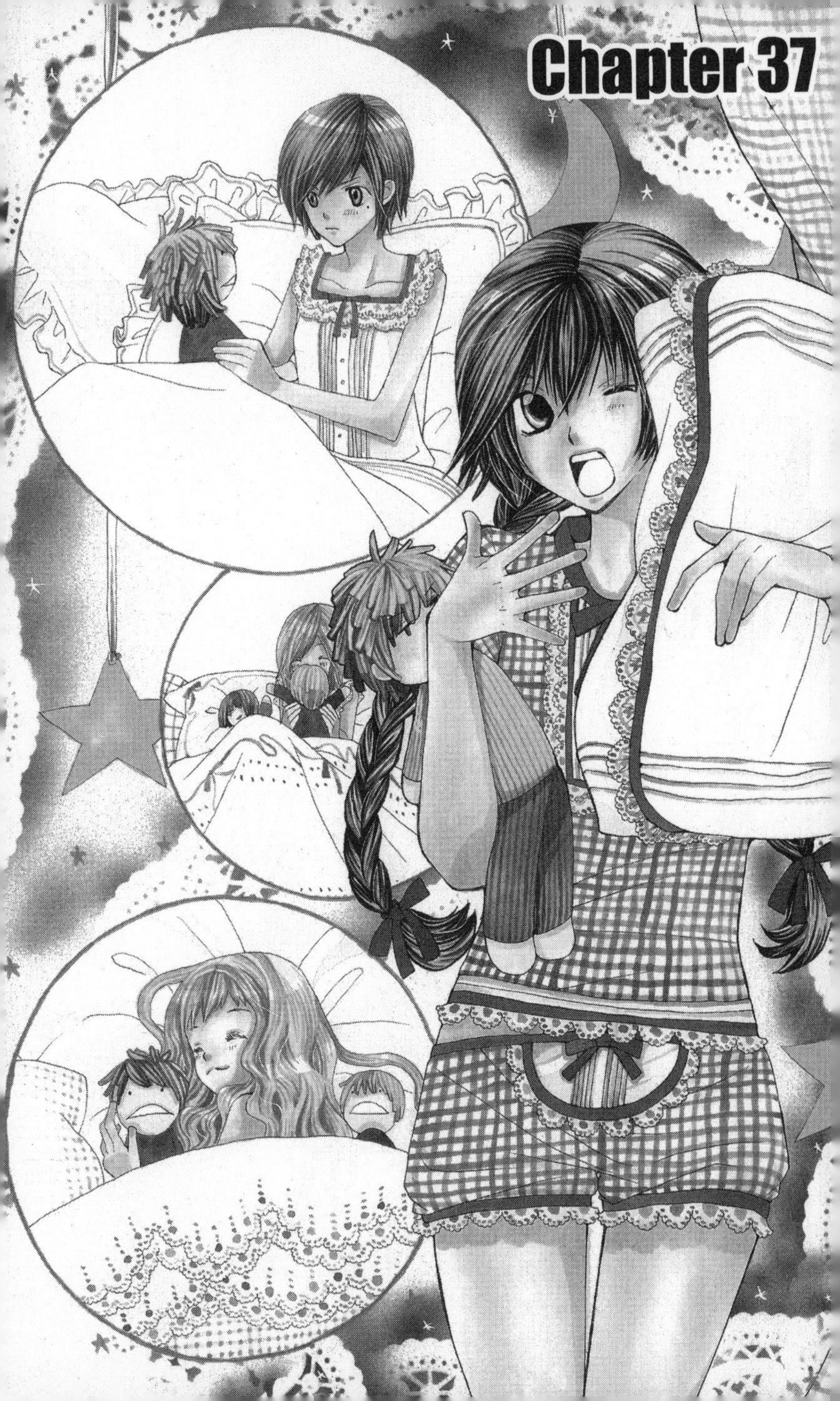
Chapter 37

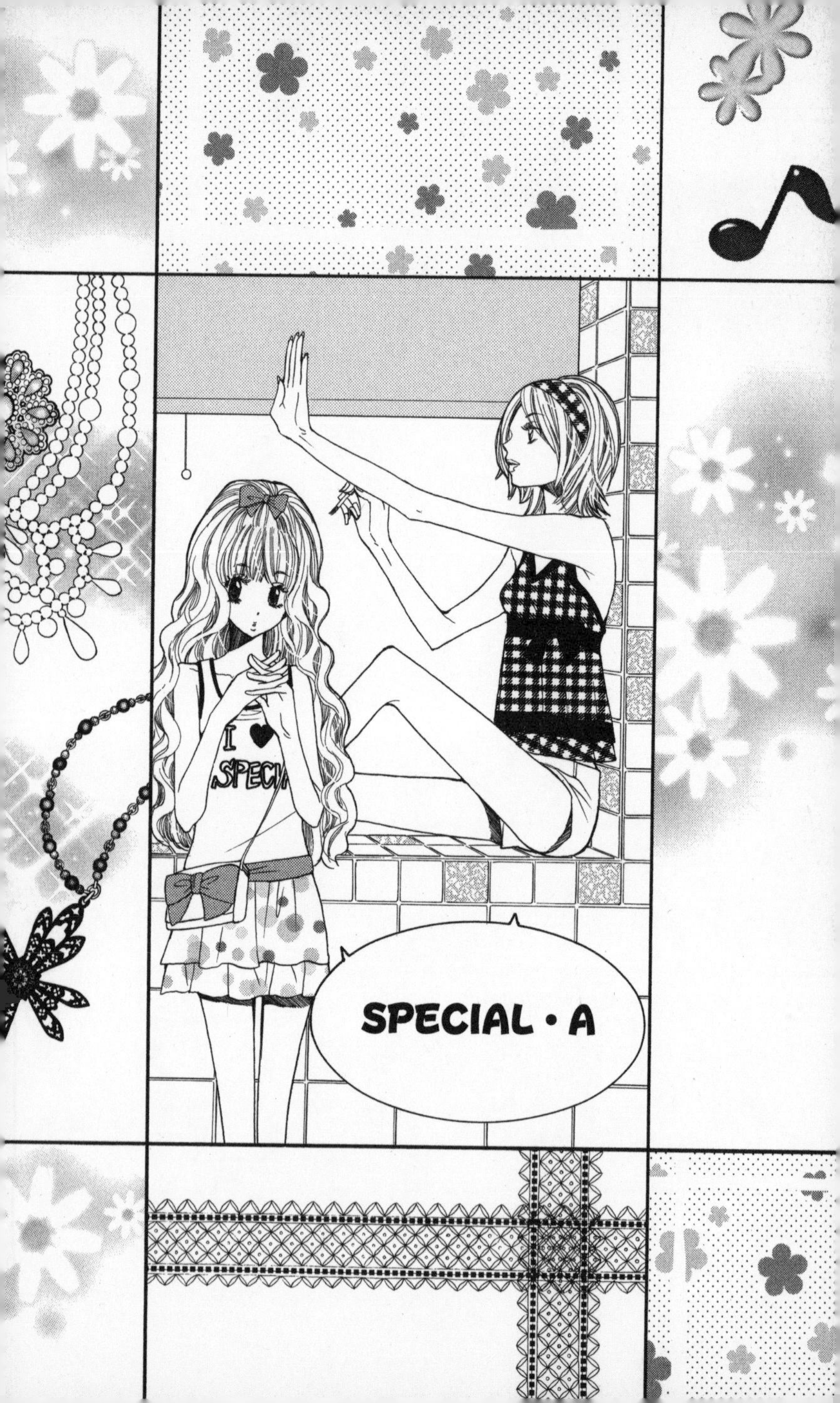
SPECIAL • A
I ♥ SPECI

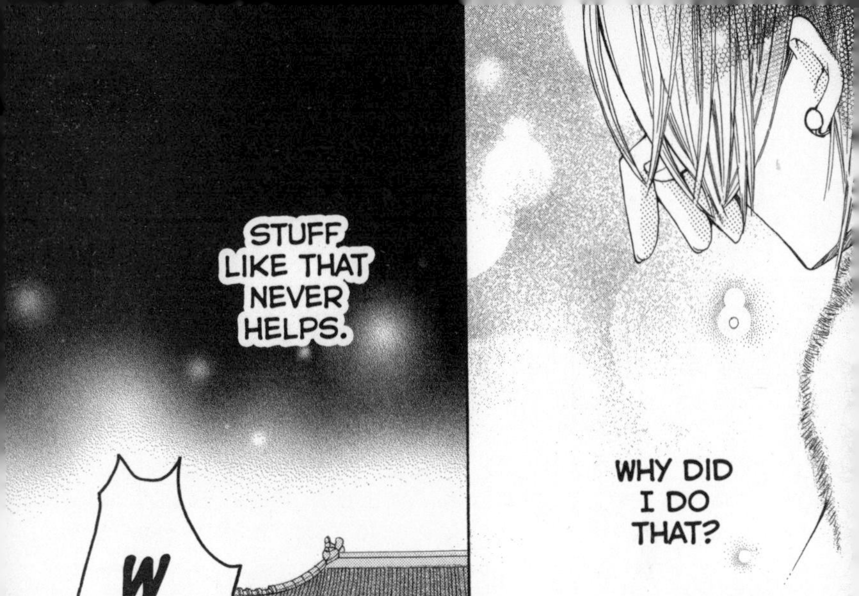
WHY DID I DO THAT?
STUFF LIKE THAT NEVER HELPS.
WHOA!

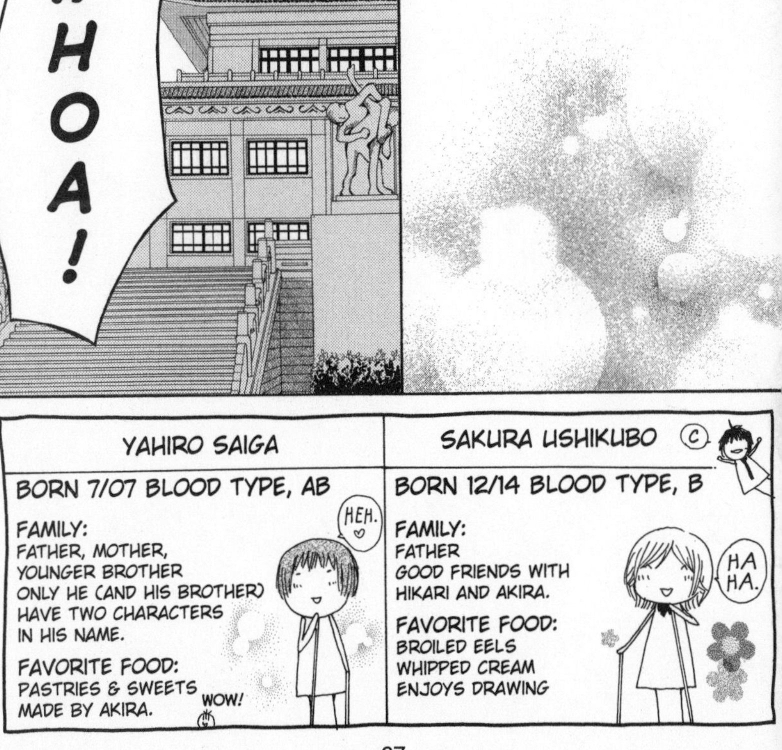
YAHIRO SAIGA
BORN 7/07 BLOOD TYPE, AB
FAMILY:
FATHER, MOTHER, YOUNGER BROTHER
ONLY HE (AND HIS BROTHER) HAVE TWO CHARACTERS IN HIS NAME.
FAVORITE FOOD:
PASTRIES & SWEETS MADE BY AKIRA.
HEH.
WOW!
SAKURA USHIKUBO ©
BORN 12/14 BLOOD TYPE, B
FAMILY:
FATHER
GOOD FRIENDS WITH HIKARI AND AKIRA.
FAVORITE FOOD:
BROILED EELS
WHIPPED CREAM
ENJOYS DRAWING
HA HA.

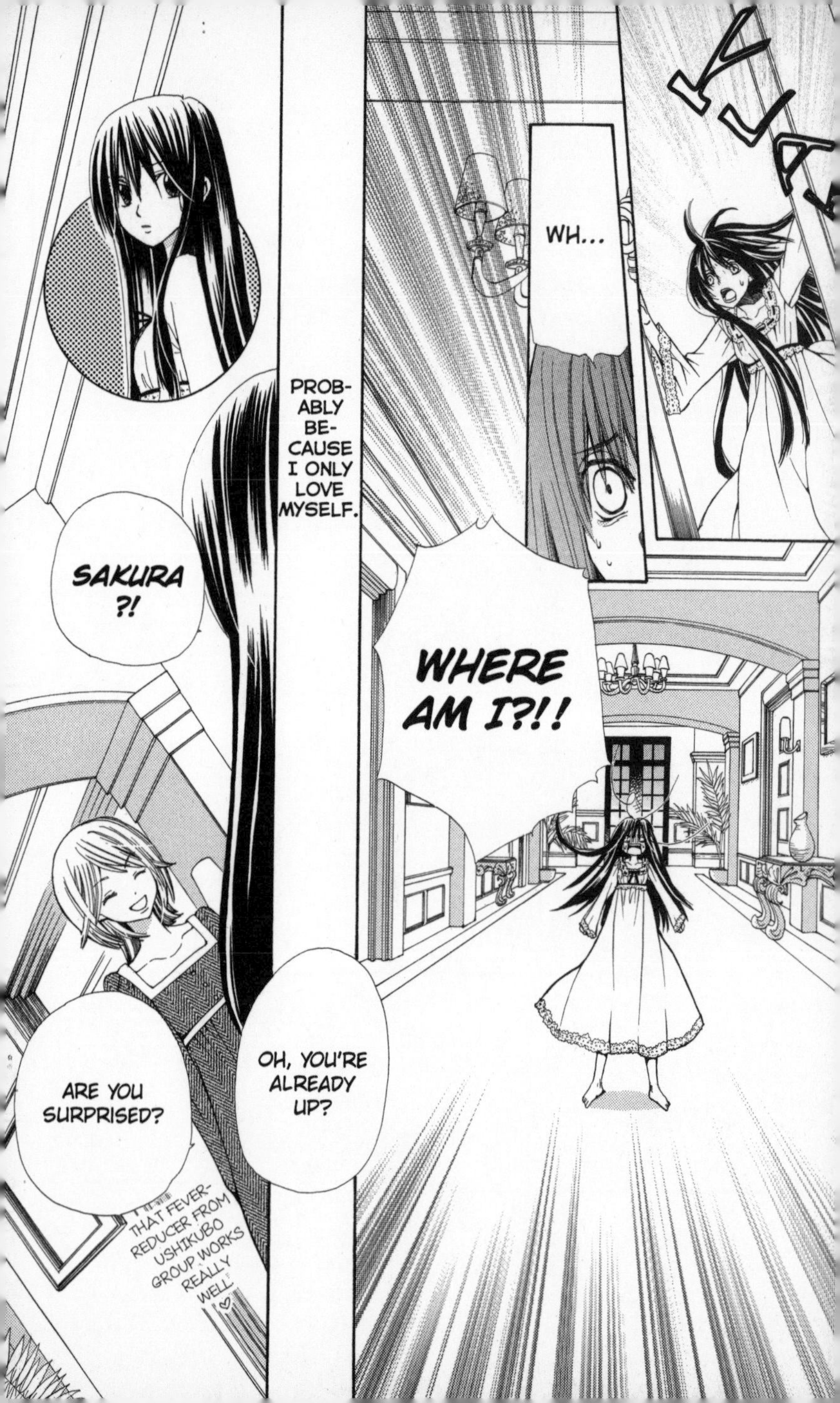
WH...
WHERE AM I?!!
PROB-ABLY BE-CAUSE I ONLY LOVE MYSELF.
OH, YOU'RE ALREADY UP?
SAKURA?!
ARE YOU SURPRISED?
THAT FEVER-REDUCER FROM USHIKUBO GROUP WORKS REALLY WELL ♡

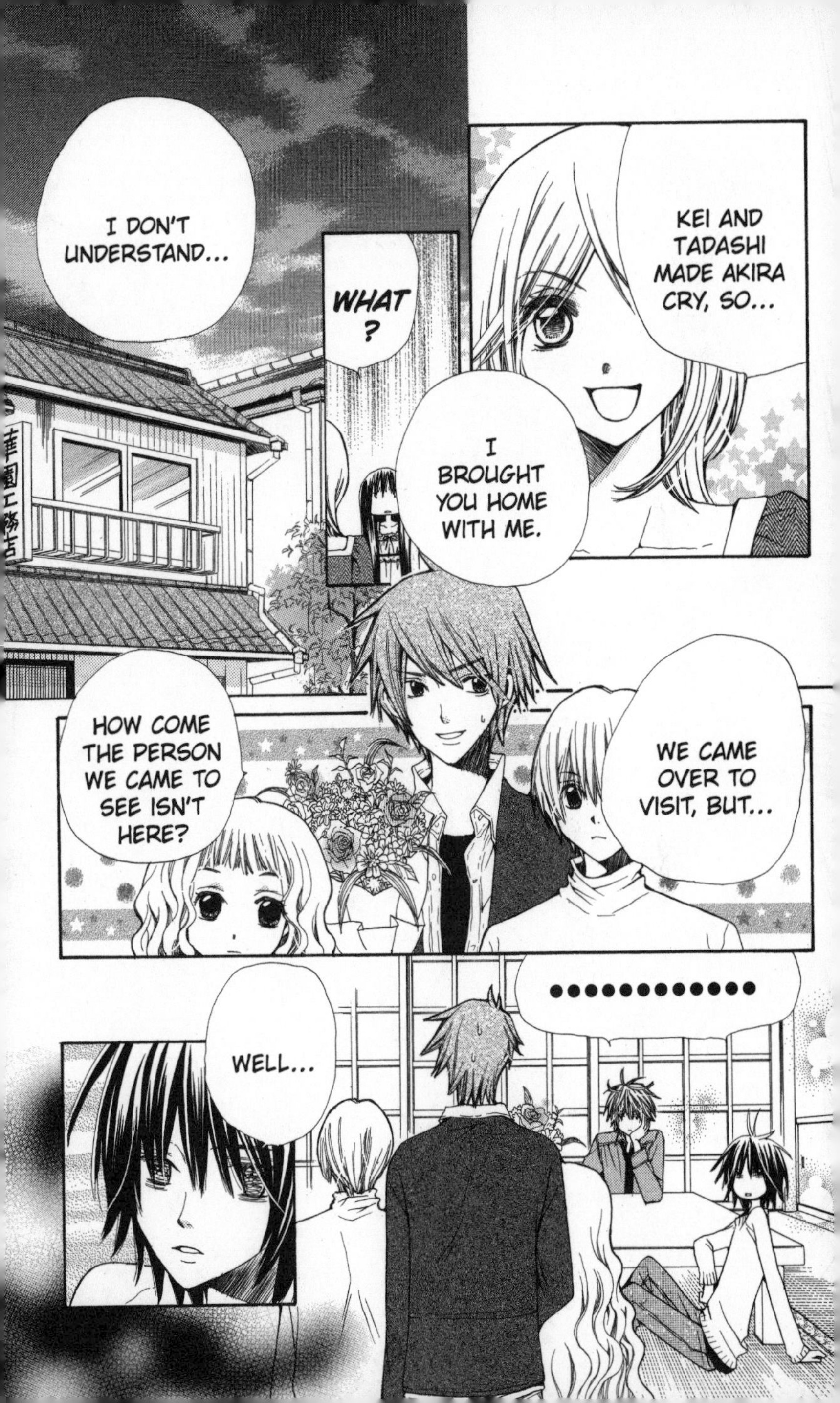
KEI AND TADASHI MADE AKIRA CRY, SO...
I BROUGHT YOU HOME WITH ME.
WHAT ?
I DON'T UNDERSTAND...
WE CAME OVER TO VISIT, BUT...
HOW COME THE PERSON WE CAME TO SEE ISN'T HERE?
....
WELL...

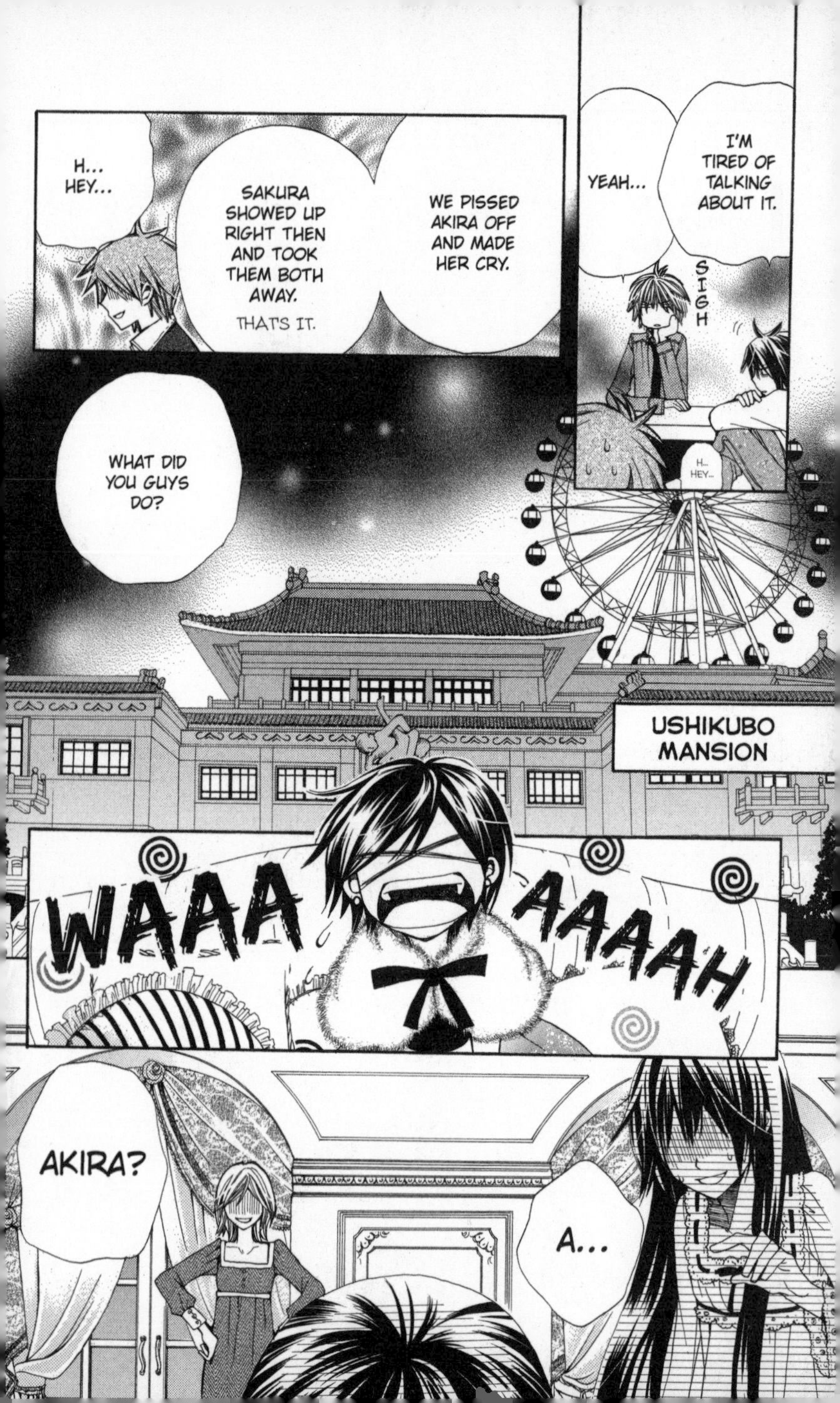
I'M TIRED OF TALKING ABOUT IT.
YEAH...
SIGH
H... HEY...
WE PISSED AKIRA OFF AND MADE HER CRY.
SAKURA SHOWED UP RIGHT THEN AND TOOK THEM BOTH AWAY.
THAT'S IT.
H... HEY...
WHAT DID YOU GUYS DO?
USHIKUBO MANSION
WAAA AAAAH
A...
AKIRA?

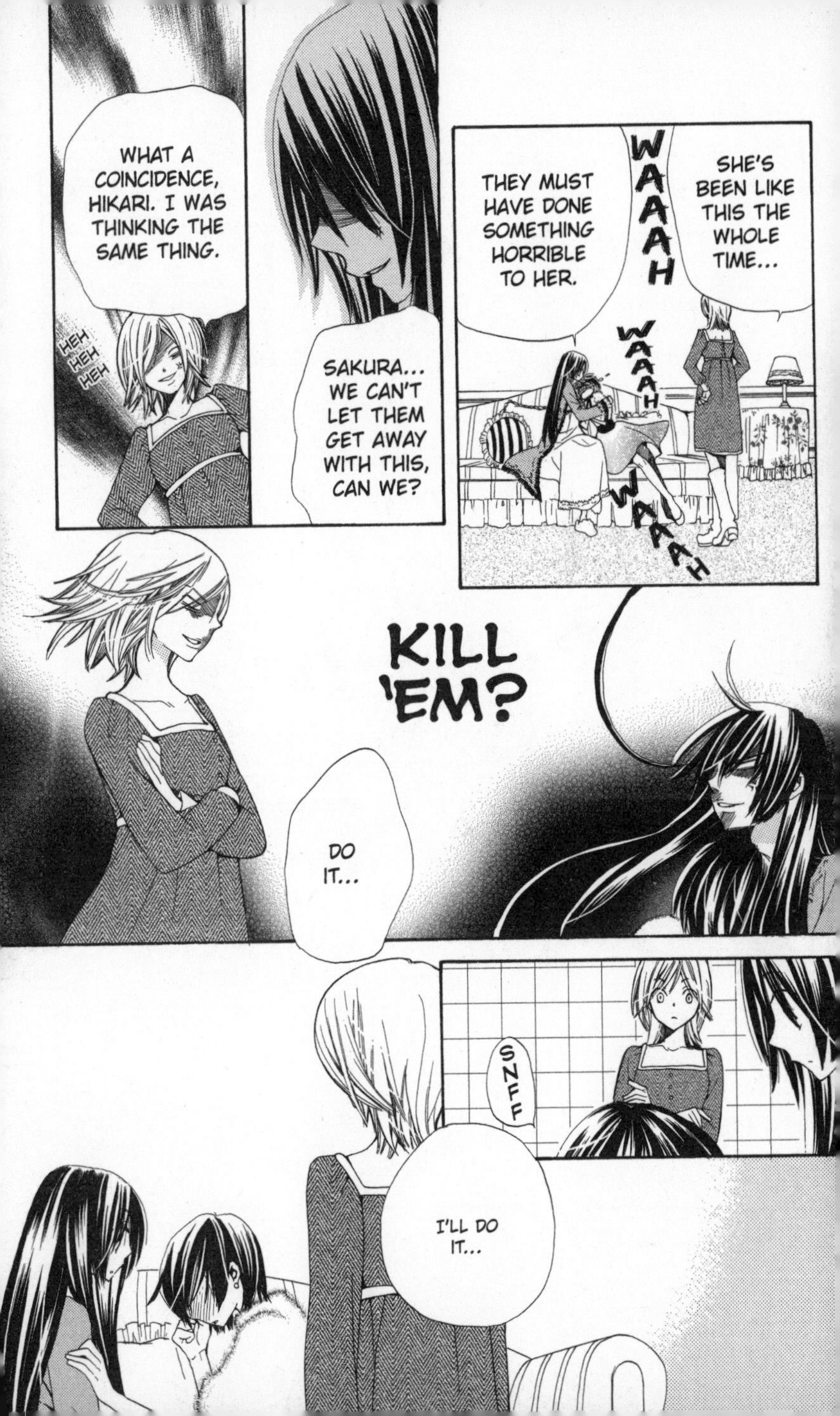
SHE'S BEEN LIKE THIS THE WHOLE TIME...
WAAAH
THEY MUST HAVE DONE SOMETHING HORRIBLE TO HER.
WAAAH
WAAAH
SAKURA... WE CAN'T LET THEM GET AWAY WITH THIS, CAN WE?
WHAT A COINCIDENCE, HIKARI. I WAS THINKING THE SAME THING.
HEH HEH HEH
KILL 'EM?
DO IT...
SNFF
I'LL DO IT...

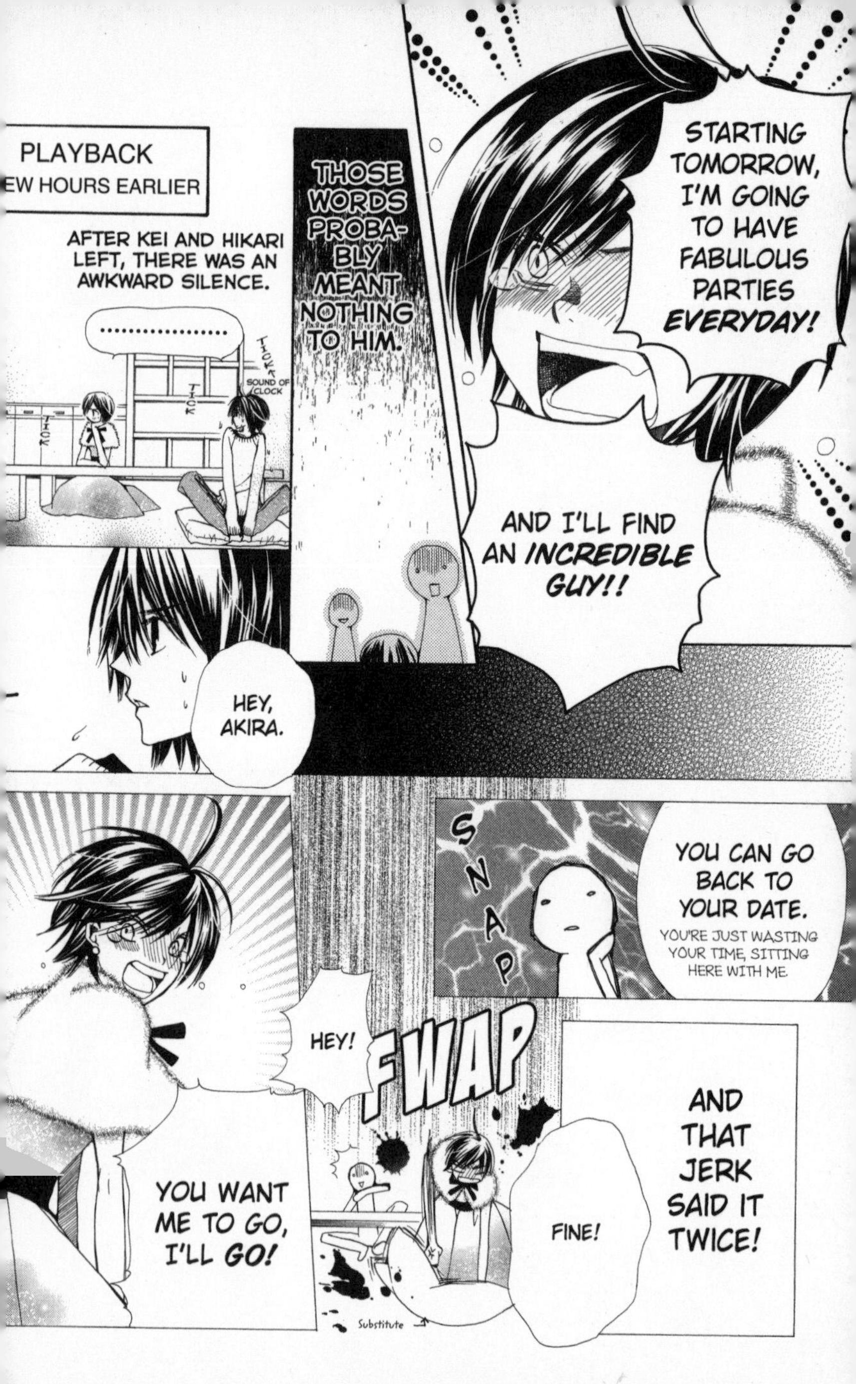
STARTING TOMORROW, I'M GOING TO HAVE FABULOUS PARTIES *EVERYDAY!*
AND I'LL FIND AN *INCREDIBLE GUY!!*
THOSE WORDS PROBA-BLY MEANT NOTHING TO HIM.
PLAYBACK
EW HOURS EARLIER
AFTER KEI AND HIKARI LEFT, THERE WAS AN AWKWARD SILENCE.
....
TICK
SOUND OF CLOCK
TICK
TICK
HEY, AKIRA.
SNAP
YOU CAN GO BACK TO YOUR DATE.
YOU'RE JUST WASTING YOUR TIME, SITTING HERE WITH ME.
AND THAT JERK SAID IT TWICE!
FINE!
FWAP
Substitute
HEY!
YOU WANT ME TO GO, I'LL *GO!*

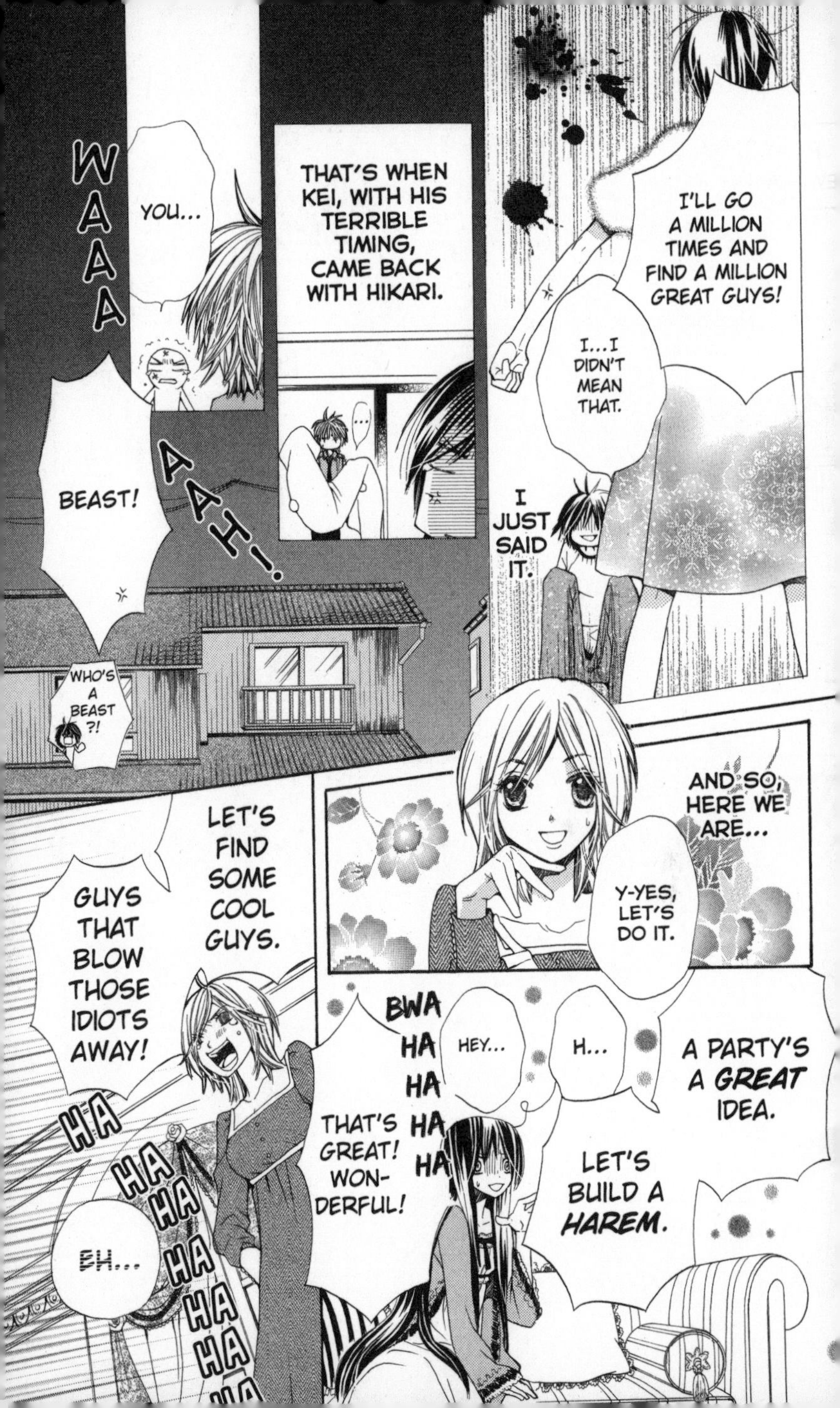

I'LL GO A MILLION TIMES AND FIND A MILLION GREAT GUYS!
I...I DIDN'T MEAN THAT.
I JUST SAID IT.
THAT'S WHEN KEI, WITH HIS TERRIBLE TIMING, CAME BACK WITH HIKARI.
...
YOU...
WAAAA
AAH-!
BEAST!
WHO'S A BEAST?!
AND SO, HERE WE ARE...
Y-YES, LET'S DO IT.
LET'S FIND SOME COOL GUYS.
GUYS THAT BLOW THOSE IDIOTS AWAY!
HA HA HA HA HA HA HA HA
EH...
A PARTY'S A GREAT IDEA.
LET'S BUILD A HAREM.
H...
HEY...
BWA HA HA HA HA HA
THAT'S GREAT! WON-DERFUL!

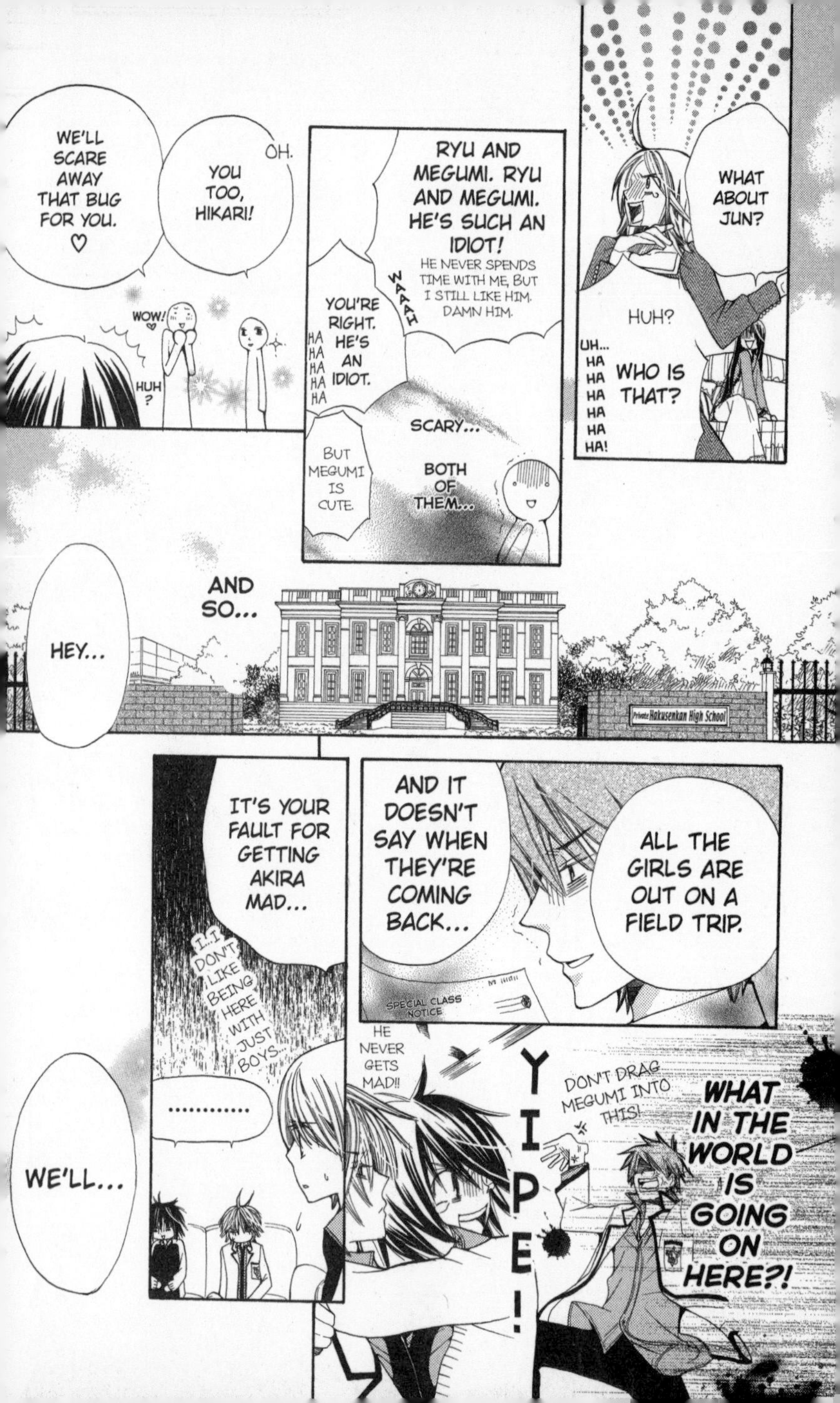
WHAT ABOUT JUN?
HUH?
WHO IS THAT?
UH... HA HA HA HA HA HA!
RYU AND MEGUMI. RYU AND MEGUMI. HE'S SUCH AN IDIOT!
HE NEVER SPENDS TIME WITH ME, BUT I STILL LIKE HIM. DAMN HIM.
WAAAAH
YOU'RE RIGHT. HE'S AN IDIOT.
HA HA HA HA HA HA
SCARY... BOTH OF THEM...
BUT MEGUMI IS CUTE.
OH.
YOU TOO, HIKARI!
WE'LL SCARE AWAY THAT BUG FOR YOU. ♡
WOW! ♡
HUH?
AND SO...
Private Hakusenkan High School
HEY...
ALL THE GIRLS ARE OUT ON A FIELD TRIP.
AND IT DOESN'T SAY WHEN THEY'RE COMING BACK...
SPECIAL CLASS NOTICE
IT'S YOUR FAULT FOR GETTING AKIRA MAD...
I..I DON'T LIKE BEING HERE WITH JUST BOYS...
WHAT IN THE WORLD IS GOING ON HERE?!
DON'T DRAG MEGUMI INTO THIS!
YIPE!
HE NEVER GETS MAD!!
....
WE'LL...

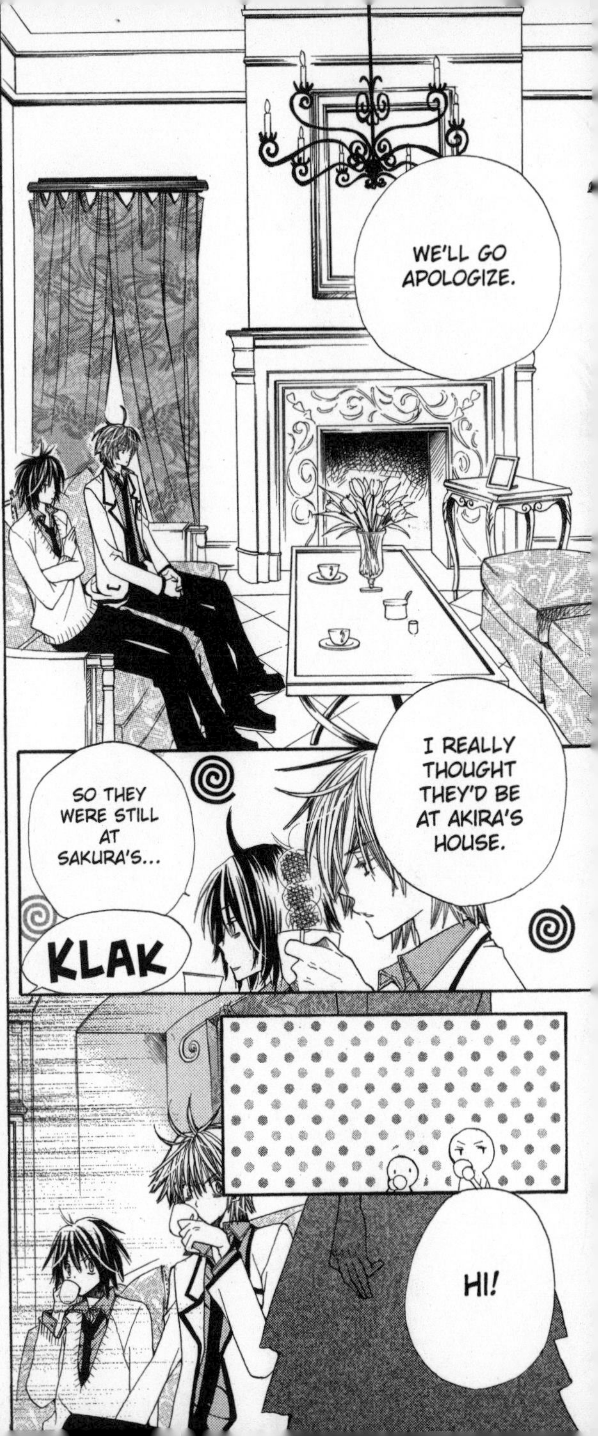

WE'LL GO APOLOGIZE.
I REALLY THOUGHT THEY'D BE AT AKIRA'S HOUSE.
SO THEY WERE STILL AT SAKURA'S...
KLAK
HI!

3

•ABOUT WORK•

THIS IS MY SCHEDULE FOR EACH CHAPTER.

A FEW DAYS FOR THE NAME

↑ THIS IS LIKE A STORYBOARD. ♥

UGH, I CAN'T WRITE...

ROUGH SKETCH, 1-2 DAYS

MY ASSISTANTS ARE COMING.

UGH

PENNING AND FINISHING, THREE NIGHTS AND FOUR DAYS AFTER THE ASSISTANTS ARRIVE.

PLEASE, DON'T ASK ME THAT!!

HOW MANY MORE PAGES?

GRIN

GRIN

THEY'RE ALL NICE PEOPLE!!

DONE.

SEE YA!

THE ASSISTANTS LEAVE REFRESHED. →

I REPEAT THIS EVERY TIME. AND ONE OR TWO DAYS AFTER THE DEADLINE, THERE IS STILL THE COLORING. WORK IS REALLY, HONESTLY FUN!! AND IT'S ALL THANKS TO YOU!!

HUP

MY DAYS ARE FULL...

MY JAPANESE IS STRANGE...

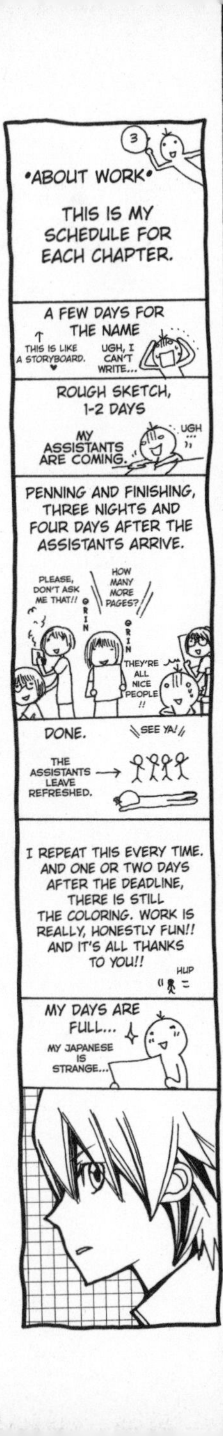

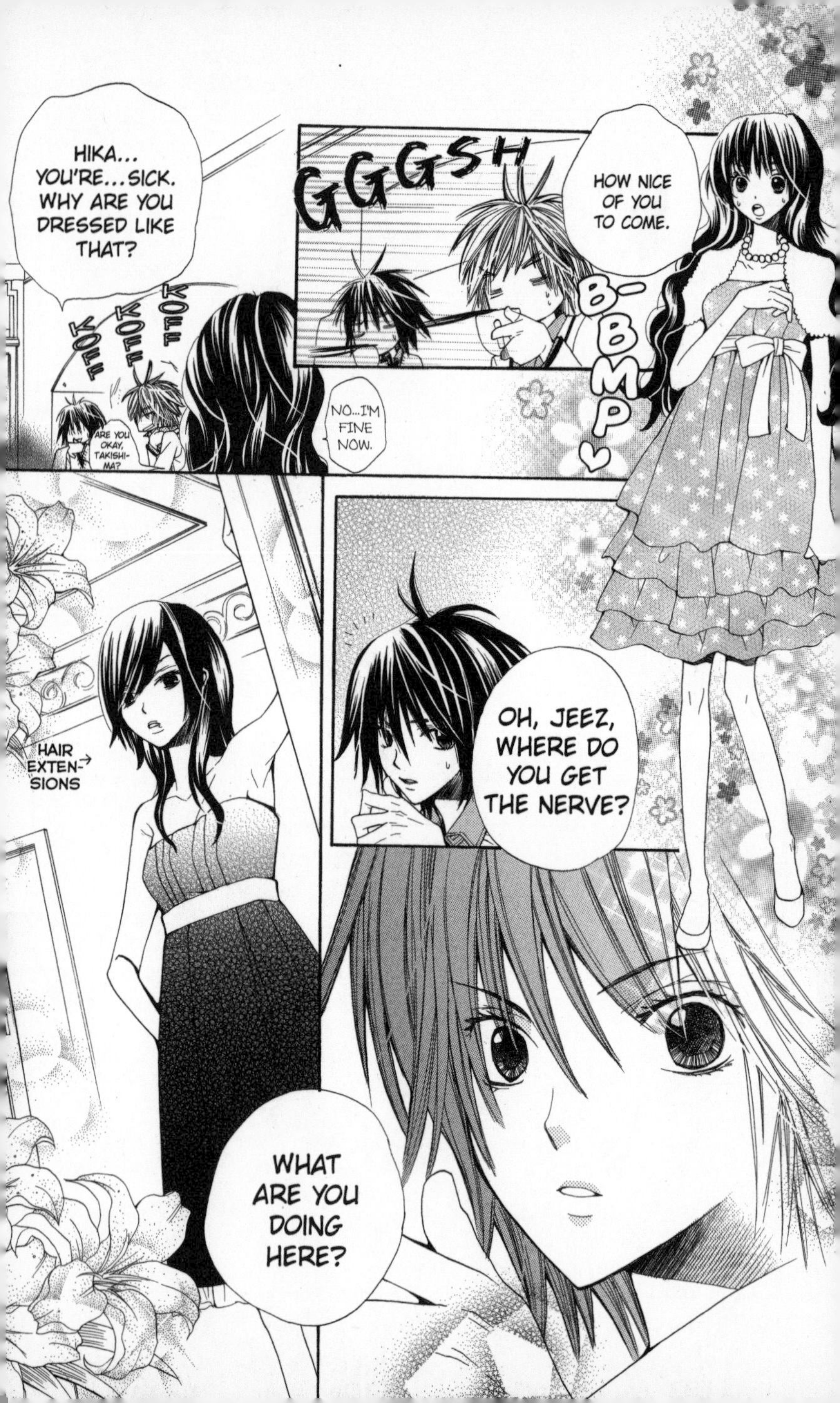
HOW NICE OF YOU TO COME.
B-BMP♥
GGGSH
HIKA... YOU'RE...SICK. WHY ARE YOU DRESSED LIKE THAT?
KOFF KOFF KOFF
NO...I'M FINE NOW.
ARE YOU OKAY, TAKISHIMA?
OH, JEEZ, WHERE DO YOU GET THE NERVE?
HAIR EXTEN-SIONS
WHAT ARE YOU DOING HERE?

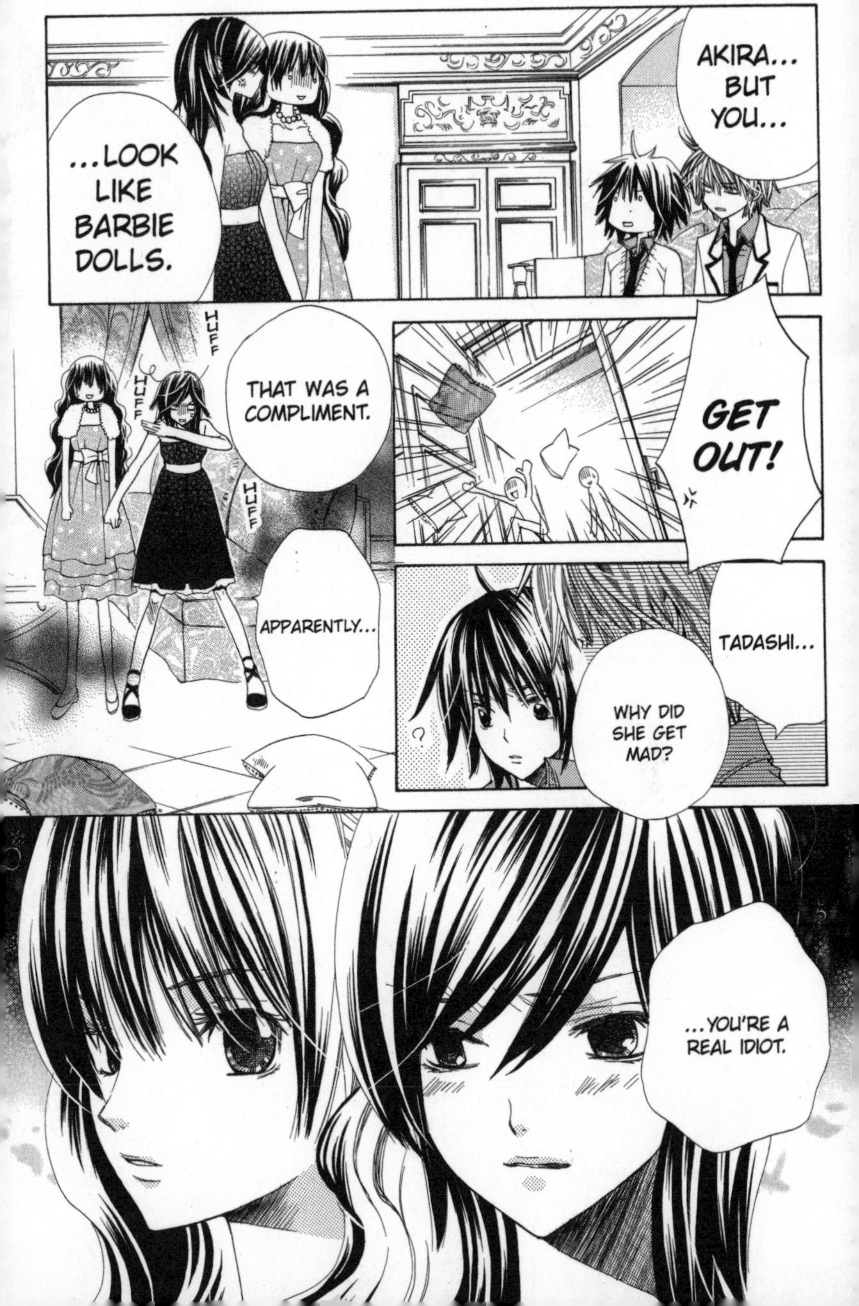
AKIRA... BUT YOU...
...LOOK LIKE BARBIE DOLLS.
GET OUT!
TADASHI...
WHY DID SHE GET MAD?
HUFF
HUFF
HUFF
THAT WAS A COMPLIMENT.
APPARENTLY...
...YOU'RE A REAL IDIOT.

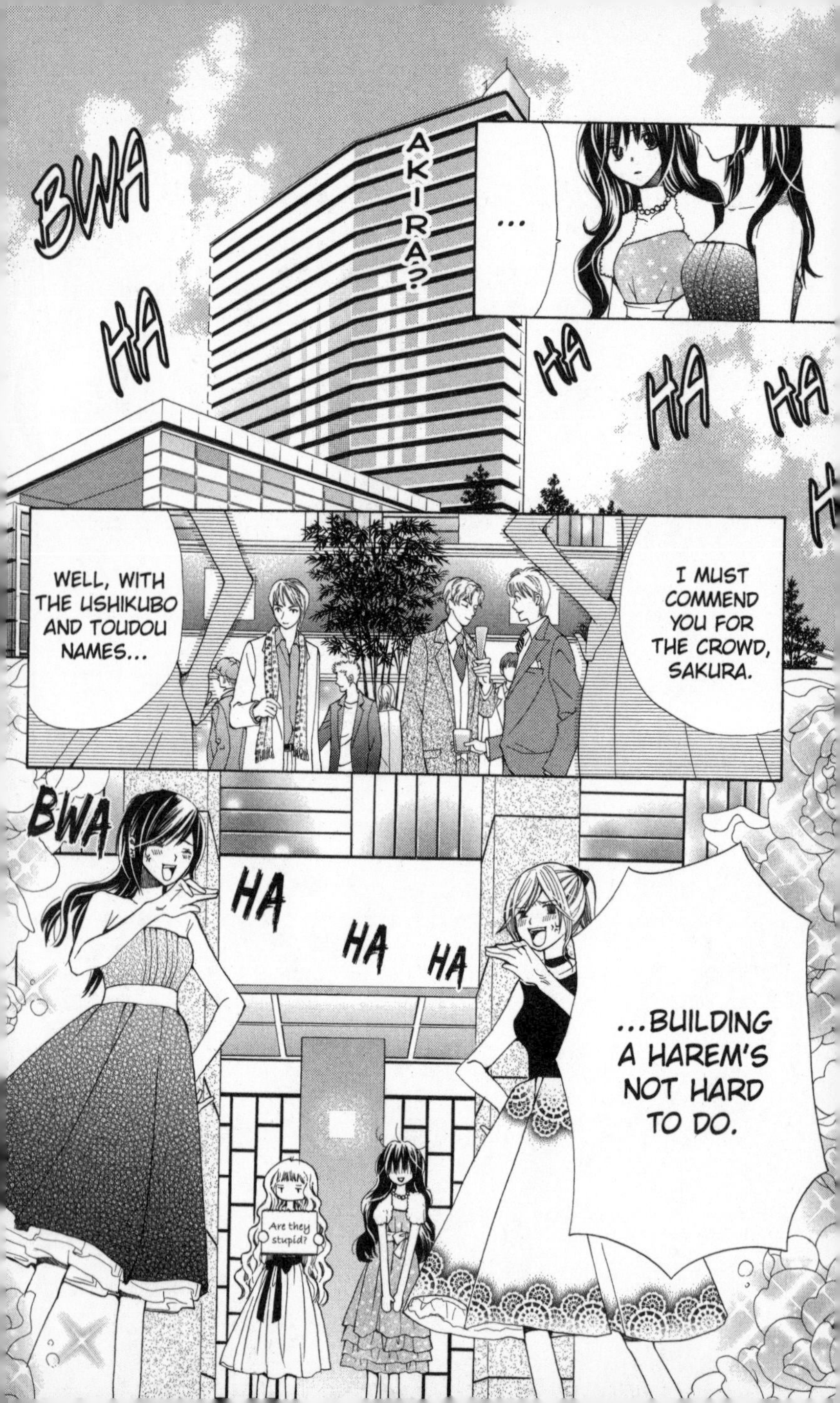
...
HA HA HA HA H
BWA HA
AKIRA?
I MUST COMMEND YOU FOR THE CROWD, SAKURA.
WELL, WITH THE USHIKUBO AND TOUDOU NAMES...
...BUILDING A HAREM'S NOT HARD TO DO.
BWA HA HA HA
Are they stupid?

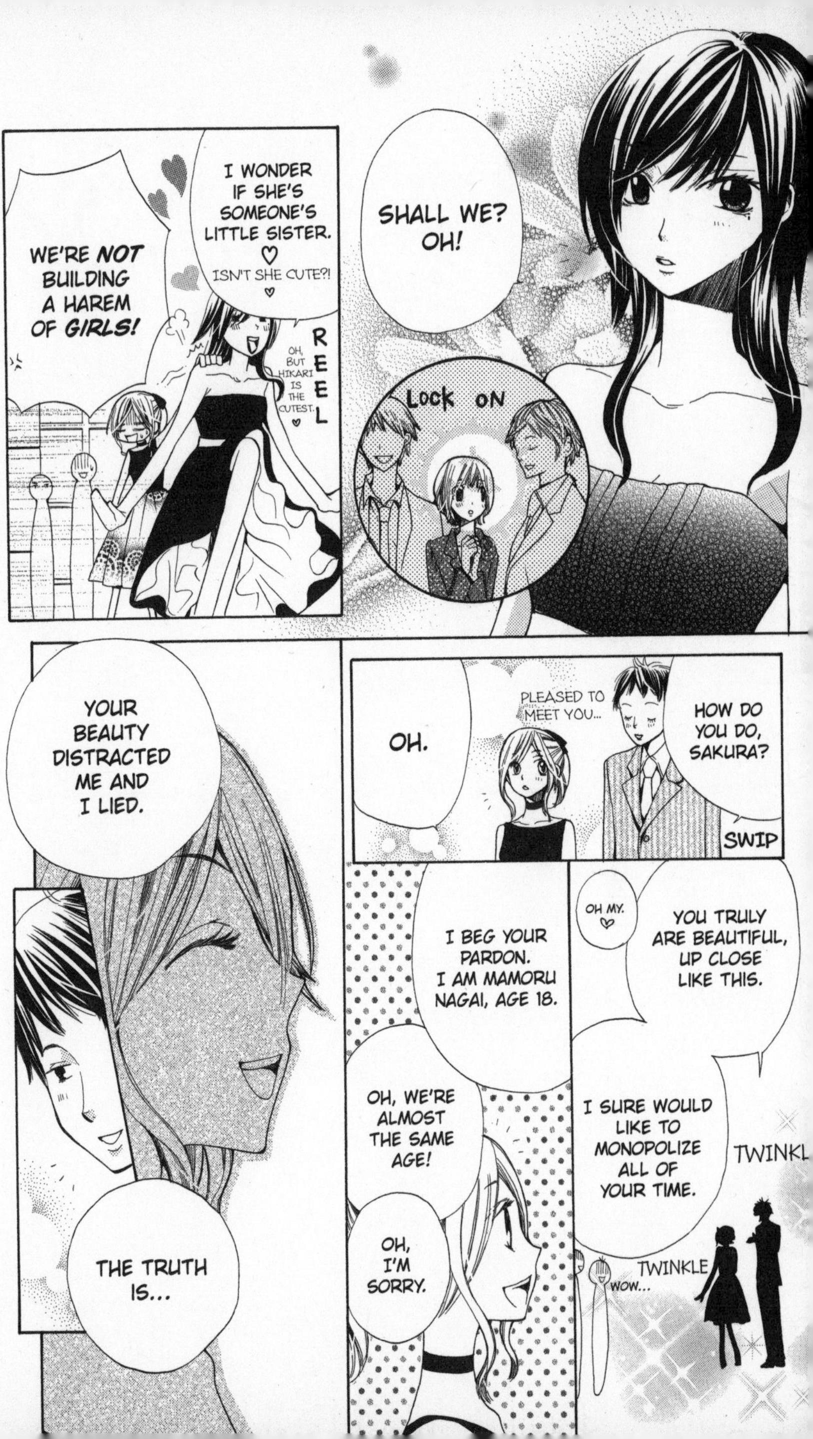
SHALL WE? OH!
LOCK ON
I WONDER IF SHE'S SOMEONE'S LITTLE SISTER. ♡
ISN'T SHE CUTE?! ♡
REEL
OH, BUT HIKARI IS THE CUTEST. ♡
WE'RE NOT BUILDING A HAREM OF GIRLS!
HOW DO YOU DO, SAKURA?
SWIP
PLEASED TO MEET YOU...
OH.
YOU TRULY ARE BEAUTIFUL, UP CLOSE LIKE THIS.
OH MY. ♡
I SURE WOULD LIKE TO MONOPOLIZE ALL OF YOUR TIME.
TWINKL
TWINKLE
WOW...
I BEG YOUR PARDON. I AM MAMORU NAGAI, AGE 18.
OH, WE'RE ALMOST THE SAME AGE!
OH, I'M SORRY.
YOUR BEAUTY DISTRACTED ME AND I LIED.
THE TRUTH IS...

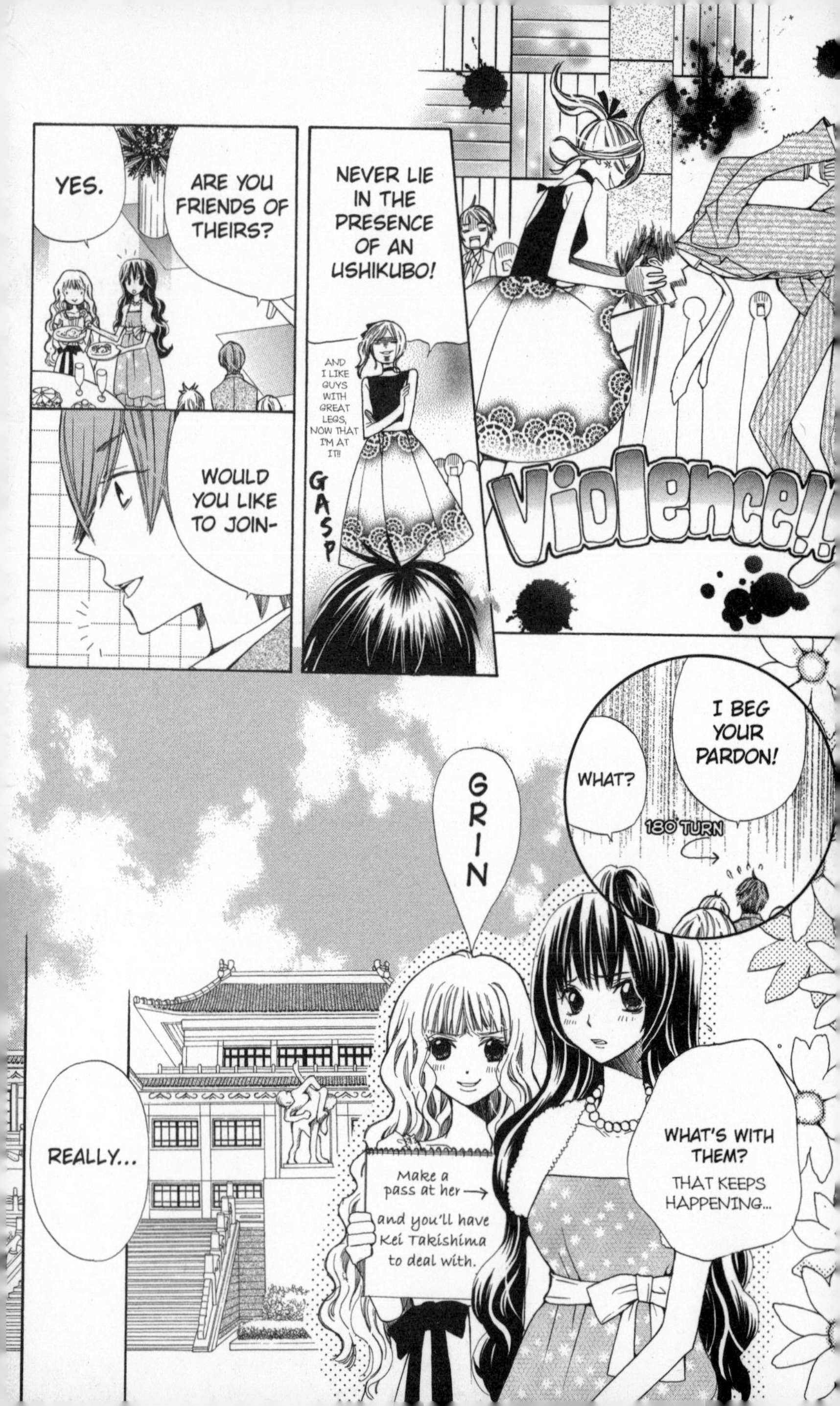
Violence!!
NEVER LIE IN THE PRESENCE OF AN USHIKUBO!
AND I LIKE GUYS WITH GREAT LEGS, NOW THAT I'M AT IT!!
GASP
ARE YOU FRIENDS OF THEIRS?
YES.
WOULD YOU LIKE TO JOIN-
I BEG YOUR PARDON!
WHAT?
180 TURN
GRIN
WHAT'S WITH THEM?
THAT KEEPS HAPPENING...
Make a pass at her →
and you'll have Kei Takishima to deal with.
REALLY...

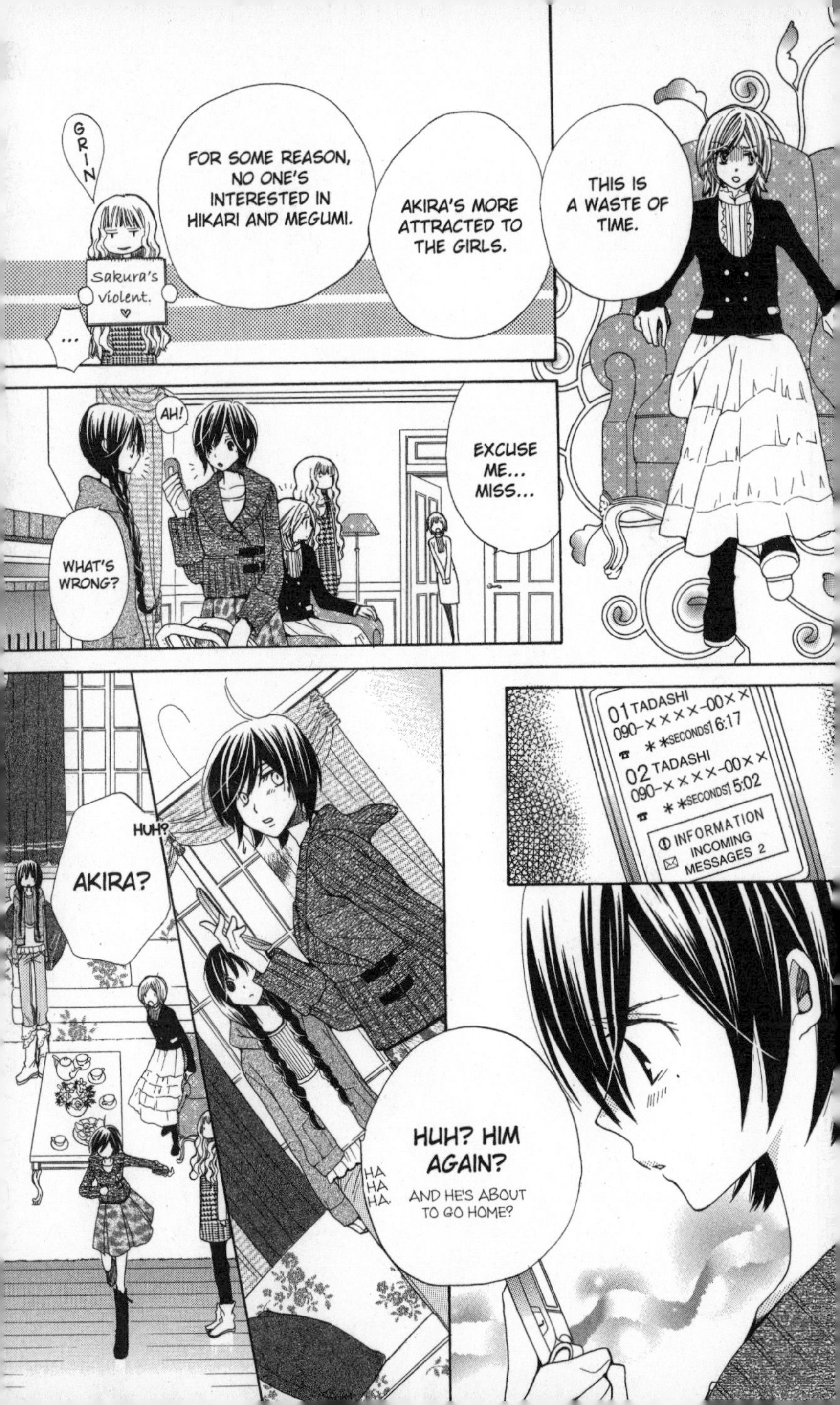
THIS IS A WASTE OF TIME.
AKIRA'S MORE ATTRACTED TO THE GIRLS.
FOR SOME REASON, NO ONE'S INTERESTED IN HIKARI AND MEGUMI.
GRIN
Sakura's violent. ♥
...
EXCUSE ME... MISS...
AH!
WHAT'S WRONG?
01 TADASHI 090-××××-00×× ✱✱SECONDS 6:17
02 TADASHI 090-××××-00×× ✱✱SECONDS 5:02
INFORMATION INCOMING MESSAGES 2
HUH? HIM AGAIN?
AND HE'S ABOUT TO GO HOME?
HA HA HA.
HUH?
AKIRA?

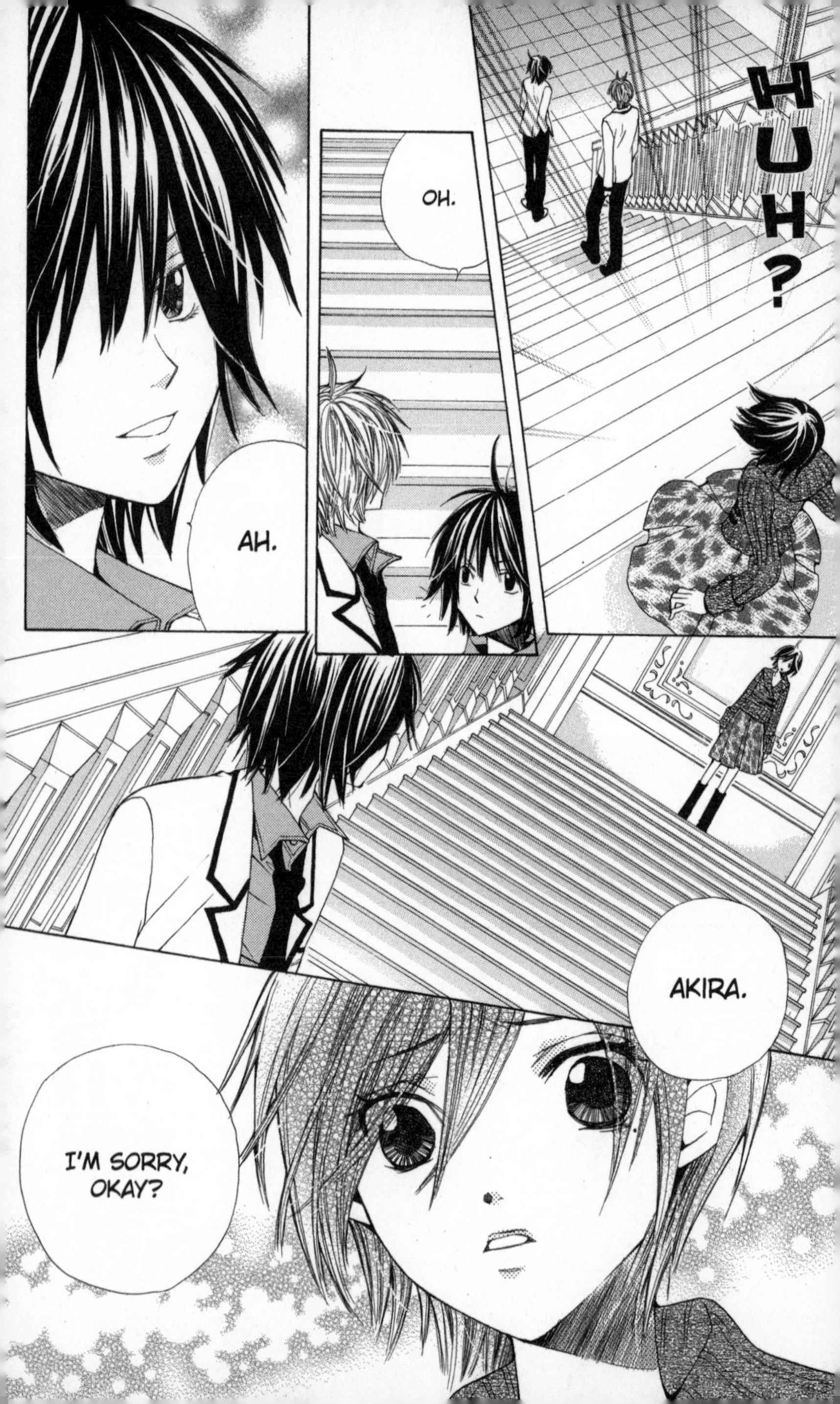
HUH?
OH.
AH.
AKIRA.
I'M SORRY, OKAY?

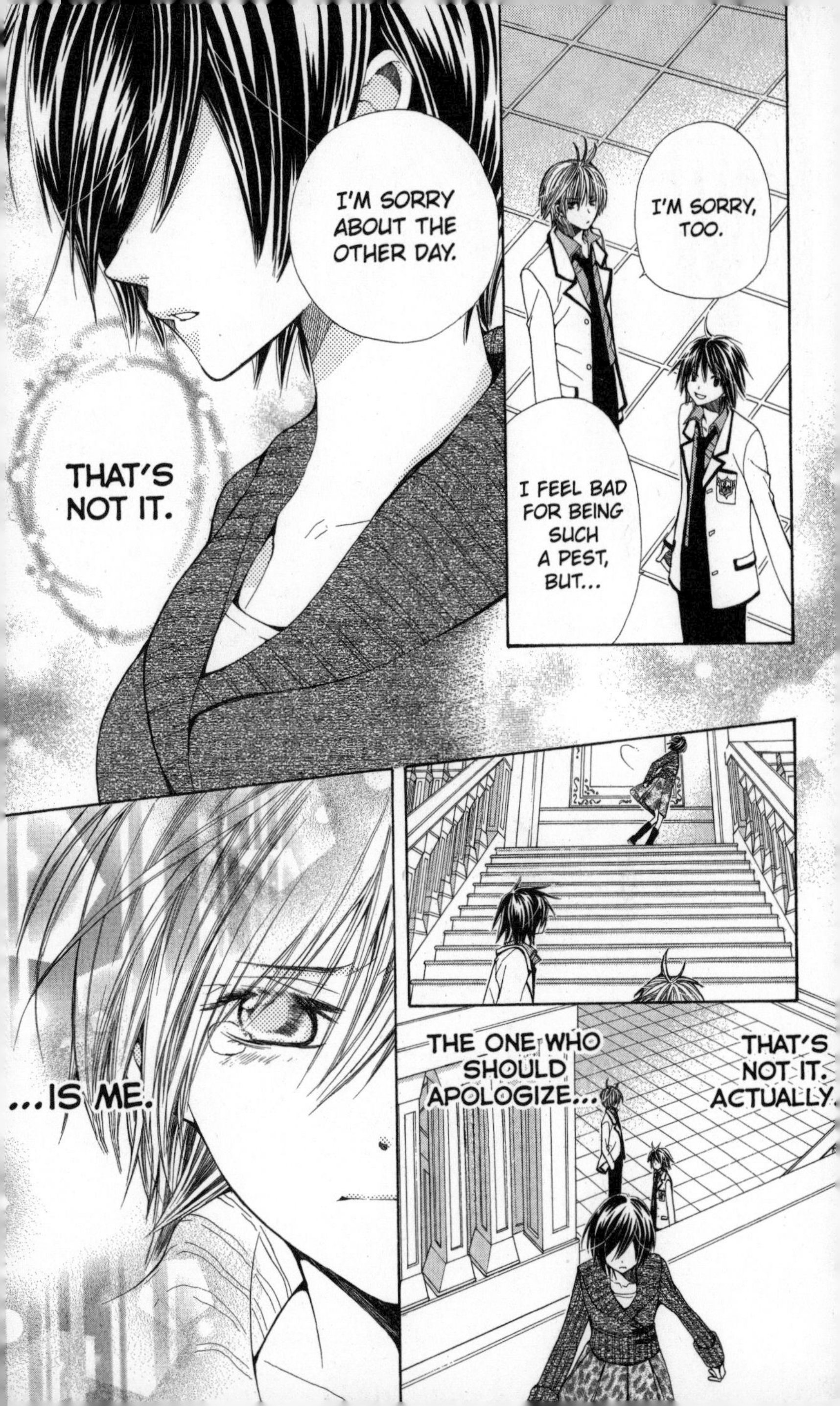
I'M SORRY, TOO.
I FEEL BAD FOR BEING SUCH A PEST, BUT...
I'M SORRY ABOUT THE OTHER DAY.
THAT'S NOT IT.
THAT'S NOT IT. ACTUALLY
THE ONE WHO SHOULD APOLOGIZE...
...IS ME.

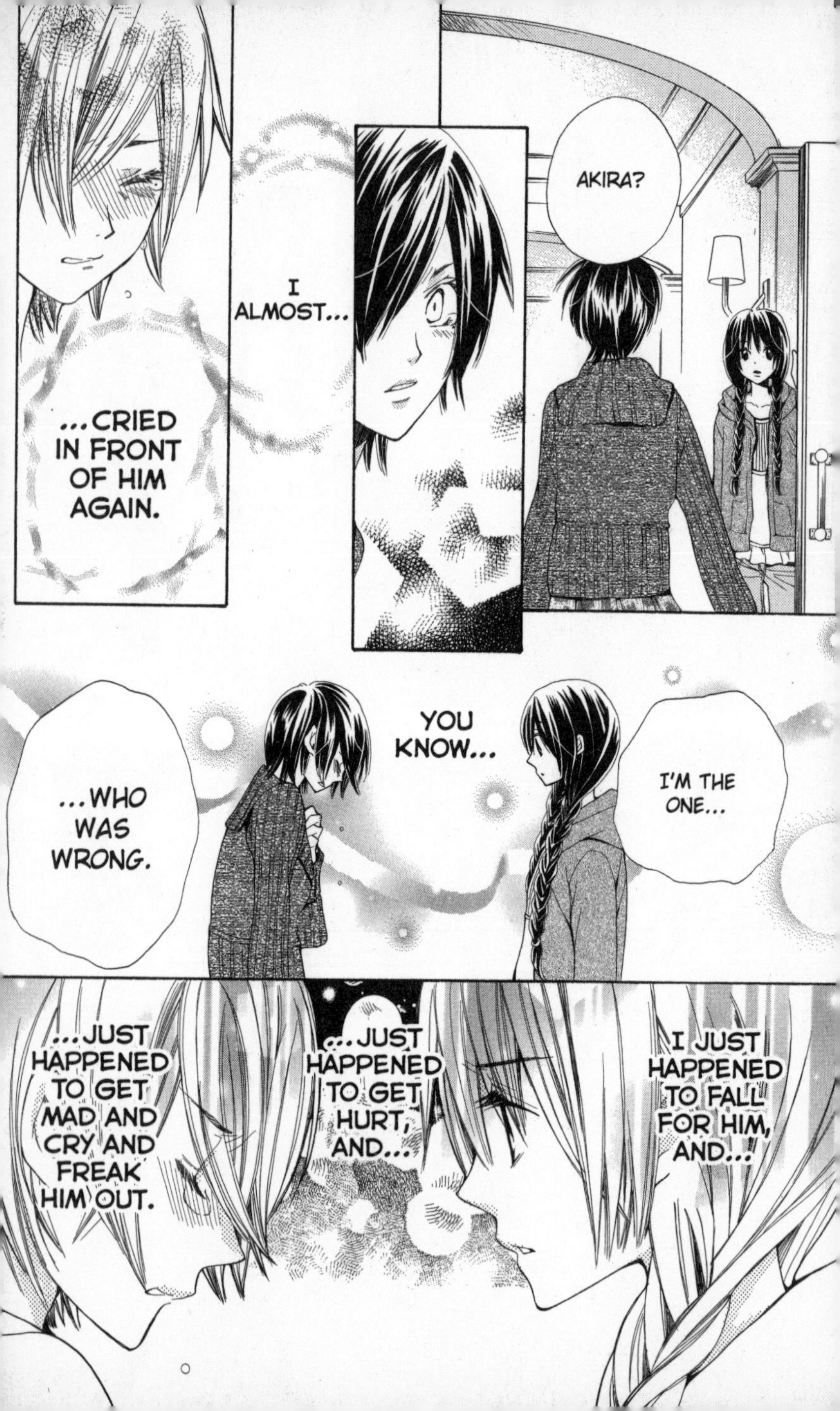
AKIRA?
I ALMOST...
...CRIED IN FRONT OF HIM AGAIN.
I'M THE ONE...
YOU KNOW...
...WHO WAS WRONG.
I JUST HAPPENED TO FALL FOR HIM, AND...
...JUST HAPPENED TO GET HURT, AND...
...JUST HAPPENED TO GET MAD AND CRY AND FREAK HIM OUT.

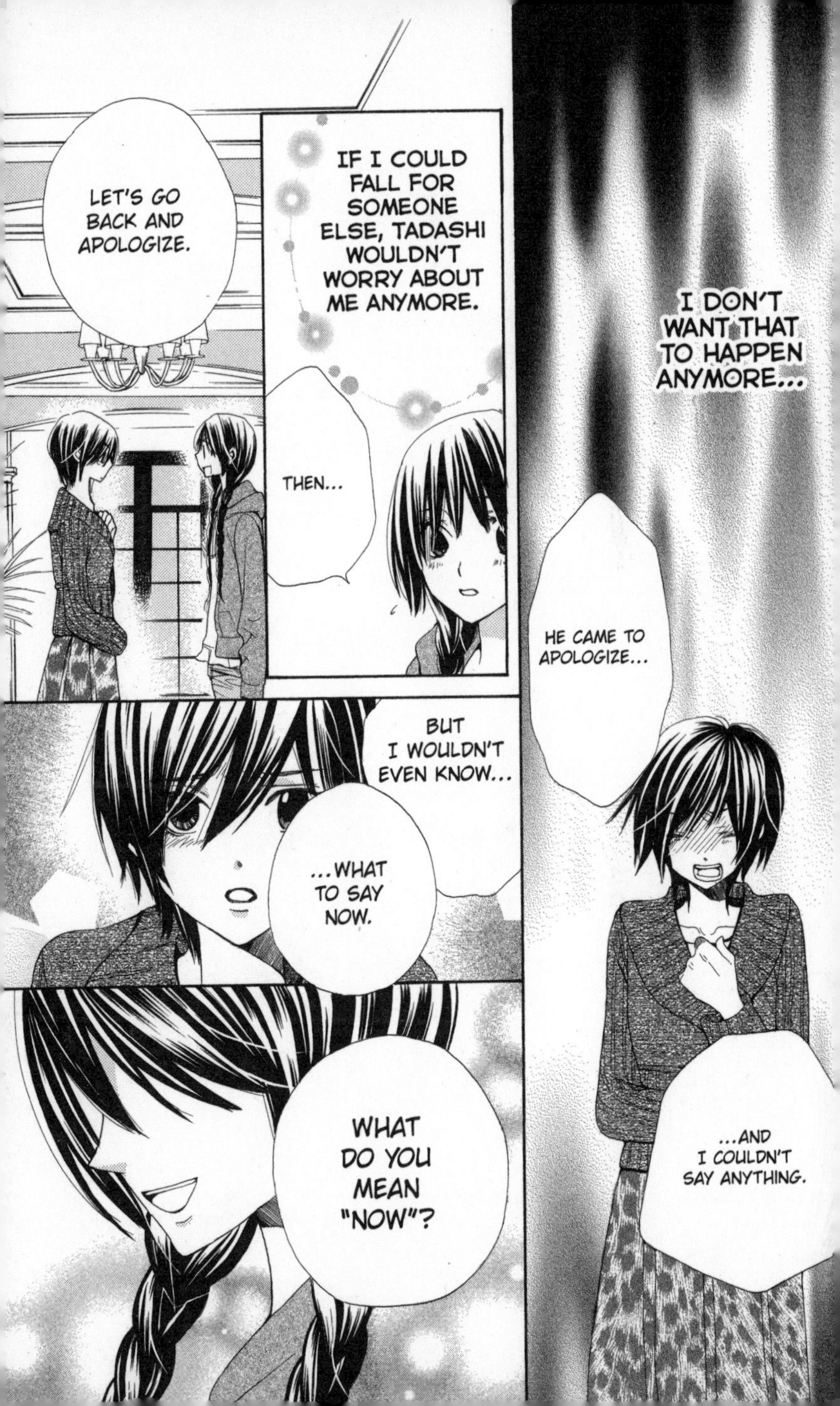
I DON'T WANT THAT TO HAPPEN ANYMORE...
HE CAME TO APOLOGIZE...
...AND I COULDN'T SAY ANYTHING.
IF I COULD FALL FOR SOMEONE ELSE, TADASHI WOULDN'T WORRY ABOUT ME ANYMORE.
THEN...
LET'S GO BACK AND APOLOGIZE.
BUT I WOULDN'T EVEN KNOW...
...WHAT TO SAY NOW.
WHAT DO YOU MEAN "NOW"?

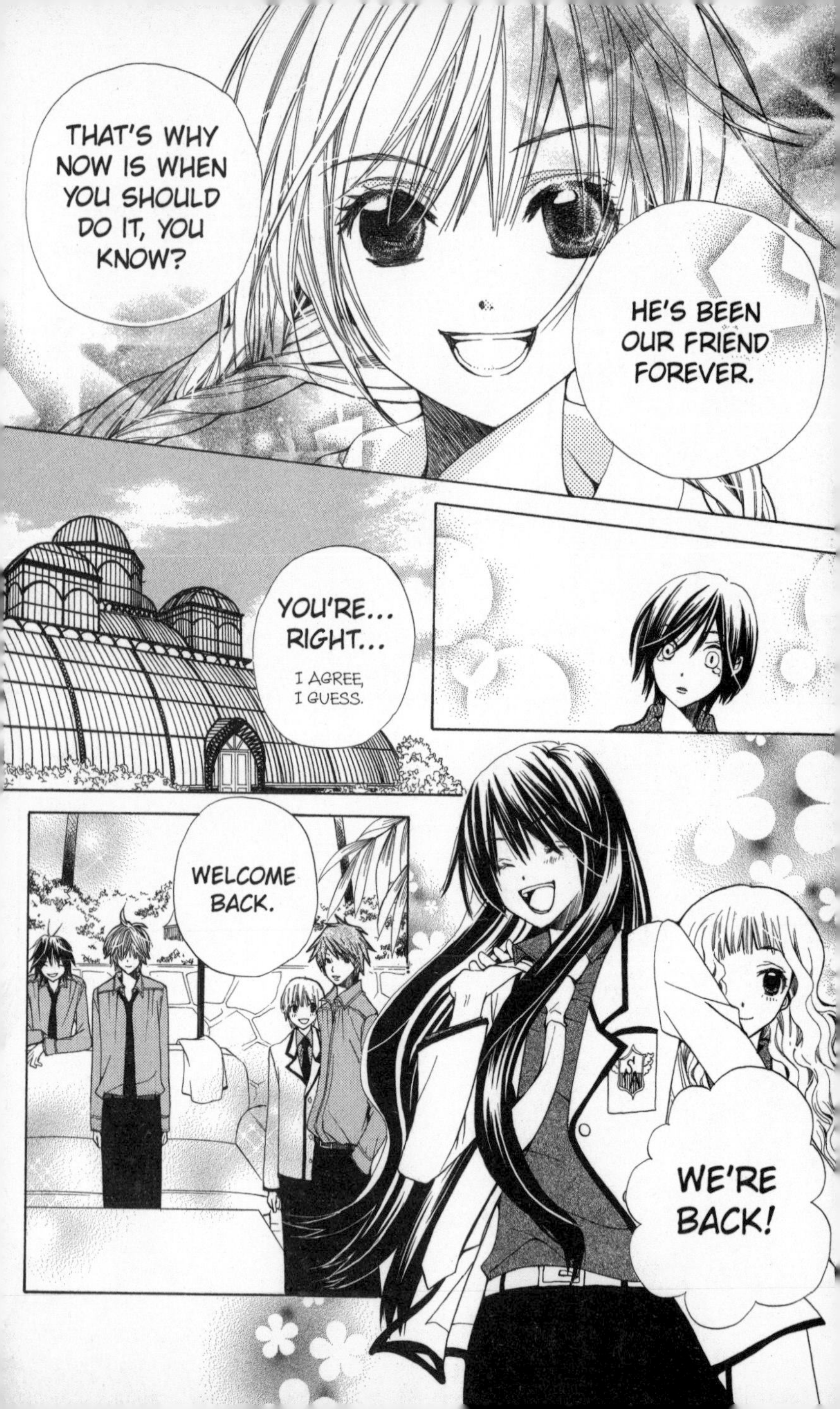

HE'S BEEN OUR FRIEND FOREVER.
THAT'S WHY NOW IS WHEN YOU SHOULD DO IT, YOU KNOW?
YOU'RE... RIGHT...
I AGREE, I GUESS.
WE'RE BACK!
WELCOME BACK.

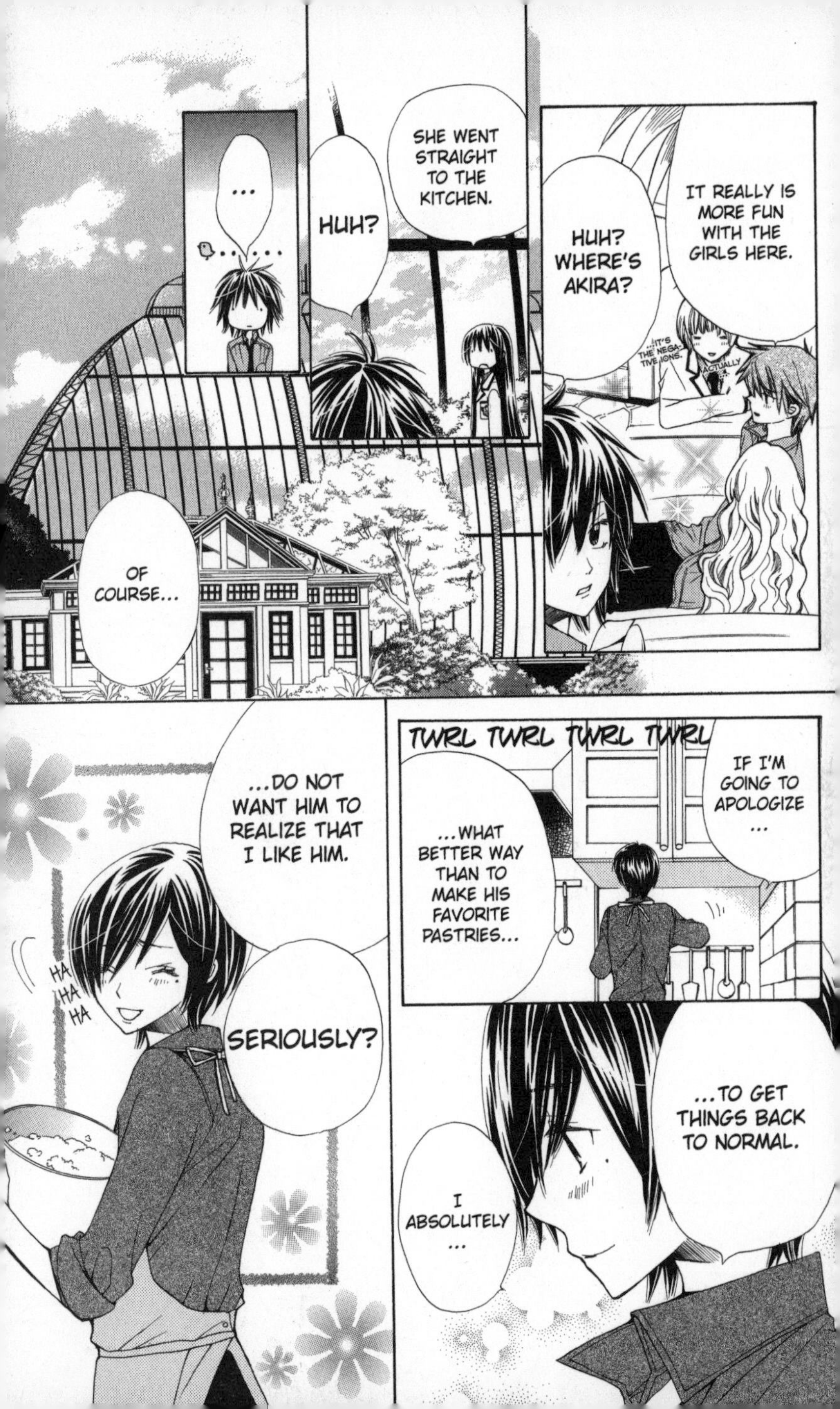
IT REALLY IS MORE FUN WITH THE GIRLS HERE.
ACTUALLY
...IT'S THE NEGATIVE IONS.
HUH? WHERE'S AKIRA?
SHE WENT STRAIGHT TO THE KITCHEN.
HUH?
...
......
OF COURSE...
TWRL TWRL TWRL TWRL
IF I'M GOING TO APOLOGIZE ...
...WHAT BETTER WAY THAN TO MAKE HIS FAVORITE PASTRIES...
...TO GET THINGS BACK TO NORMAL.
I ABSOLUTELY ...
...DO NOT WANT HIM TO REALIZE THAT I LIKE HIM.
HA HA HA
SERIOUSLY?

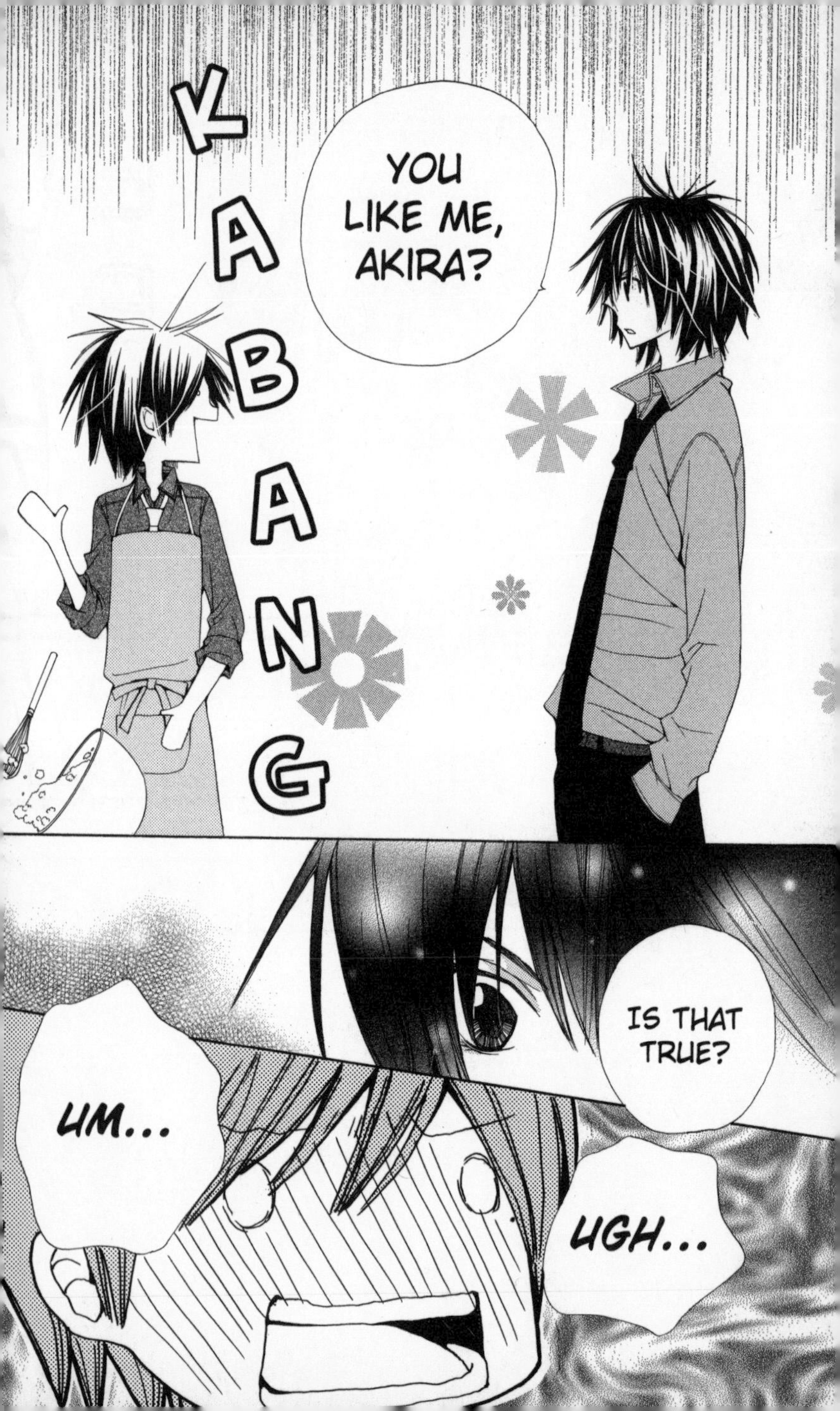
YOU LIKE ME, AKIRA?
KABANG
IS THAT TRUE?
UGH...
UM...

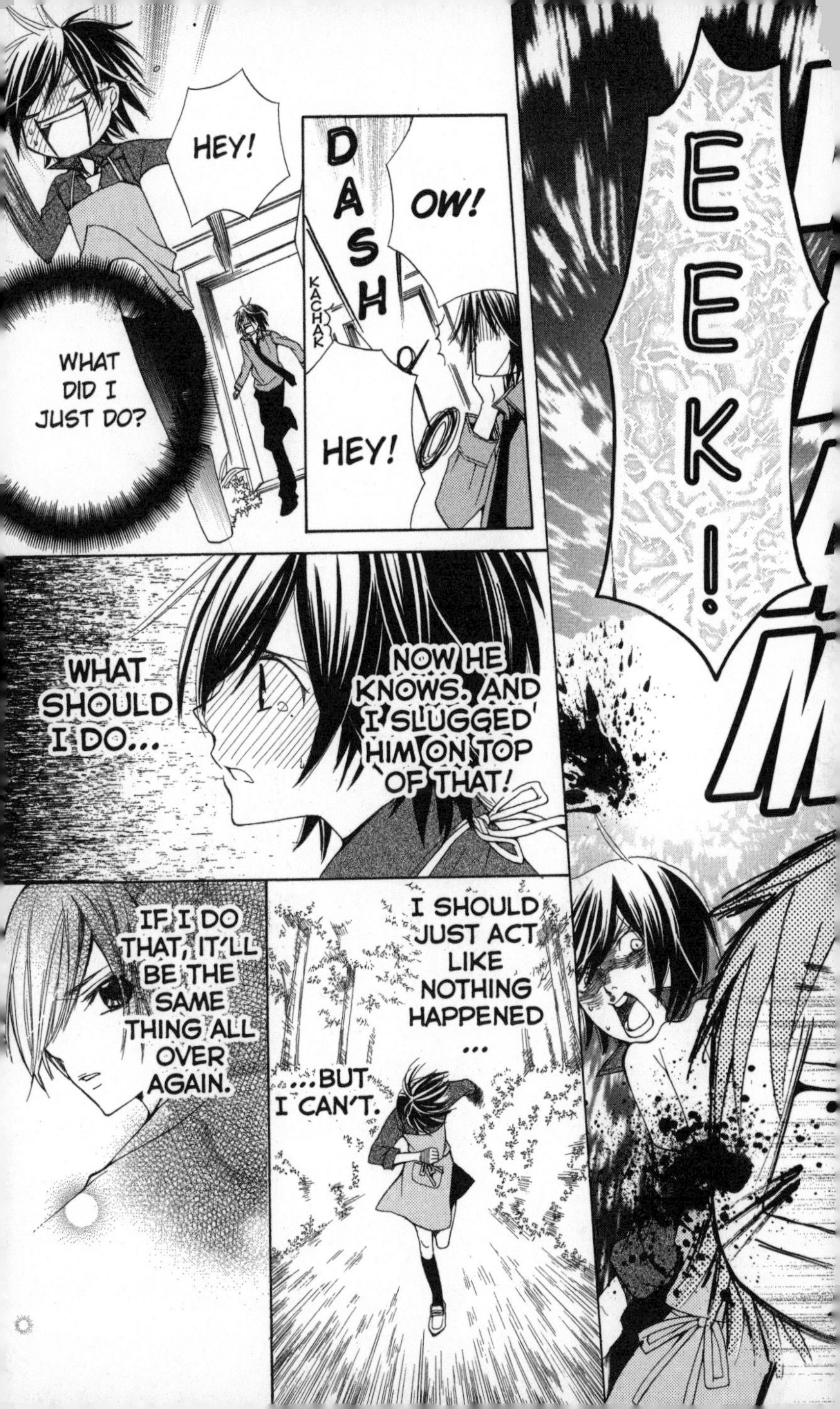
EEEK!
DASH
OW!
KACHAK
HEY!
HEY!
WHAT DID I JUST DO?
NOW HE KNOWS. AND I SLUGGED HIM ON TOP OF THAT!
WHAT SHOULD I DO...
I SHOULD JUST ACT LIKE NOTHING HAPPENED...
...BUT I CAN'T.
IF I DO THAT, IT'LL BE THE SAME THING ALL OVER AGAIN.

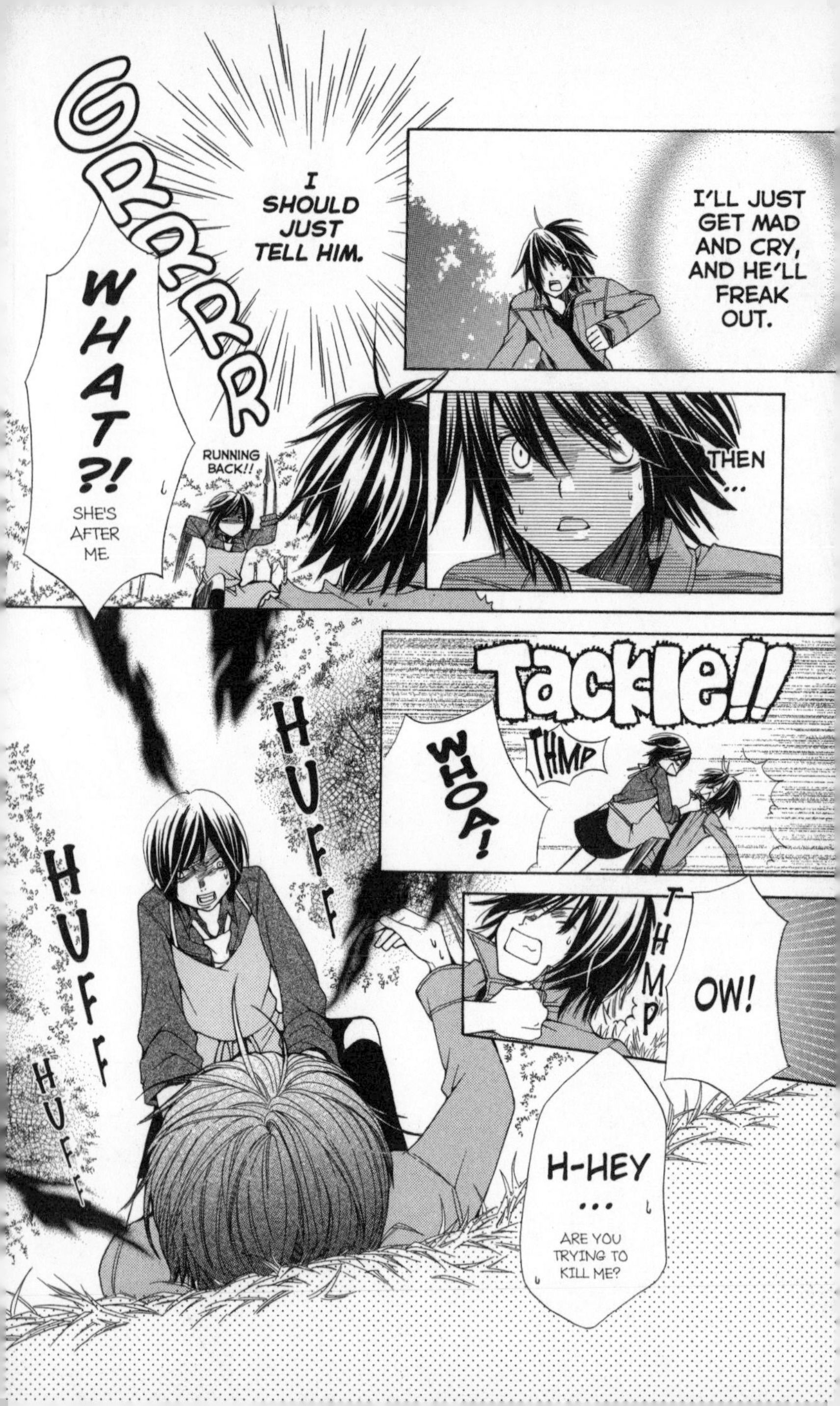
I'LL JUST GET MAD AND CRY, AND HE'LL FREAK OUT.
I SHOULD JUST TELL HIM.
THEN ...
GRRRR
WHAT?!
SHE'S AFTER ME.
RUNNING BACK!!
Tackle!!
THMP
WHOA!
THMP
OW!
H-HEY ...
ARE YOU TRYING TO KILL ME?
HUFF
HUFF
HUFF

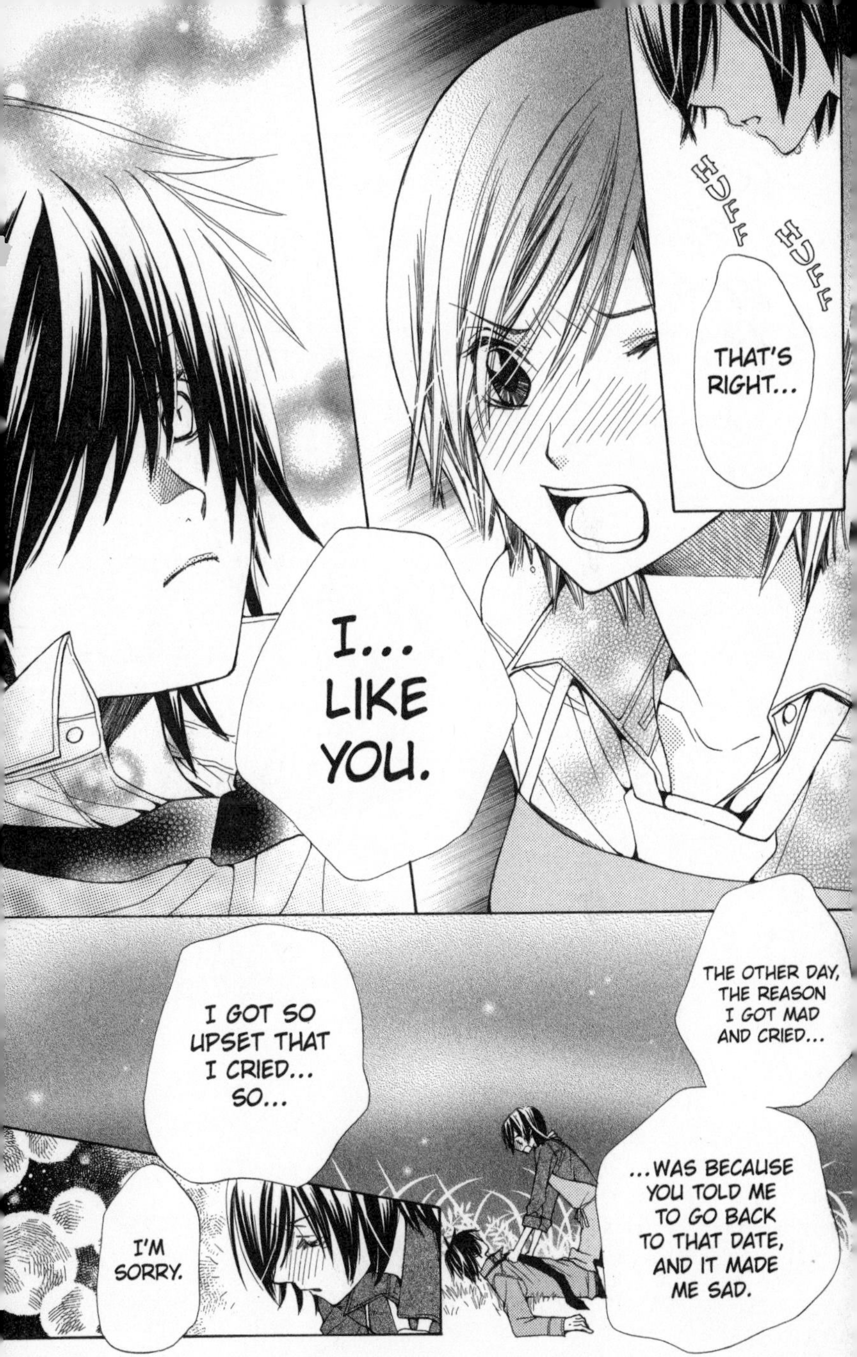
HUFF
HUFF
THAT'S RIGHT...
I... LIKE YOU.
THE OTHER DAY, THE REASON I GOT MAD AND CRIED...
...WAS BECAUSE YOU TOLD ME TO GO BACK TO THAT DATE, AND IT MADE ME SAD.
I GOT SO UPSET THAT I CRIED... SO...
I'M SORRY.

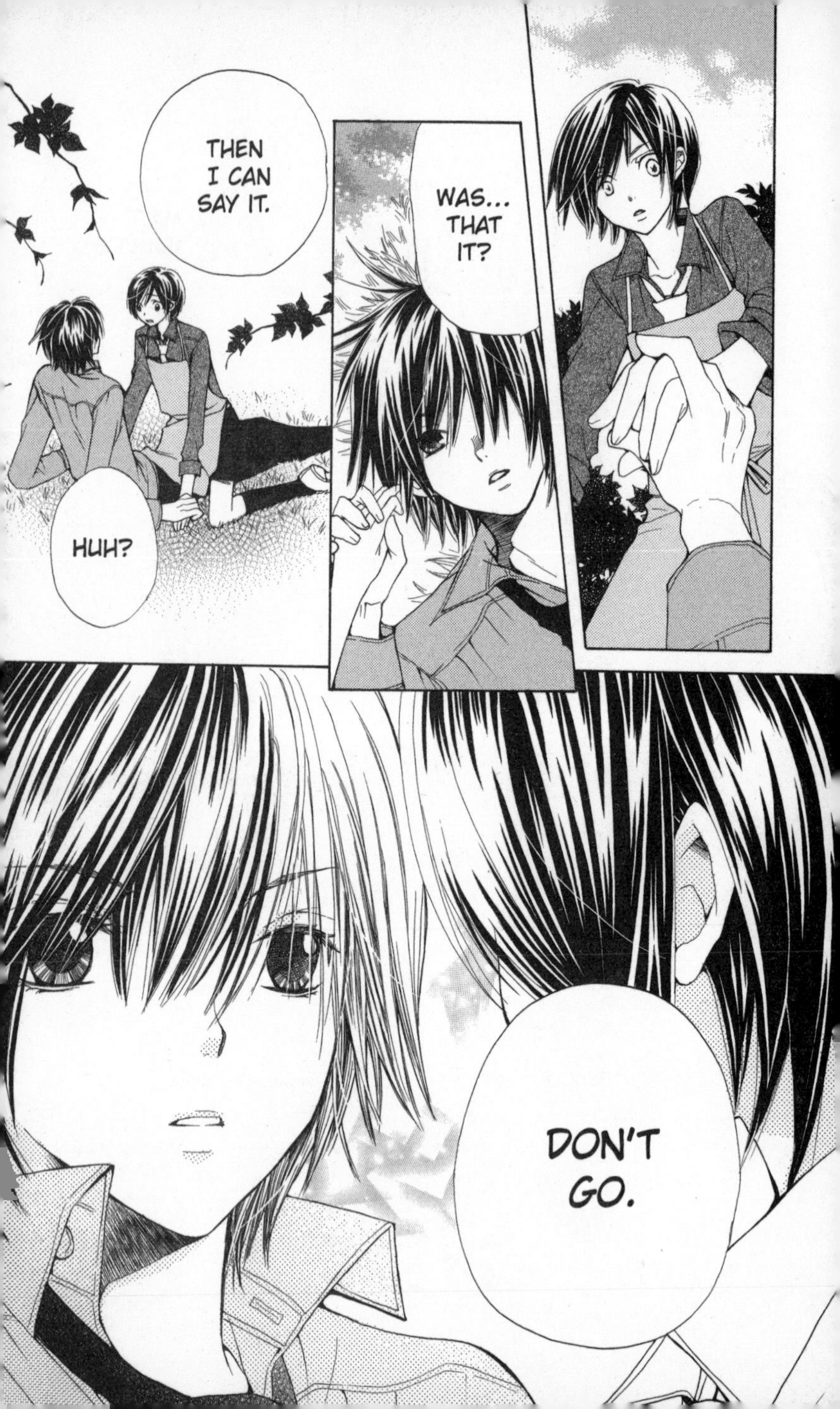
WAS... THAT IT?
THEN I CAN SAY IT.
HUH?
DON'T GO.

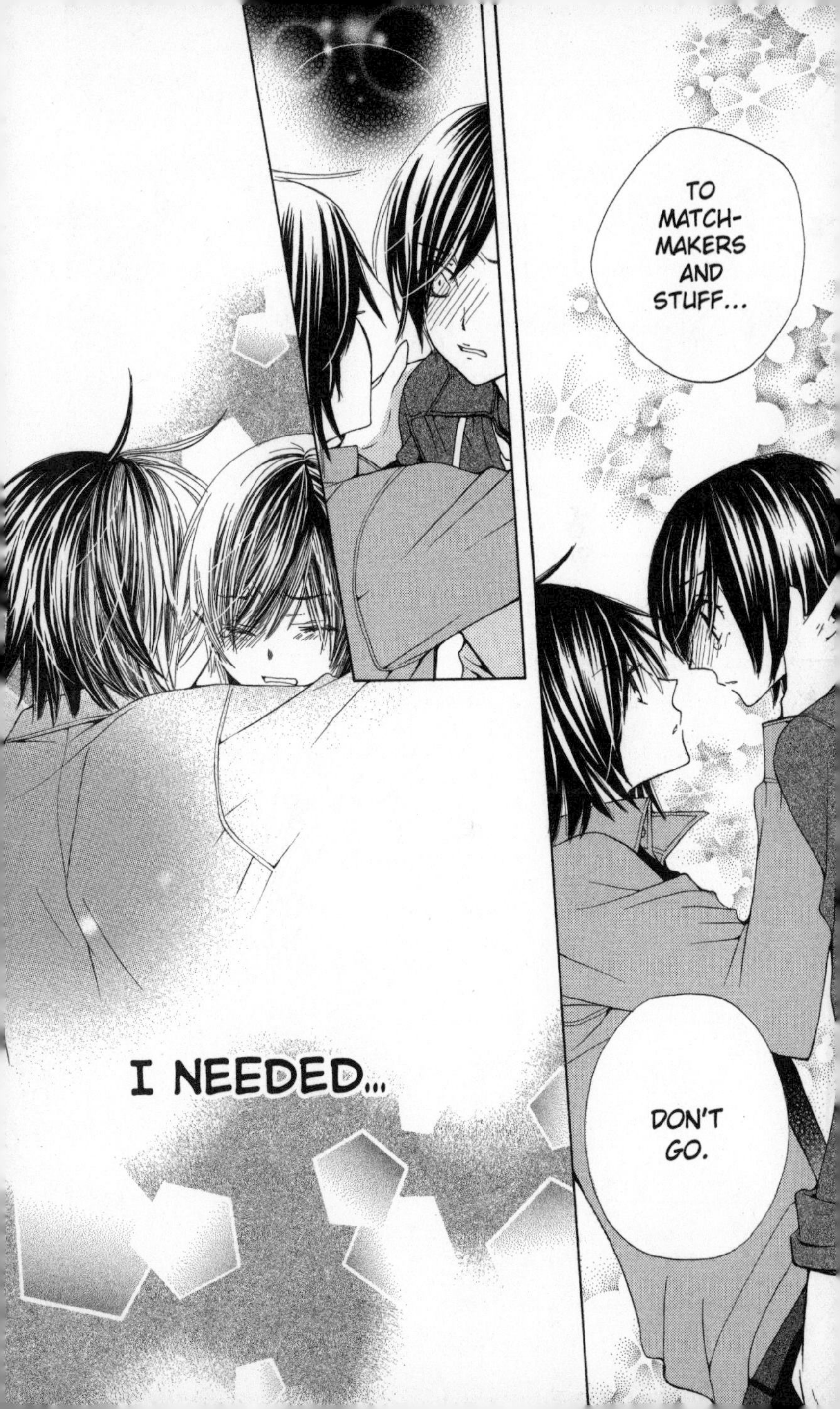
TO MATCH-MAKERS AND STUFF...
DON'T GO.
I NEEDED...

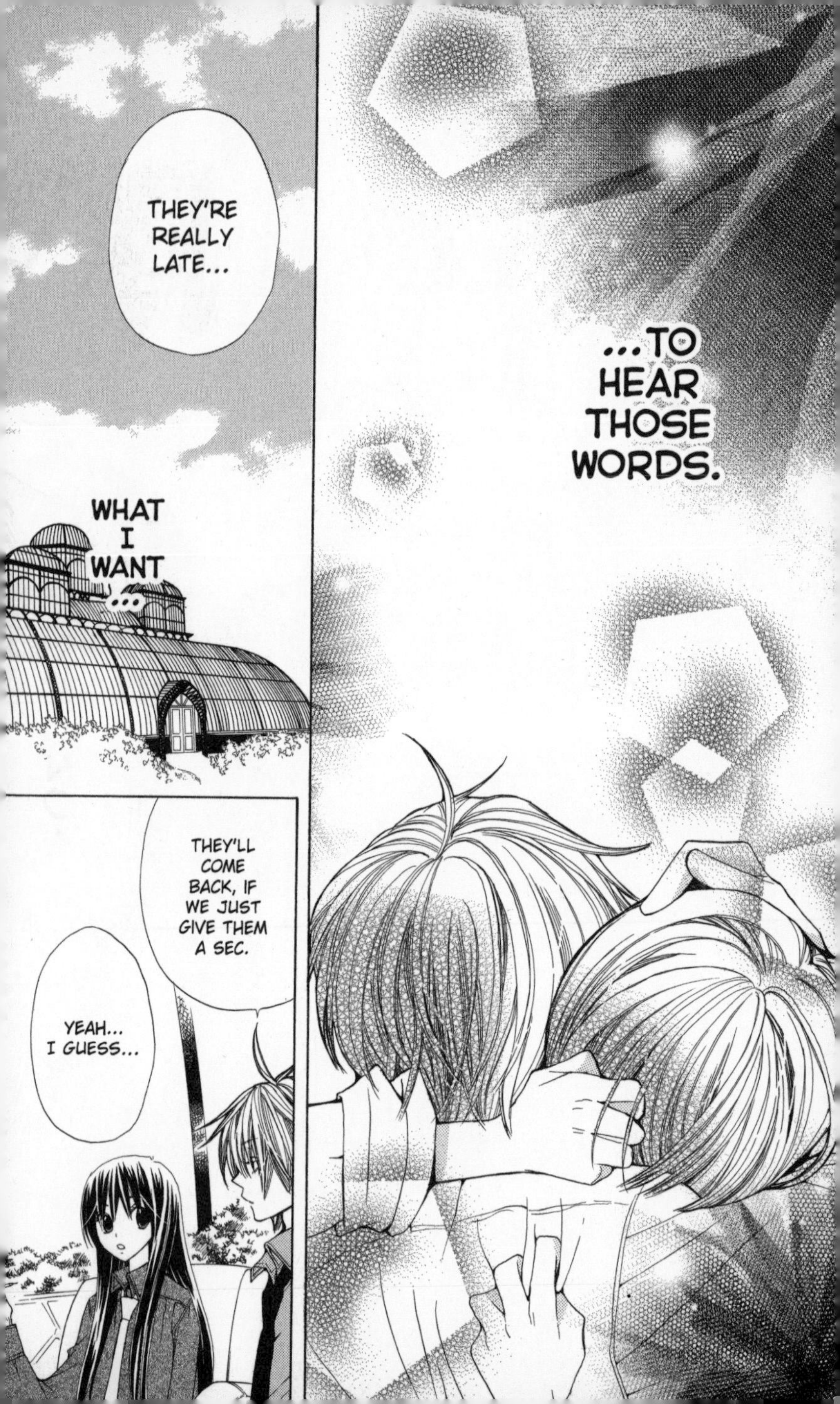
...TO HEAR THOSE WORDS.
THEY'RE REALLY LATE...
WHAT I WANT...
THEY'LL COME BACK, IF WE JUST GIVE THEM A SEC.
YEAH... I GUESS...

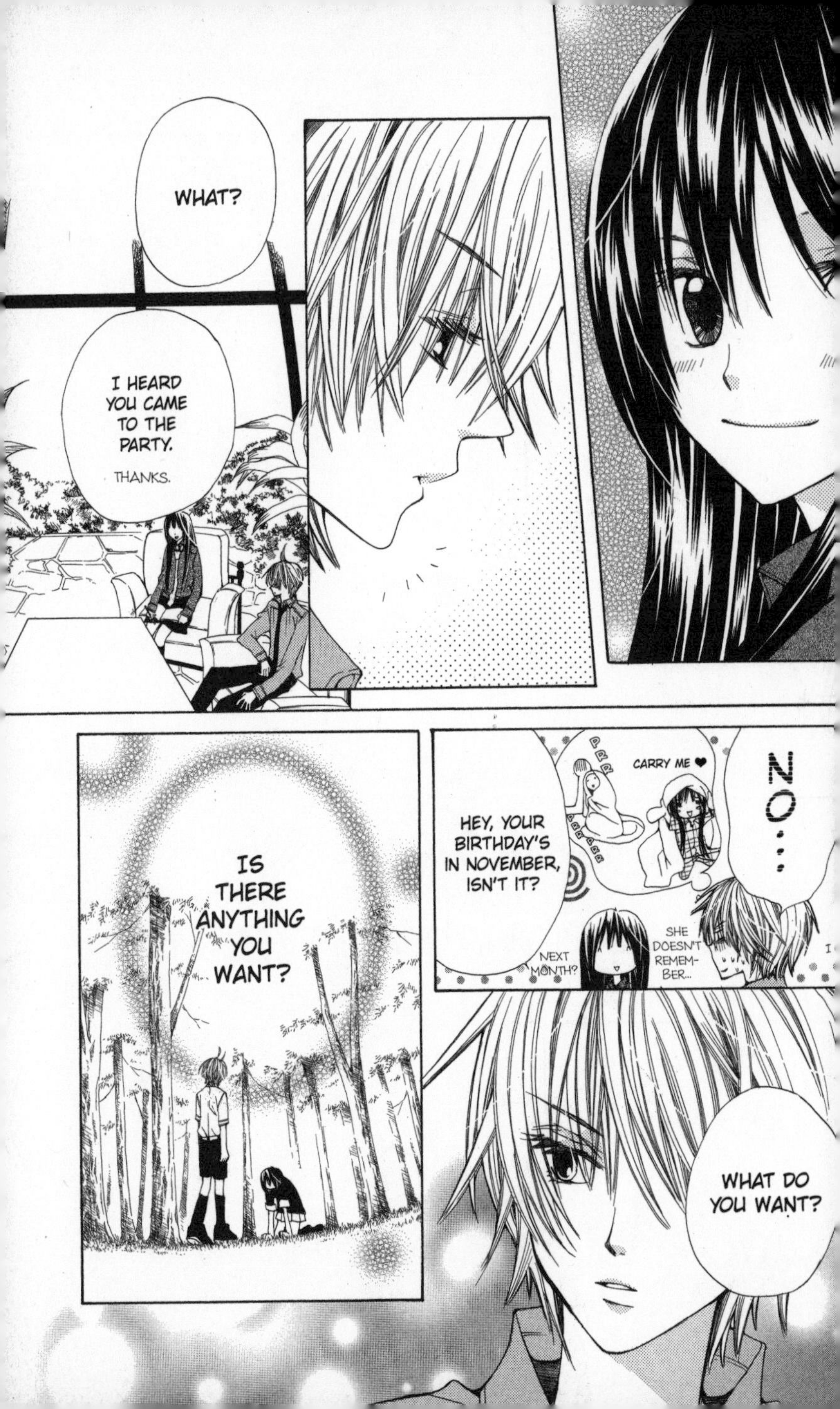

WHAT?
I HEARD YOU CAME TO THE PARTY.
THANKS.
NO...
I
CARRY ME ❤
HEY, YOUR BIRTHDAY'S IN NOVEMBER, ISN'T IT?
SHE DOESN'T REMEMBER...
NEXT MONTH?
WHAT DO YOU WANT?
IS THERE ANYTHING YOU WANT?

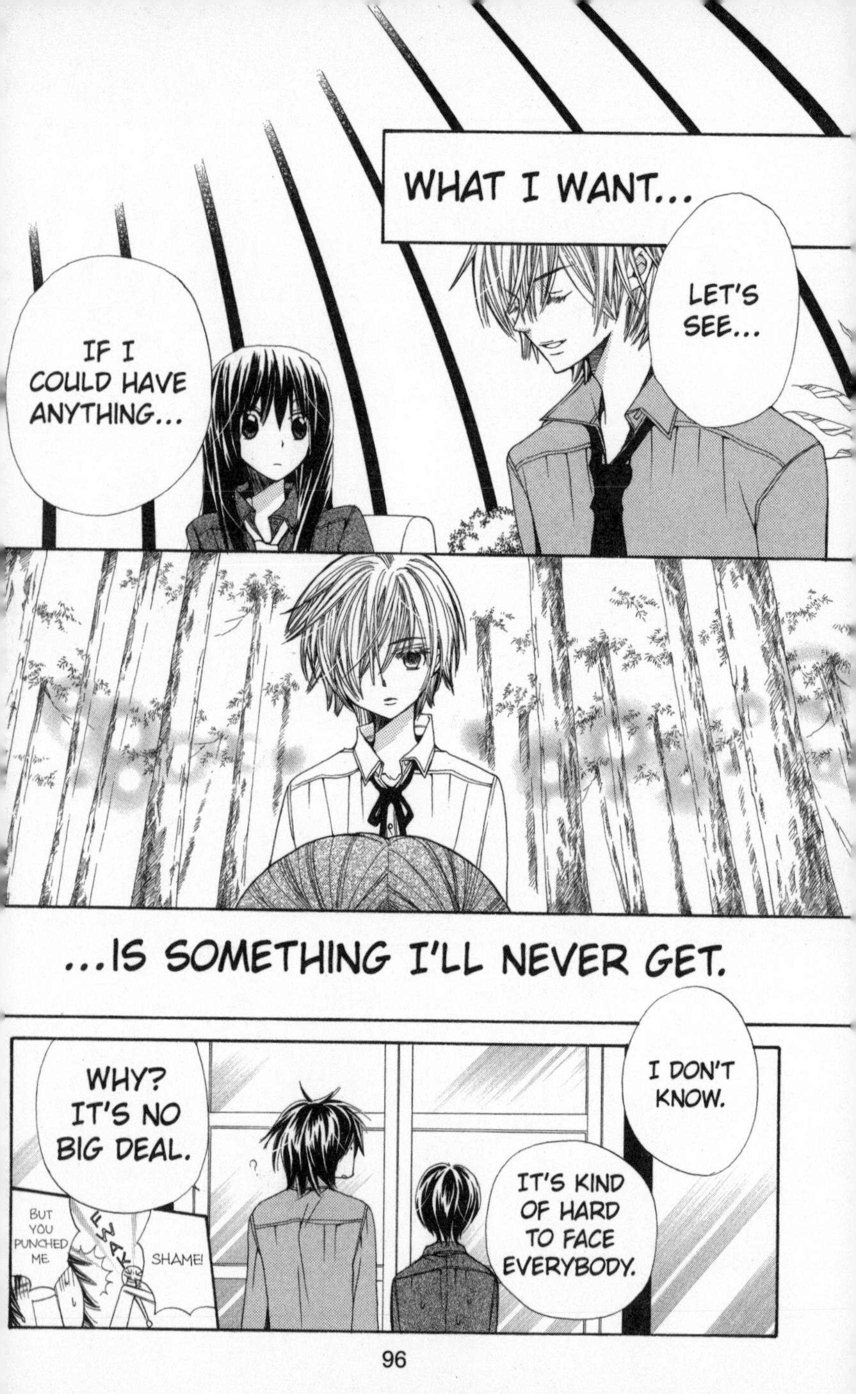
WHAT I WANT...
LET'S SEE...
IF I COULD HAVE ANYTHING...
...IS SOMETHING I'LL NEVER GET.
I DON'T KNOW.
IT'S KIND OF HARD TO FACE EVERYBODY.
WHY? IT'S NO BIG DEAL.
SHAME!
BUT YOU PUNCHED ME.

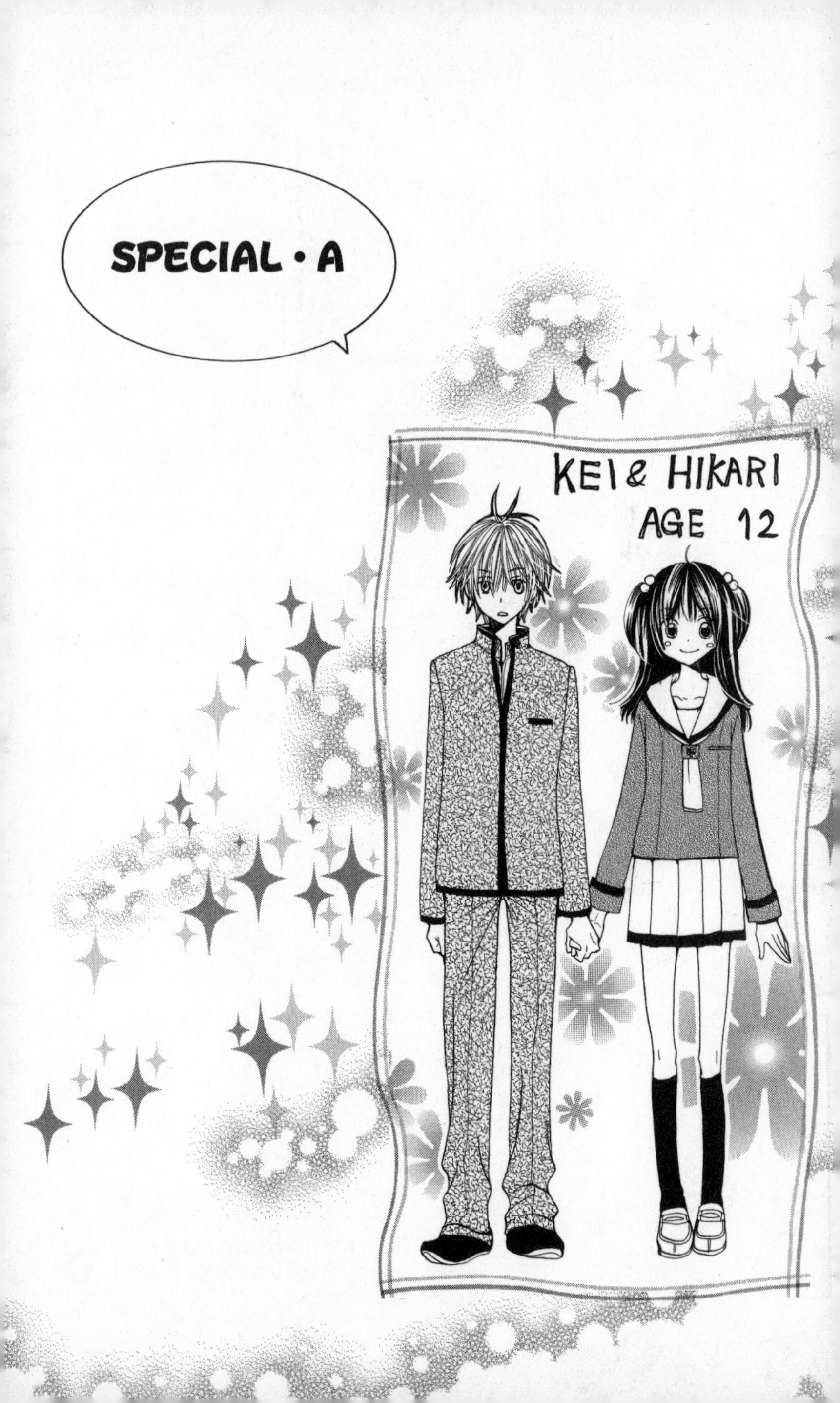
SPECIAL • A
KEI & HIKARI
AGE 12

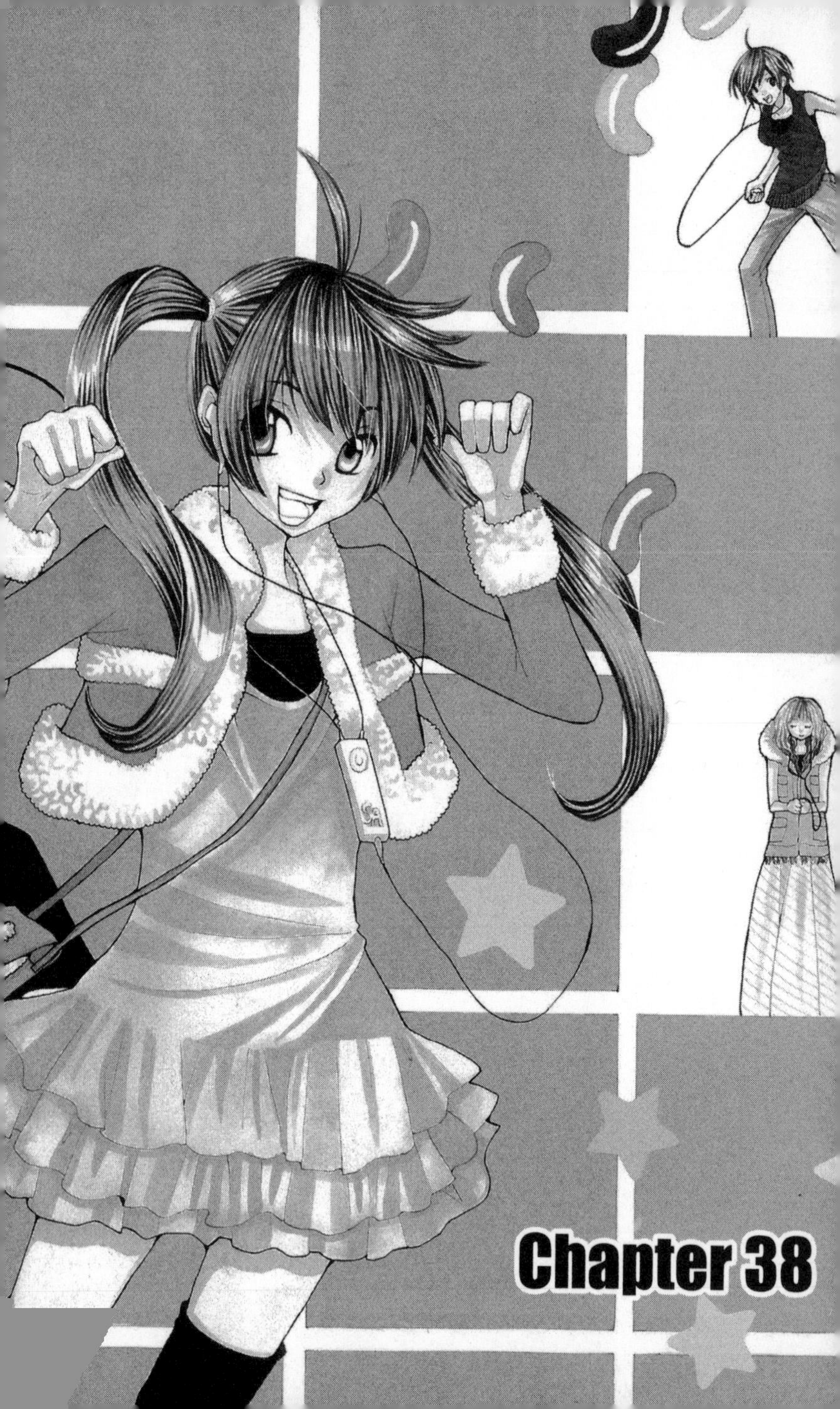
Chapter 38

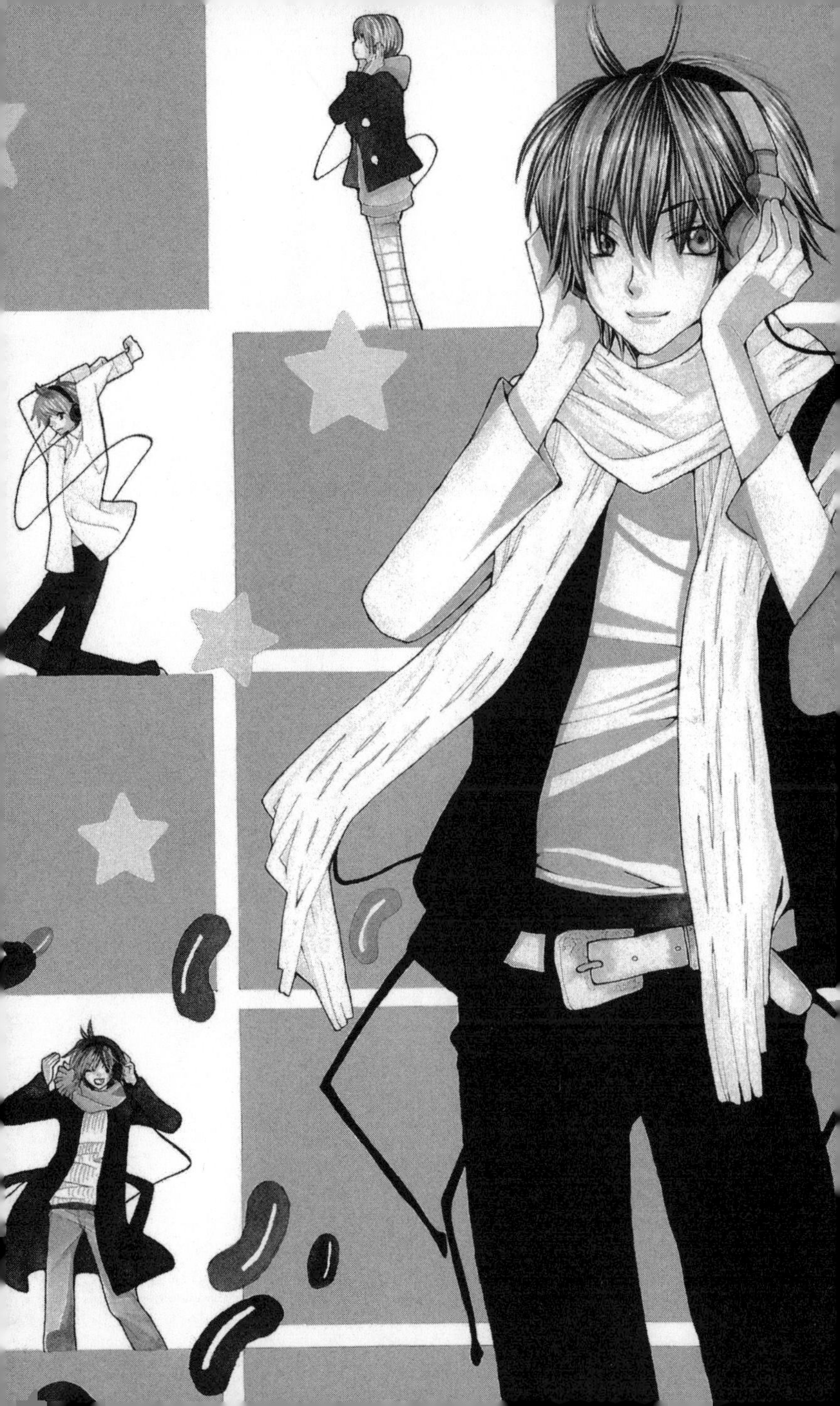

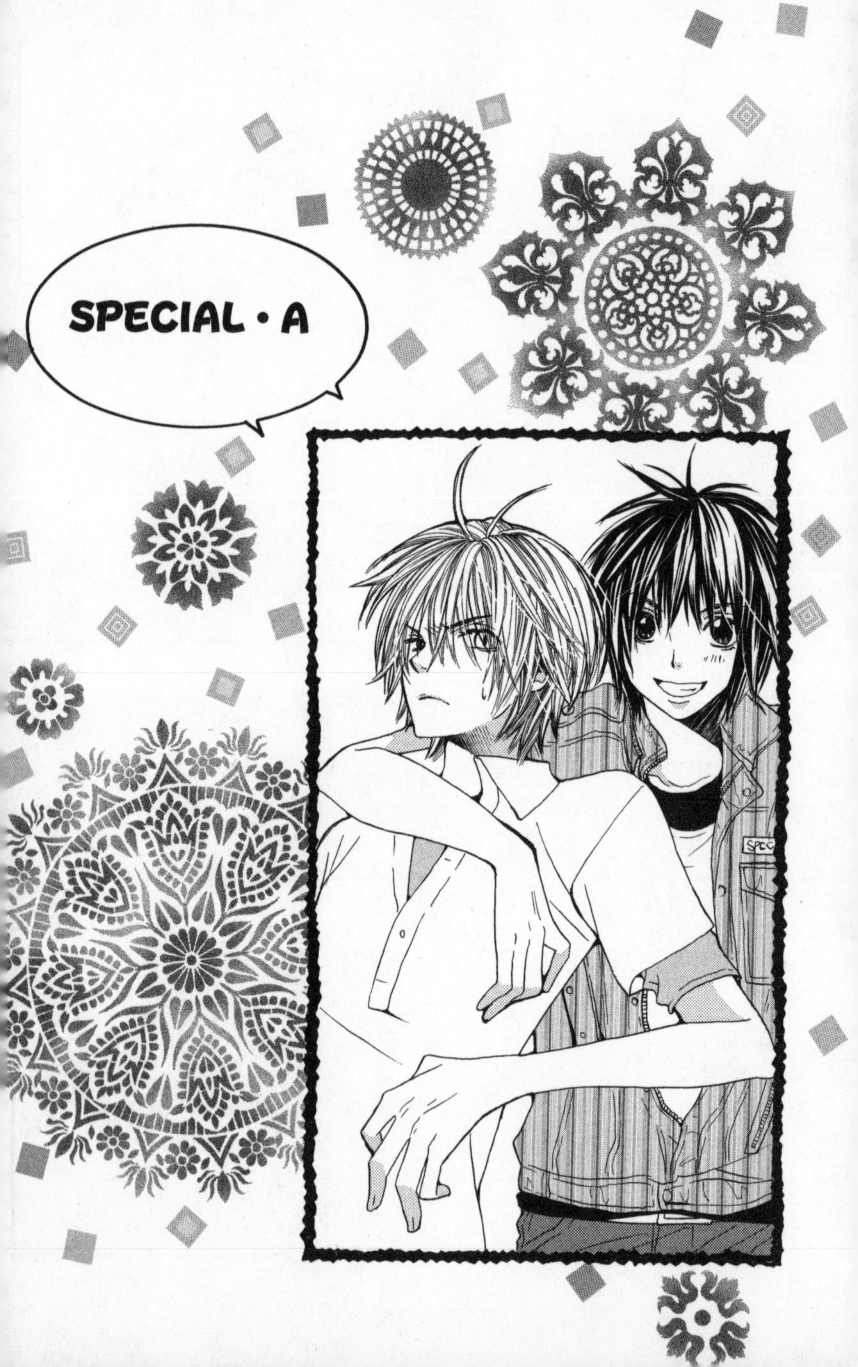
SPECIAL • A

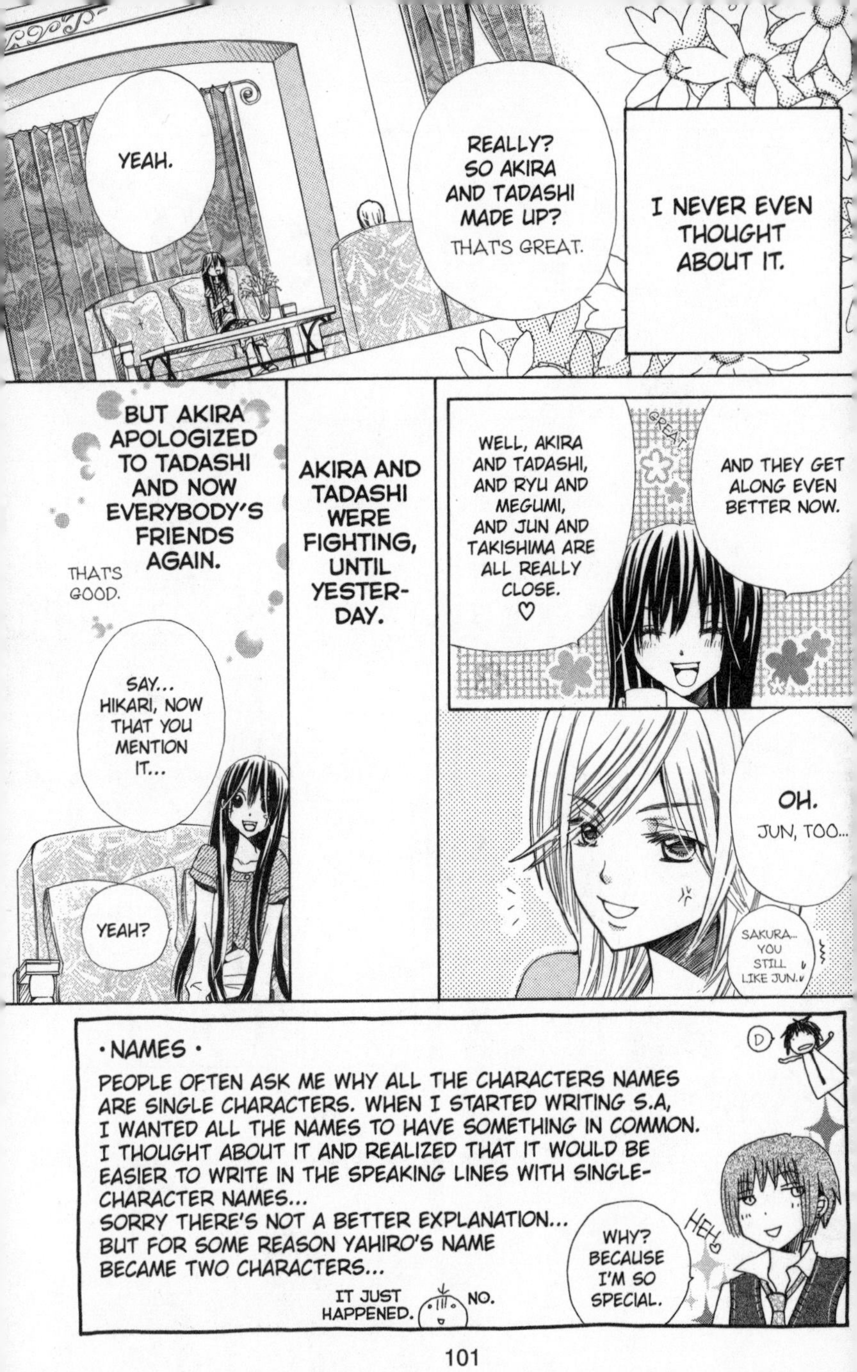
I NEVER EVEN THOUGHT ABOUT IT.
REALLY? SO AKIRA AND TADASHI MADE UP?
THAT'S GREAT.
YEAH.
AND THEY GET ALONG EVEN BETTER NOW.
GREAT.
WELL, AKIRA AND TADASHI, AND RYU AND MEGUMI, AND JUN AND TAKISHIMA ARE ALL REALLY CLOSE. ♡
OH.
JUN, TOO...
SAKURA... YOU STILL LIKE JUN.
AKIRA AND TADASHI WERE FIGHTING, UNTIL YESTER-DAY.
BUT AKIRA APOLOGIZED TO TADASHI AND NOW EVERYBODY'S FRIENDS AGAIN.
THAT'S GOOD.
SAY... HIKARI, NOW THAT YOU MENTION IT...
YEAH?

• NAMES •

PEOPLE OFTEN ASK ME WHY ALL THE CHARACTERS NAMES ARE SINGLE CHARACTERS. WHEN I STARTED WRITING S.A, I WANTED ALL THE NAMES TO HAVE SOMETHING IN COMMON. I THOUGHT ABOUT IT AND REALIZED THAT IT WOULD BE EASIER TO WRITE IN THE SPEAKING LINES WITH SINGLE-CHARACTER NAMES...
SORRY THERE'S NOT A BETTER EXPLANATION...
BUT FOR SOME REASON YAHIRO'S NAME BECAME TWO CHARACTERS...

IT JUST HAPPENED. NO.

WHY? BECAUSE I'M SO SPECIAL.

HEH ♡

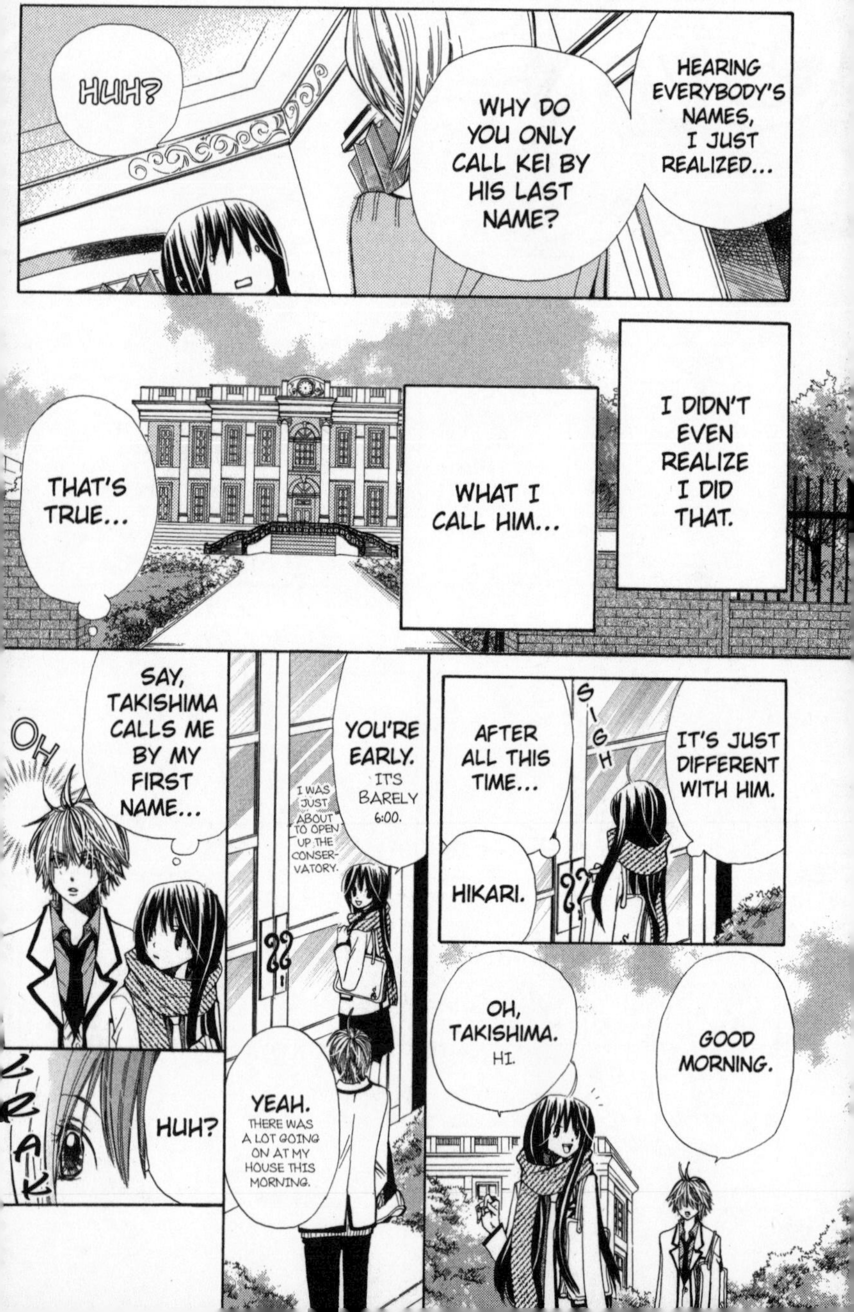
HEARING EVERYBODY'S NAMES, I JUST REALIZED...
WHY DO YOU ONLY CALL KEI BY HIS LAST NAME?
HUH?
I DIDN'T EVEN REALIZE I DID THAT.
WHAT I CALL HIM...
THAT'S TRUE...
IT'S JUST DIFFERENT WITH HIM.
SIGH
AFTER ALL THIS TIME...
HIKARI.
GOOD MORNING.
OH, TAKISHIMA. HI.
YOU'RE EARLY. IT'S BARELY 6:00.
I WAS JUST ABOUT TO OPEN UP THE CONSERVATORY.
YEAH. THERE WAS A LOT GOING ON AT MY HOUSE THIS MORNING.
SAY, TAKISHIMA CALLS ME BY MY FIRST NAME...
OH
HUH?
RAK

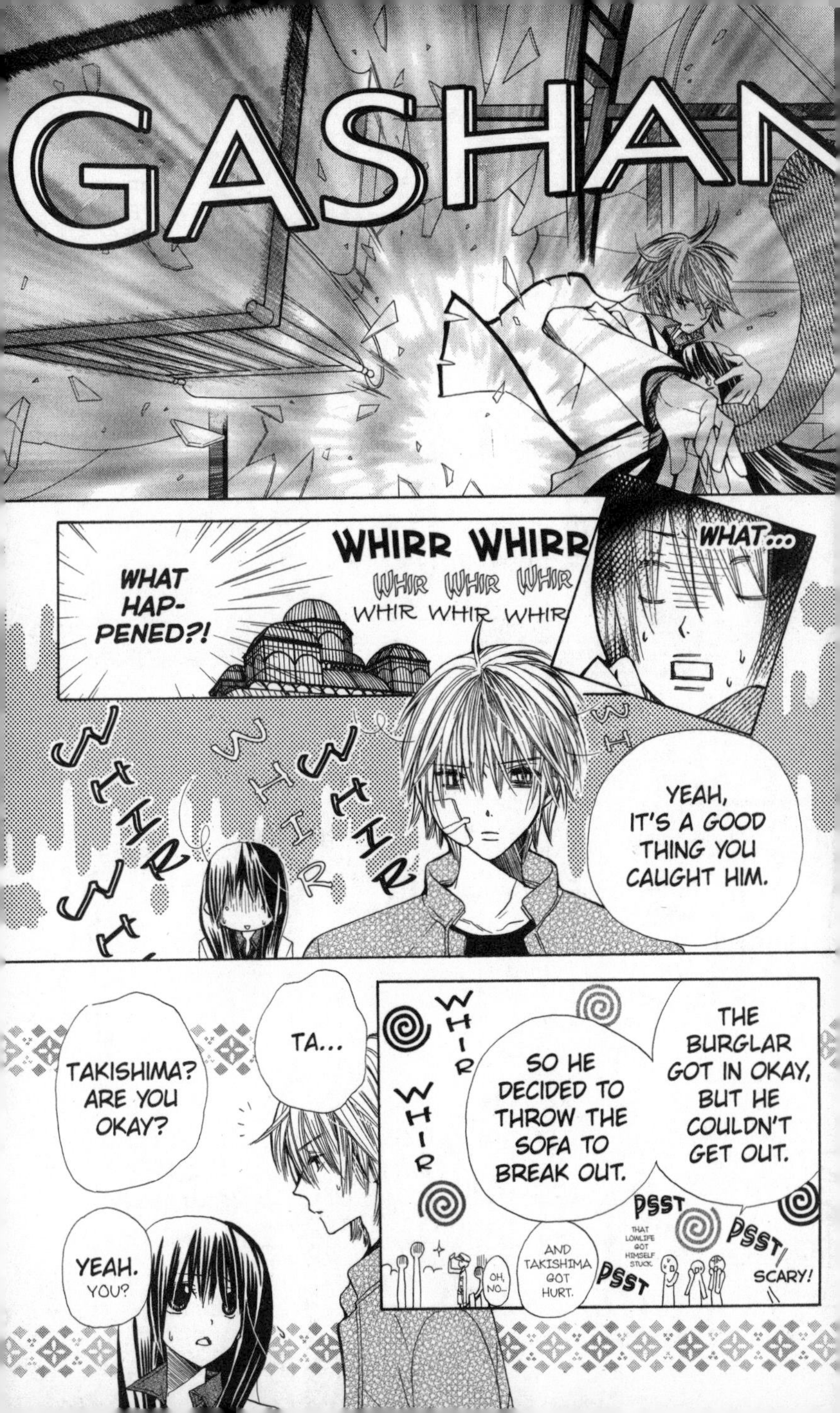
GASHAN
WHAT...
WHAT HAPPENED?!
WHIRR WHIRR
WHIR WHIR WHIR
WHIR WHIR WHIR
WHIRR
WHIRR
WHIR
WHIR
YEAH, IT'S A GOOD THING YOU CAUGHT HIM.
THE BURGLAR GOT IN OKAY, BUT HE COULDN'T GET OUT.
SO HE DECIDED TO THROW THE SOFA TO BREAK OUT.
WHIR
WHIR
PSST
PSST
THAT LOWLIFE GOT HIMSELF STUCK.
SCARY!
AND TAKISHIMA GOT HURT.
PSST
OH, NO...
TA...
TAKISHIMA? ARE YOU OKAY?
YEAH. YOU?

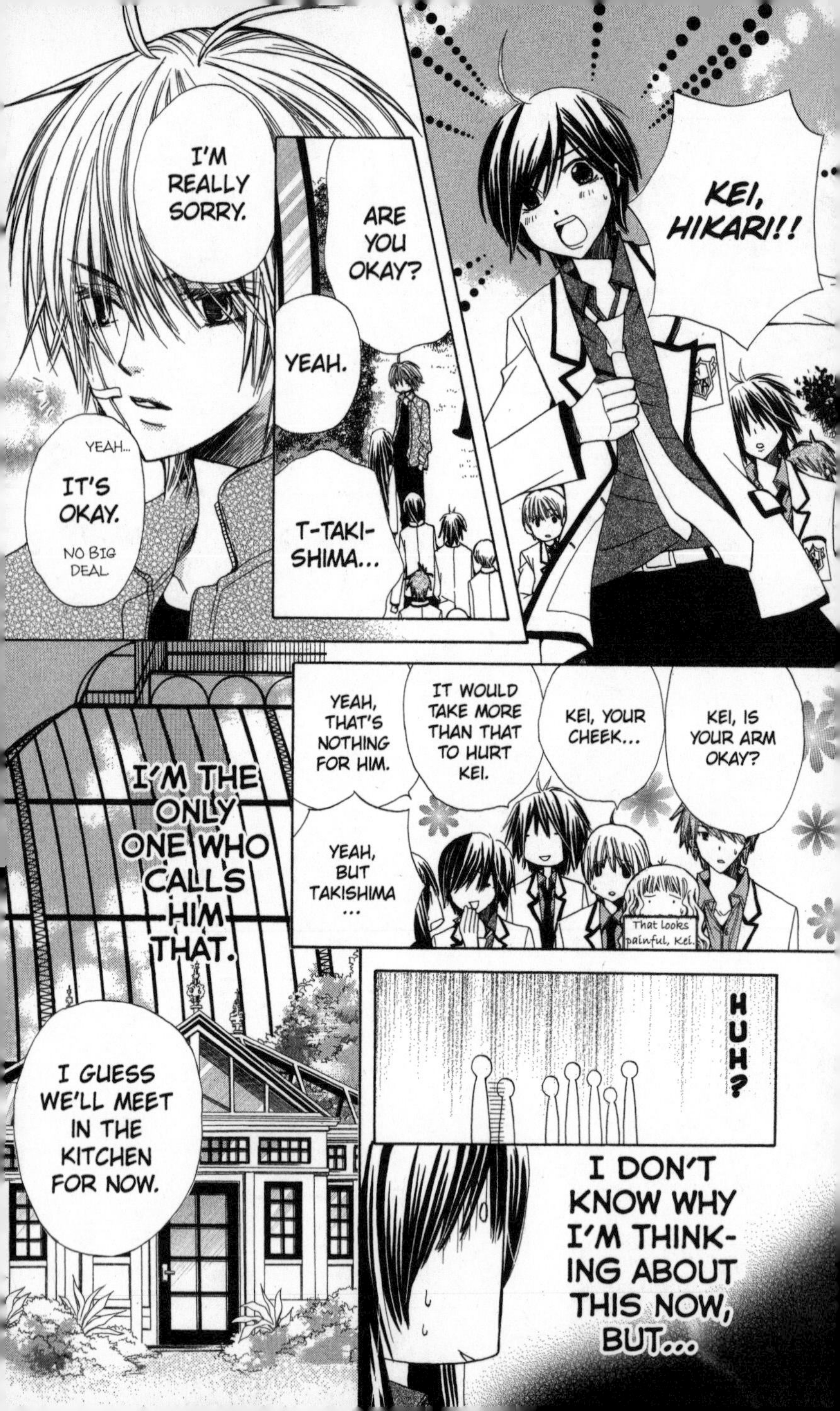
KEI, HIKARI!!
ARE YOU OKAY?
YEAH.
T-TAKI-SHIMA...
I'M REALLY SORRY.
YEAH... IT'S OKAY. NO BIG DEAL.
KEI, IS YOUR ARM OKAY?
KEI, YOUR CHEEK...
IT WOULD TAKE MORE THAN THAT TO HURT KEI.
YEAH, THAT'S NOTHING FOR HIM.
YEAH, BUT TAKISHIMA...
That looks painful, Kei.
HUH?
I DON'T KNOW WHY I'M THINKING ABOUT THIS NOW, BUT...
I'M THE ONLY ONE WHO CALLS HIM THAT.
I GUESS WE'LL MEET IN THE KITCHEN FOR NOW.

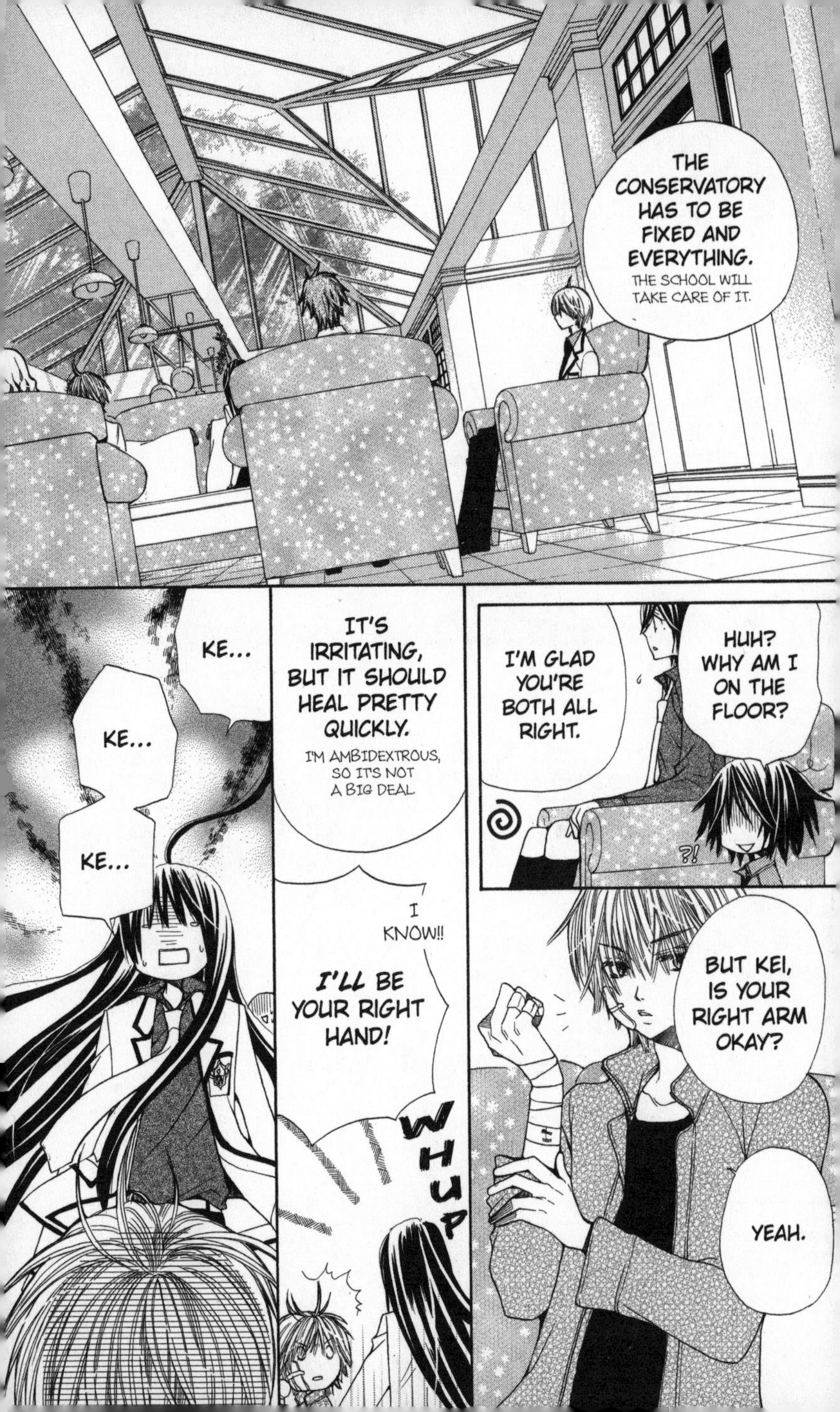
THE CONSERVATORY HAS TO BE FIXED AND EVERYTHING.
THE SCHOOL WILL TAKE CARE OF IT.
HUH? WHY AM I ON THE FLOOR?
I'M GLAD YOU'RE BOTH ALL RIGHT.
?!
BUT KEI, IS YOUR RIGHT ARM OKAY?
YEAH.
IT'S IRRITATING, BUT IT SHOULD HEAL PRETTY QUICKLY.
I'M AMBIDEXTROUS, SO IT'S NOT A BIG DEAL
I KNOW!!
I'LL BE YOUR RIGHT HAND!
WHUP
KE...
KE...
KE...

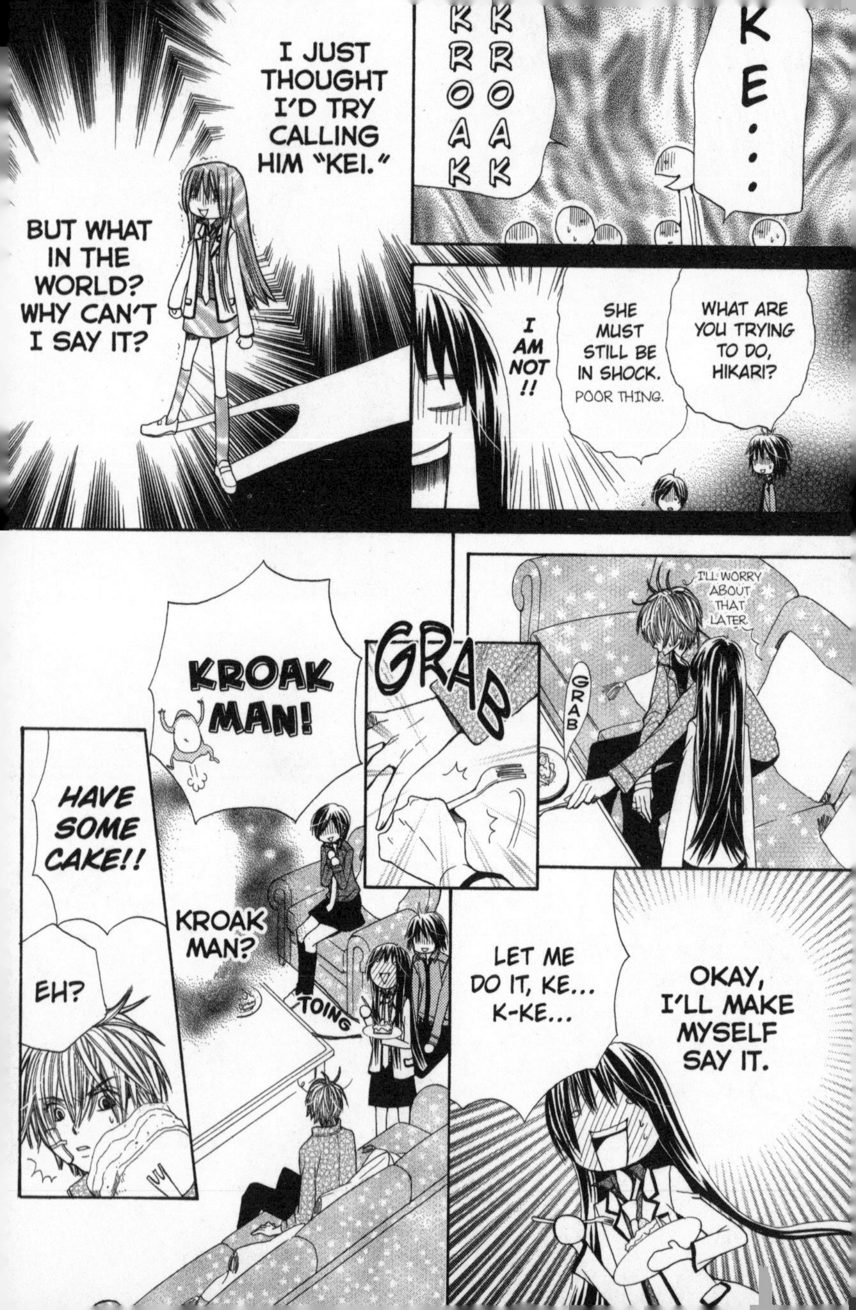
KE...
KROAK KROAK
WHAT ARE YOU TRYING TO DO, HIKARI?
SHE MUST STILL BE IN SHOCK.
POOR THING.
I AM NOT!!
I JUST THOUGHT I'D TRY CALLING HIM "KEI."
BUT WHAT IN THE WORLD? WHY CAN'T I SAY IT?
I'LL WORRY ABOUT THAT LATER.
GRAB
OKAY, I'LL MAKE MYSELF SAY IT.
LET ME DO IT, KE... K-KE...
GRAB
KROAK MAN!
HAVE SOME CAKE!!
KROAK MAN?
TOING
EH?

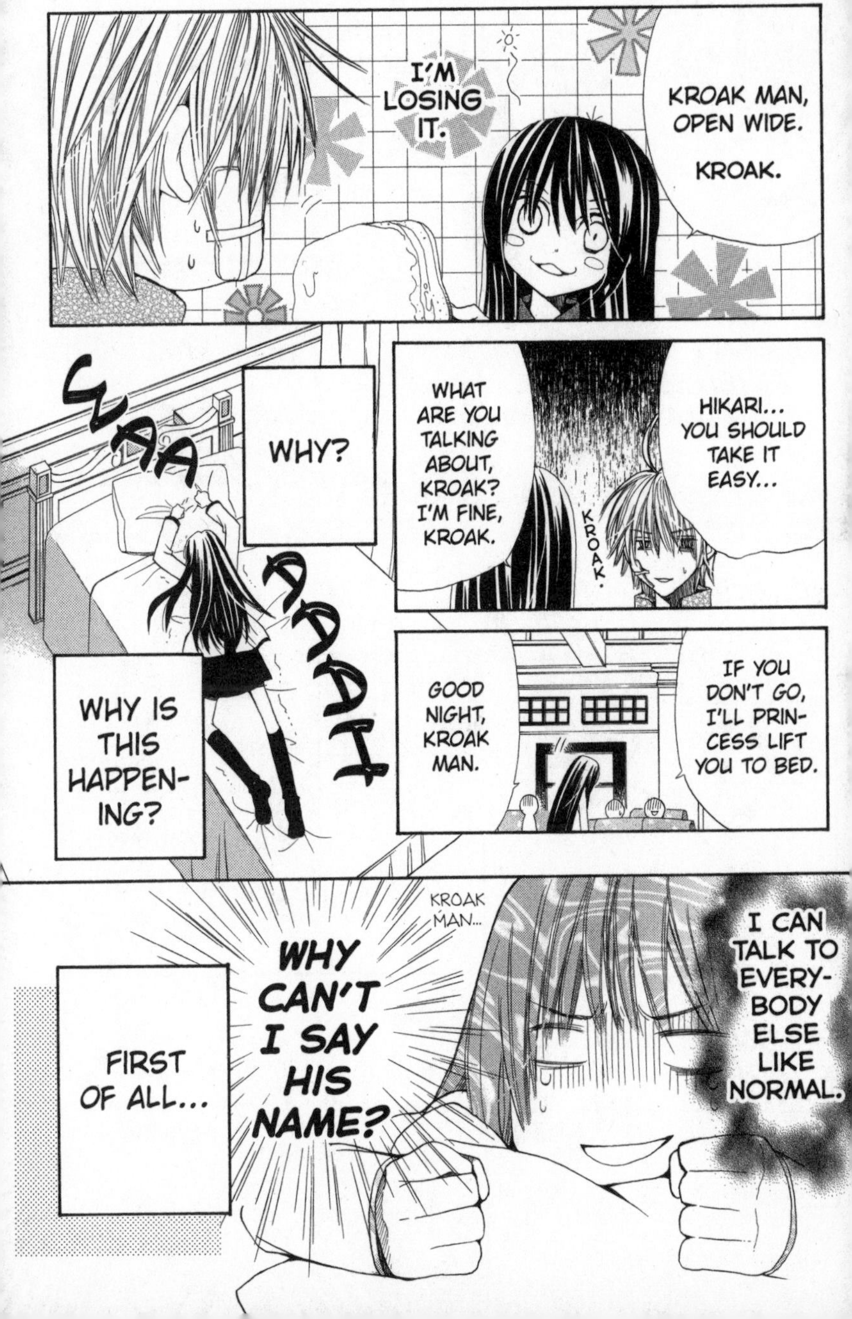
KROAK MAN, OPEN WIDE.
KROAK.
I'M LOSING IT.
HIKARI... YOU SHOULD TAKE IT EASY...
WHAT ARE YOU TALKING ABOUT, KROAK? I'M FINE, KROAK.
KROAK.
IF YOU DON'T GO, I'LL PRINCESS LIFT YOU TO BED.
GOOD NIGHT, KROAK MAN.
WHY?
WAA
AAAI
WHY IS THIS HAPPENING?
I CAN TALK TO EVERYBODY ELSE LIKE NORMAL.
KROAK MAN...
WHY CAN'T I SAY HIS NAME?
FIRST OF ALL...

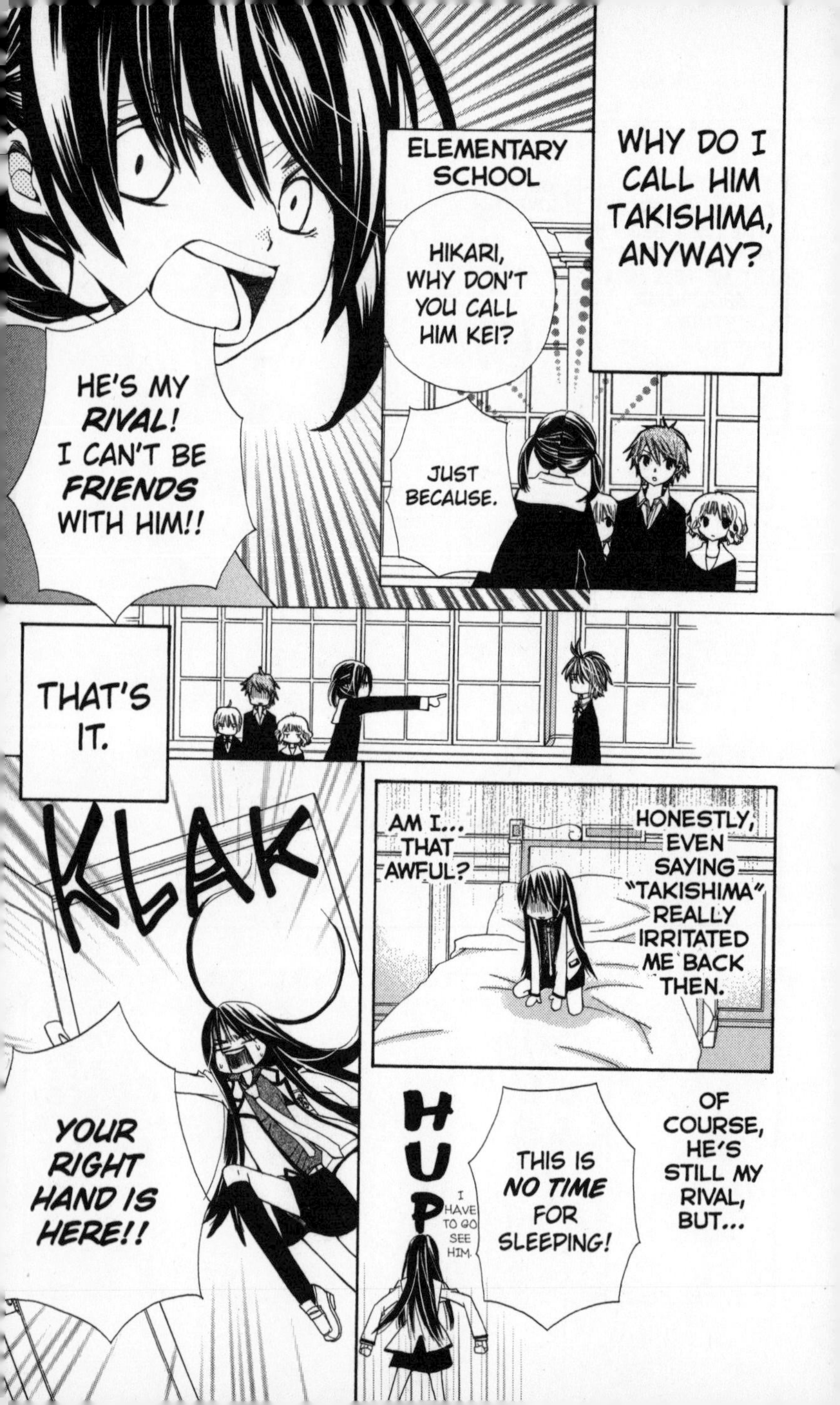

WHY DO I CALL HIM TAKISHIMA, ANYWAY?
ELEMENTARY SCHOOL
HIKARI, WHY DON'T YOU CALL HIM KEI?
JUST BECAUSE.
HE'S MY *RIVAL*! I CAN'T BE *FRIENDS* WITH HIM!!
THAT'S IT.
HONESTLY, EVEN SAYING "TAKISHIMA" REALLY IRRITATED ME BACK THEN.
AM I... THAT AWFUL?
OF COURSE, HE'S STILL MY RIVAL, BUT...
THIS IS *NO TIME* FOR SLEEPING!
HUP
I HAVE TO GO SEE HIM.
KLAK
YOUR RIGHT HAND IS HERE!!

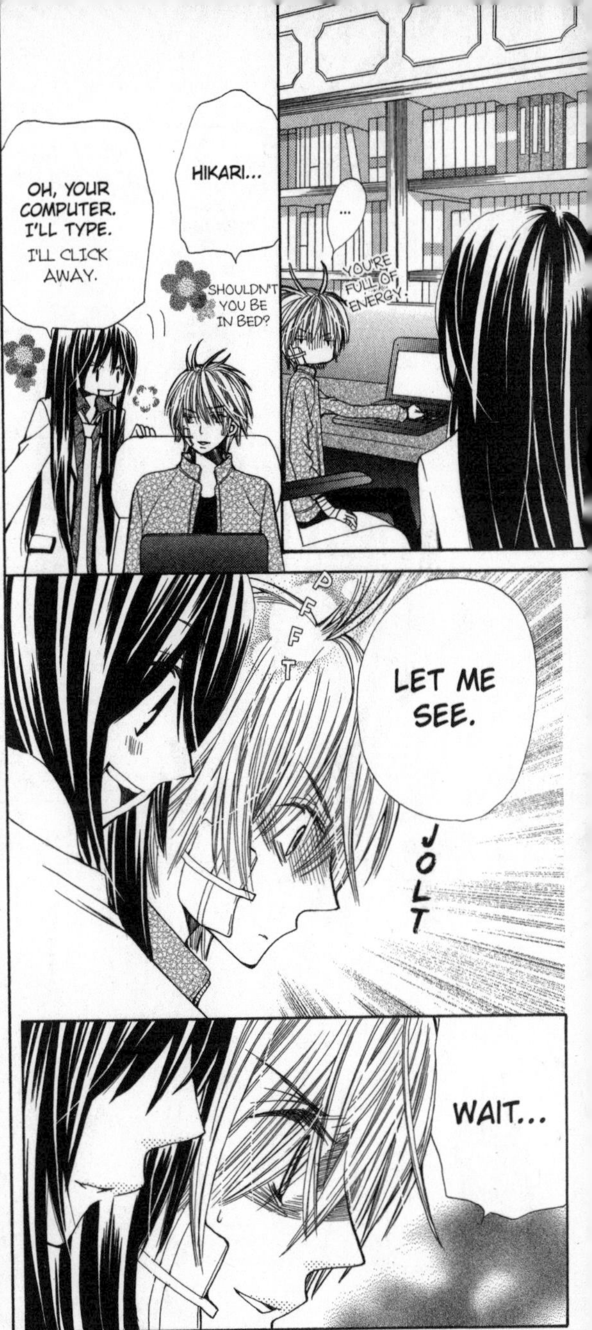
...
YOU'RE FULL OF ENERGY.
HIKARI...
OH, YOUR COMPUTER. I'LL TYPE.
I'LL CLICK AWAY.
SHOULDN'T YOU BE IN BED?
PFFT
LET ME SEE.
JOLT
WAIT...

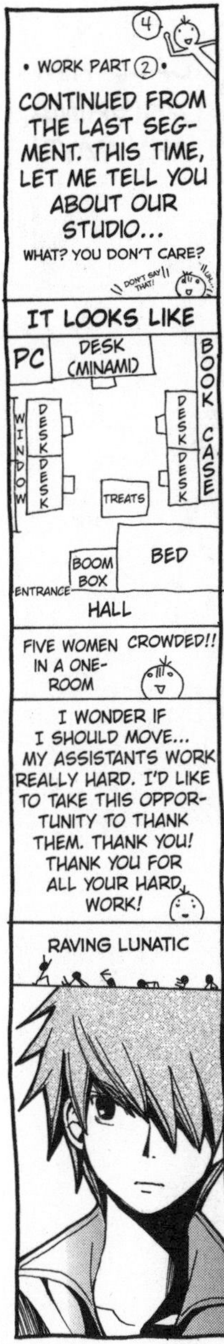
4
• WORK PART 2 •
CONTINUED FROM THE LAST SEGMENT. THIS TIME, LET ME TELL YOU ABOUT OUR STUDIO...
WHAT? YOU DON'T CARE?
DON'T SAY THAT!
IT LOOKS LIKE
PC
DESK (MINAMI)
BOOK CASE
WINDOW
DESK
DESK
DESK
DESK
TREATS
BED
BOOM BOX
ENTRANCE
HALL
FIVE WOMEN IN A ONE-ROOM
CROWDED!!
I WONDER IF I SHOULD MOVE... MY ASSISTANTS WORK REALLY HARD. I'D LIKE TO TAKE THIS OPPORTUNITY TO THANK THEM. THANK YOU! THANK YOU FOR ALL YOUR HARD WORK!
RAVING LUNATIC

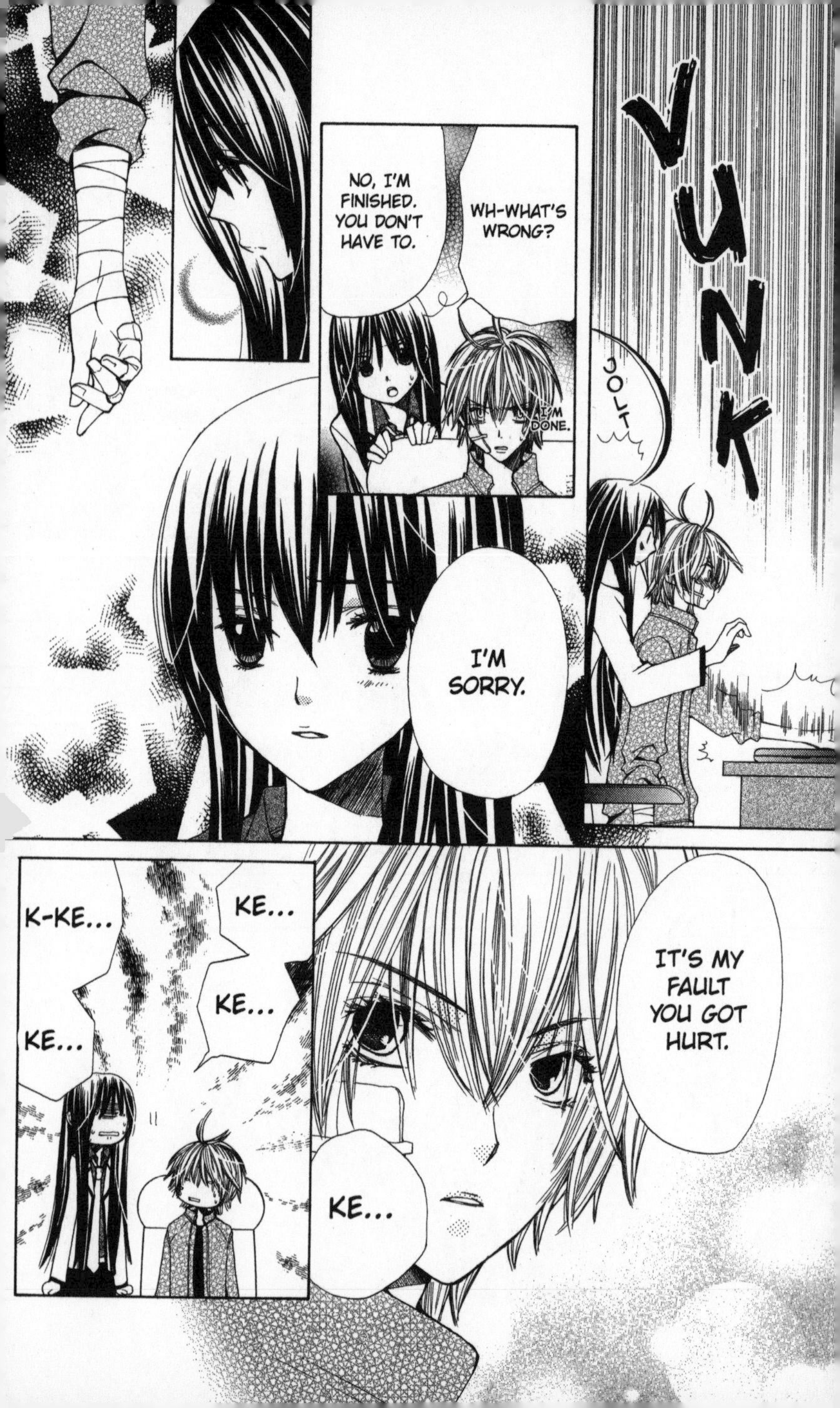
VUNK
JOLT
WH-WHAT'S WRONG?
NO, I'M FINISHED. YOU DON'T HAVE TO.
I'M DONE.
I'M SORRY.
IT'S MY FAULT YOU GOT HURT.
KE...
KE...
KE...
K-KE...
KE...

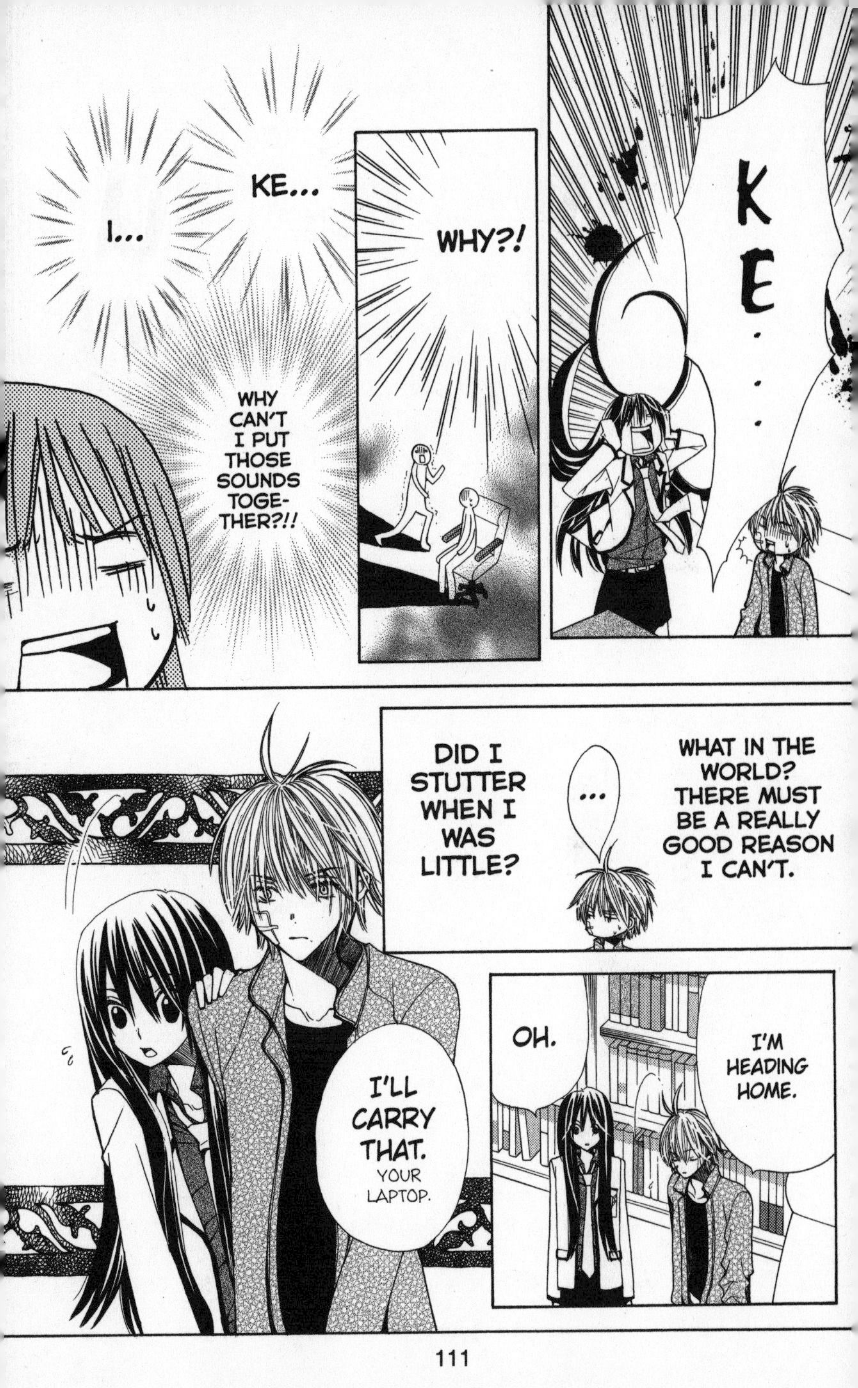
KE...
WHY?!
KE...
I...
WHY CAN'T I PUT THOSE SOUNDS TOGE-THER?!!
WHAT IN THE WORLD? THERE MUST BE A REALLY GOOD REASON I CAN'T.
...
DID I STUTTER WHEN I WAS LITTLE?
I'M HEADING HOME.
OH.
I'LL CARRY THAT.
YOUR LAPTOP.

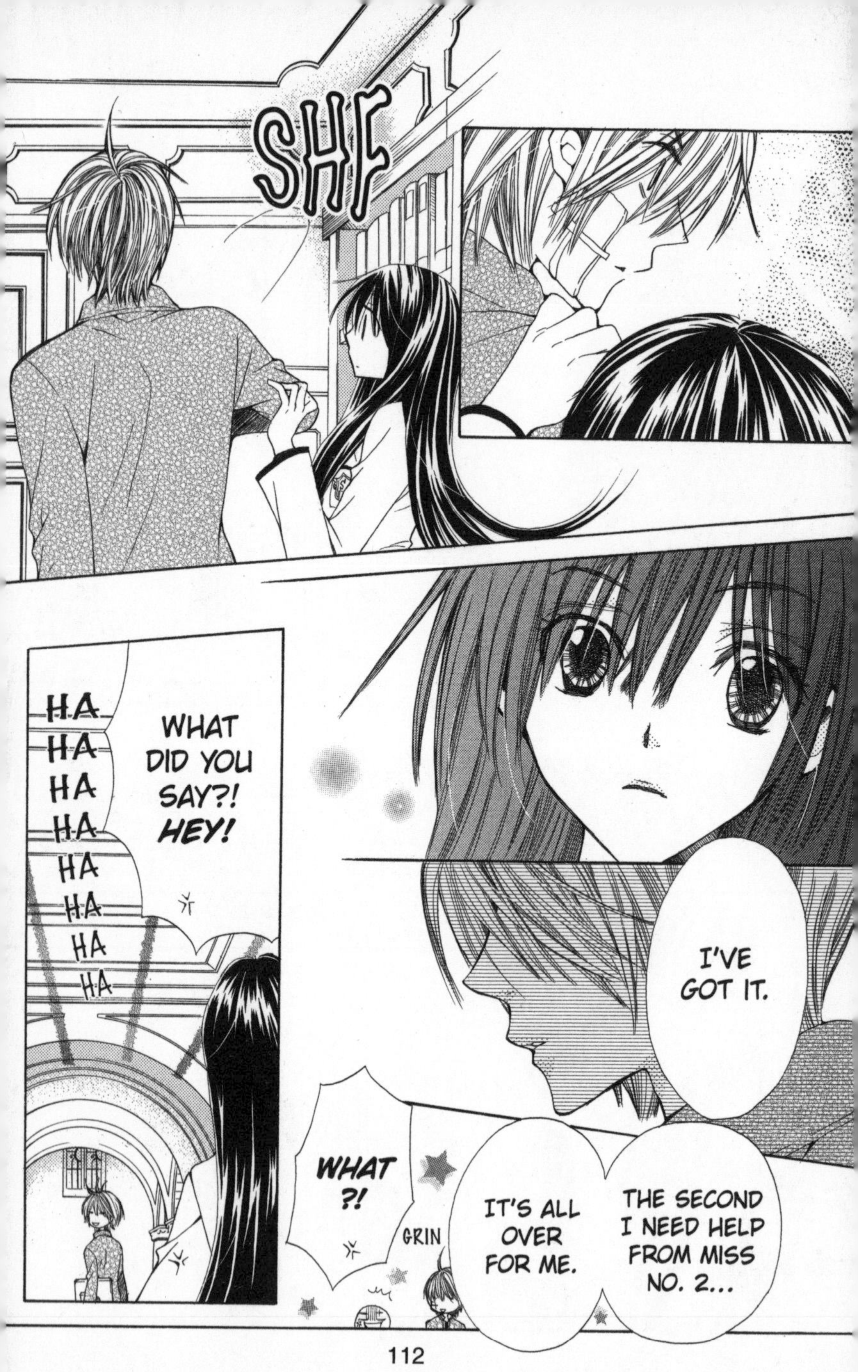
SHF
WHAT DID YOU SAY?! HEY!
HA HA HA HA HA HA HA HA
I'VE GOT IT.
THE SECOND I NEED HELP FROM MISS NO. 2...
IT'S ALL OVER FOR ME.
WHAT ?!
GRIN

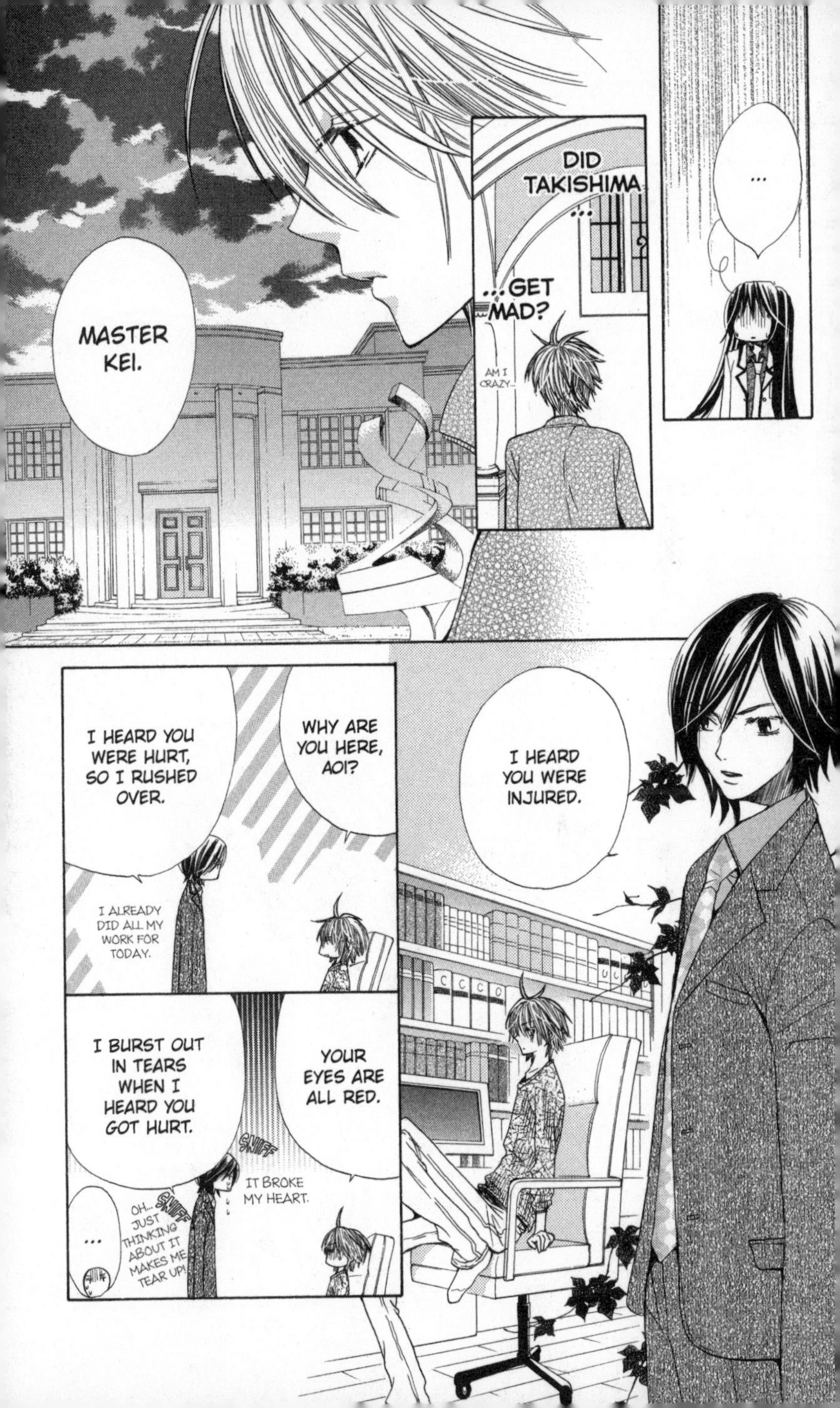
...
DID TAKISHIMA ...
...GET MAD?
AM I CRAZY...
MASTER KEI.
I HEARD YOU WERE INJURED.
WHY ARE YOU HERE, AOI?
I HEARD YOU WERE HURT, SO I RUSHED OVER.
I ALREADY DID ALL MY WORK FOR TODAY.
YOUR EYES ARE ALL RED.
I BURST OUT IN TEARS WHEN I HEARD YOU GOT HURT.
IT BROKE MY HEART.
SNIFF
SNIFF
OH... JUST THINKING ABOUT IT MAKES ME TEAR UP!
...

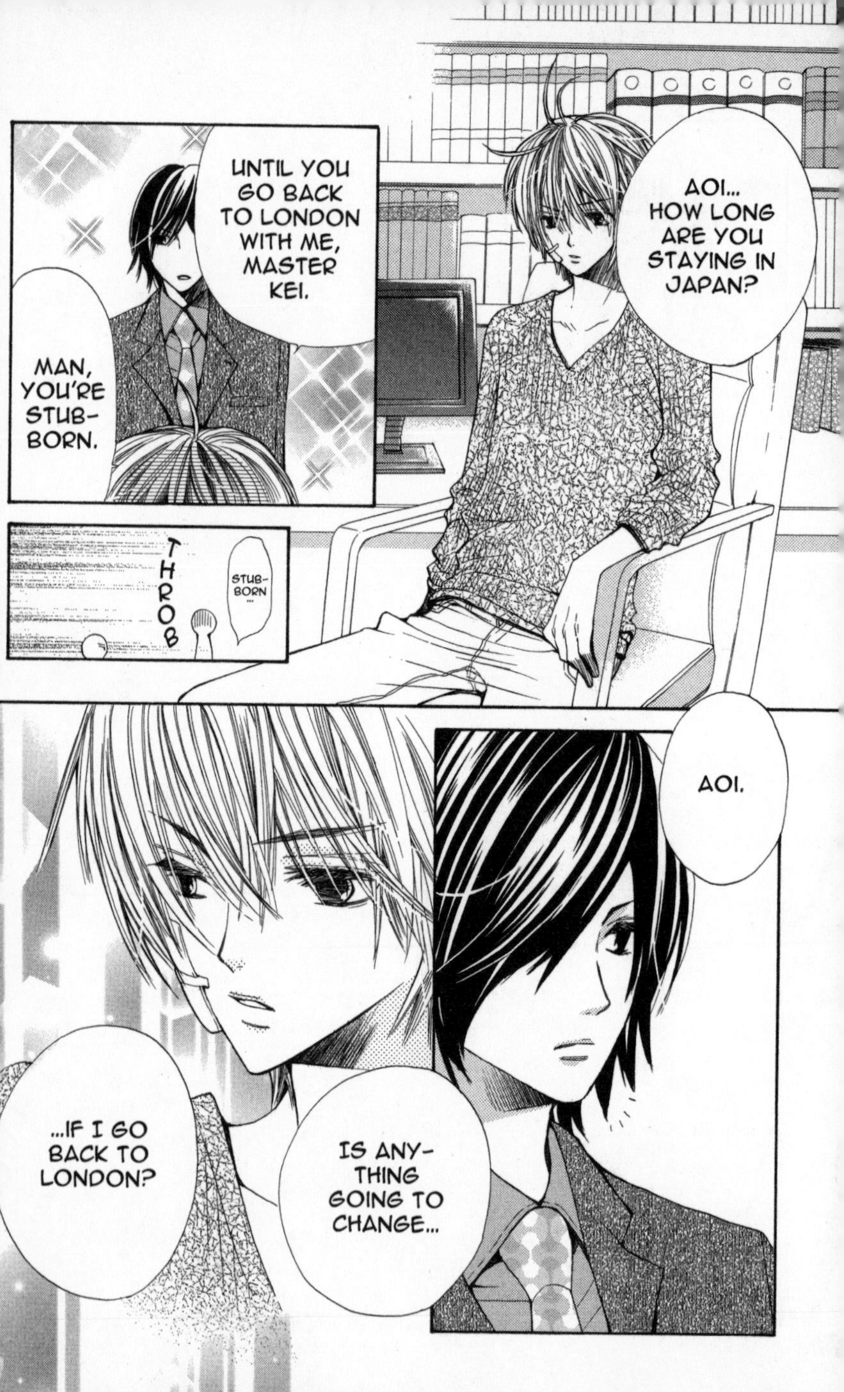
AOI... HOW LONG ARE YOU STAYING IN JAPAN?
UNTIL YOU GO BACK TO LONDON WITH ME, MASTER KEI.
MAN, YOU'RE STUB-BORN.
STUB-BORN...
THROB
AOI.
IS ANY-THING GOING TO CHANGE...
...IF I GO BACK TO LONDON?

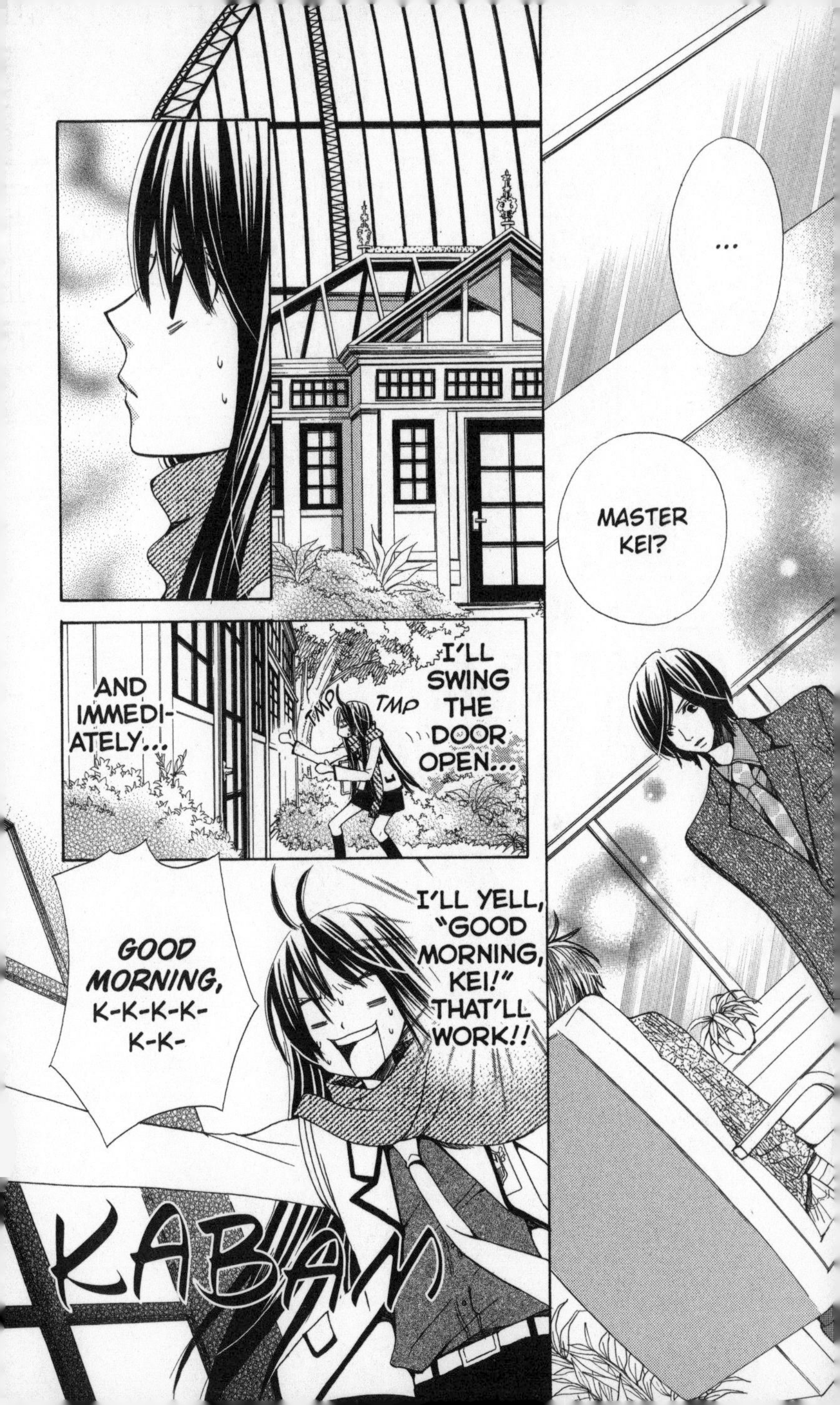
...
MASTER KEI?
I'LL SWING THE DOOR OPEN...
TMP TMP
AND IMMEDIATELY...
I'LL YELL, "GOOD MORNING, KEI!" THAT'LL WORK!!
GOOD MORNING, K-K-K-K-K-K-
KABAM

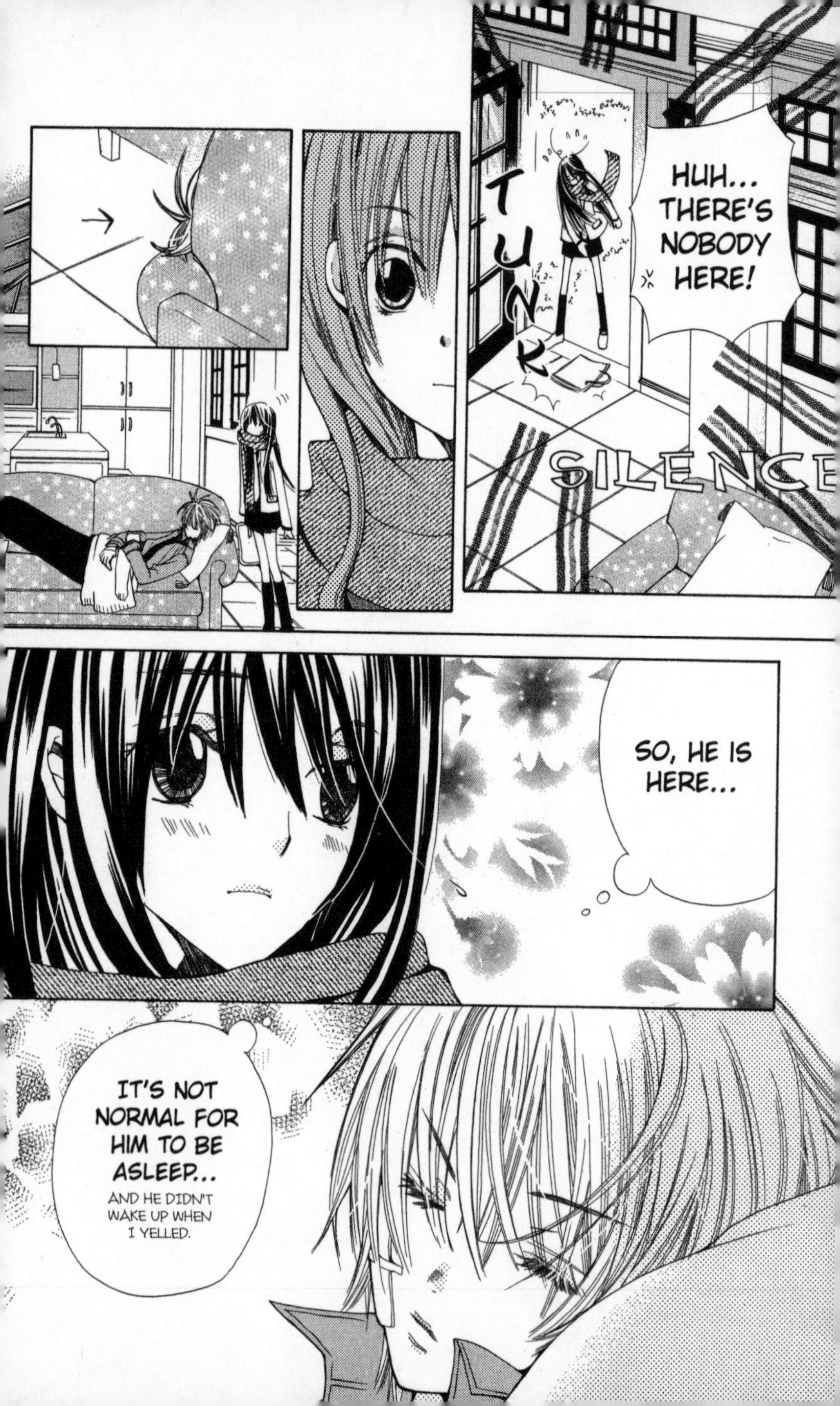
HUH... THERE'S NOBODY HERE!
TUNK
SILENCE
SO, HE IS HERE...
IT'S NOT NORMAL FOR HIM TO BE ASLEEP...
AND HE DIDN'T WAKE UP WHEN I YELLED.

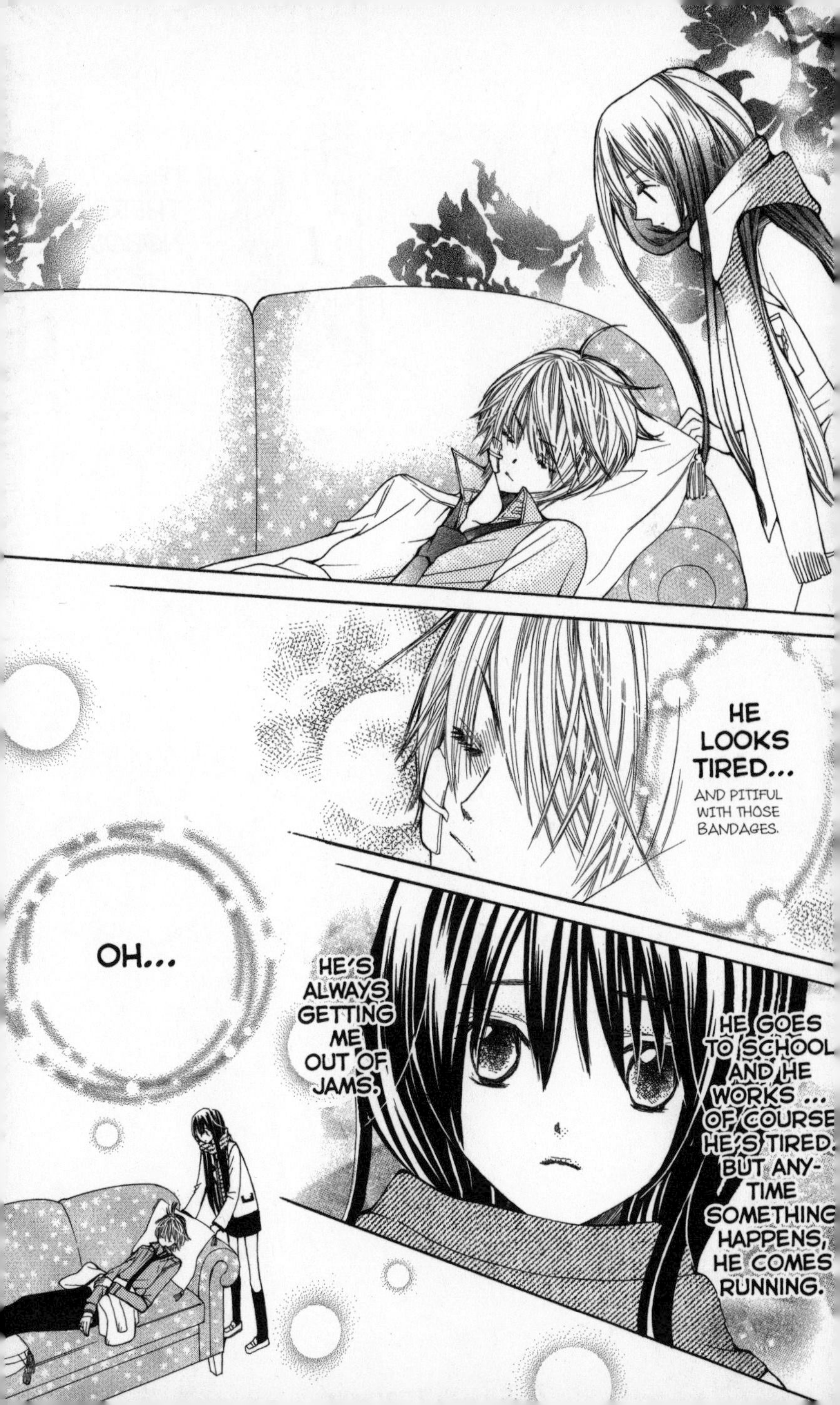
HE LOOKS TIRED...
AND PITIFUL WITH THOSE BANDAGES.
HE GOES TO SCHOOL AND HE WORKS ... OF COURSE HE'S TIRED. BUT ANY-TIME SOMETHING HAPPENS, HE COMES RUNNING.
HE'S ALWAYS GETTING ME OUT OF JAMS.
OH...

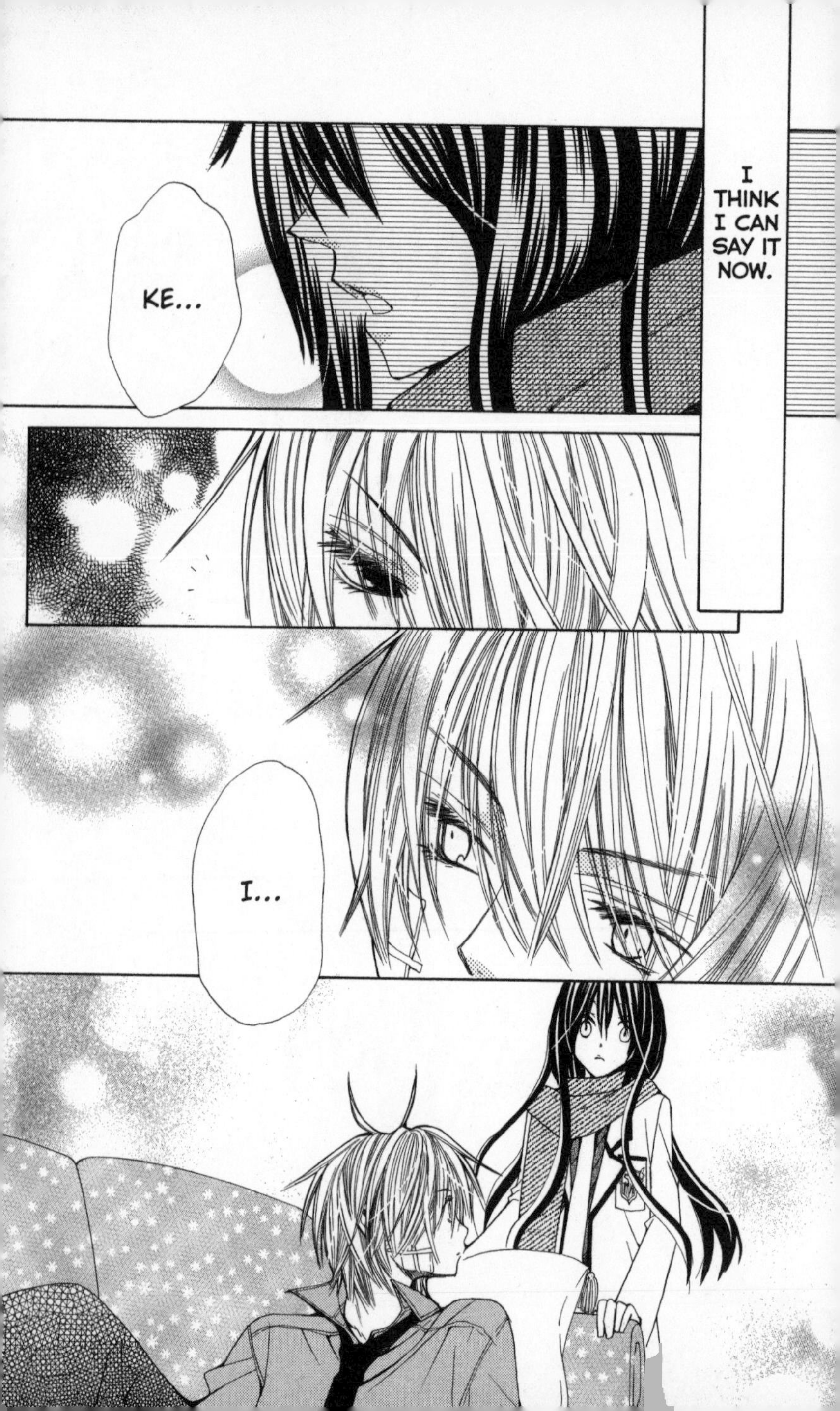
I THINK I CAN SAY IT NOW.
KE...
I...

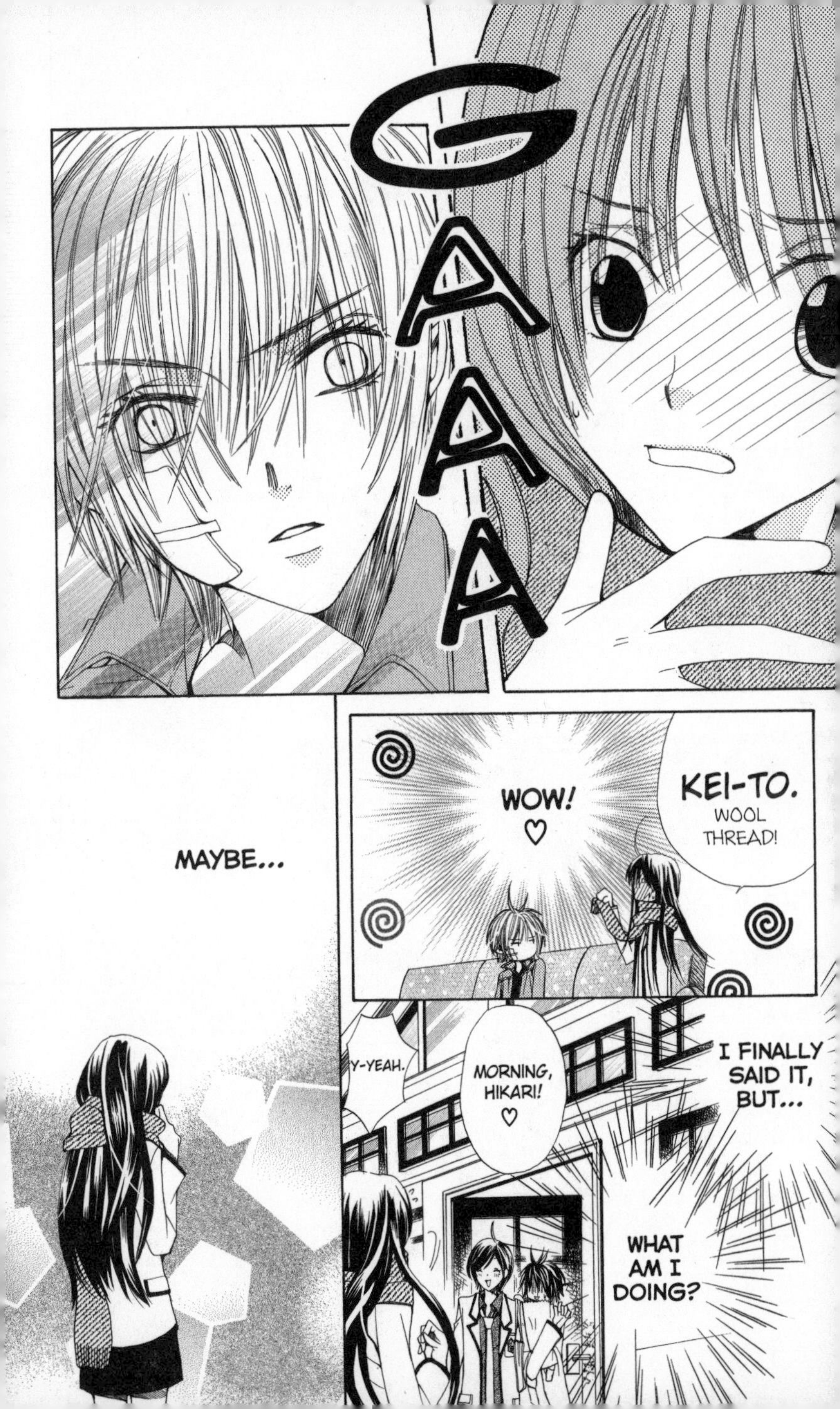
GAAAA
KEI-TO. WOOL THREAD!
WOW! ♡
I FINALLY SAID IT, BUT...
MORNING, HIKARI! ♡
Y-YEAH.
WHAT AM I DOING?
MAYBE...

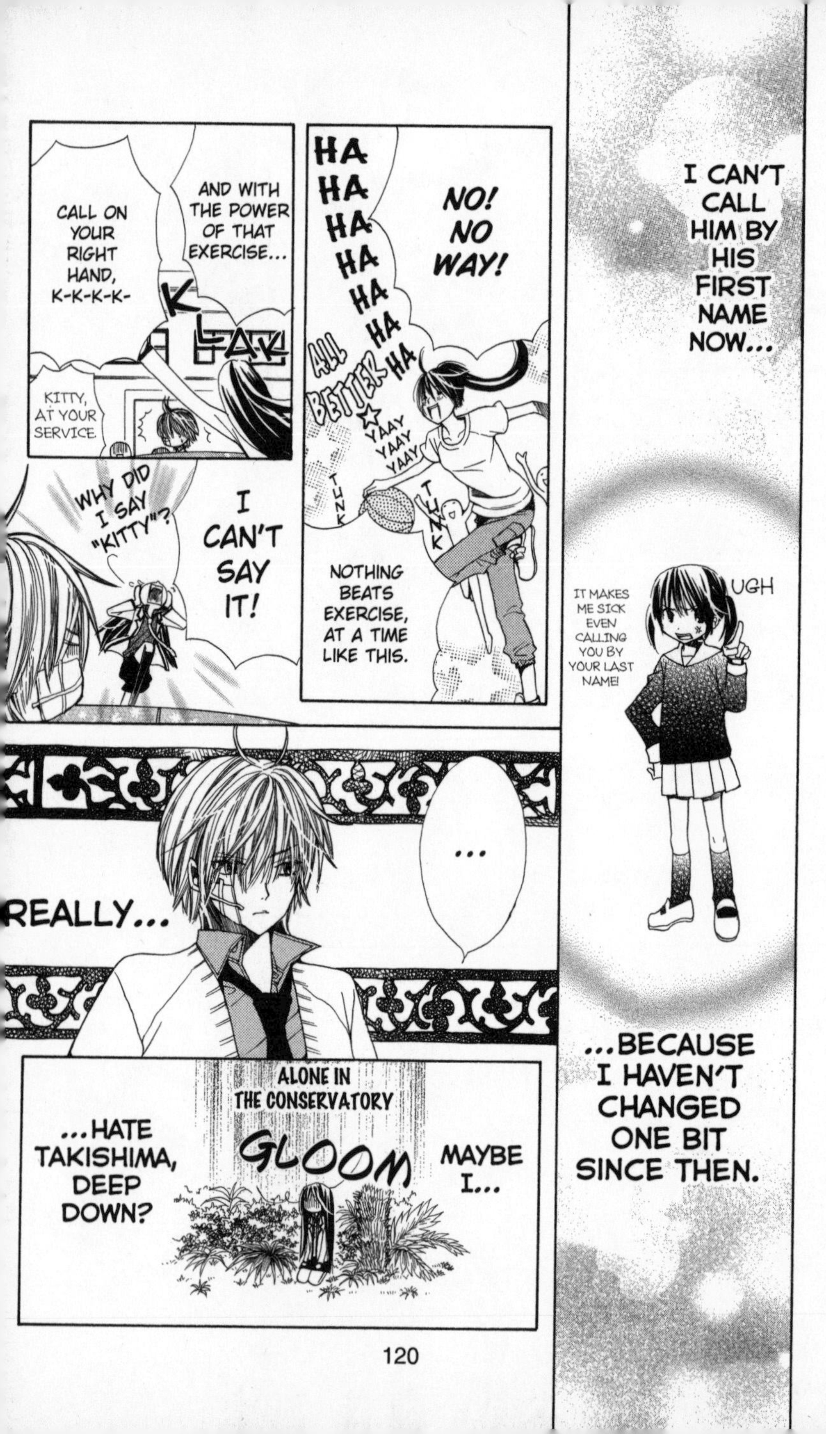
I CAN'T CALL HIM BY HIS FIRST NAME NOW...
IT MAKES ME SICK EVEN CALLING YOU BY YOUR LAST NAME!
UGH
...BECAUSE I HAVEN'T CHANGED ONE BIT SINCE THEN.
NO! NO WAY!
HA HA HA HA HA HA HA HA
ALL BETTER☆
YAAY YAAY YAAY
THUNK
THUNK
NOTHING BEATS EXERCISE, AT A TIME LIKE THIS.
AND WITH THE POWER OF THAT EXERCISE...
CALL ON YOUR RIGHT HAND, K-K-K-K-
KLAK
KITTY, AT YOUR SERVICE
I CAN'T SAY IT!
WHY DID I SAY "KITTY"?
...
REALLY...
MAYBE I...
ALONE IN THE CONSERVATORY
GLOOM
...HATE TAKISHIMA, DEEP DOWN?

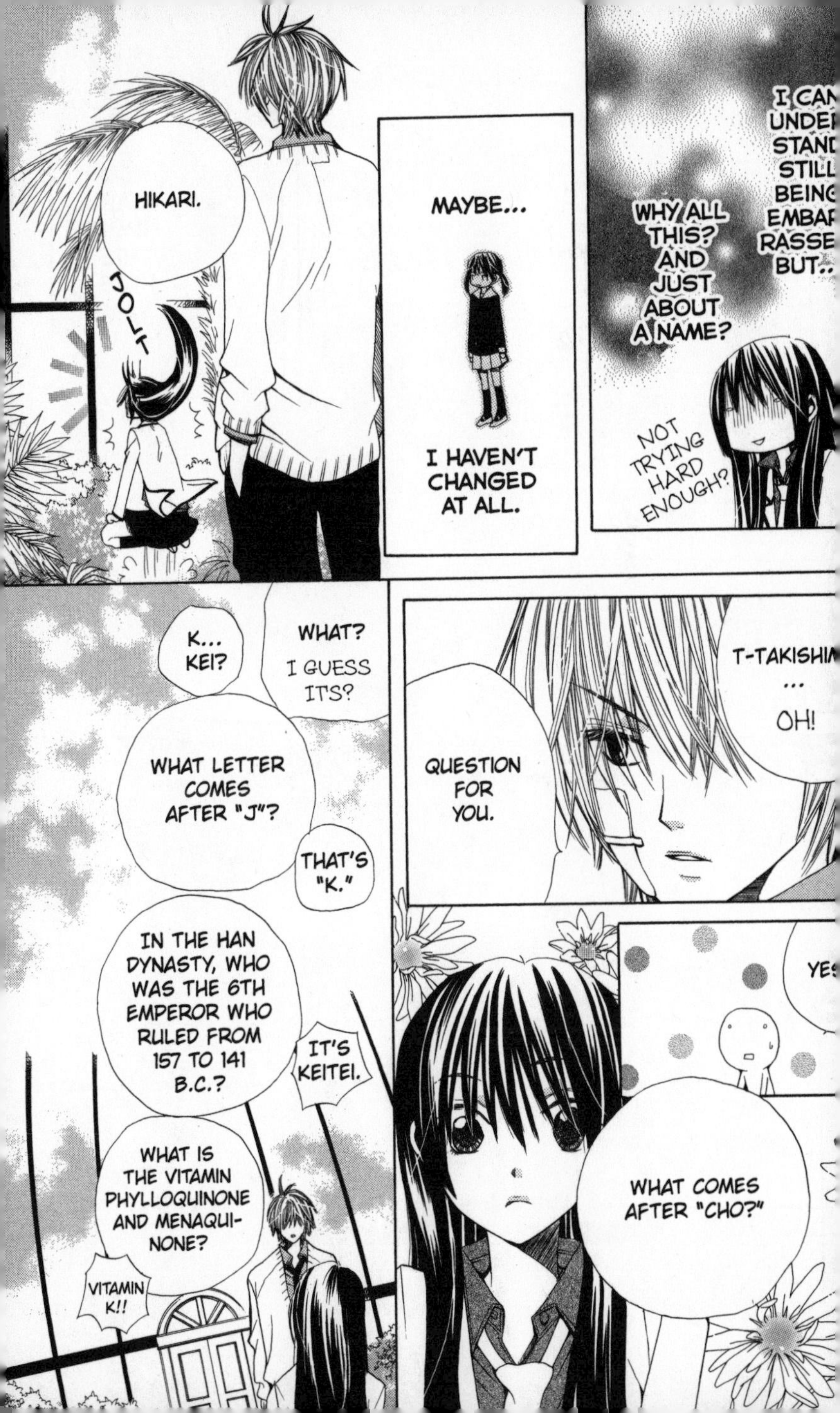
I CAN UNDER STAND STILL BEING EMBAR RASSE BUT...
WHY ALL THIS? AND JUST ABOUT A NAME?
NOT TRYING HARD ENOUGH?
MAYBE...
I HAVEN'T CHANGED AT ALL.
HIKARI.
JOLT
T-TAKISHIM ... OH!
QUESTION FOR YOU.
YE
WHAT COMES AFTER "CHO?"
WHAT? I GUESS ITS?
K... KEI?
WHAT LETTER COMES AFTER "J"?
THAT'S "K."
IN THE HAN DYNASTY, WHO WAS THE 6TH EMPEROR WHO RULED FROM 157 TO 141 B.C.?
IT'S KEITEI.
WHAT IS THE VITAMIN PHYLLOQUINONE AND MENAQUINONE?
VITAMIN K!!

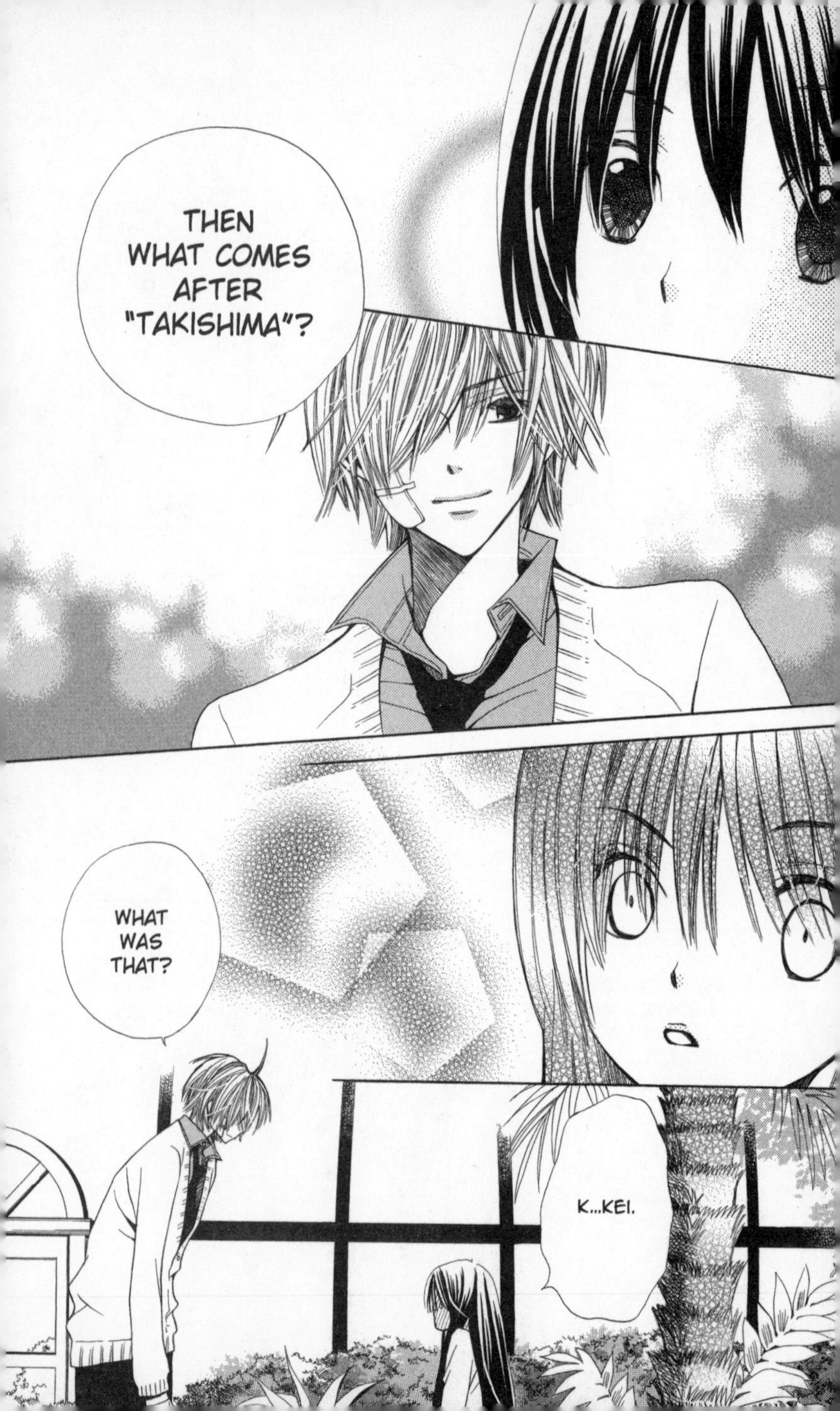
THEN WHAT COMES AFTER "TAKISHIMA"?
WHAT WAS THAT?
K...KEI.

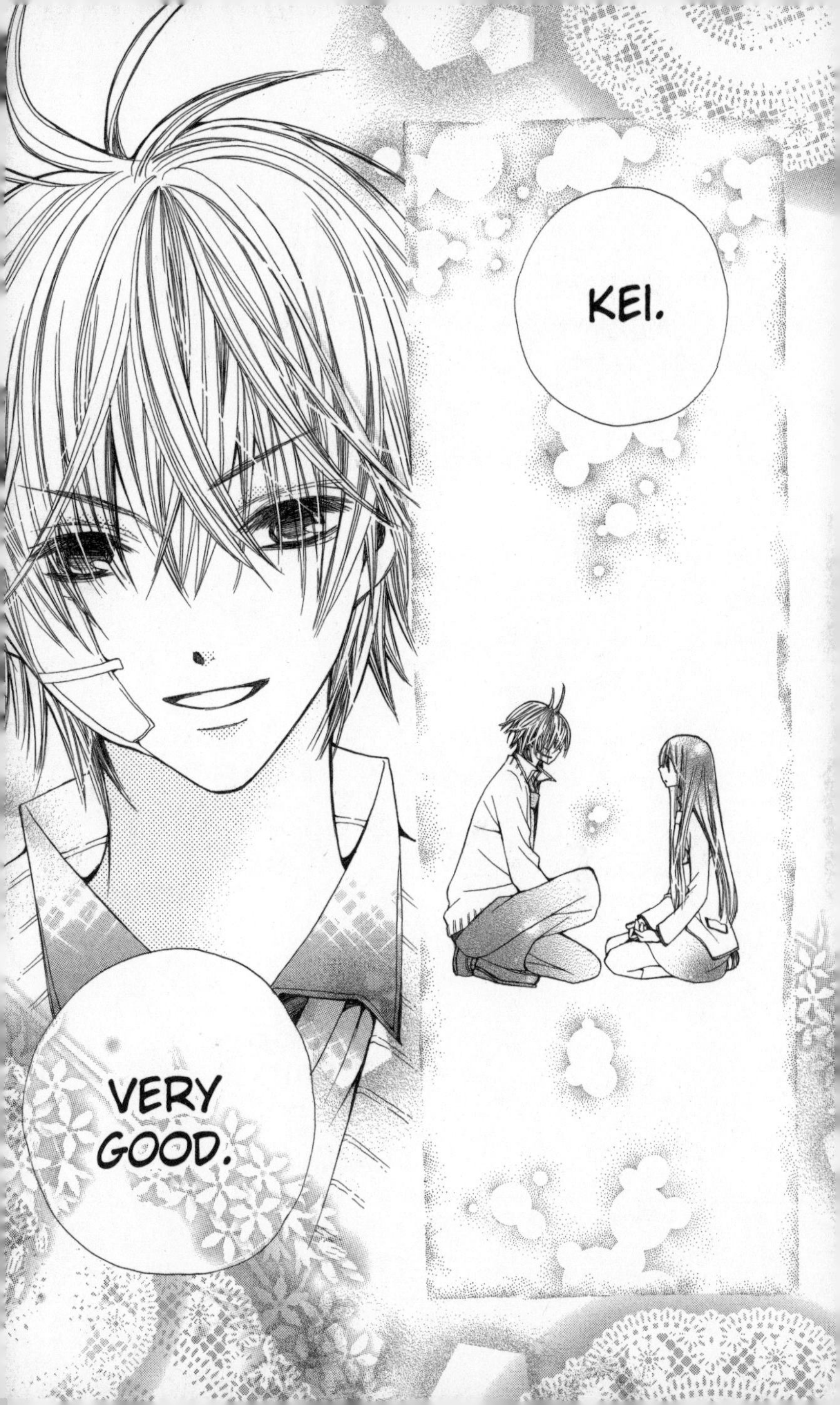
KEI.
VERY GOOD.

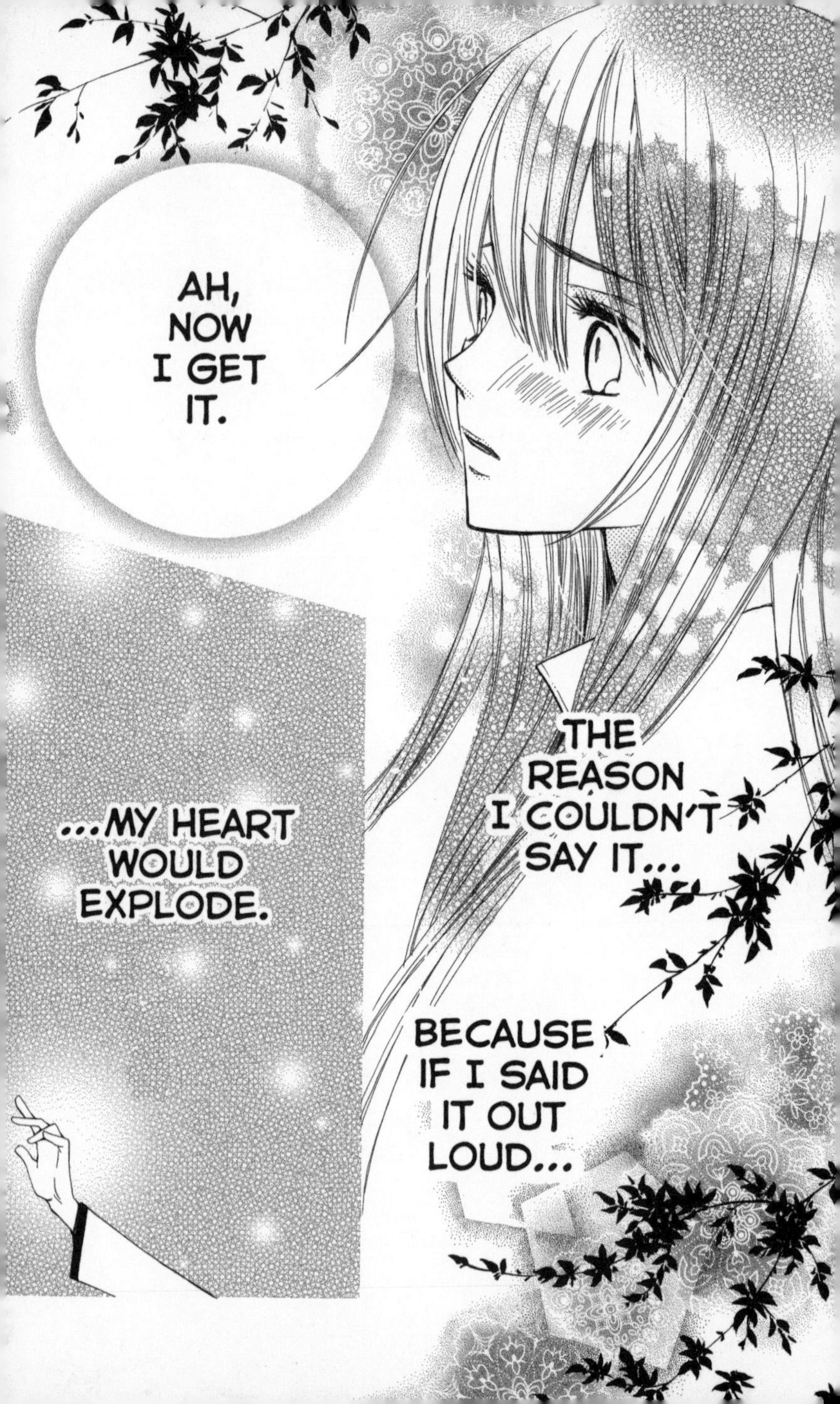
AH, NOW I GET IT.
THE REASON I COULDN'T SAY IT...
BECAUSE IF I SAID IT OUT LOUD...
...MY HEART WOULD EXPLODE.

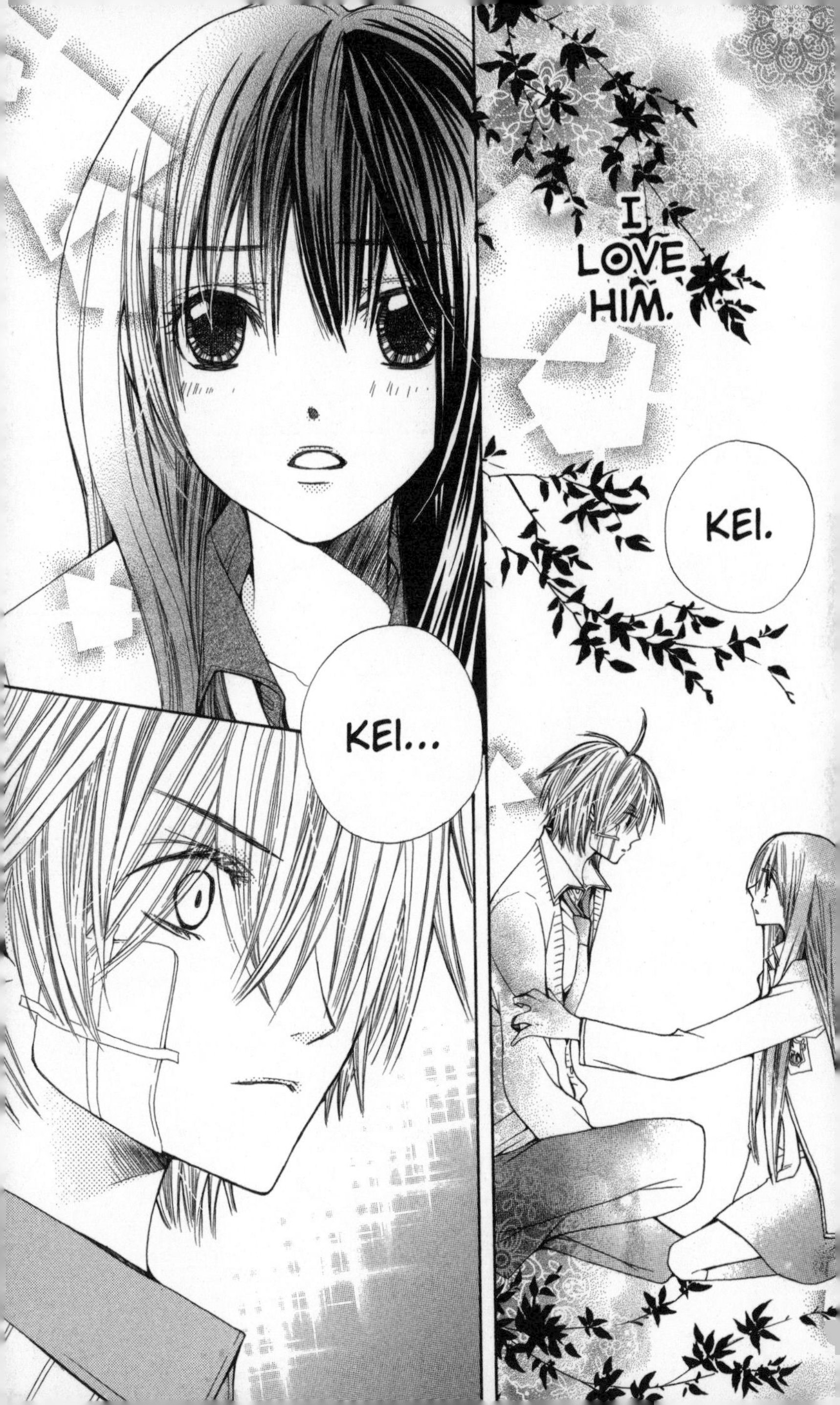
I LOVE HIM.
KEI.
KEI...

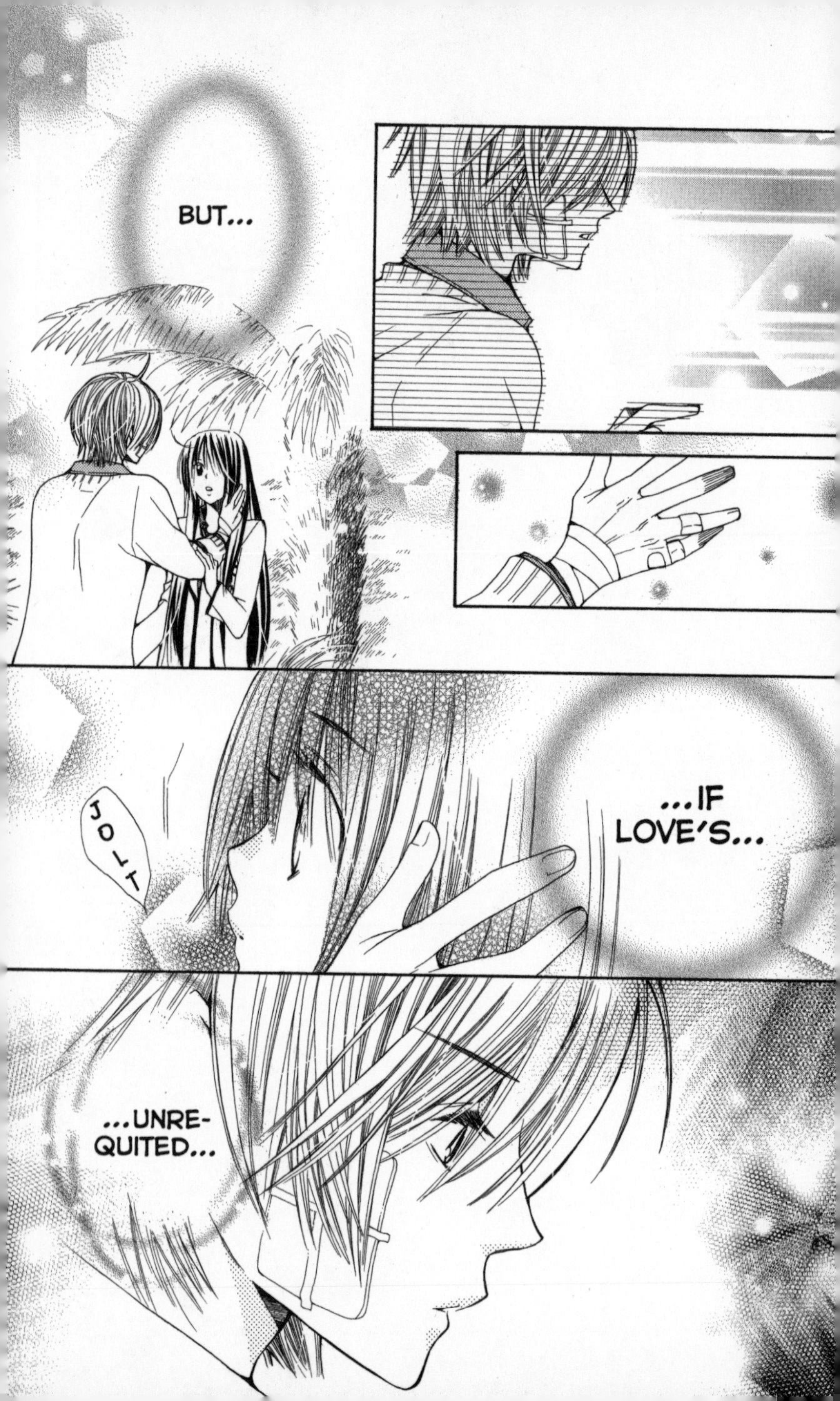
BUT...
...IF LOVE'S...
JOLT
...UNRE-QUITED...

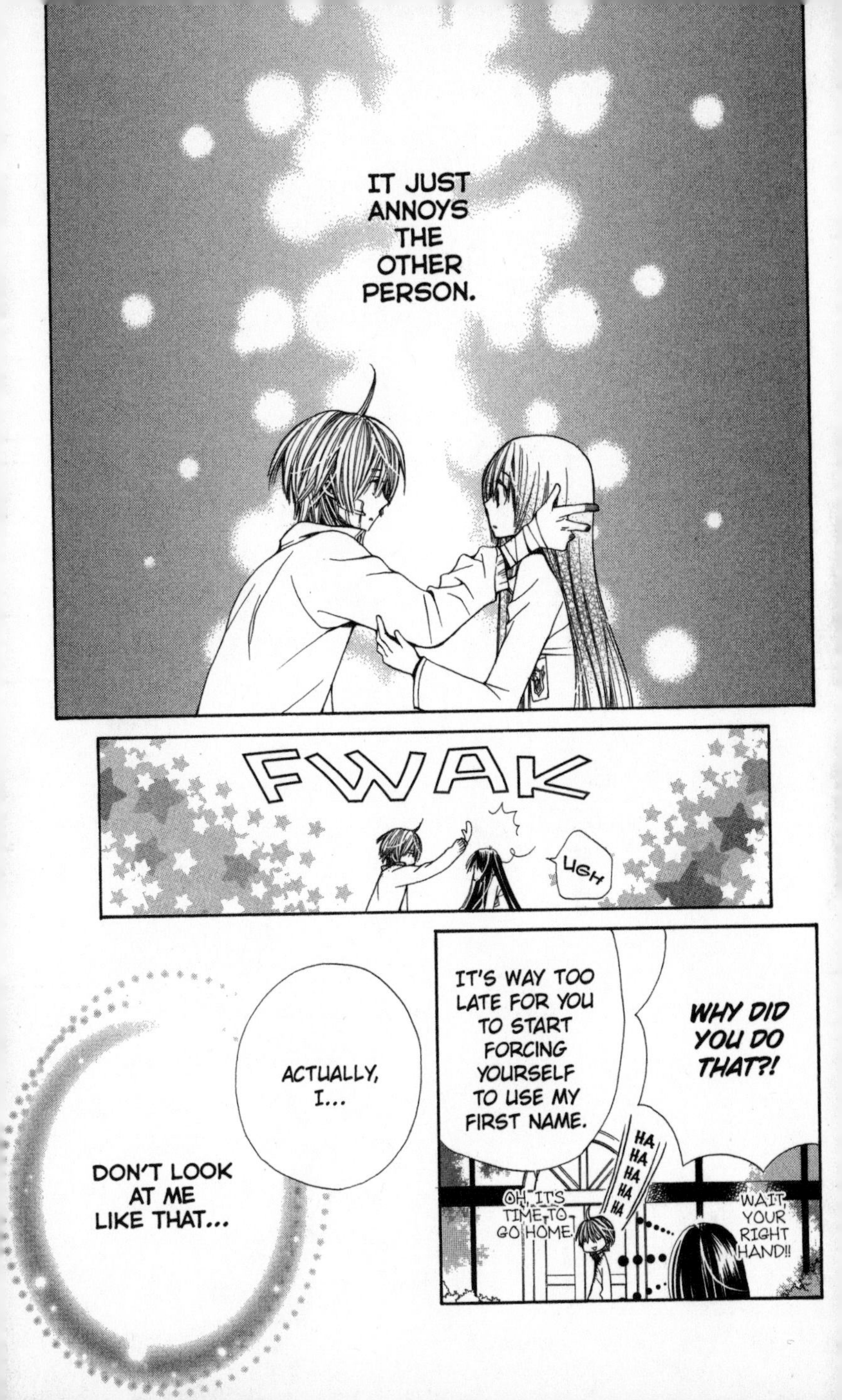
IT JUST ANNOYS THE OTHER PERSON.
FWAK
UGH
WHY DID YOU DO THAT?!
IT'S WAY TOO LATE FOR YOU TO START FORCING YOURSELF TO USE MY FIRST NAME.
WAIT, YOUR RIGHT HAND!!
HA HA HA HA HA
OH, IT'S TIME TO GO HOME.
ACTUALLY, I...
DON'T LOOK AT ME LIKE THAT...

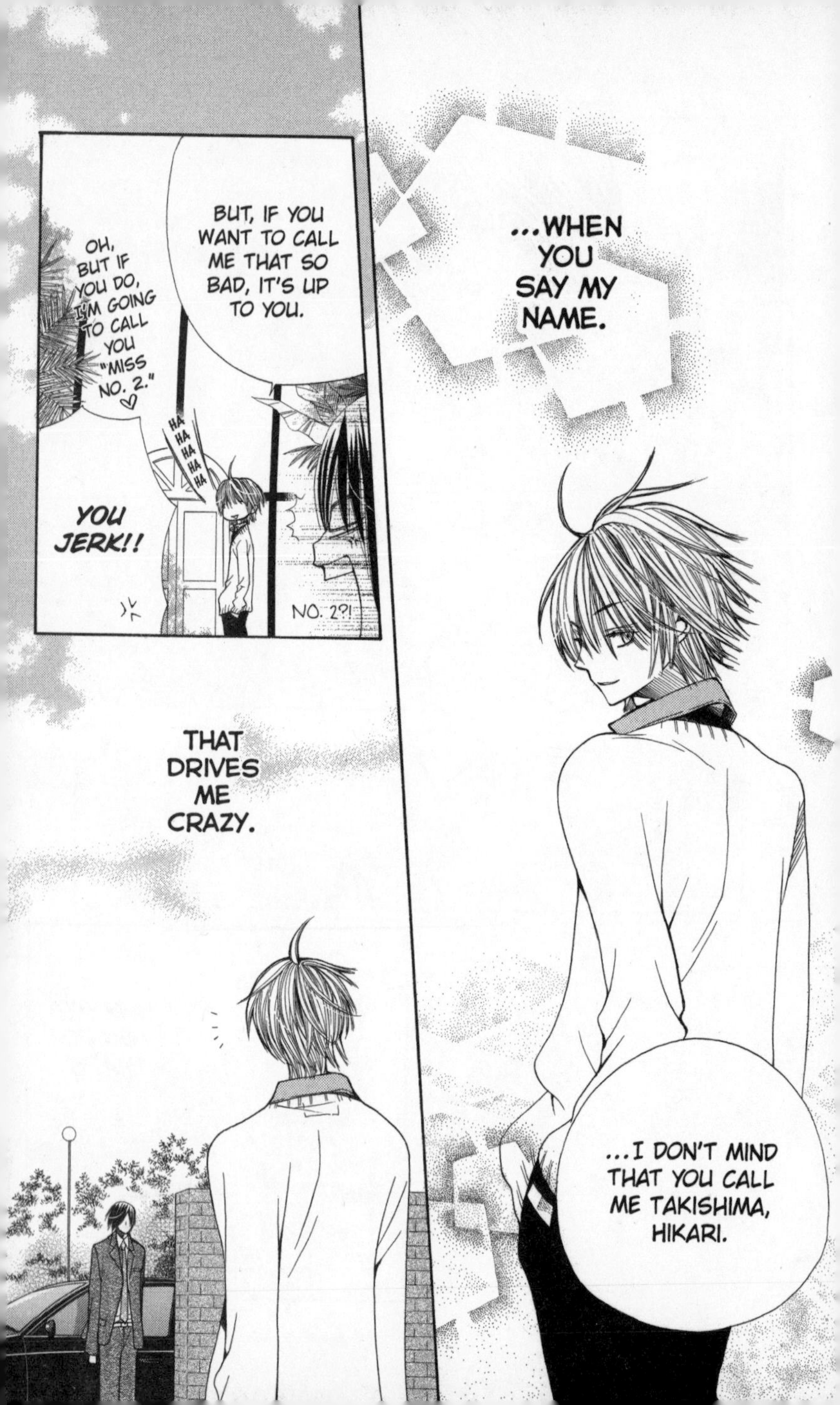
...WHEN YOU SAY MY NAME.
...I DON'T MIND THAT YOU CALL ME TAKISHIMA, HIKARI.
BUT, IF YOU WANT TO CALL ME THAT SO BAD, IT'S UP TO YOU.
OH, BUT IF YOU DO, I'M GOING TO CALL YOU "MISS NO. 2." ♡
HA HA HA HA HA HA
NO. 2?!
YOU JERK!!
THAT DRIVES ME CRAZY.

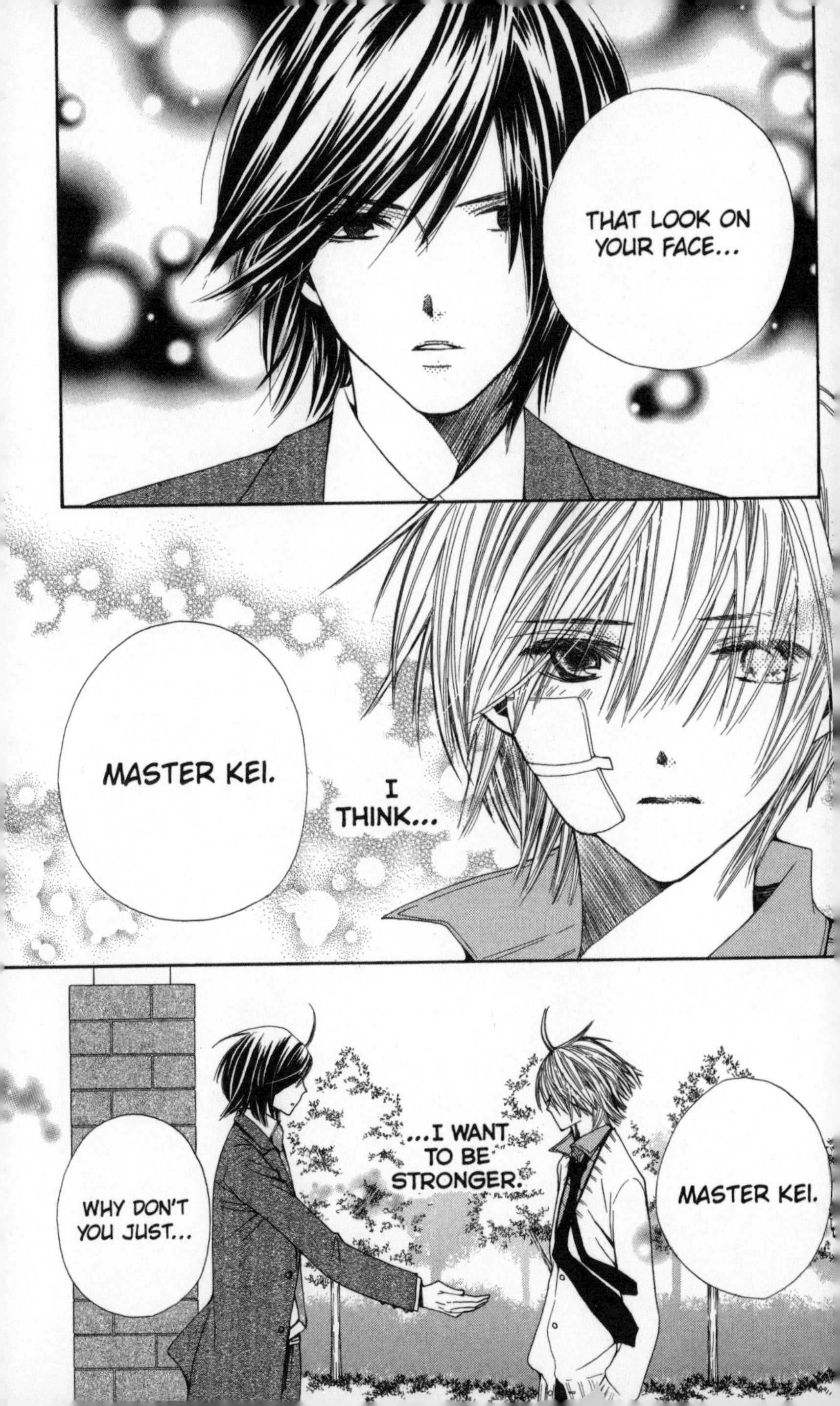
THAT LOOK ON YOUR FACE...
I THINK...
MASTER KEI.
MASTER KEI.
...I WANT TO BE STRONGER.
WHY DON'T YOU JUST...

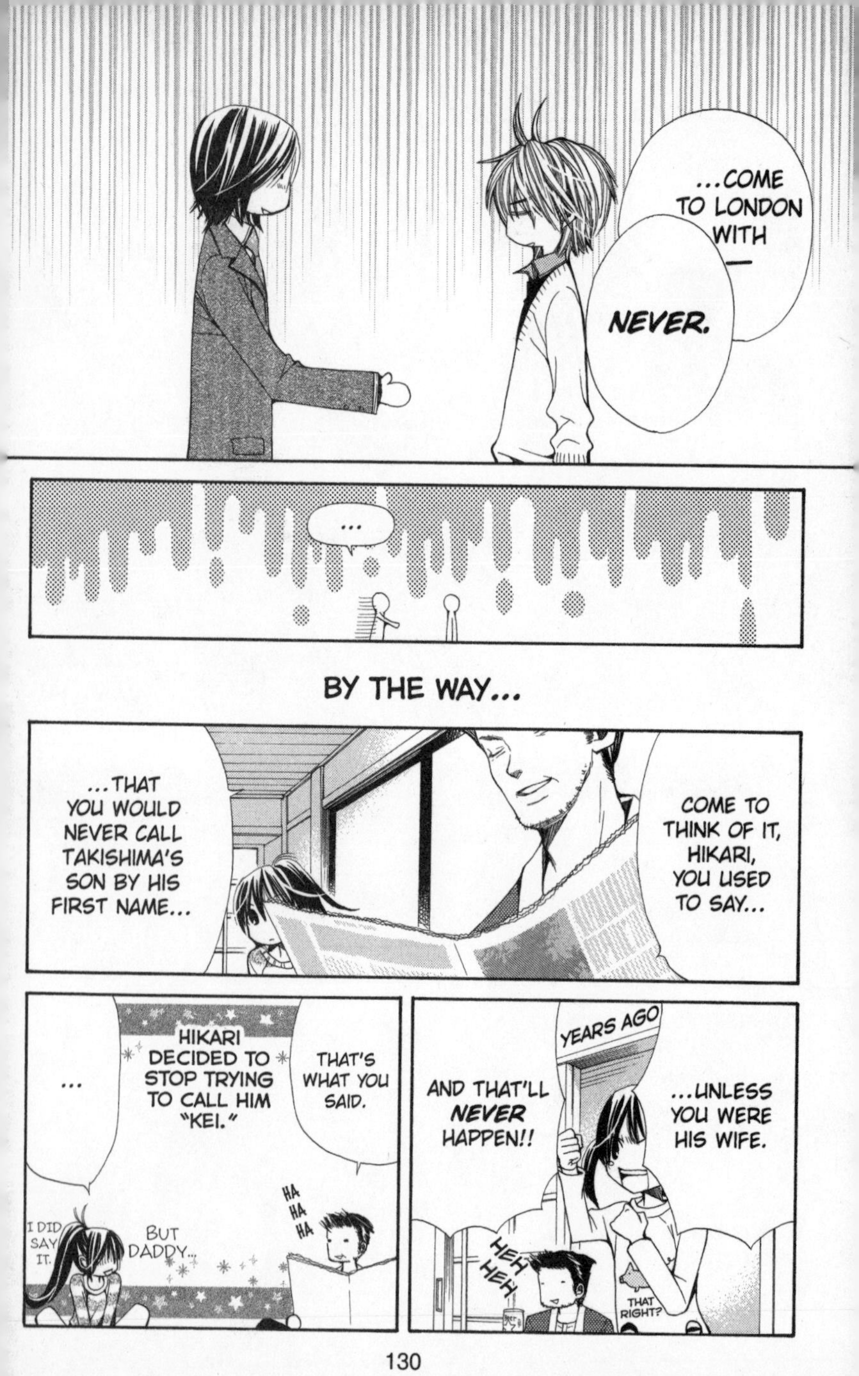

...COME TO LONDON WITH —
NEVER.
...
BY THE WAY...
COME TO THINK OF IT, HIKARI, YOU USED TO SAY...
...THAT YOU WOULD NEVER CALL TAKISHIMA'S SON BY HIS FIRST NAME...
YEARS AGO
...UNLESS YOU WERE HIS WIFE.
AND THAT'LL NEVER HAPPEN!!
HEH HEH
THAT RIGHT?
THAT'S WHAT YOU SAID.
HA HA HA
HIKARI DECIDED TO STOP TRYING TO CALL HIM "KEI."
...
BUT DADDY...
I DID SAY IT.

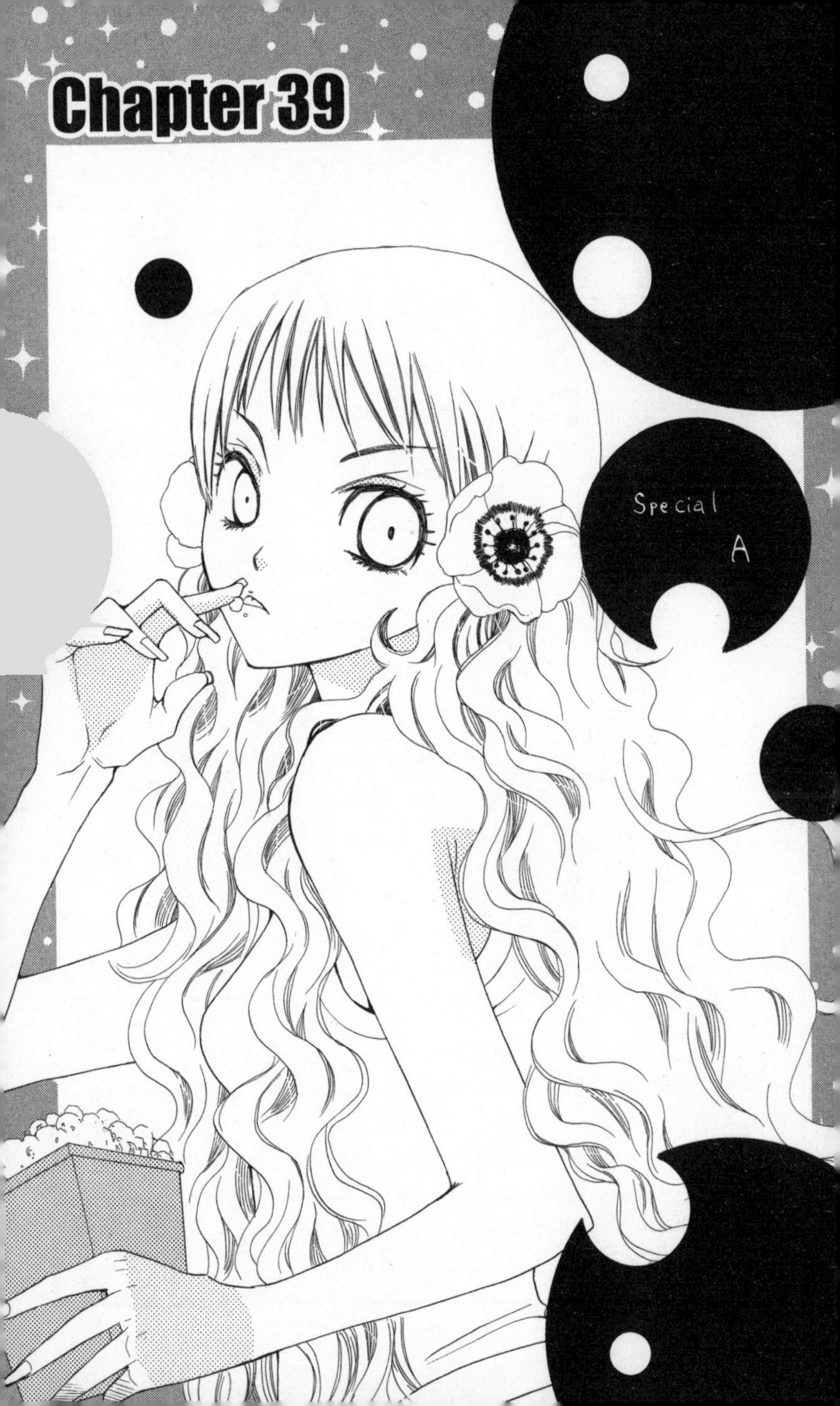
Chapter 39
Special A

I LOVE OUR GROUP!

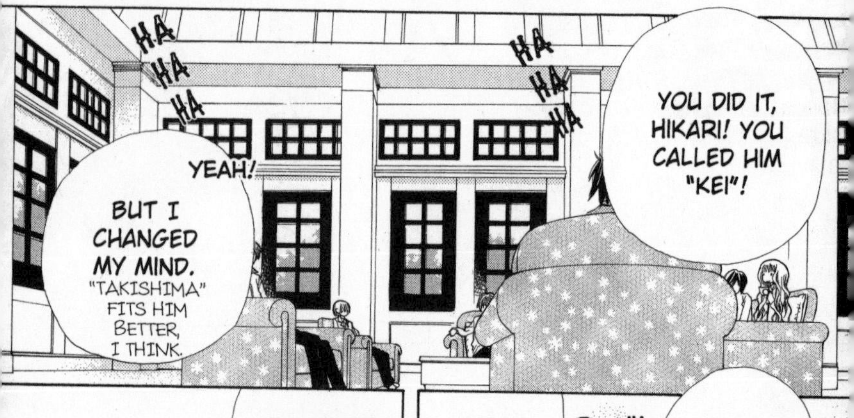
YOU DID IT, HIKARI! YOU CALLED HIM "KEI"!
HA HA HA
HA HA HA
YEAH!
BUT I CHANGED MY MIND. "TAKISHIMA" FITS HIM BETTER, I THINK.
WHAT A SHAME, KEI.
HA HA HA
GRIN
WHAT'S A SHAME?
I DON'T CARE. HA HA HA!
HA HA HA
YOU'RE AWFUL!
HEY...
SO...
WHILE WE'RE ALL HERE, I'VE BEEN WANTING TO TELL YOU SOMETHING...

· COUPLES ·

THE FIRST COUPLE COMES TOGETHER IN VOL. 7.
LOVE STORIES, ALTHOUGH THEY ARE STILL NEW TO ME, ARE FUN TO WRITE.
I WANT TO WRITE MORE MUSHY STORIES, IF I CAN. I WILL TRY REALLY HARD! S.A'S FIRST COUPLE WAS TOTALLY UNPLANNED, BUT BY THE END OF THE STORY, THEY WERE TOGETHER... YOU NEVER KNOW!

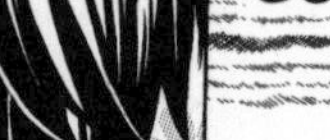
...I'M BRAINLESS...
YOU COULD ALSO SAY...

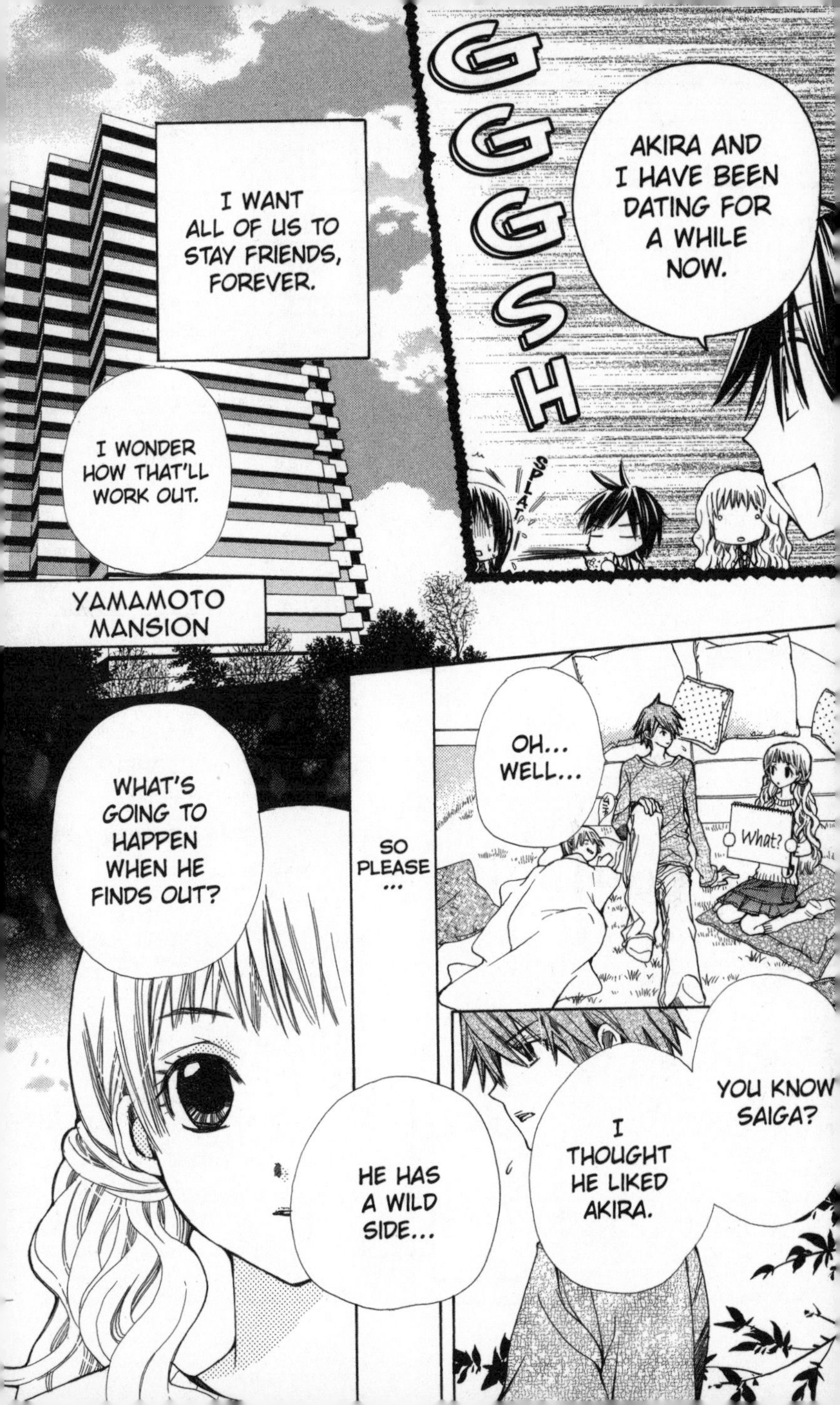
AKIRA AND I HAVE BEEN DATING FOR A WHILE NOW.
GGGSH
SPLAT
I WANT ALL OF US TO STAY FRIENDS, FOREVER.
I WONDER HOW THAT'LL WORK OUT.
YAMAMOTO MANSION
OH... WELL...
What?
YOU KNOW SAIGA?
I THOUGHT HE LIKED AKIRA.
HE HAS A WILD SIDE...
SO PLEASE...
WHAT'S GOING TO HAPPEN WHEN HE FINDS OUT?

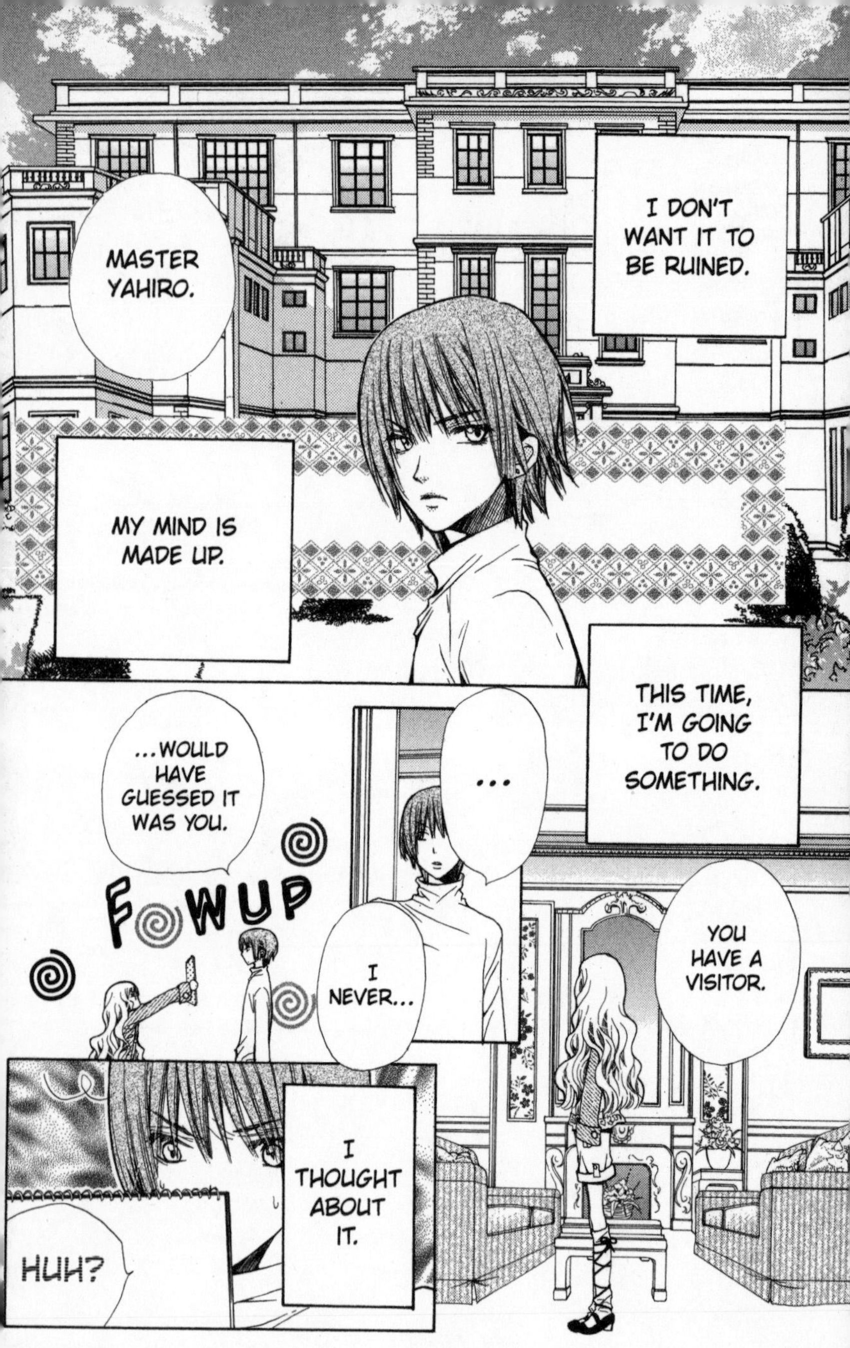

I DON'T WANT IT TO BE RUINED.
MASTER YAHIRO.
MY MIND IS MADE UP.
THIS TIME, I'M GOING TO DO SOMETHING.
YOU HAVE A VISITOR.
...
I NEVER...
...WOULD HAVE GUESSED IT WAS YOU.
FWUP
I THOUGHT ABOUT IT.
HUH?

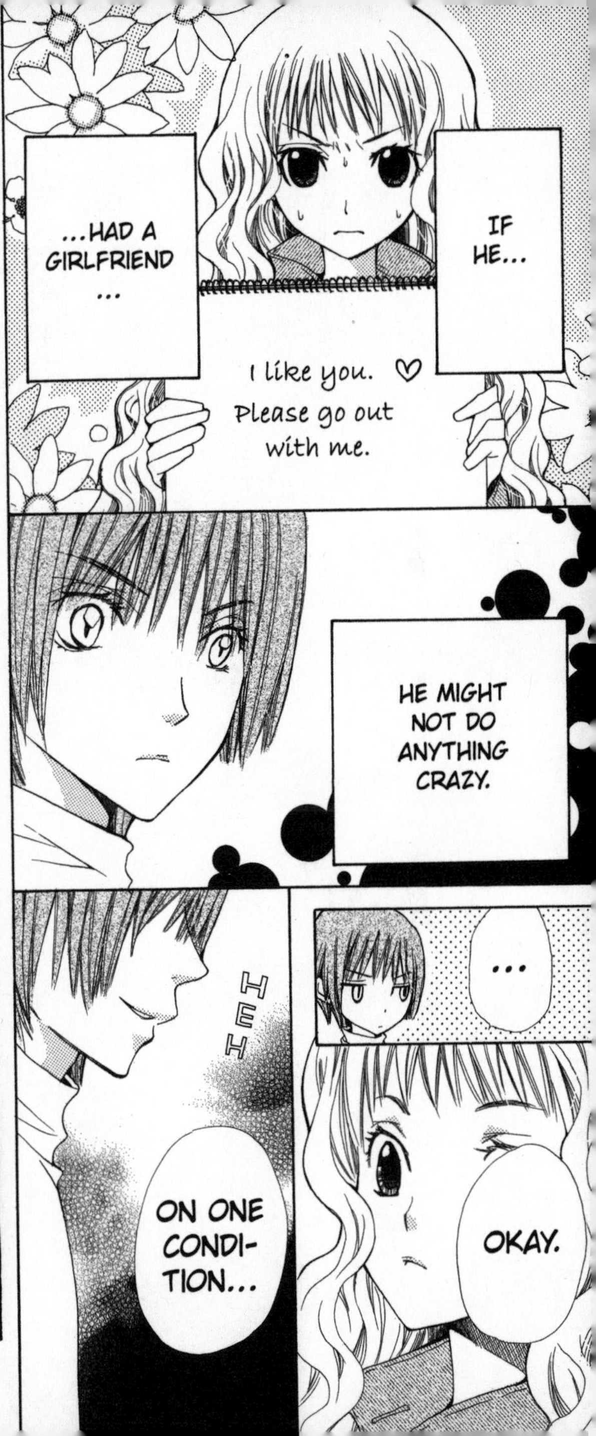
IF HE...
...HAD A GIRLFRIEND ...
I like you. ♡ Please go out with me.
HE MIGHT NOT DO ANYTHING CRAZY.
...
OKAY.
HEH
ON ONE CONDITION...

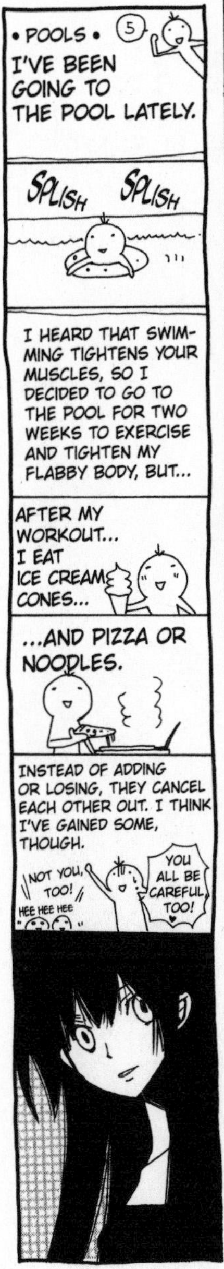
• POOLS • 5
I'VE BEEN GOING TO THE POOL LATELY.
SPLISH SPLISH
I HEARD THAT SWIMMING TIGHTENS YOUR MUSCLES, SO I DECIDED TO GO TO THE POOL FOR TWO WEEKS TO EXERCISE AND TIGHTEN MY FLABBY BODY, BUT...
AFTER MY WORKOUT... I EAT ICE CREAM CONES...
...AND PIZZA OR NOODLES.
INSTEAD OF ADDING OR LOSING, THEY CANCEL EACH OTHER OUT. I THINK I'VE GAINED SOME, THOUGH.
YOU ALL BE CAREFUL TOO! ♥
NOT YOU, TOO!
HEE HEE HEE

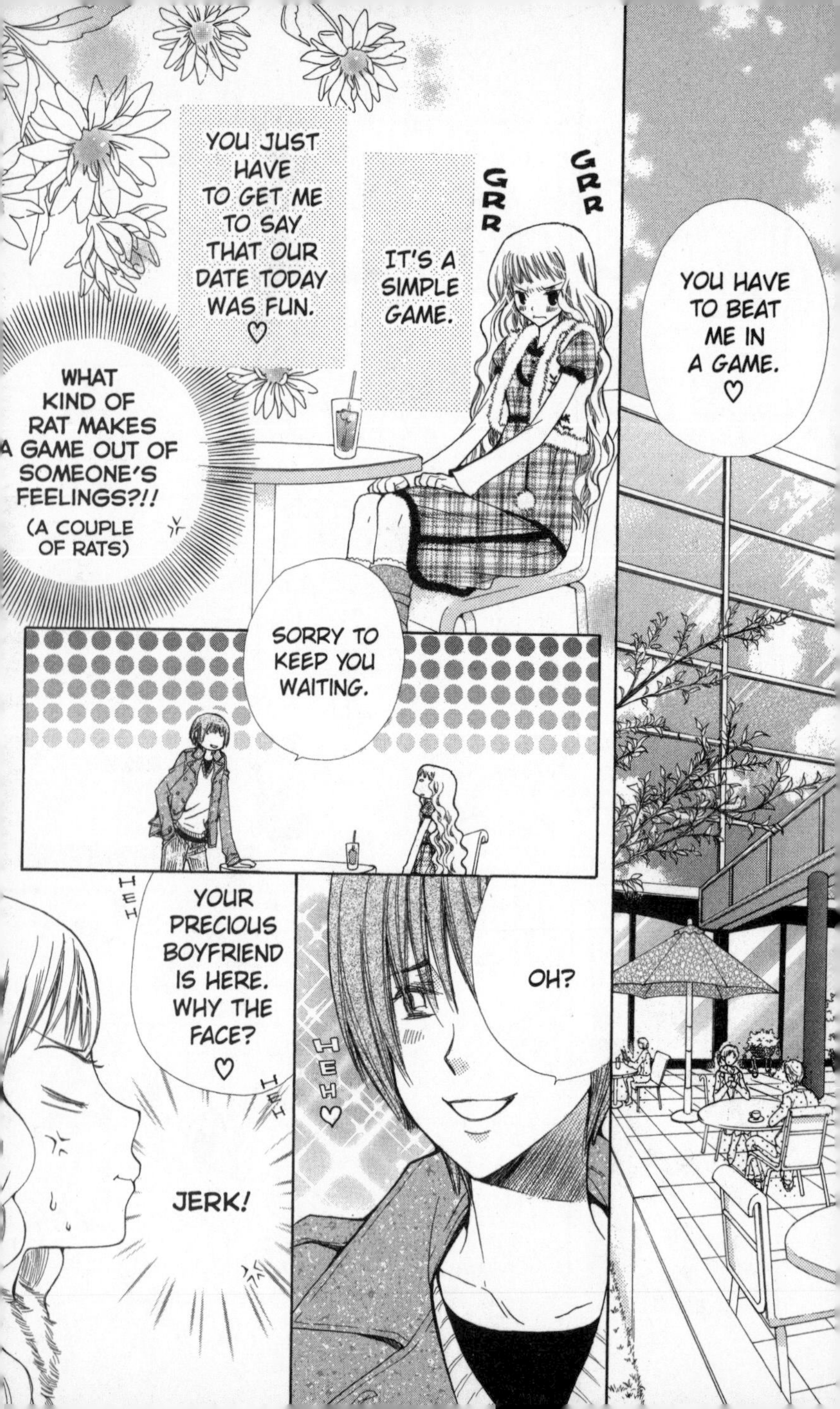
YOU HAVE TO BEAT ME IN A GAME. ♡
GRR
GRR
IT'S A SIMPLE GAME.
YOU JUST HAVE TO GET ME TO SAY THAT OUR DATE TODAY WAS FUN. ♡
WHAT KIND OF RAT MAKES A GAME OUT OF SOMEONE'S FEELINGS?!!
(A COUPLE OF RATS)
SORRY TO KEEP YOU WAITING.
OH?
HEH HEH ♡
YOUR PRECIOUS BOYFRIEND IS HERE. WHY THE FACE? ♡
HEH
HEH
JERK!

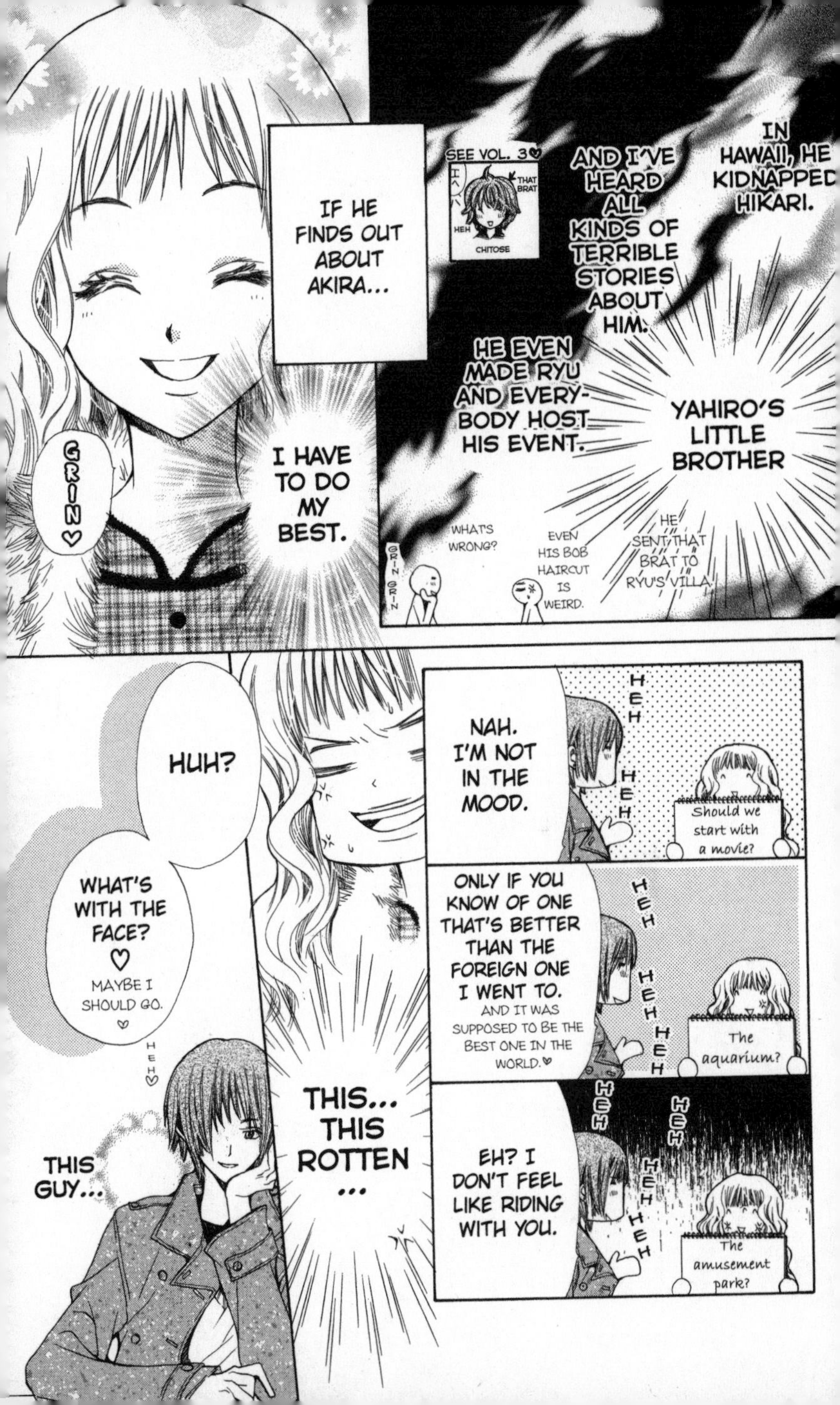
IN HAWAII, HE KIDNAPPED HIKARI.
AND I'VE HEARD ALL KINDS OF TERRIBLE STORIES ABOUT HIM.
SEE VOL. 3♡
THAT BRAT
HEH
CHITOSE
HE EVEN MADE RYU AND EVERY-BODY HOST HIS EVENT.
YAHIRO'S LITTLE BROTHER
HE SENT THAT BRAT TO RYU'S VILLA.
EVEN HIS BOB HAIRCUT IS WEIRD.
WHAT'S WRONG?
GRIN GRIN
IF HE FINDS OUT ABOUT AKIRA...
I HAVE TO DO MY BEST.
GRIN♡
HEH HEH
Should we start with a movie?
NAH. I'M NOT IN THE MOOD.
HEH HEH HEH HEH
The aquarium?
ONLY IF YOU KNOW OF ONE THAT'S BETTER THAN THE FOREIGN ONE I WENT TO.
AND IT WAS SUPPOSED TO BE THE BEST ONE IN THE WORLD.♡
HEH HEH HEH HEH HEH
The amusement park?
EH? I DON'T FEEL LIKE RIDING WITH YOU.
HUH?
THIS... THIS ROTTEN...
WHAT'S WITH THE FACE? ♡
MAYBE I SHOULD GO. ♡
HEH♡
THIS GUY...

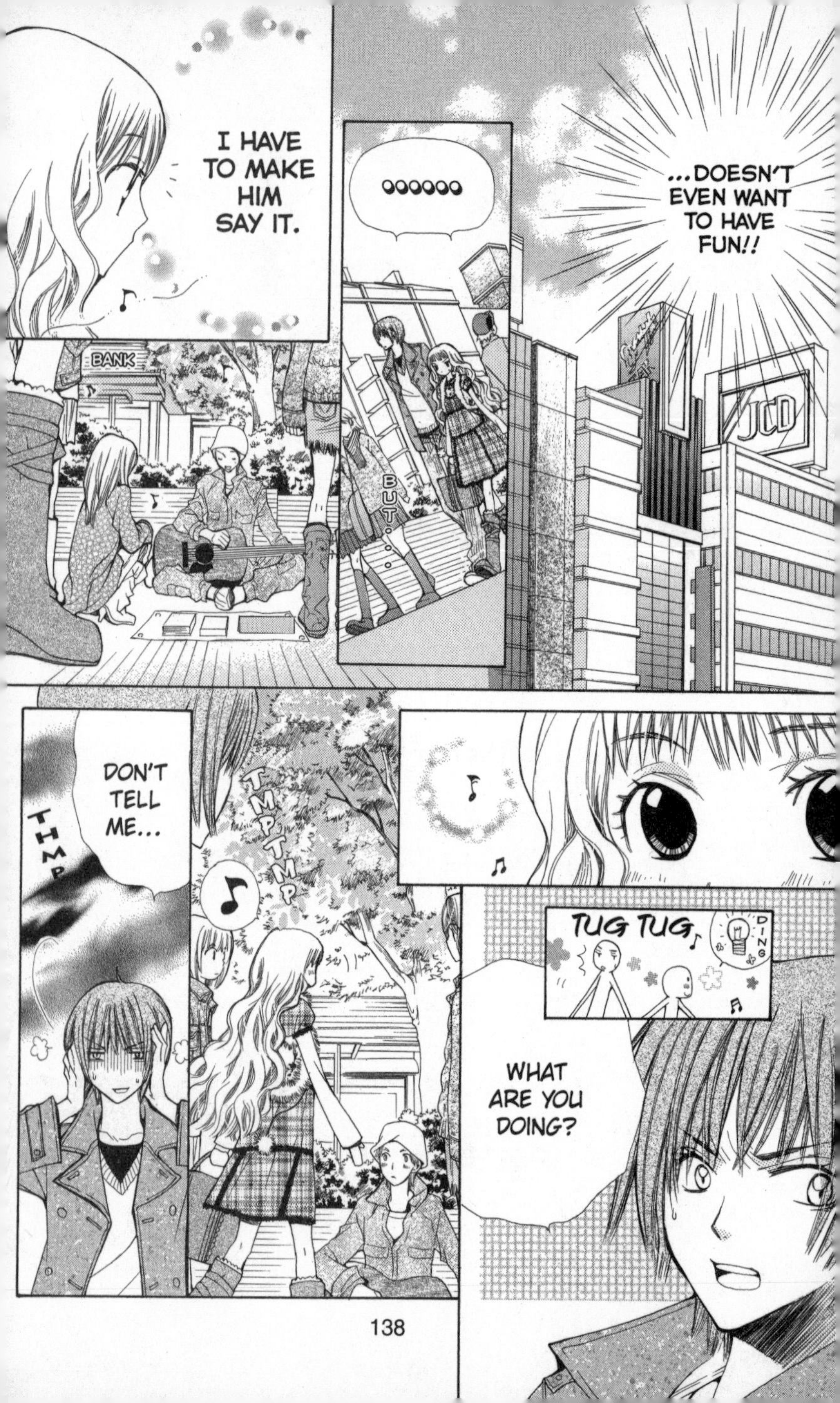
...DOESN'T EVEN WANT TO HAVE FUN!!
JCD
......
BUT...
I HAVE TO MAKE HIM SAY IT.
BANK
TUG TUG
DING
WHAT ARE YOU DOING?
TMPTMPTMP
DON'T TELL ME...
THMP

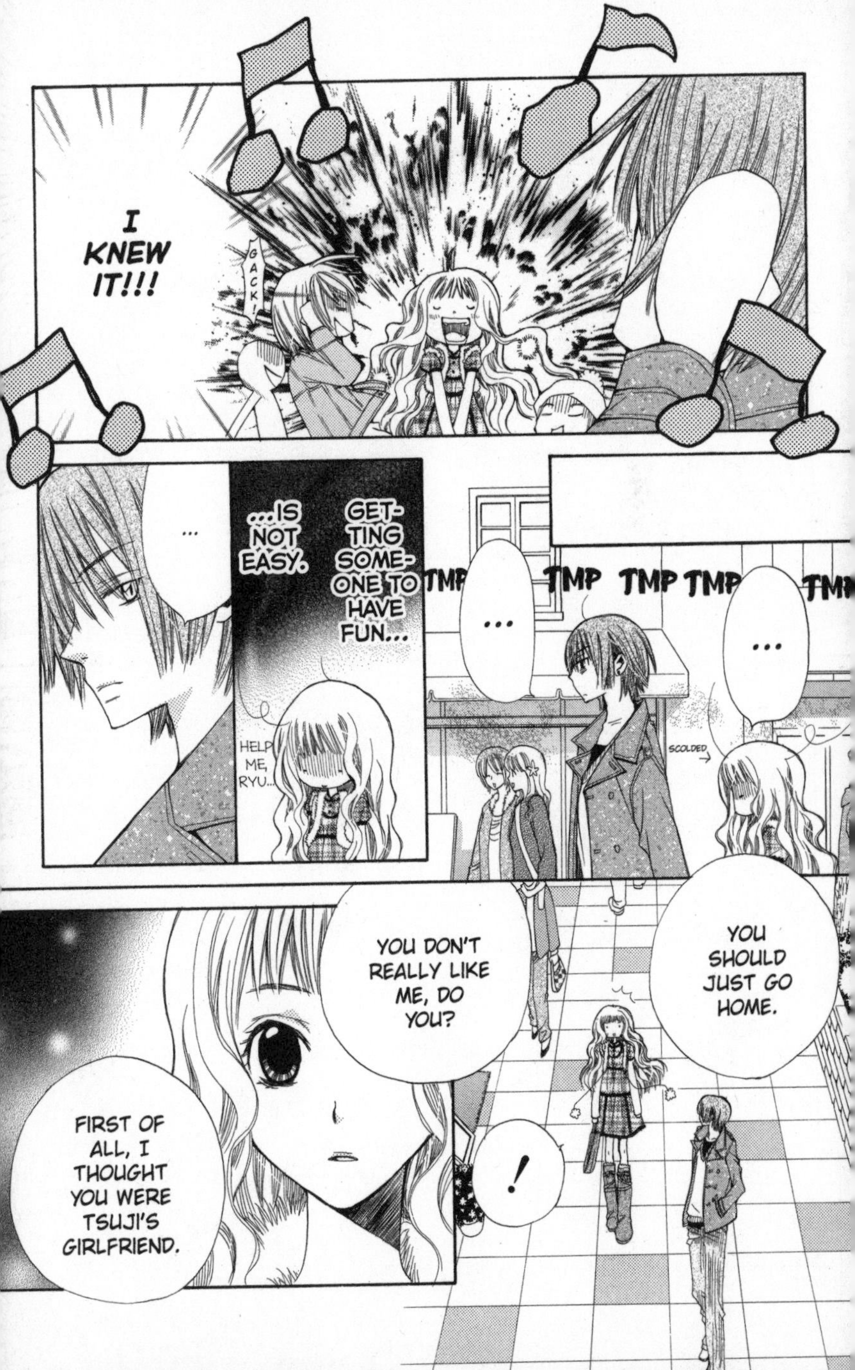
GACK!
I KNEW IT!!!
TMP TMP TMP TMP TMP
...
...
SCOLDED
GET-TING SOME-ONE TO HAVE FUN...
...IS NOT EASY.
HELP ME, RYU...
...
YOU SHOULD JUST GO HOME.
YOU DON'T REALLY LIKE ME, DO YOU?
!
FIRST OF ALL, I THOUGHT YOU WERE TSUJI'S GIRLFRIEND.

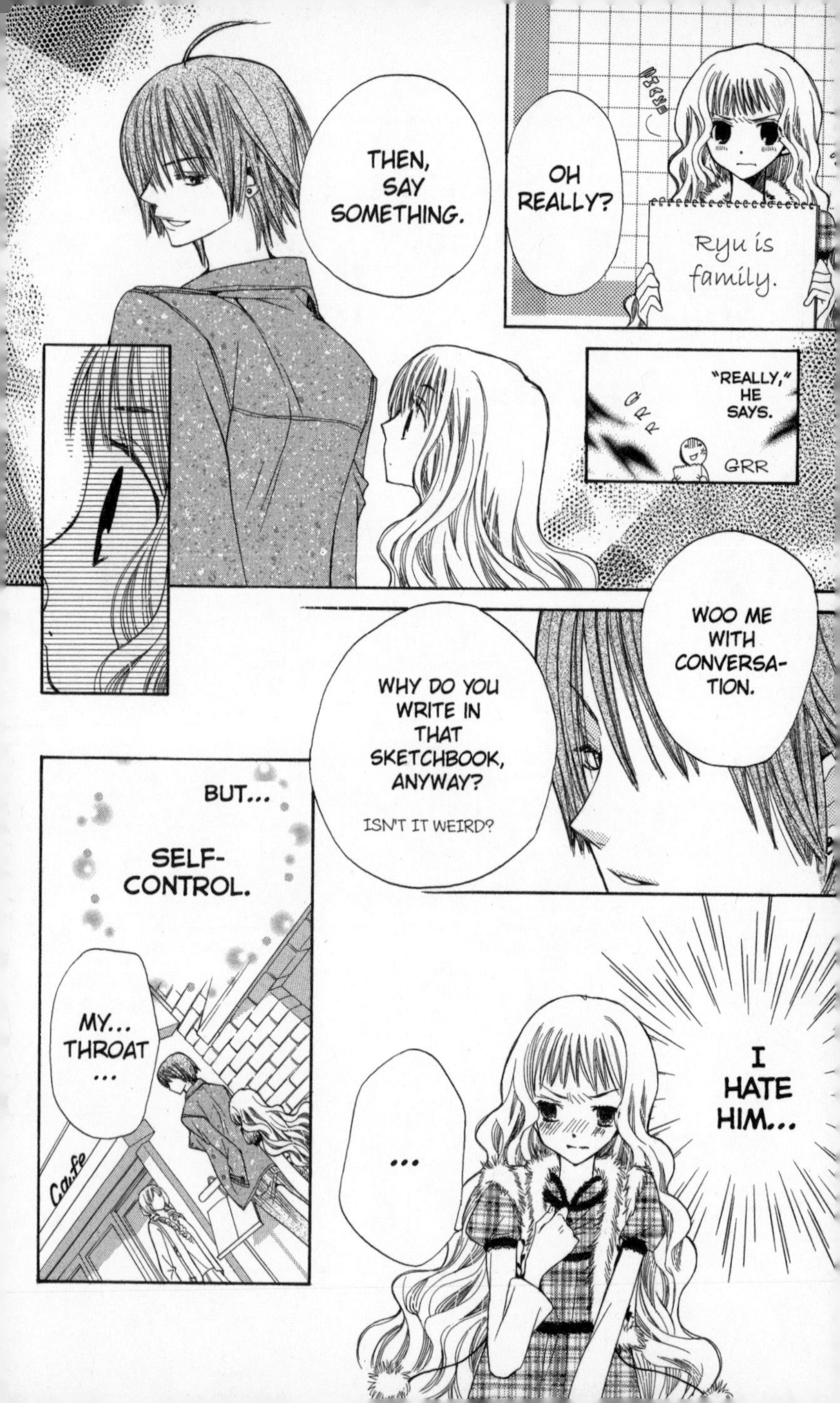

Ryu is family.
OH REALLY?
THEN, SAY SOMETHING.
"REALLY," HE SAYS.
GRR
GRR
WOO ME WITH CONVERSATION.
WHY DO YOU WRITE IN THAT SKETCHBOOK, ANYWAY?
ISN'T IT WEIRD?
I HATE HIM...
...
BUT...
SELF-CONTROL.
MY... THROAT ...
Cafe

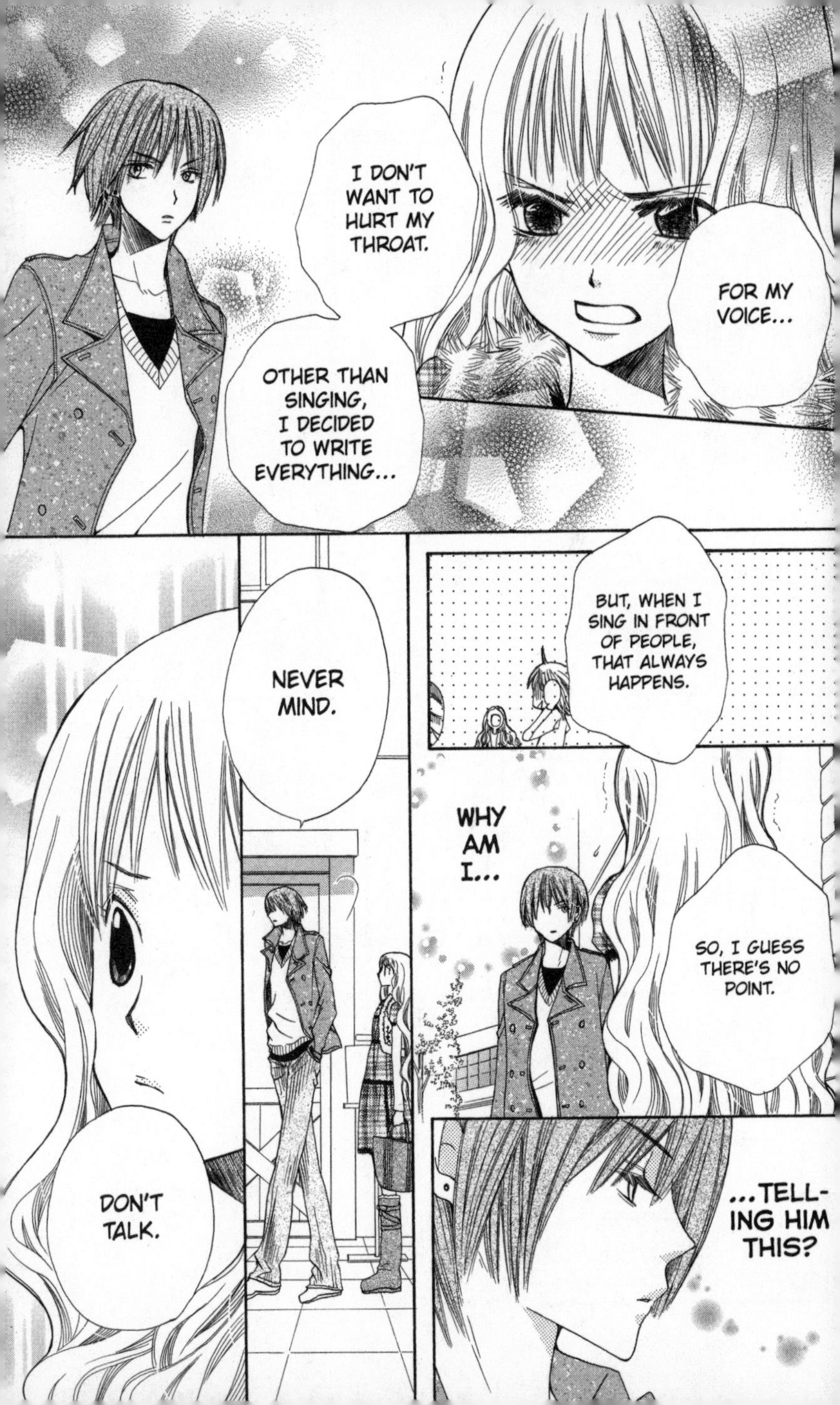
FOR MY VOICE...
I DON'T WANT TO HURT MY THROAT.
OTHER THAN SINGING, I DECIDED TO WRITE EVERYTHING...
BUT, WHEN I SING IN FRONT OF PEOPLE, THAT ALWAYS HAPPENS.
SO, I GUESS THERE'S NO POINT.
WHY AM I...
...TELL-ING HIM THIS?
NEVER MIND.
DON'T TALK.

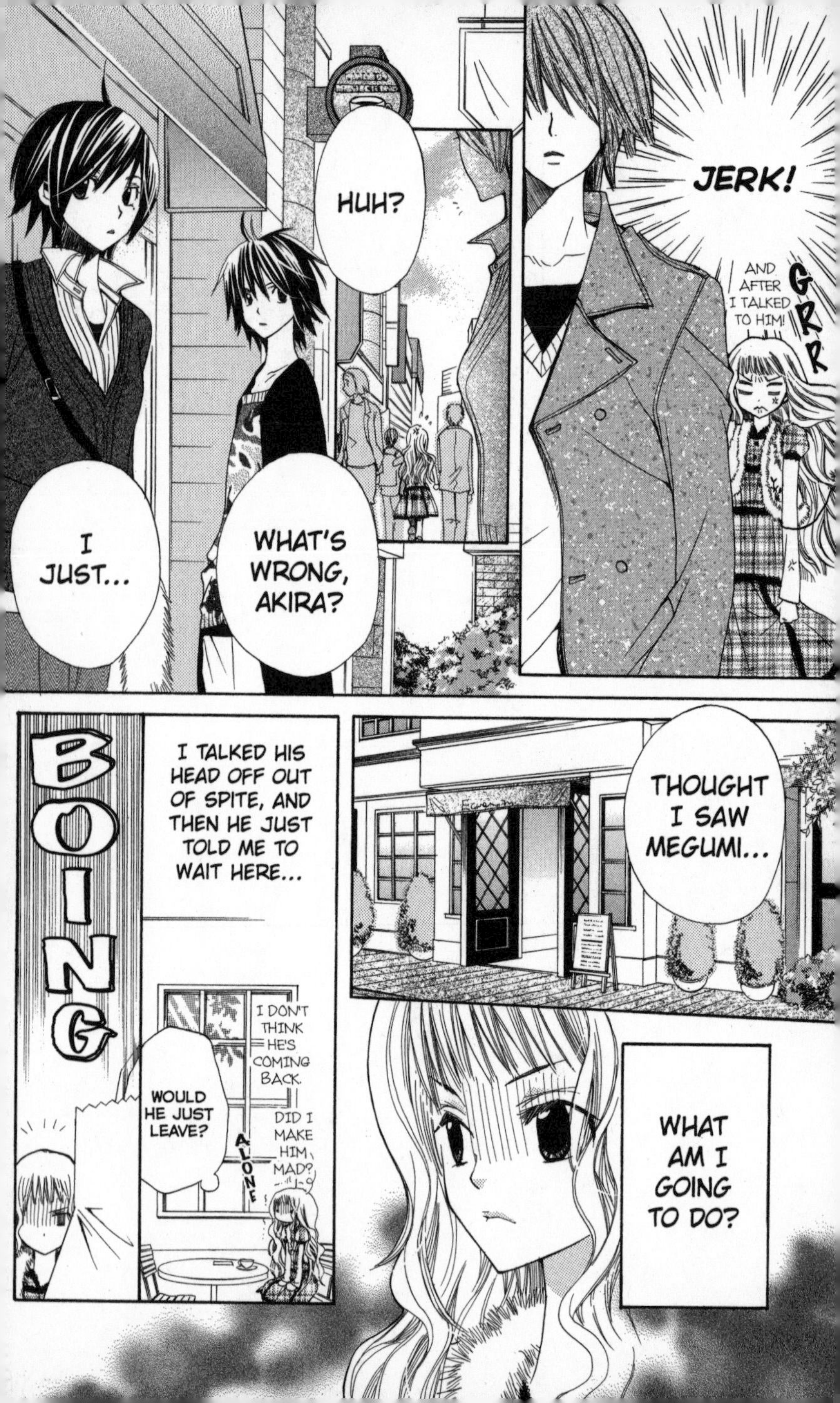
JERK!
AND AFTER I TALKED TO HIM!
GRR
HUH?
WHAT'S WRONG, AKIRA?
I JUST...
THOUGHT I SAW MEGUMI...
WHAT AM I GOING TO DO?
I TALKED HIS HEAD OFF OUT OF SPITE, AND THEN HE JUST TOLD ME TO WAIT HERE...
BOING
I DON'T THINK HE'S COMING BACK.
WOULD HE JUST LEAVE?
DID I MAKE HIM MAD?
ALONE

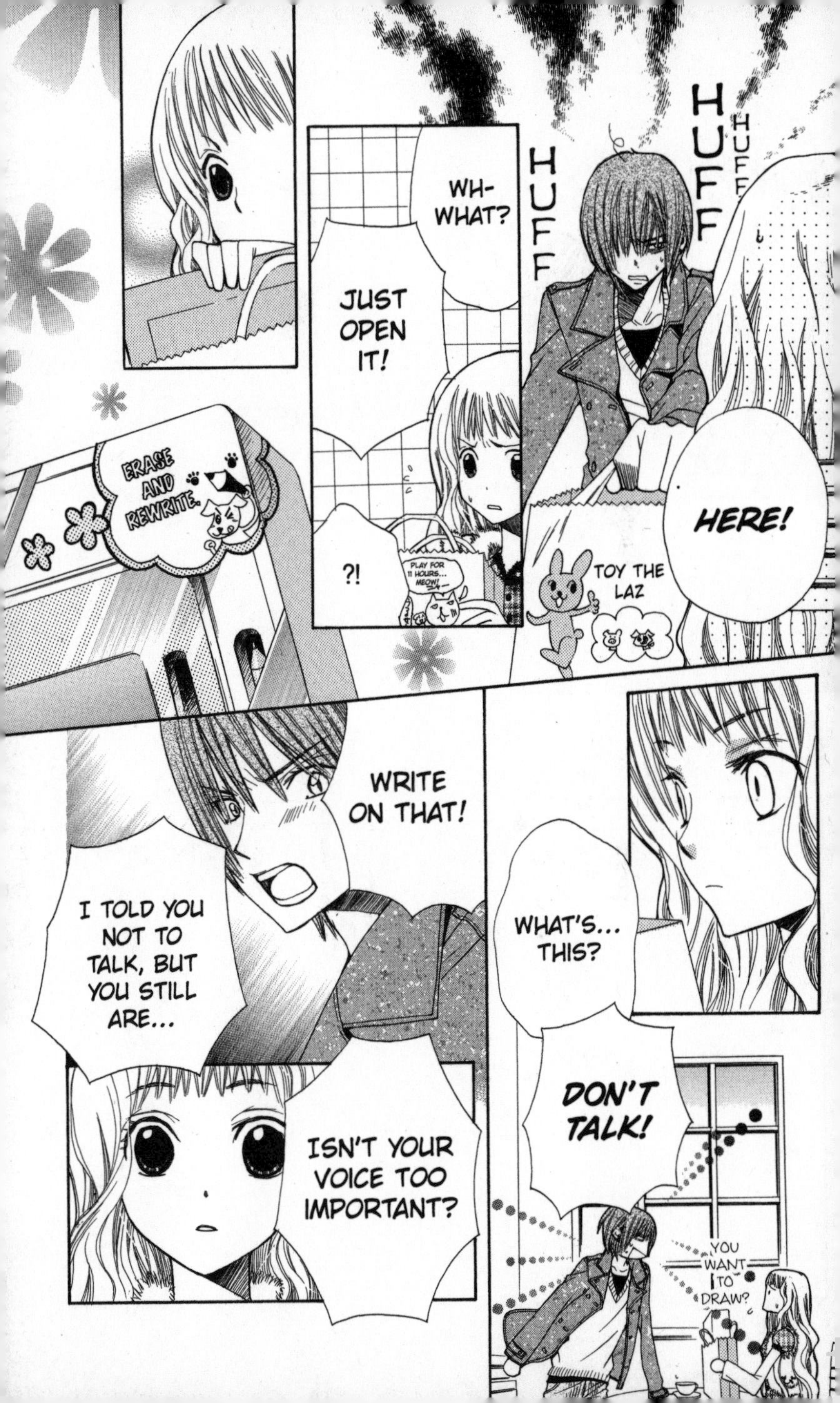
HUFF
HUFF
HUFF
HERE!
TOY THE LAZ
WH-WHAT?
JUST OPEN IT!
?!
PLAY FOR 11 HOURS... MEOW!
ERASE AND REWRITE.
WHAT'S... THIS?
DON'T TALK!
YOU WANT TO DRAW?
WRITE ON THAT!
I TOLD YOU NOT TO TALK, BUT YOU STILL ARE...
ISN'T YOUR VOICE TOO IMPORTANT?

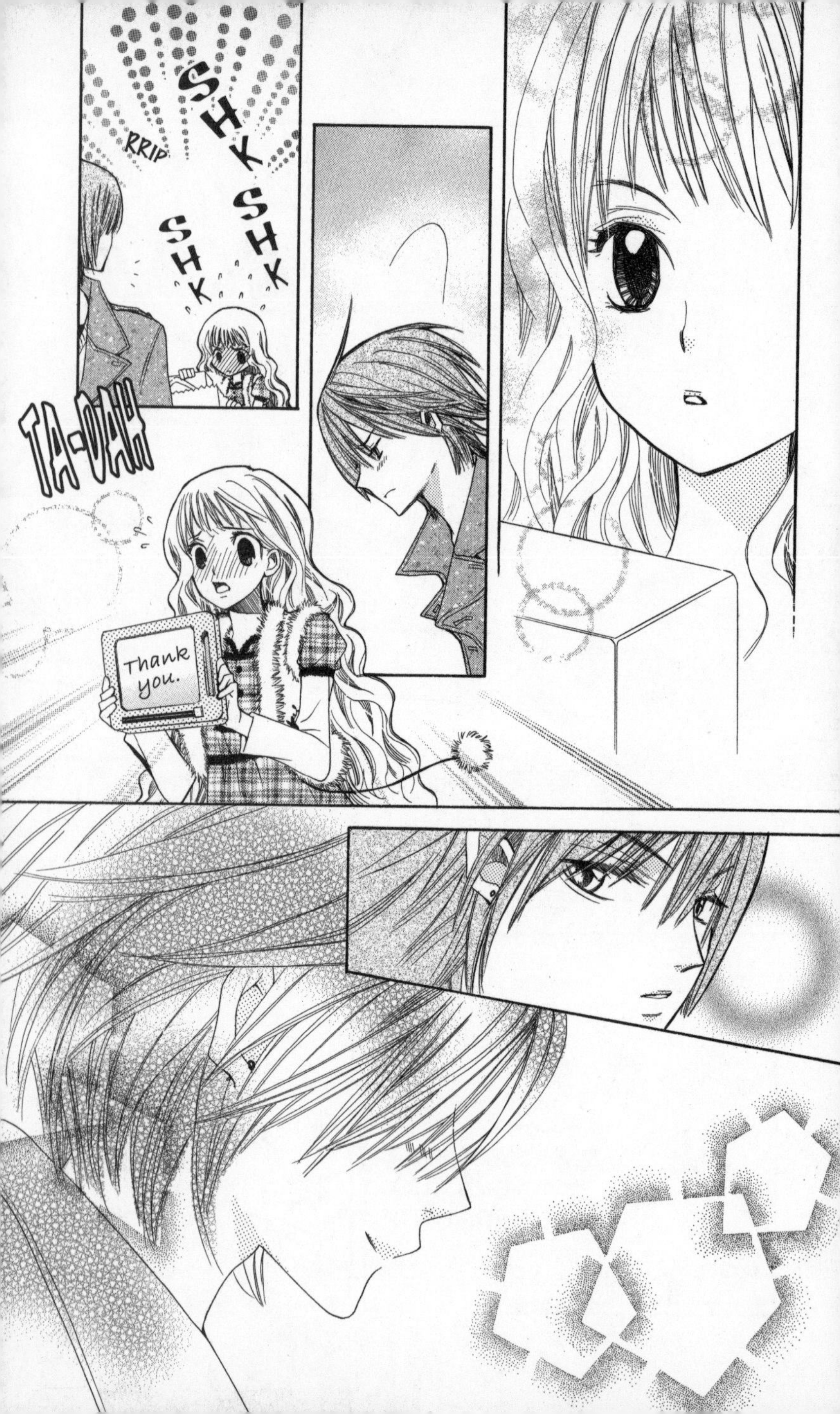
SHK
SHK
SHK
SHK
RRIP
TA-DAH!
Thank you.

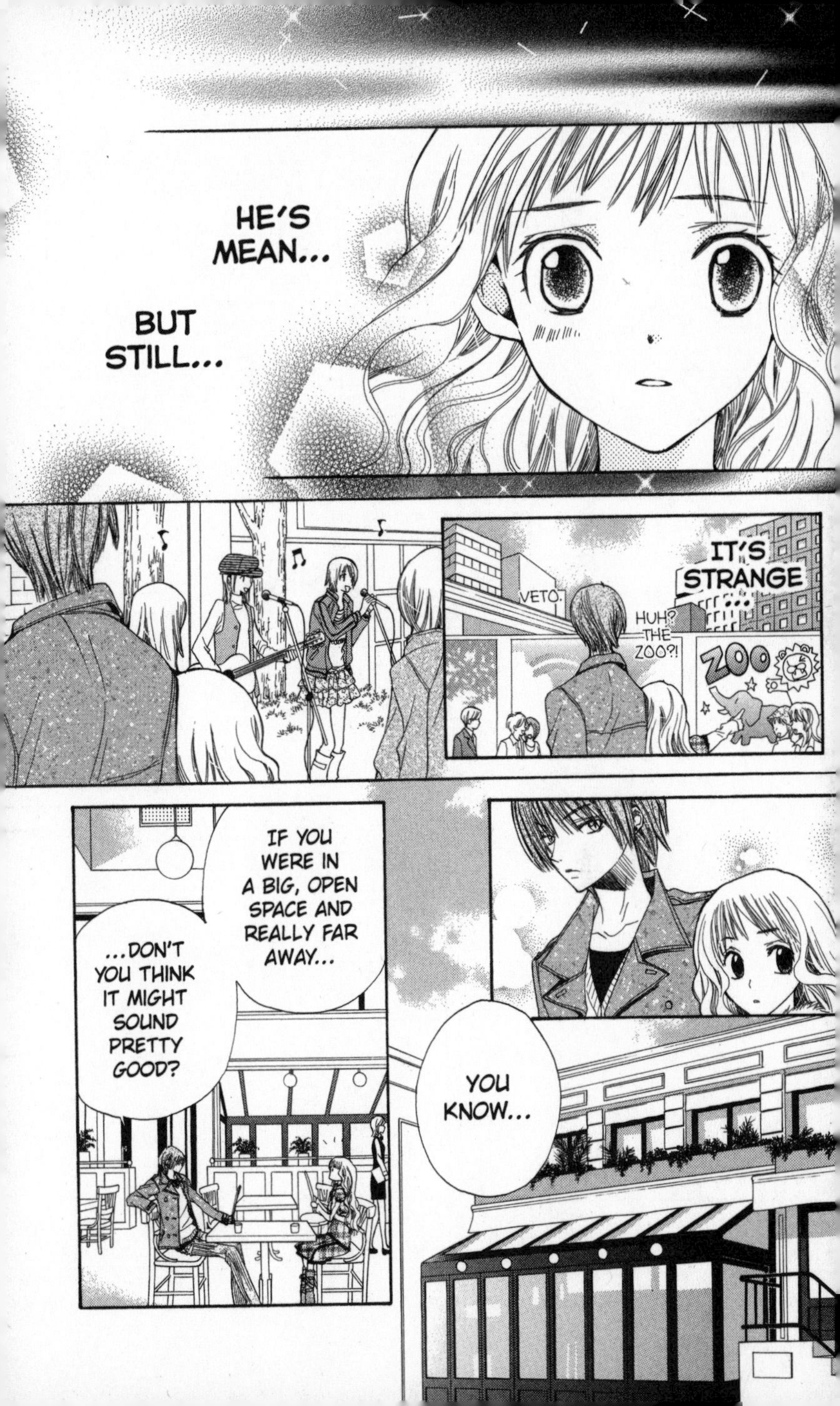
HE'S MEAN...
BUT STILL...
IT'S STRANGE...
VETO.
HUH? THE ZOO?!
ZOO
YOU KNOW...
IF YOU WERE IN A BIG, OPEN SPACE AND REALLY FAR AWAY...
...DON'T YOU THINK IT MIGHT SOUND PRETTY GOOD?

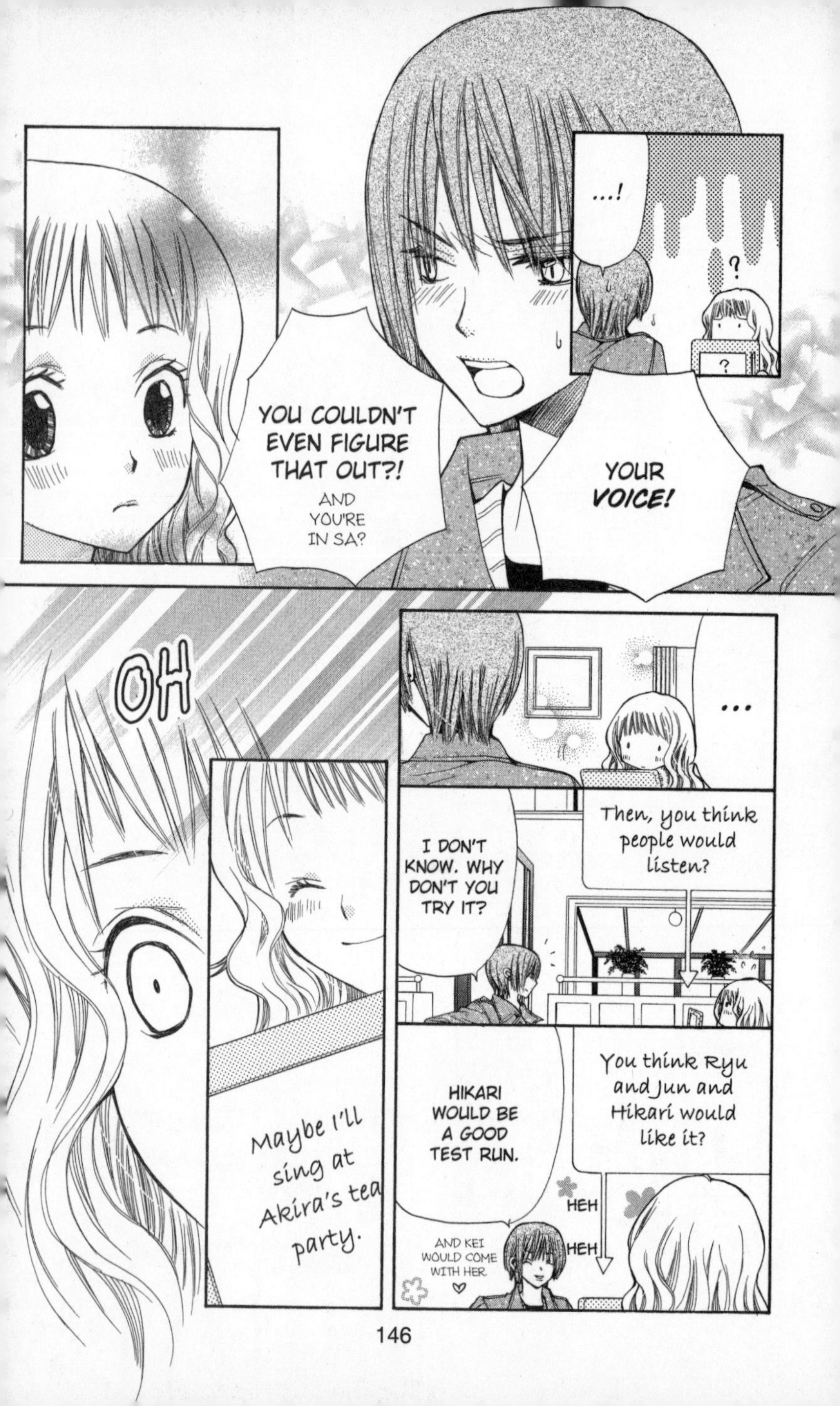

...!
?
?
YOUR VOICE!
YOU COULDN'T EVEN FIGURE THAT OUT?!
AND YOU'RE IN SA?
...
Then, you think people would listen?
I DON'T KNOW. WHY DON'T YOU TRY IT?
You think Ryu and Jun and Hikari would like it?
HIKARI WOULD BE A GOOD TEST RUN.
HEH
HEH
AND KEI WOULD COME WITH HER.
Maybe I'll sing at Akira's tea party.
OH

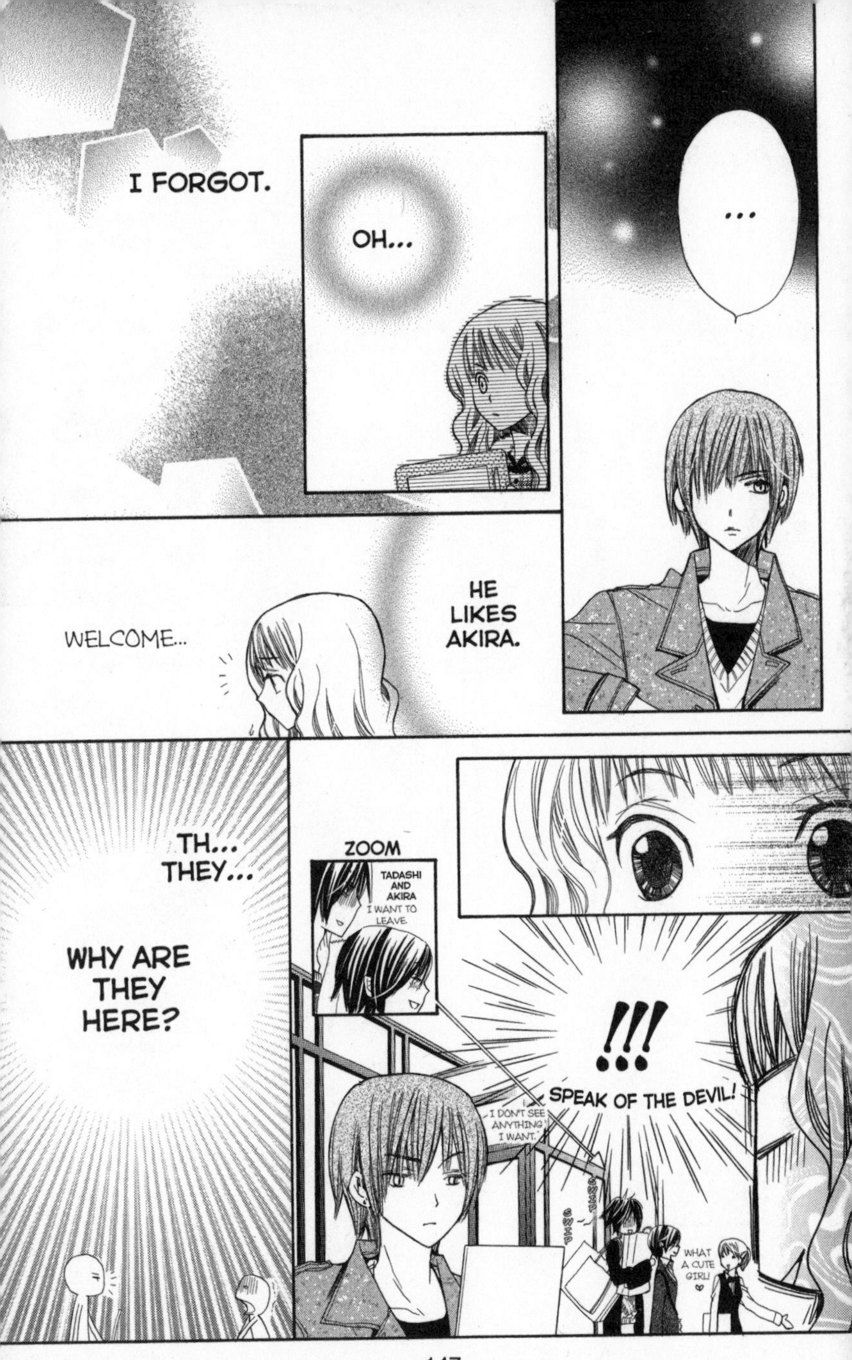
...
OH...
I FORGOT.
HE LIKES AKIRA.
WELCOME...
!!!
SPEAK OF THE DEVIL!
ZOOM
TADASHI AND AKIRA
I WANT TO LEAVE.
I DON'T SEE ANYTHING I WANT.
SWIP
SWIP
WHAT A CUTE GIRL!
TH... THEY...
WHY ARE THEY HERE?

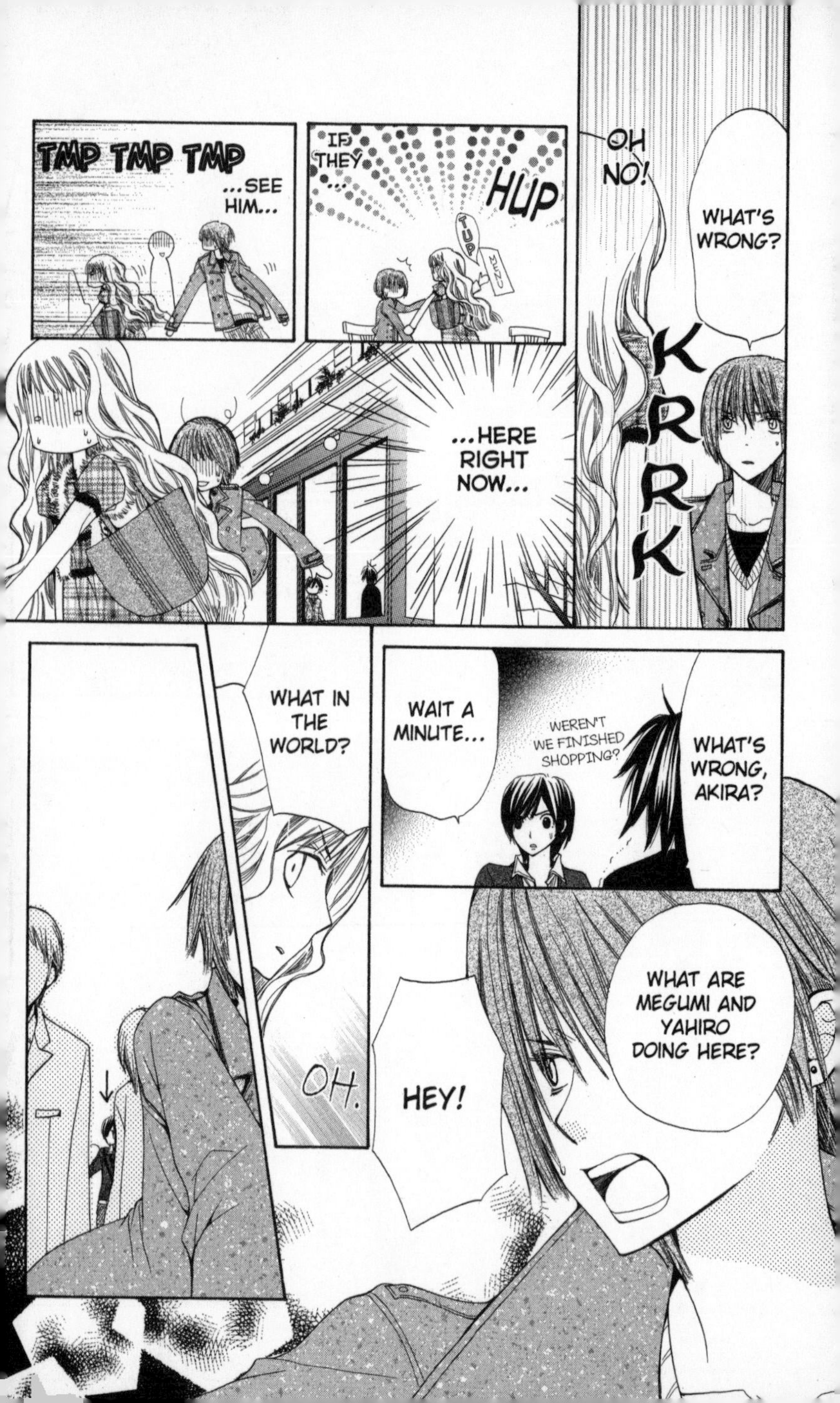
WHAT'S WRONG?
OH NO!
KRRK
IF THEY...
HUP
TUP
MENU
TMP TMP TMP
...SEE HIM...
...HERE RIGHT NOW...
WHAT'S WRONG, AKIRA?
WEREN'T WE FINISHED SHOPPING?
WAIT A MINUTE...
WHAT IN THE WORLD?
WHAT ARE MEGUMI AND YAHIRO DOING HERE?
HEY!
OH.

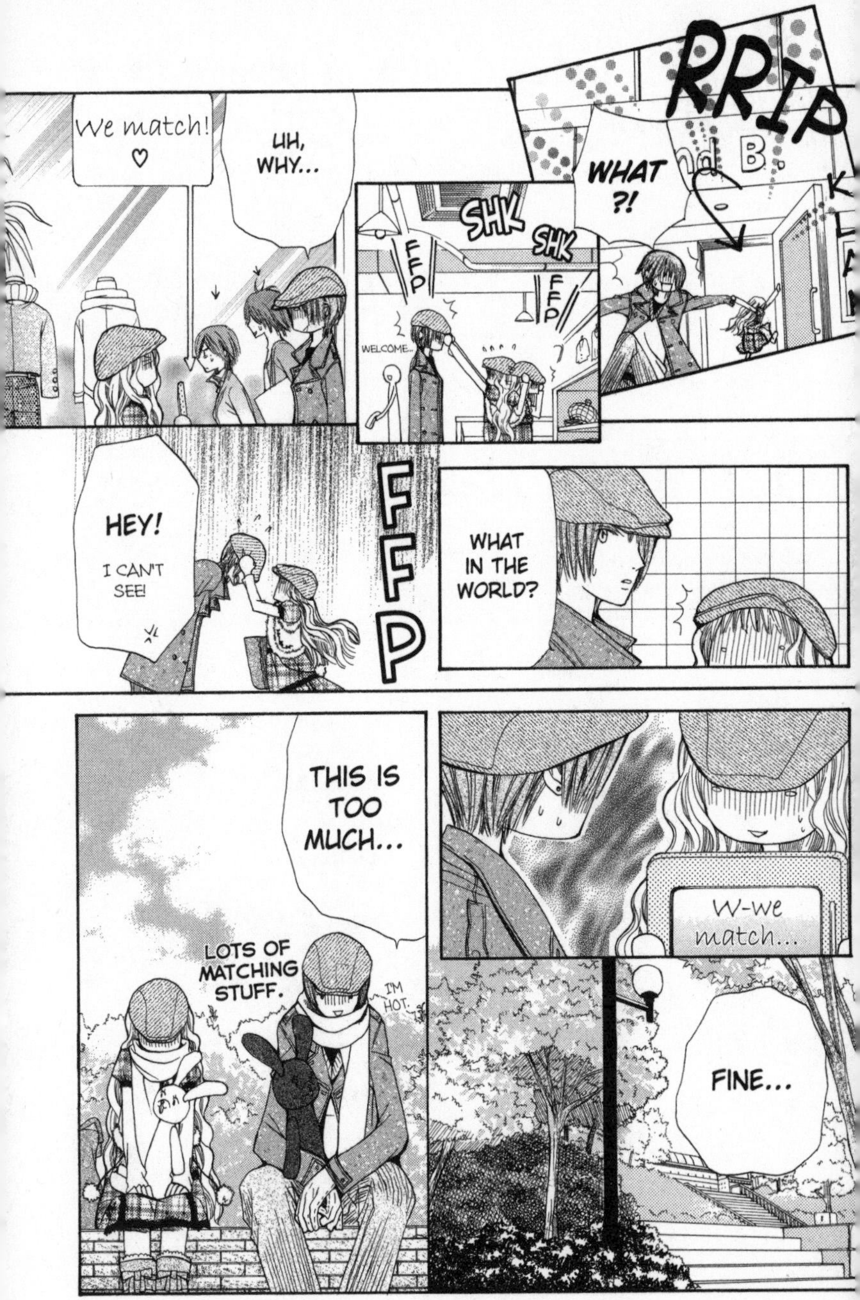
RRIP
WHAT ?!
B
KLAK
SHK
SHK
FFP
FFP
WELCOME...
UH, WHY...
We match! ♡
WHAT IN THE WORLD?
FFP
HEY!
I CAN'T SEE!
W-we match...
THIS IS TOO MUCH...
FINE...
I'M HOT.
LOTS OF MATCHING STUFF.

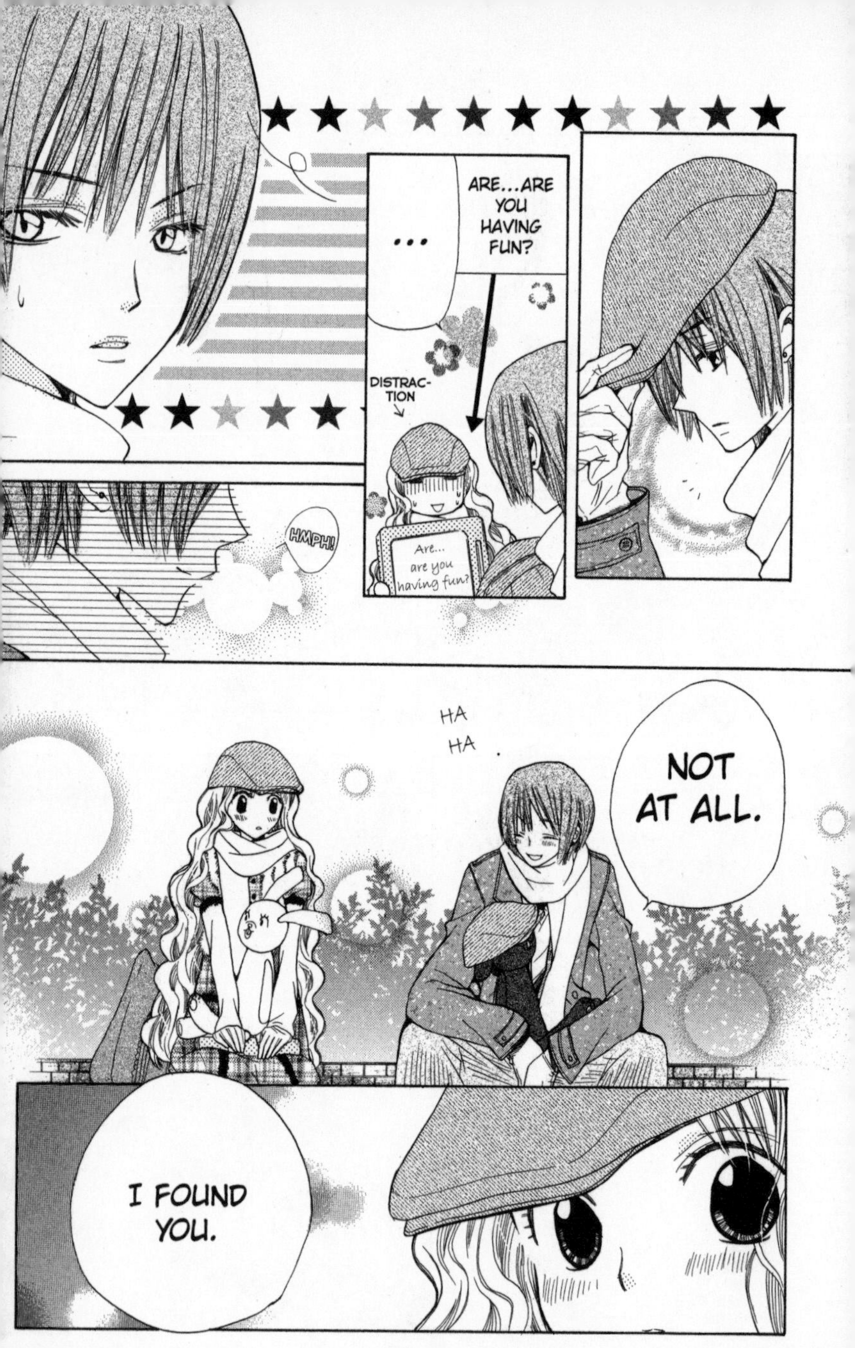

ARE...ARE YOU HAVING FUN?
...
DISTRACTION
Are... are you having fun?
HMPH!
HA HA
NOT AT ALL.
I FOUND YOU.

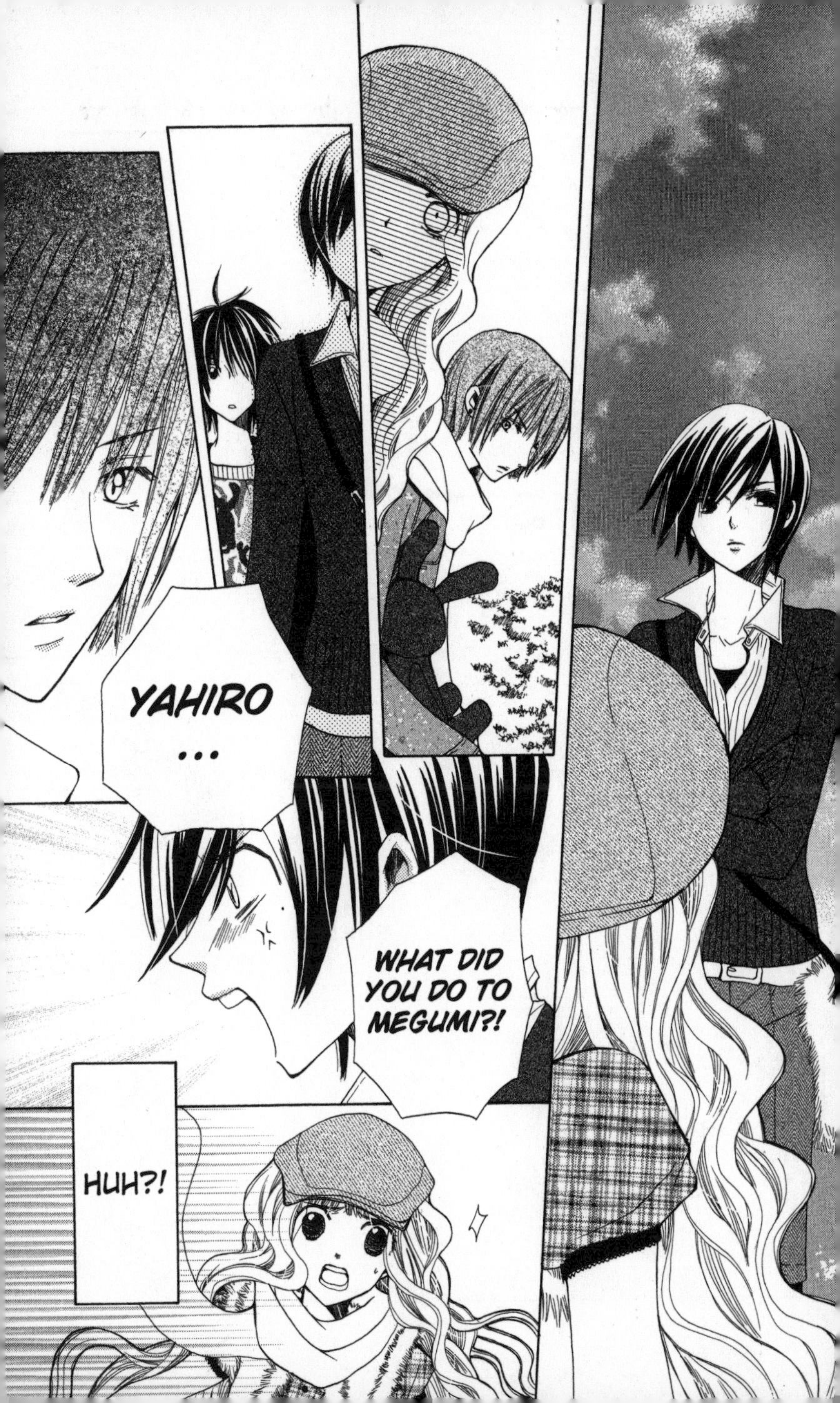
YAHIRO ...
WHAT DID YOU DO TO MEGUMI?!
HUH?!

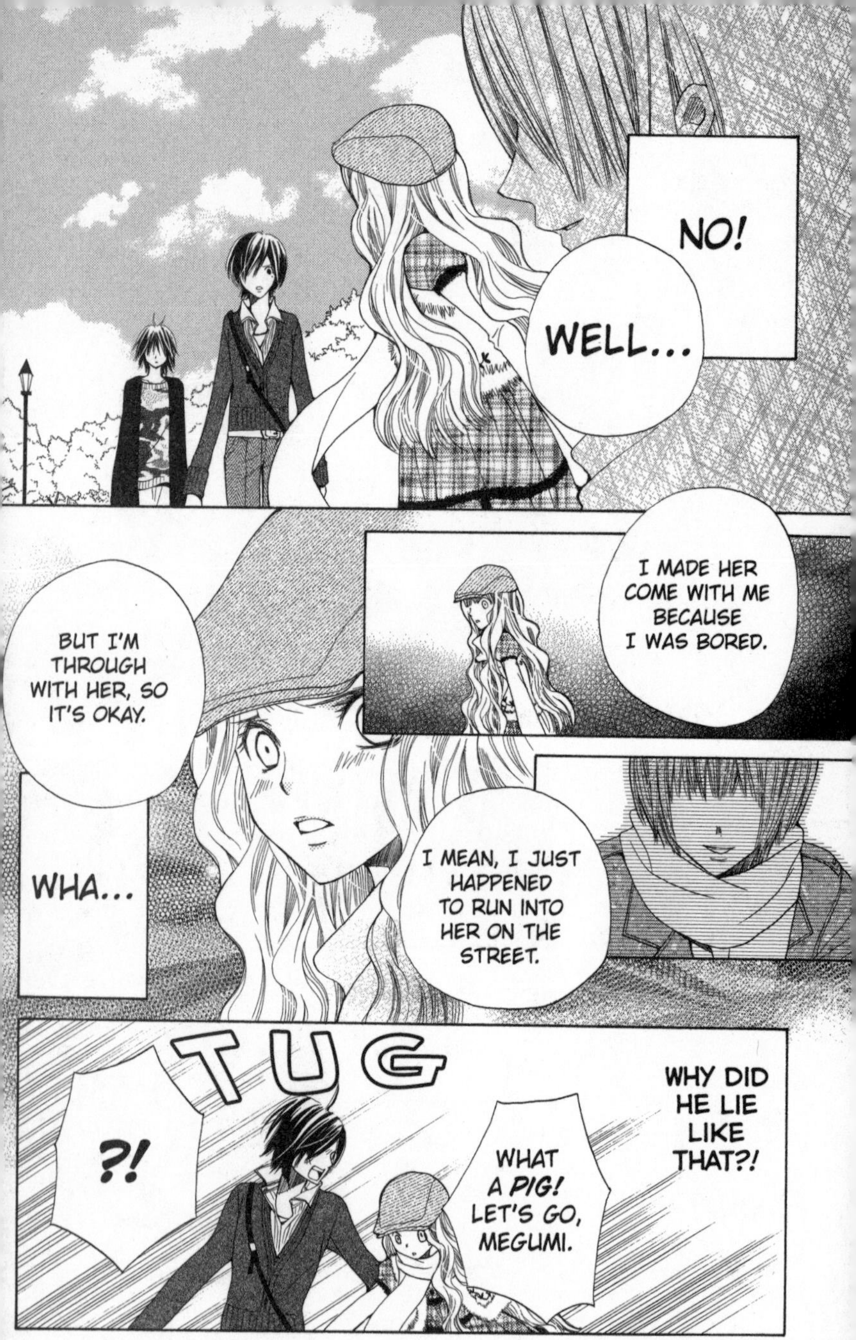
NO!
WELL...
I MADE HER COME WITH ME BECAUSE I WAS BORED.
BUT I'M THROUGH WITH HER, SO IT'S OKAY.
I MEAN, I JUST HAPPENED TO RUN INTO HER ON THE STREET.
WHA...
WHY DID HE LIE LIKE THAT?!
TUG
WHAT A *PIG!* LET'S GO, MEGUMI.
?!

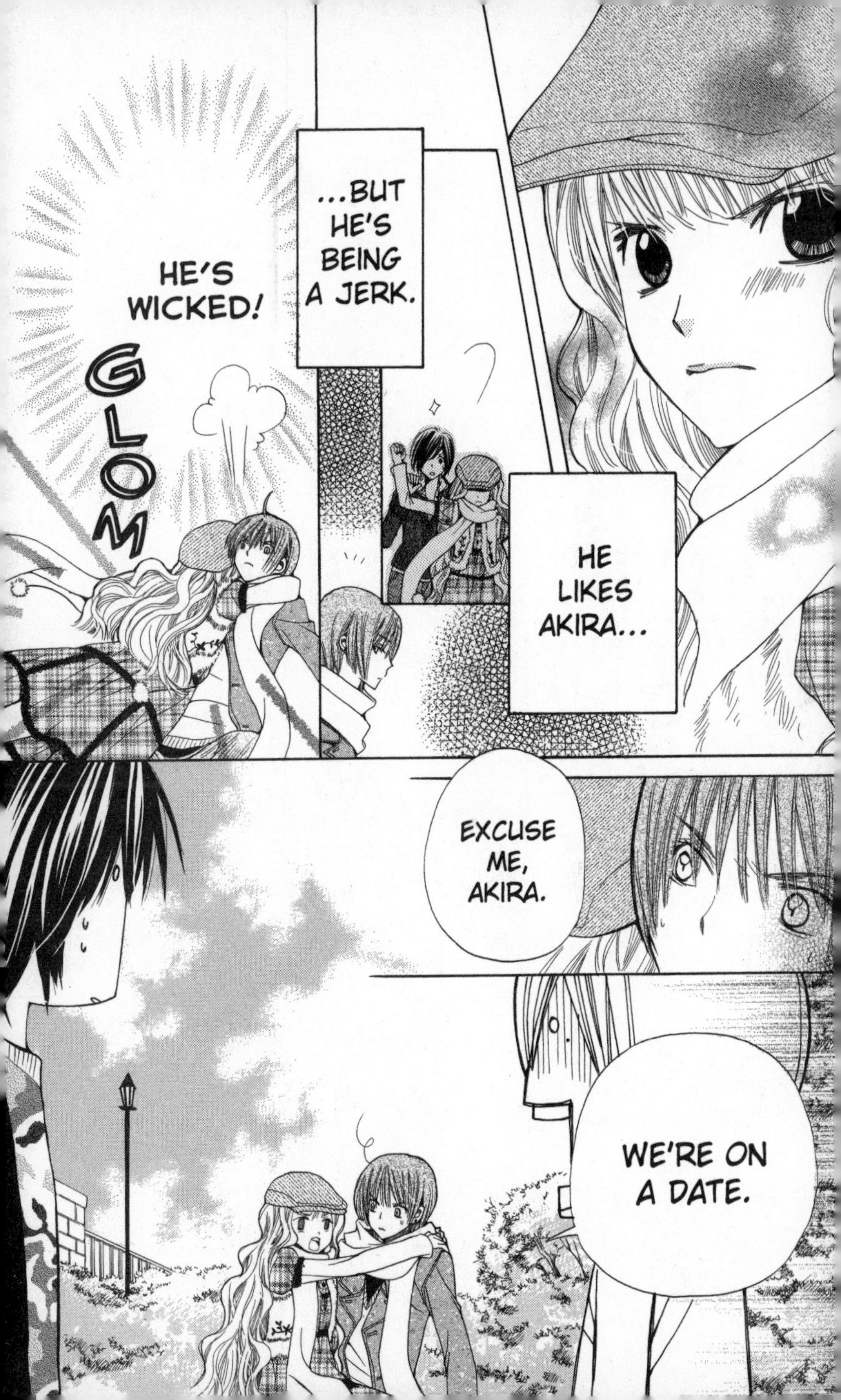
HE LIKES AKIRA...
...BUT HE'S BEING A JERK.
HE'S WICKED!
GLOM
EXCUSE ME, AKIRA.
WE'RE ON A DATE.

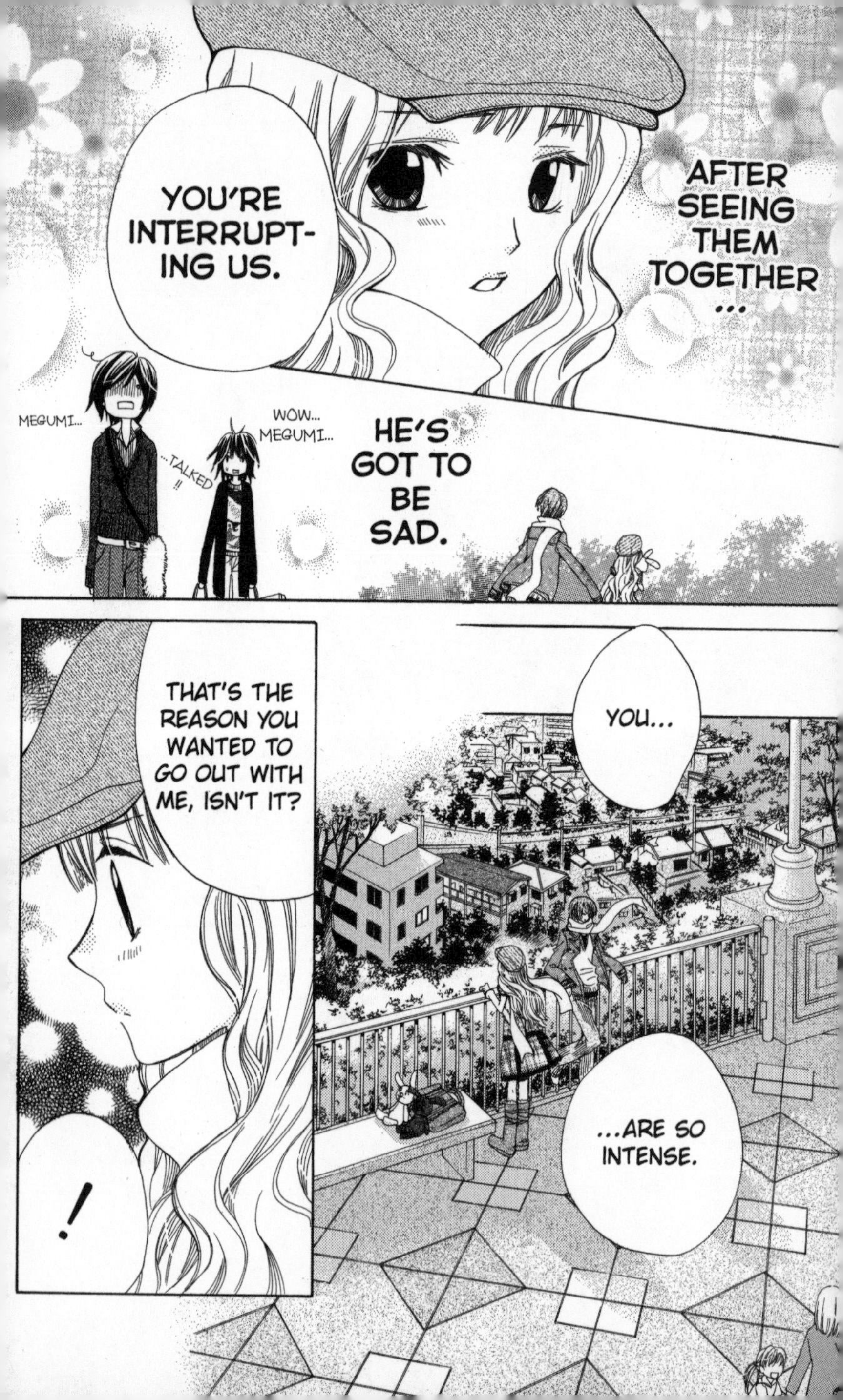
AFTER SEEING THEM TOGETHER...
YOU'RE INTERRUPTING US.
HE'S GOT TO BE SAD.
WOW... MEGUMI...
...TALKED!!
MEGUMI...
YOU...
...ARE SO INTENSE.
THAT'S THE REASON YOU WANTED TO GO OUT WITH ME, ISN'T IT?
!

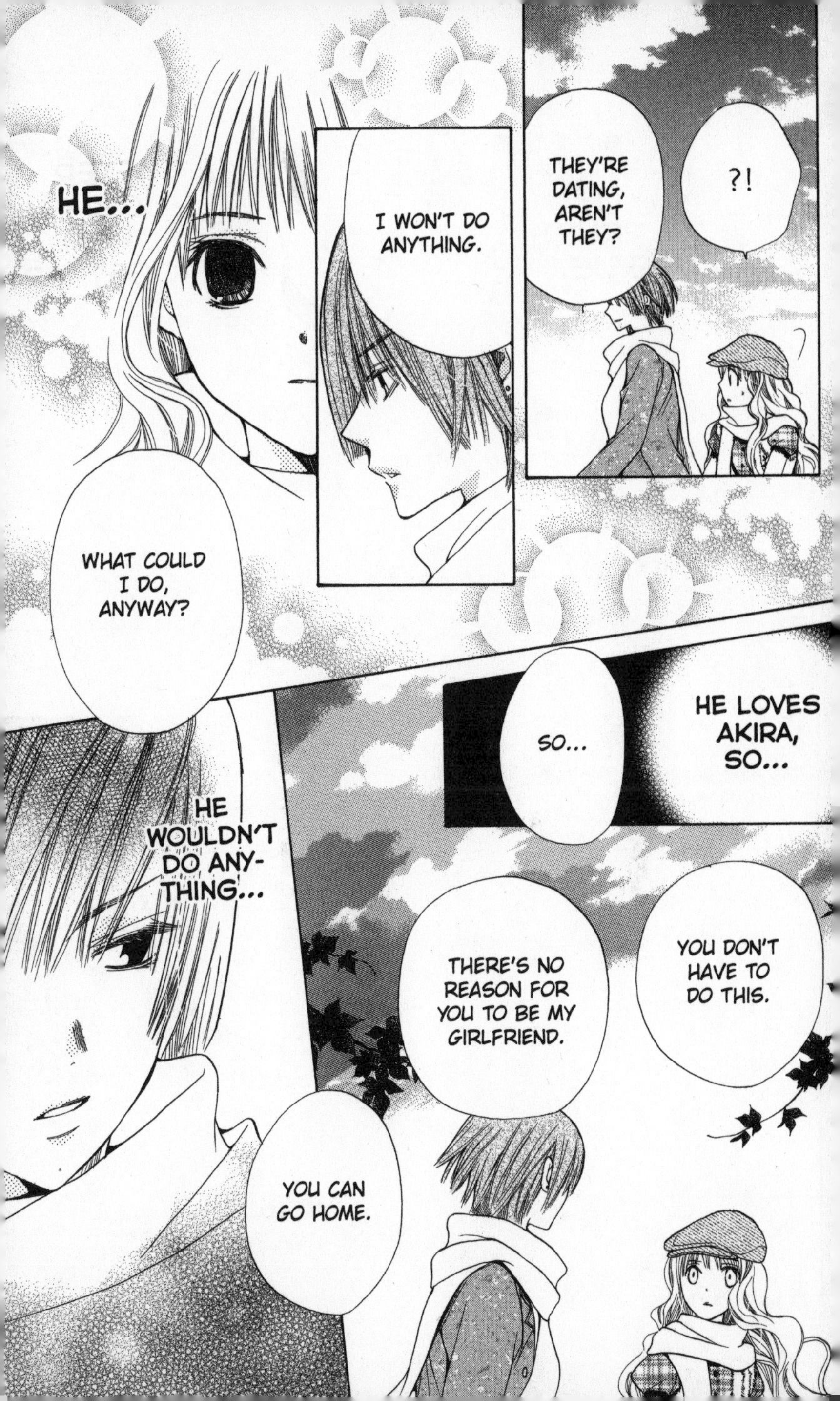
THEY'RE DATING, AREN'T THEY?
?!
I WON'T DO ANYTHING.
HE...
WHAT COULD I DO, ANYWAY?
HE LOVES AKIRA, SO...
SO...
YOU DON'T HAVE TO DO THIS.
THERE'S NO REASON FOR YOU TO BE MY GIRLFRIEND.
YOU CAN GO HOME.
HE WOULDN'T DO ANY-THING...

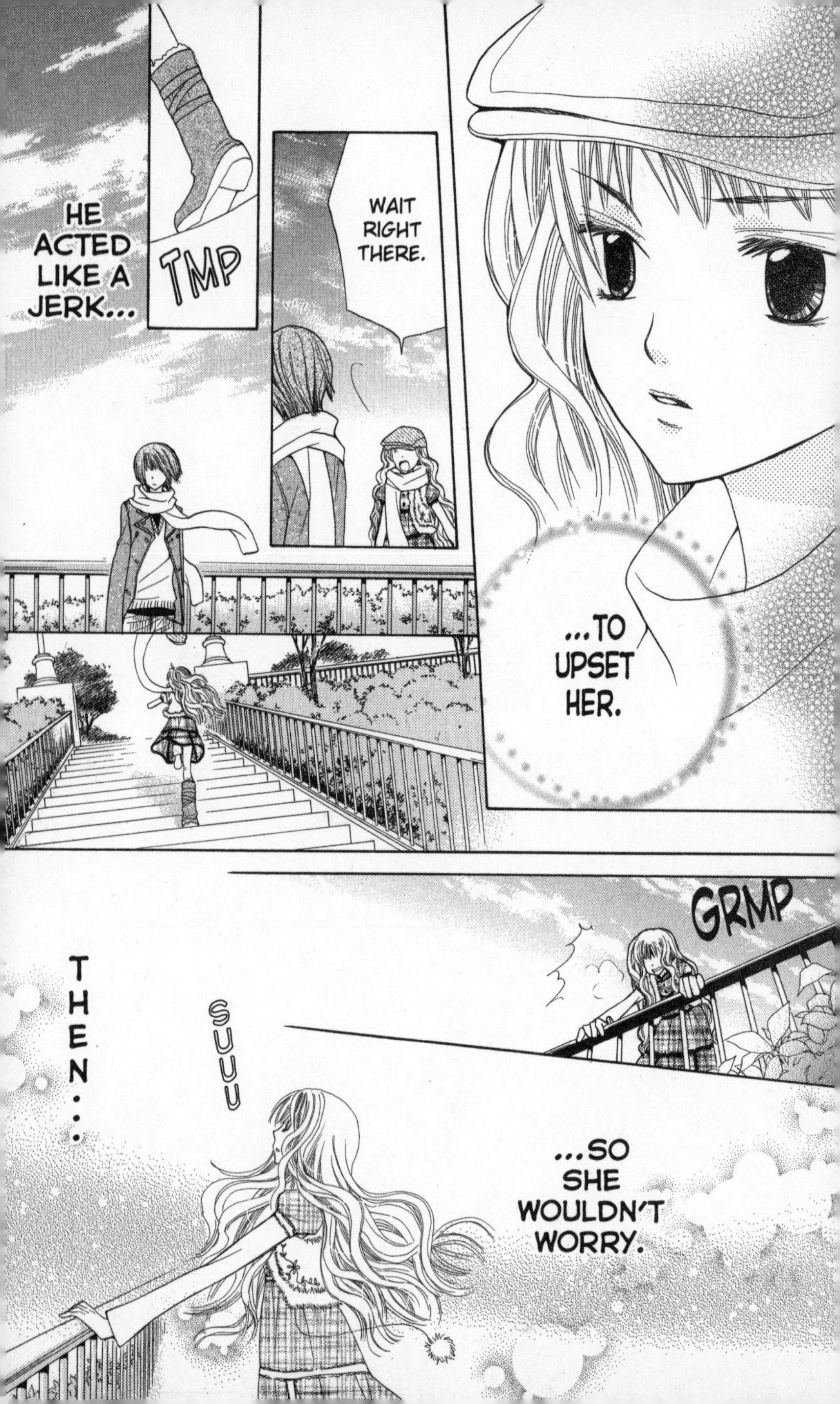

...TO UPSET HER.
WAIT RIGHT THERE.
TMP
HE ACTED LIKE A JERK...
GRMP
...SO SHE WOULDN'T WORRY.
SUUU
THEN...

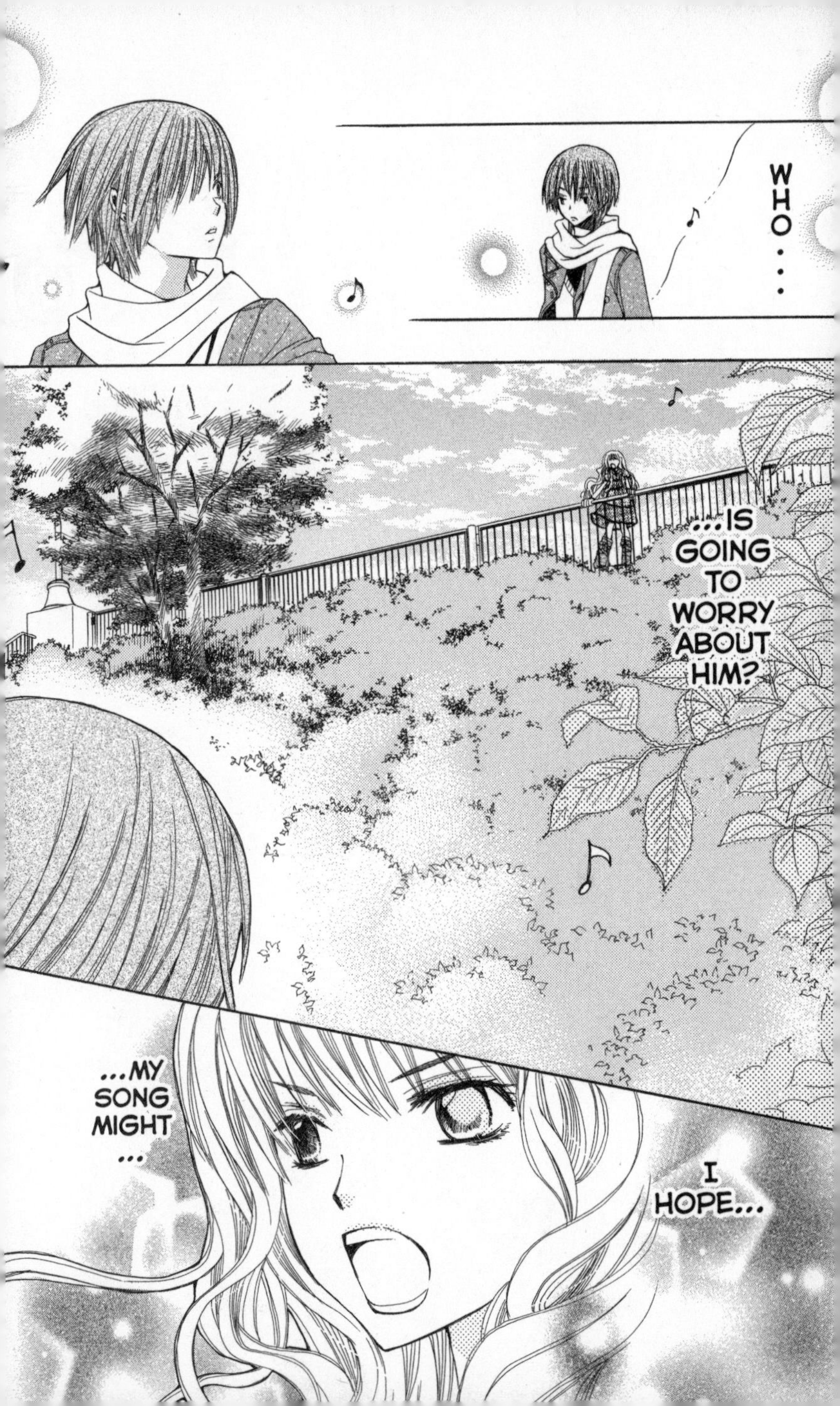
WHO...
...IS GOING TO WORRY ABOUT HIM?
I HOPE...
...MY SONG MIGHT...

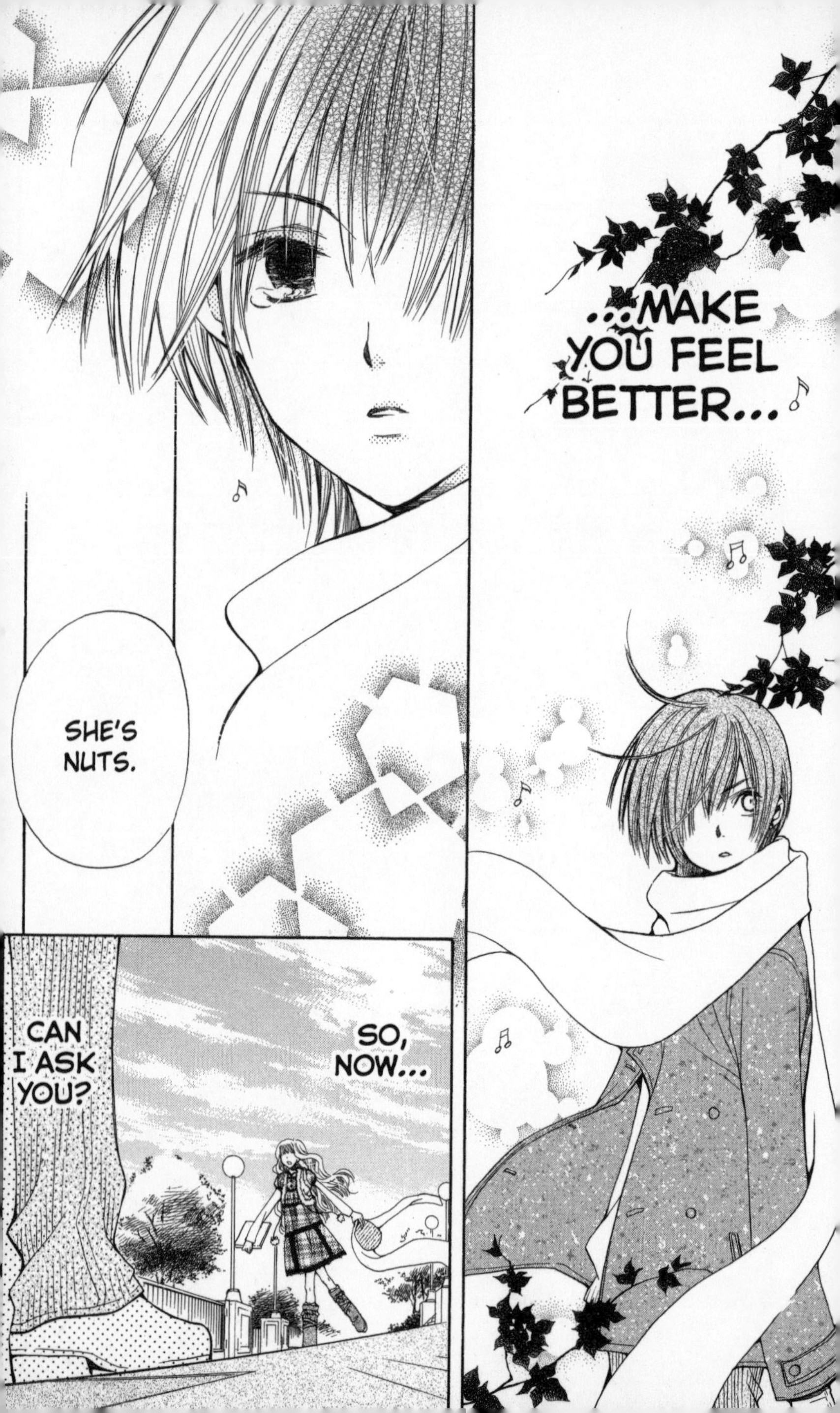
...MAKE YOU FEEL BETTER...
SHE'S NUTS.
SO, NOW...
CAN I ASK YOU?

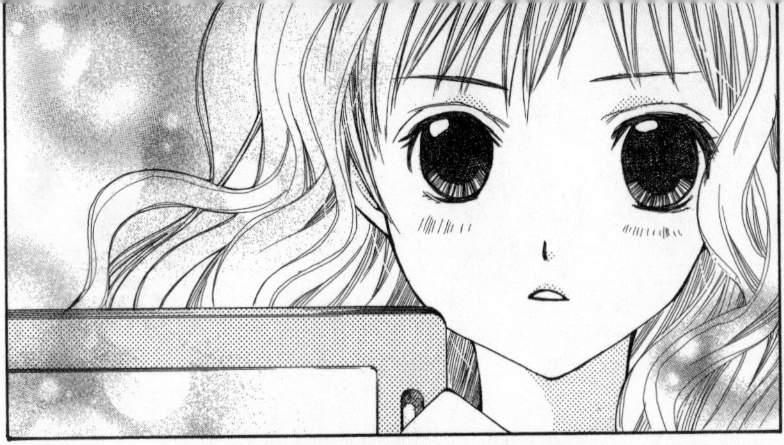

"WAS IT FUN?"

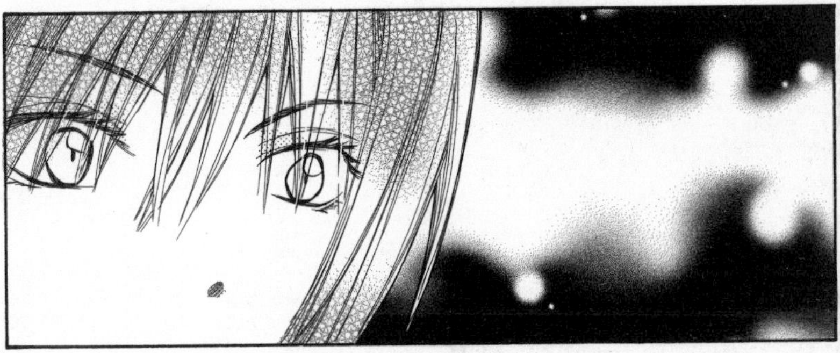

THE GAME'S NOT OVER YET, IS IT?

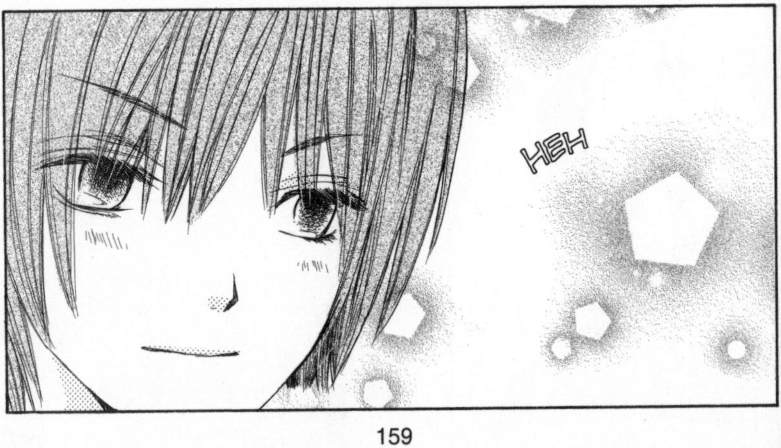
HEH

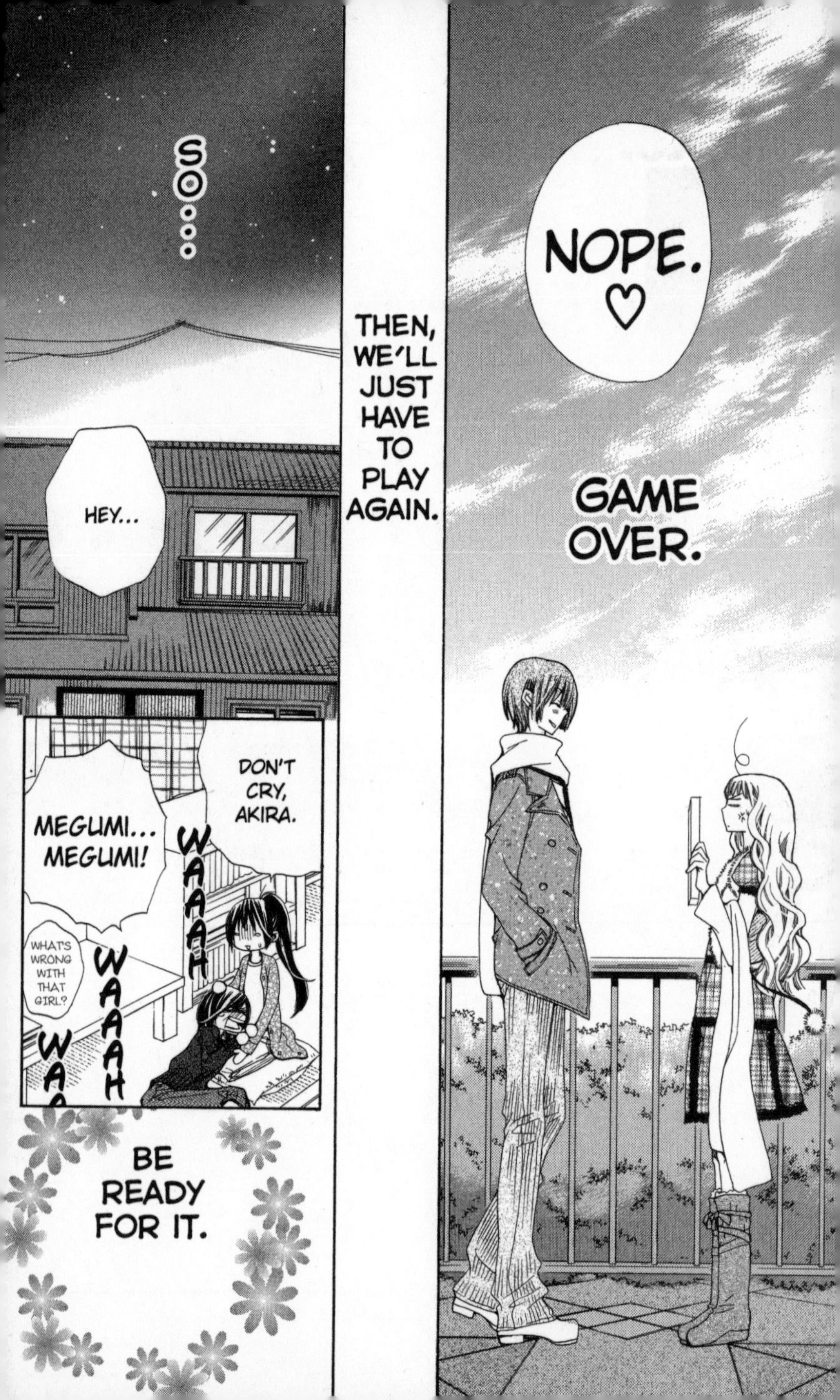
NOPE. ♡
GAME OVER.
THEN, WE'LL JUST HAVE TO PLAY AGAIN.
SO....
HEY...
DON'T CRY, AKIRA.
MEGUMI... MEGUMI!
WAAAAH
WHAT'S WRONG WITH THAT GIRL?
WAAAAH
WAA
BE READY FOR IT.

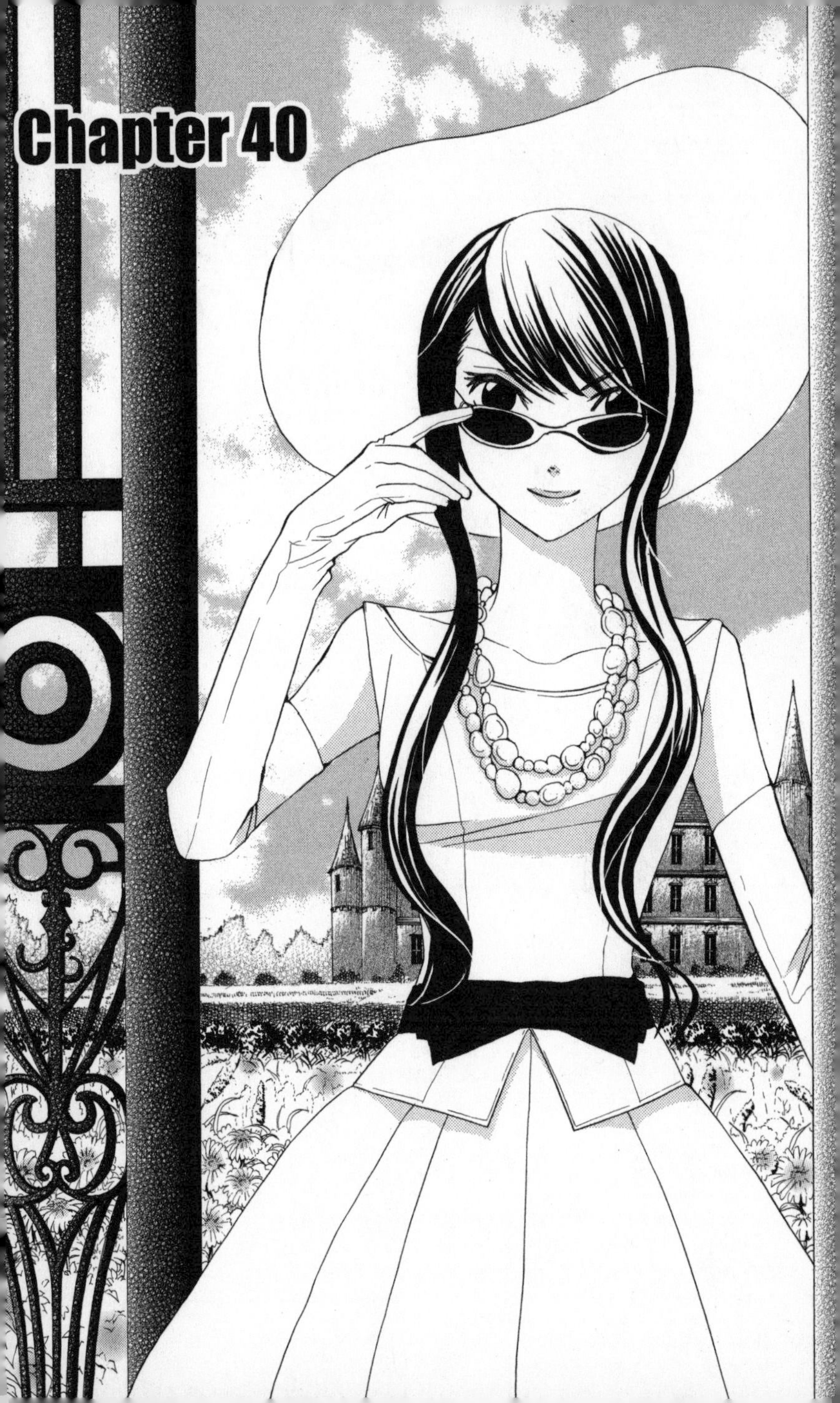
Chapter 40

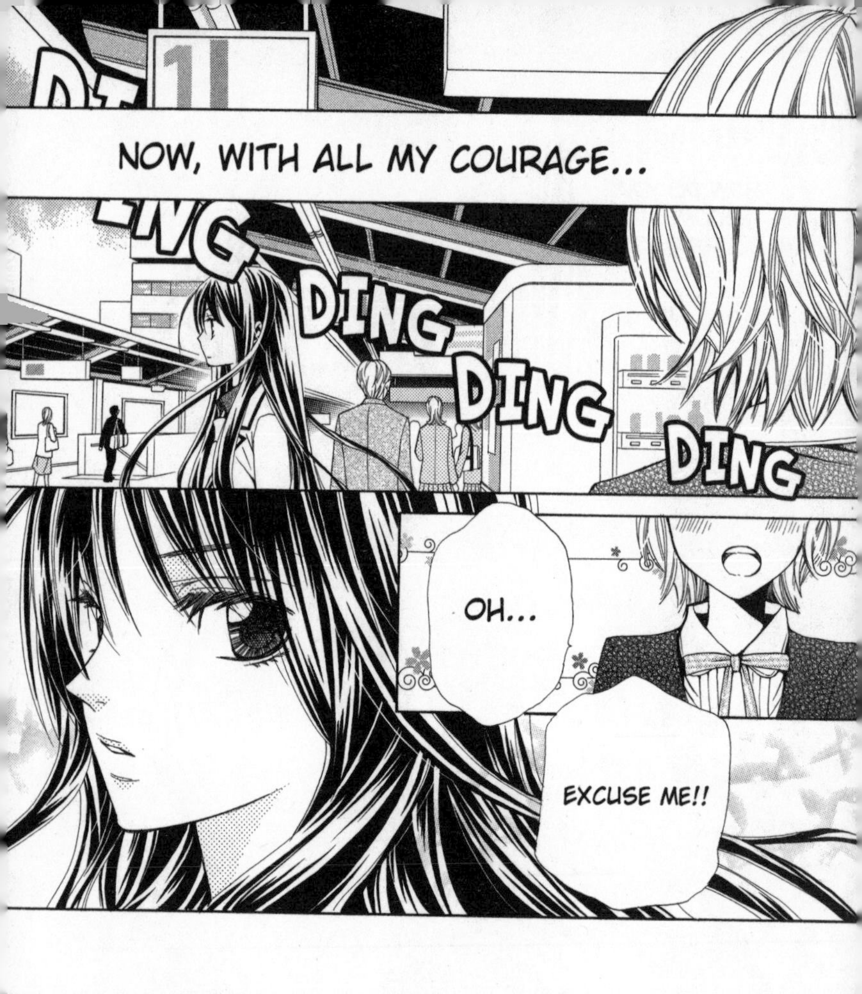
NOW, WITH ALL MY COURAGE...
DING
DING
DING
DING
OH...
EXCUSE ME!!

·THIS AND THAT

·THIS IS THE LAST BOTTOM-QUARTER PAGE. THE OTHER DAY, A FRIEND OF MINE FROM ELEMENTARY SCHOOL READ MY BOOK. IT MADE ME FEEL SILLY AND HAPPY. I'M GLAD I BECAME A MANGA WRITER.

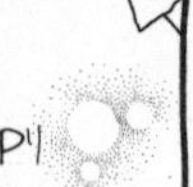
F

·I USED YOUR REQUESTS TO DO THE BONUS PAGES AGAIN THIS TIME. THANKS FOR MAKING ALL THOSE SUGGESTIONS!

·I'VE HAD REQUESTS FOR THE BOTTOM-QUARTER PAGES, TOO. I'LL TRY TO DO THOSE IN THE NEXT BOOK!! YAY!! WELL, THANK YOU SO MUCH FOR STICKING WITH ME THIS FAR!!

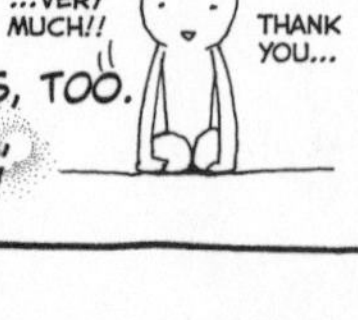
HUP!!
THANK YOU...
...VERY MUCH!!

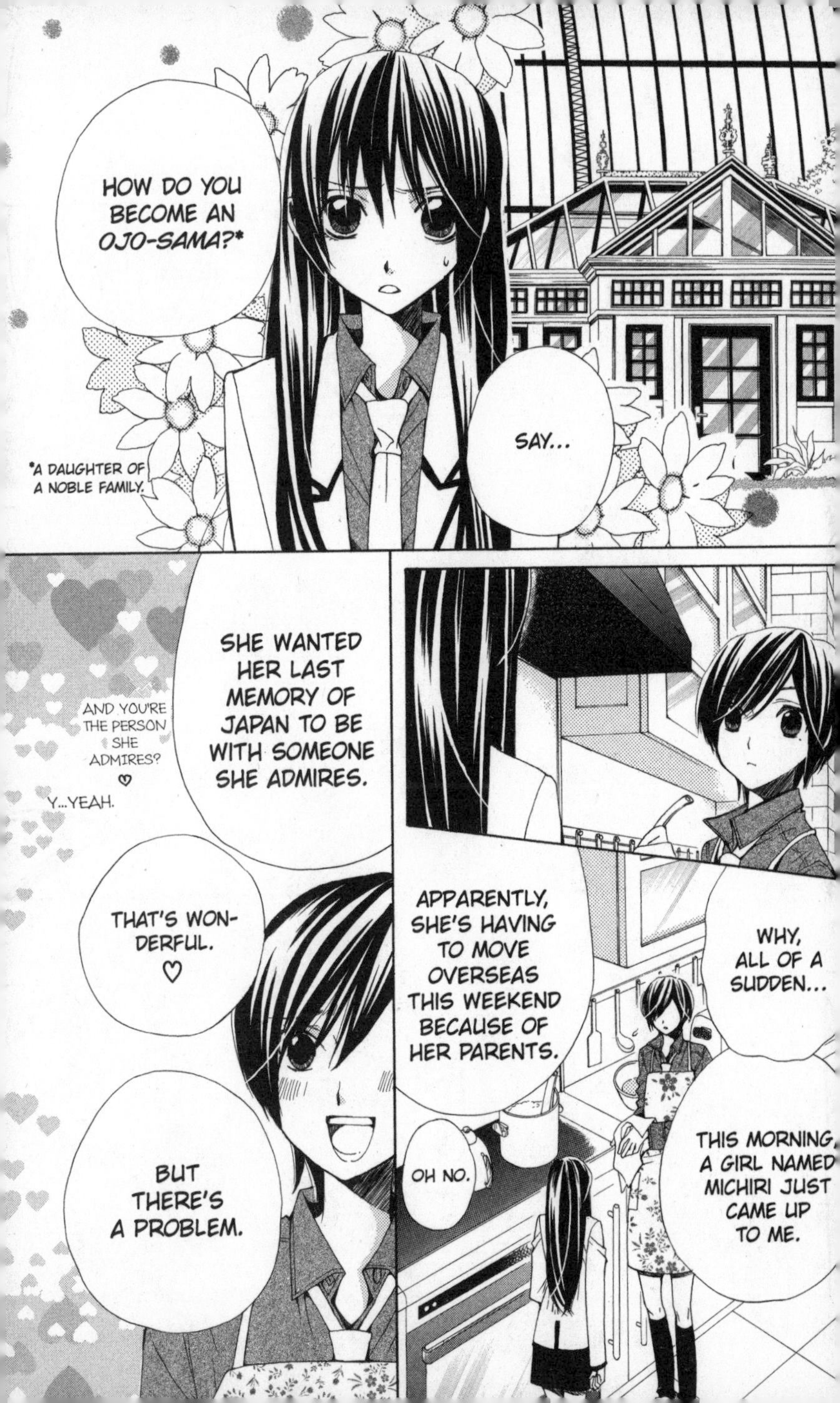

SAY...
HOW DO YOU BECOME AN OJO-SAMA?*
*A DAUGHTER OF A NOBLE FAMILY.
WHY, ALL OF A SUDDEN...
THIS MORNING, A GIRL NAMED MICHIRI JUST CAME UP TO ME.
APPARENTLY, SHE'S HAVING TO MOVE OVERSEAS THIS WEEKEND BECAUSE OF HER PARENTS.
OH NO.
SHE WANTED HER LAST MEMORY OF JAPAN TO BE WITH SOMEONE SHE ADMIRES.
AND YOU'RE THE PERSON SHE ADMIRES? ♡
Y...YEAH.
THAT'S WON-DERFUL. ♡
BUT THERE'S A PROBLEM.

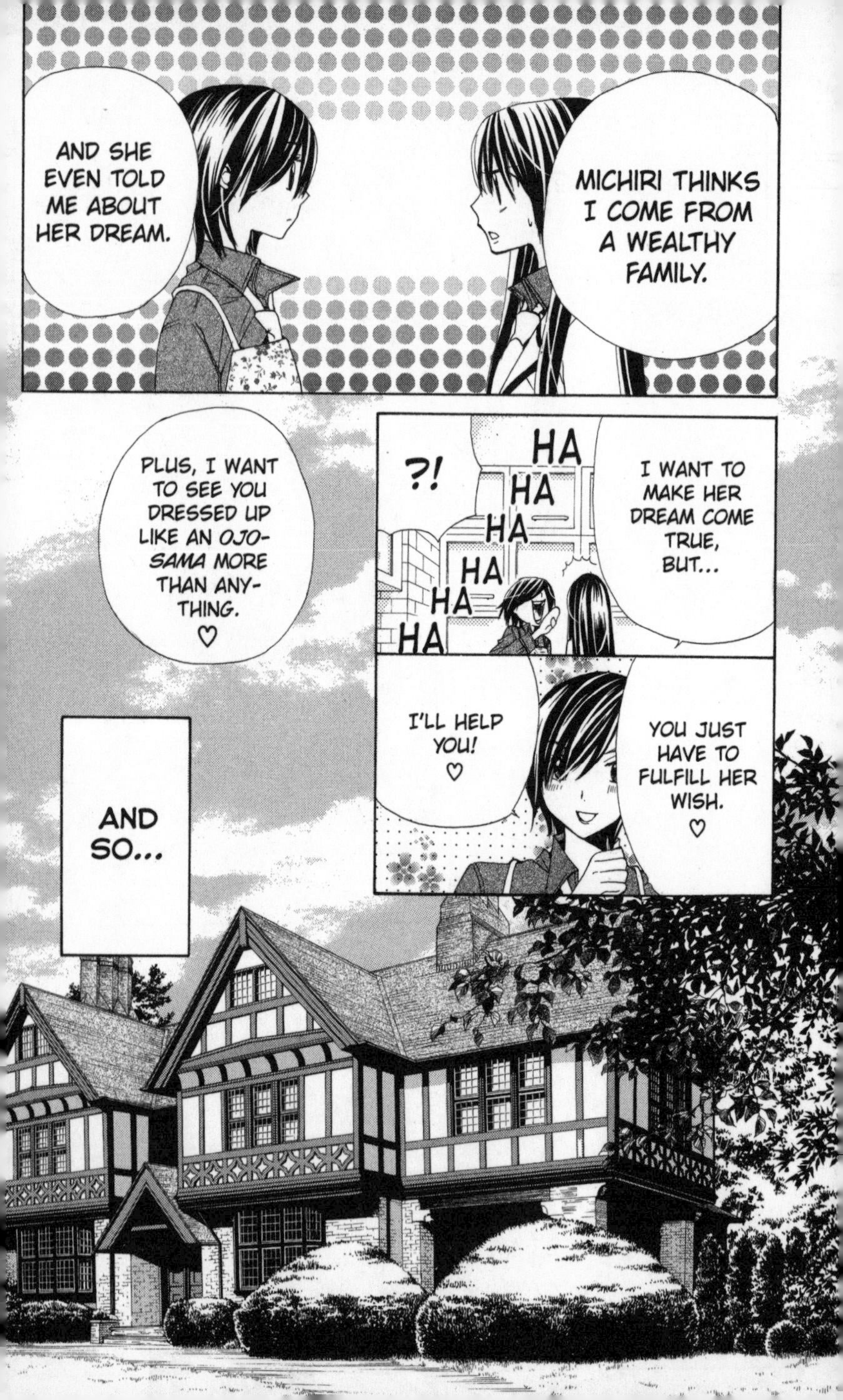
MICHIRI THINKS I COME FROM A WEALTHY FAMILY.
AND SHE EVEN TOLD ME ABOUT HER DREAM.
I WANT TO MAKE HER DREAM COME TRUE, BUT...
HA HA HA HA HA HA
?!
YOU JUST HAVE TO FULFILL HER WISH. ♡
I'LL HELP YOU! ♡
PLUS, I WANT TO SEE YOU DRESSED UP LIKE AN *OJO-SAMA* MORE THAN ANY-THING. ♡
AND SO...

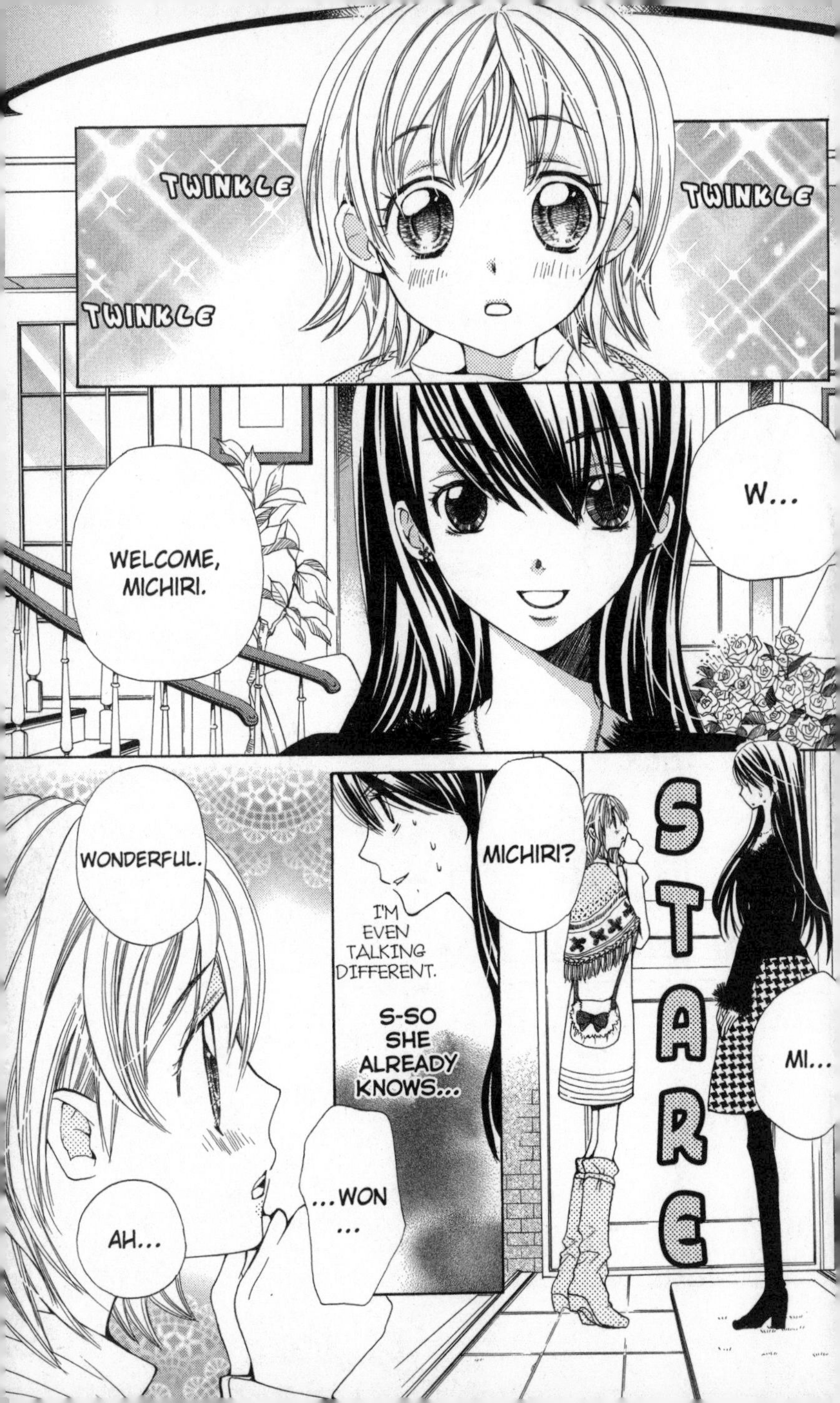
TWINKLE
TWINKLE
TWINKLE
W...
WELCOME, MICHIRI.
STARE
MI...
MICHIRI?
I'M EVEN TALKING DIFFERENT.
S-SO SHE ALREADY KNOWS...
...WON...
AH...
WONDERFUL.

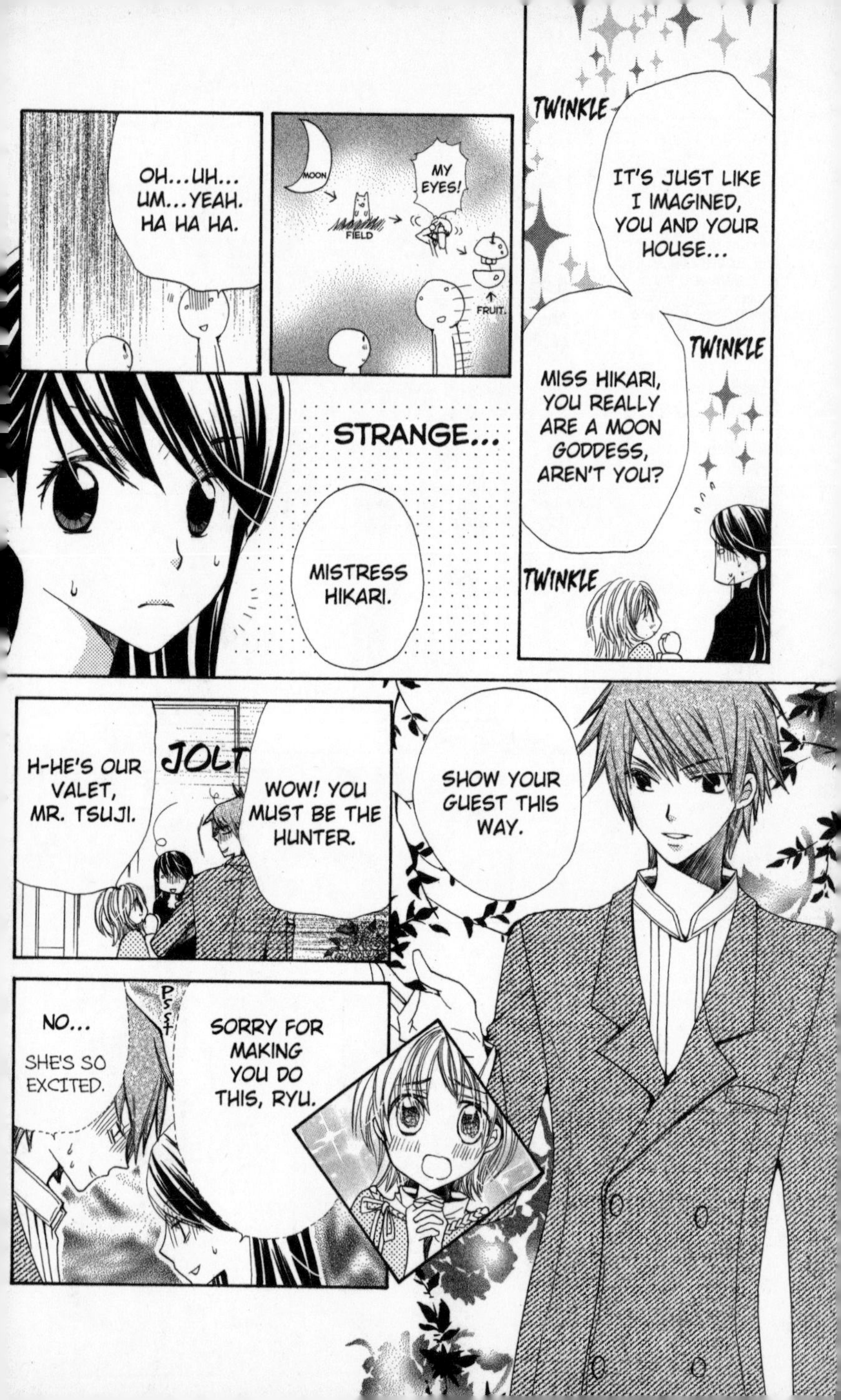
TWINKLE
IT'S JUST LIKE I IMAGINED, YOU AND YOUR HOUSE...
TWINKLE
MISS HIKARI, YOU REALLY ARE A MOON GODDESS, AREN'T YOU?
TWINKLE
MY EYES!
MOON
FIELD
FRUIT.
OH...UH... UM...YEAH. HA HA HA.
STRANGE...
MISTRESS HIKARI.
SHOW YOUR GUEST THIS WAY.
WOW! YOU MUST BE THE HUNTER.
JOLT
H-HE'S OUR VALET, MR. TSUJI.
PSST
SORRY FOR MAKING YOU DO THIS, RYU.
NO...
SHE'S SO EXCITED.

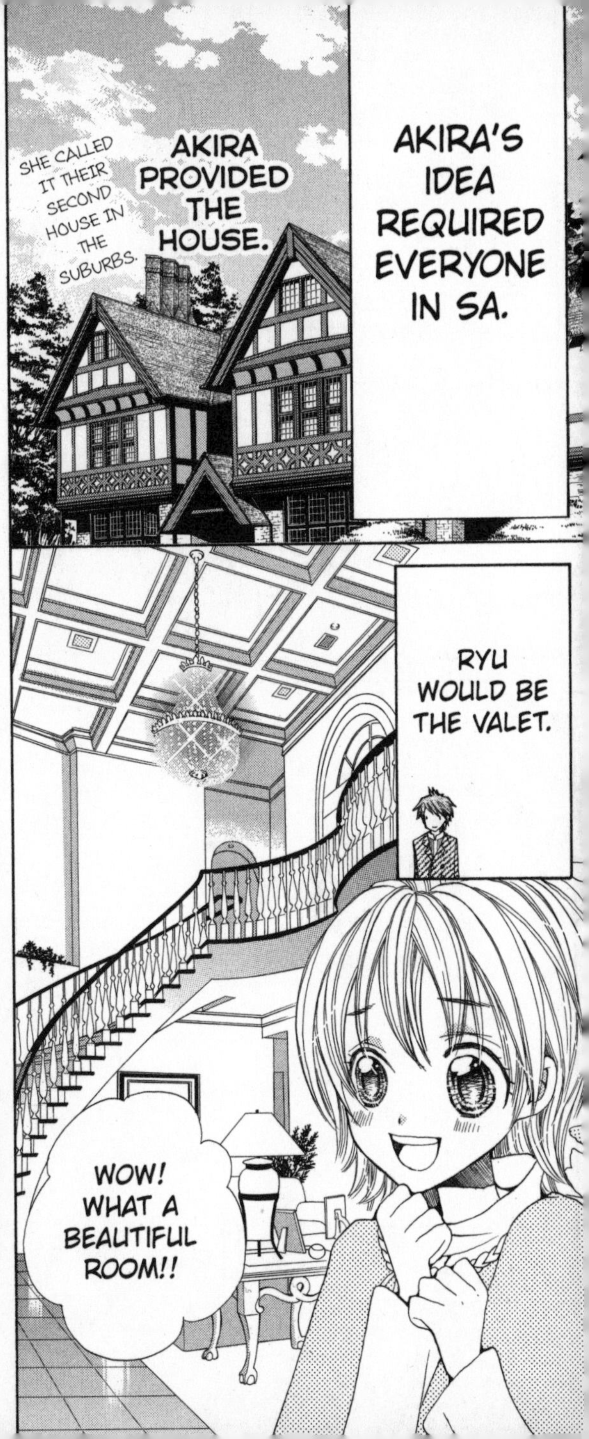
AKIRA'S IDEA REQUIRED EVERYONE IN SA.
AKIRA PROVIDED THE HOUSE.
SHE CALLED IT THEIR SECOND HOUSE IN THE SUBURBS.
RYU WOULD BE THE VALET.
WOW! WHAT A BEAUTIFUL ROOM!!

6

• THIS AND THAT •

- THIS IS THE LAST QUARTER PAGE. THANK YOU SO MUCH FOR STICKING WITH ME ALL THIS WAY!

- ONE OF THE LETTERS I GOT SAID, "I'M STILL IN JUNIOR HIGH. IS IT TOO EARLY TO START WORKING TOWARD MY DREAM?"

  I DON'T THINK IT'S EVER TOO EARLY OR TOO LATE TO START GOING FOR YOUR DREAMS.

  I THINK IT'S WONDERFUL TO HAVE SOMETHING TO WORK TOWARD! PEOPLE WHO DON'T HAVE GOALS HAVE WAY TOO MANY OPTIONS. THAT'S JUST MY OPINION, BUT I REALLY BELIEVE IT. I HOPE ALL YOUR WONDERFUL DREAMS COME TRUE!!

- THIS VOLUME HAS EIGHT BONUS PAGES! I HOPE YOU LIKE THEM!!

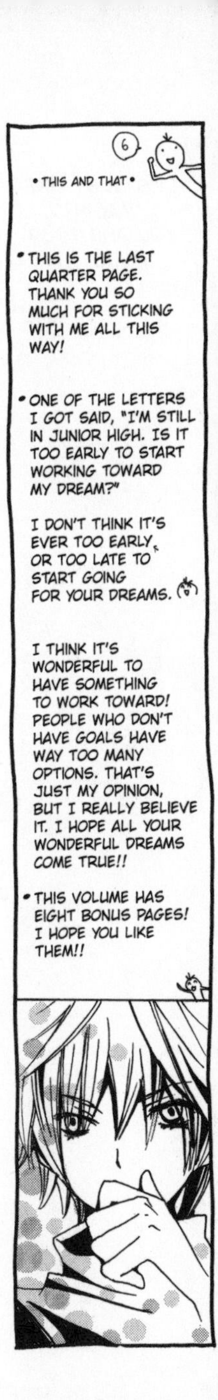

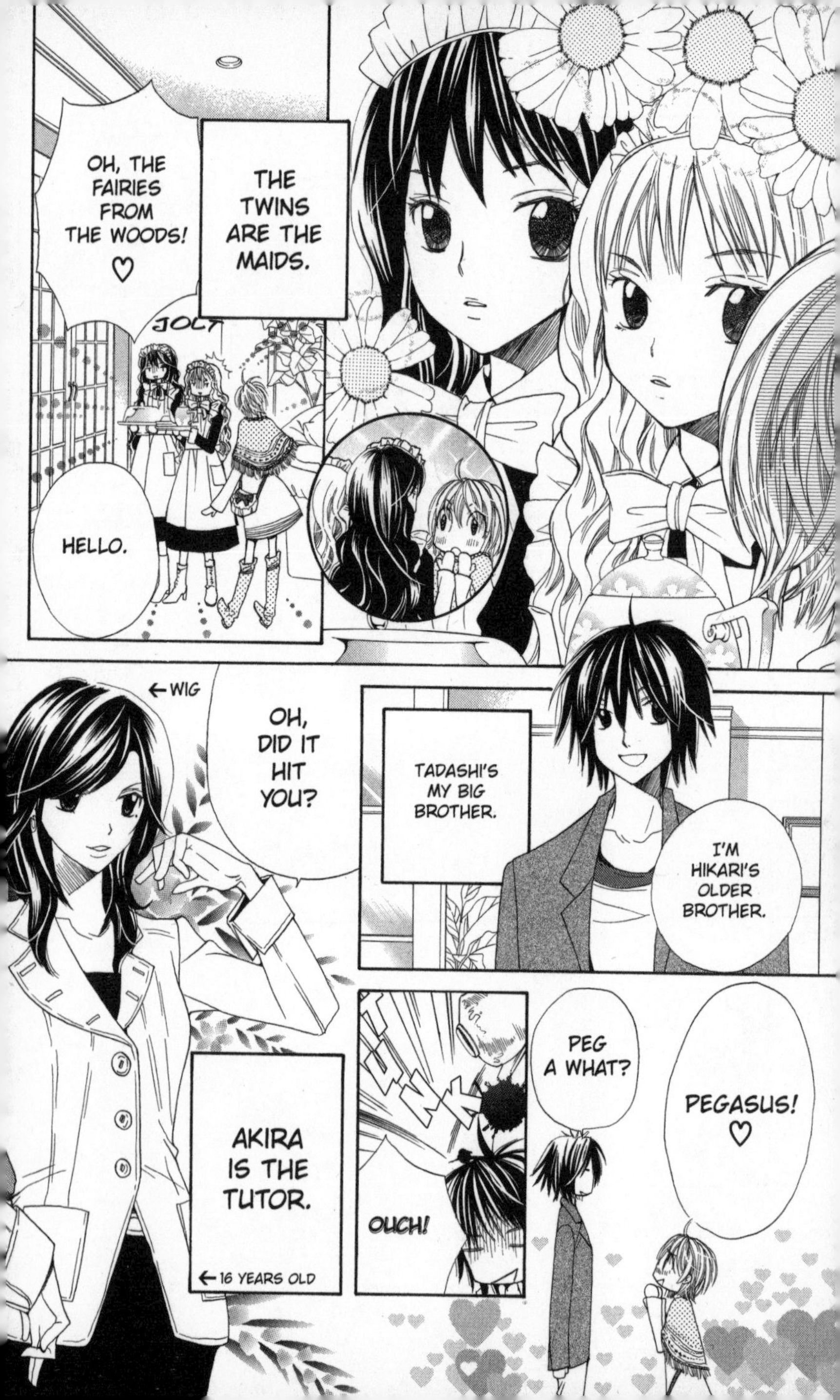
THE TWINS ARE THE MAIDS.
OH, THE FAIRIES FROM THE WOODS! ♡
JOLT
HELLO.
TADASHI'S MY BIG BROTHER.
I'M HIKARI'S OLDER BROTHER.
PEGASUS! ♡
PEG A WHAT?
OUCH!
← WIG
OH, DID IT HIT YOU?
AKIRA IS THE TUTOR.
← 16 YEARS OLD

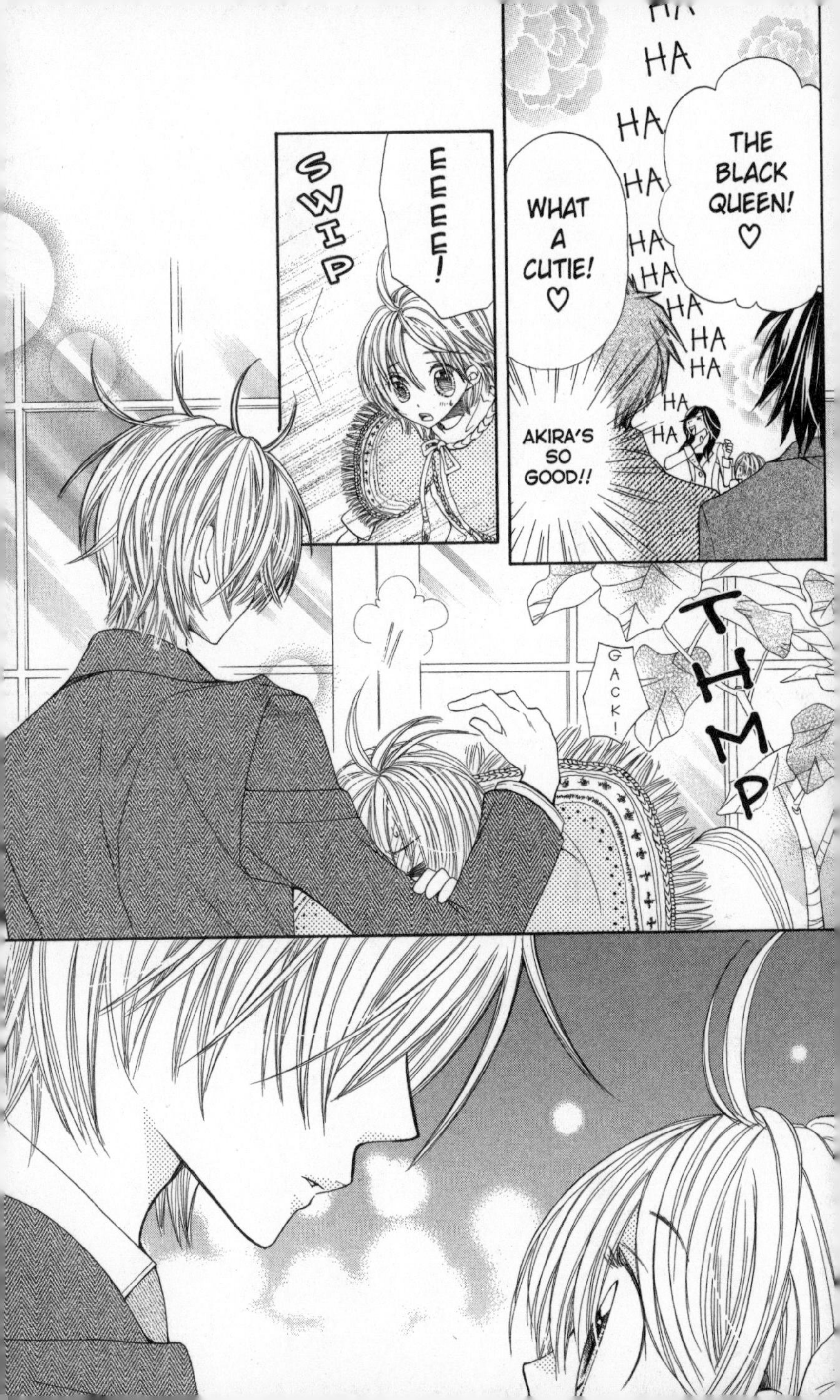

THE BLACK QUEEN! ♡
HA HA HA HA HA HA HA HA HA HA
WHAT A CUTIE! ♡
AKIRA'S SO GOOD!!
EEEE!
SWIP
THMP
GACK!

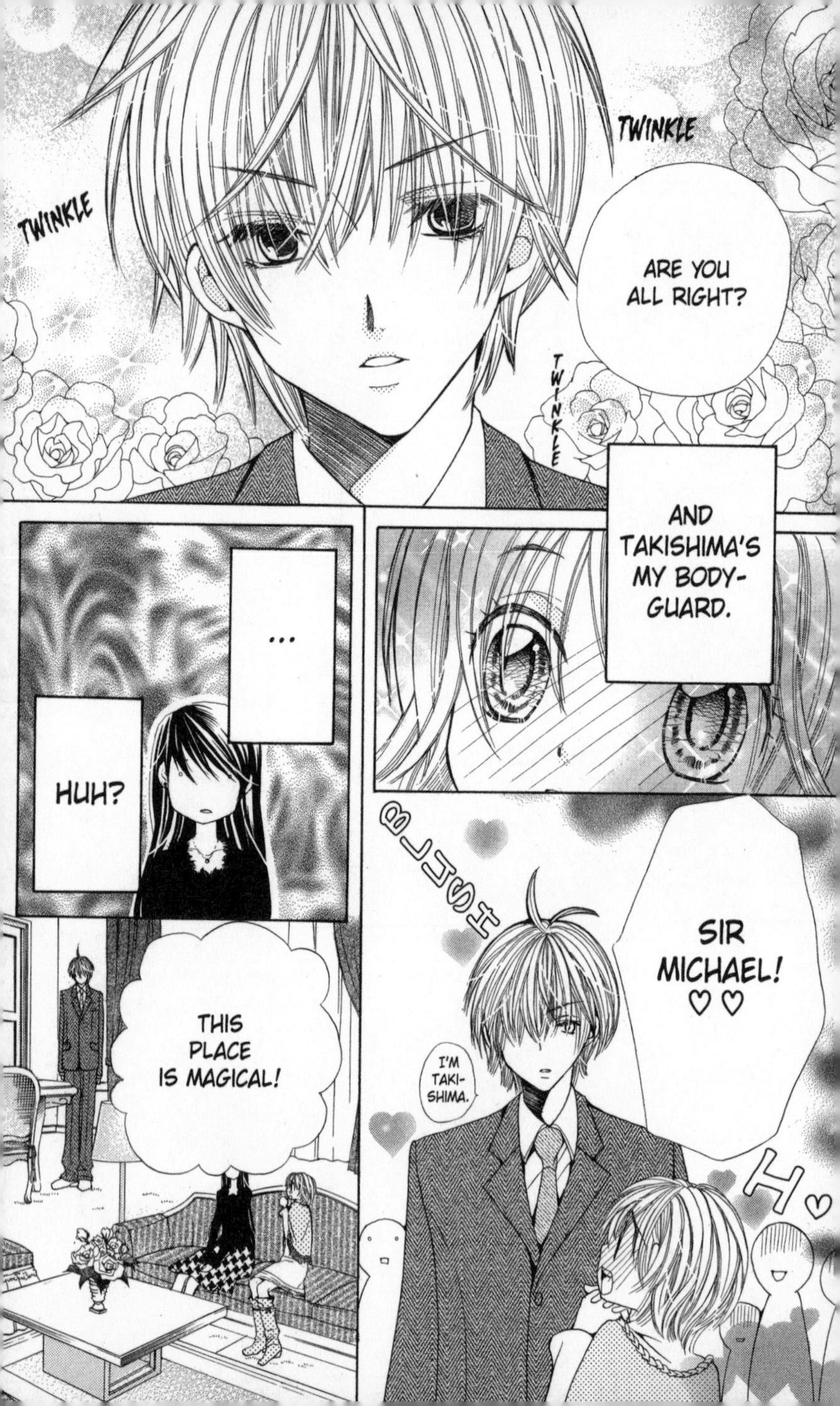

TWINKLE
ARE YOU ALL RIGHT?
TWINKLE
TWINKLE
AND TAKISHIMA'S MY BODY-GUARD.
...
HUH?
SIR MICHAEL! ♡ ♡
I'M TAKI-SHIMA.
THIS PLACE IS MAGICAL!

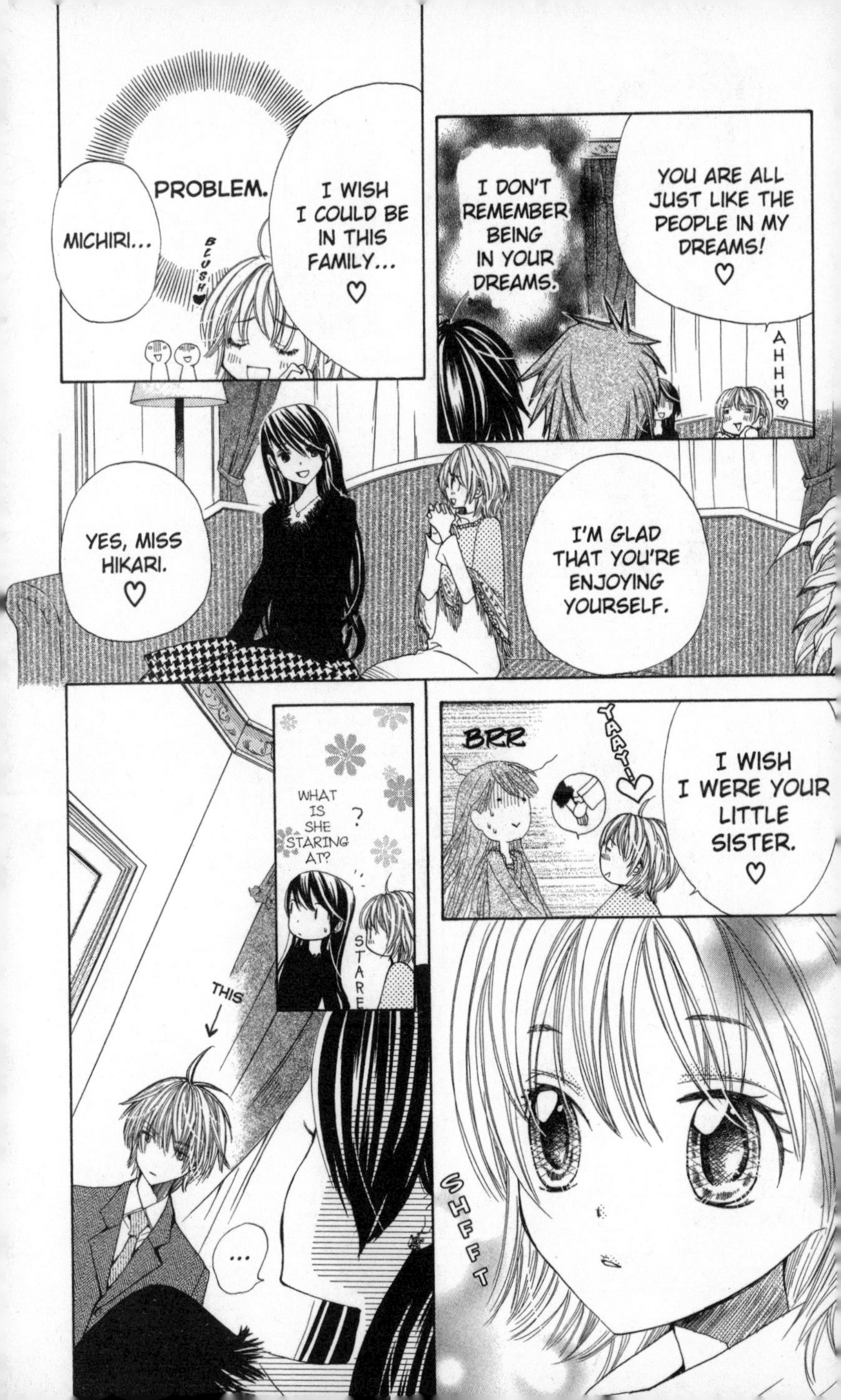
YOU ARE ALL JUST LIKE THE PEOPLE IN MY DREAMS! ♡
AHHH♡
I DON'T REMEMBER BEING IN YOUR DREAMS.
I WISH I COULD BE IN THIS FAMILY... ♡
PROBLEM.
BLUSH♥
MICHIRI...
I'M GLAD THAT YOU'RE ENJOYING YOURSELF.
YES, MISS HIKARI. ♡
I WISH I WERE YOUR LITTLE SISTER. ♡
YAAAY!♥
BRR
WHAT IS SHE STARING AT?
STARE
SHFFT
THIS
...

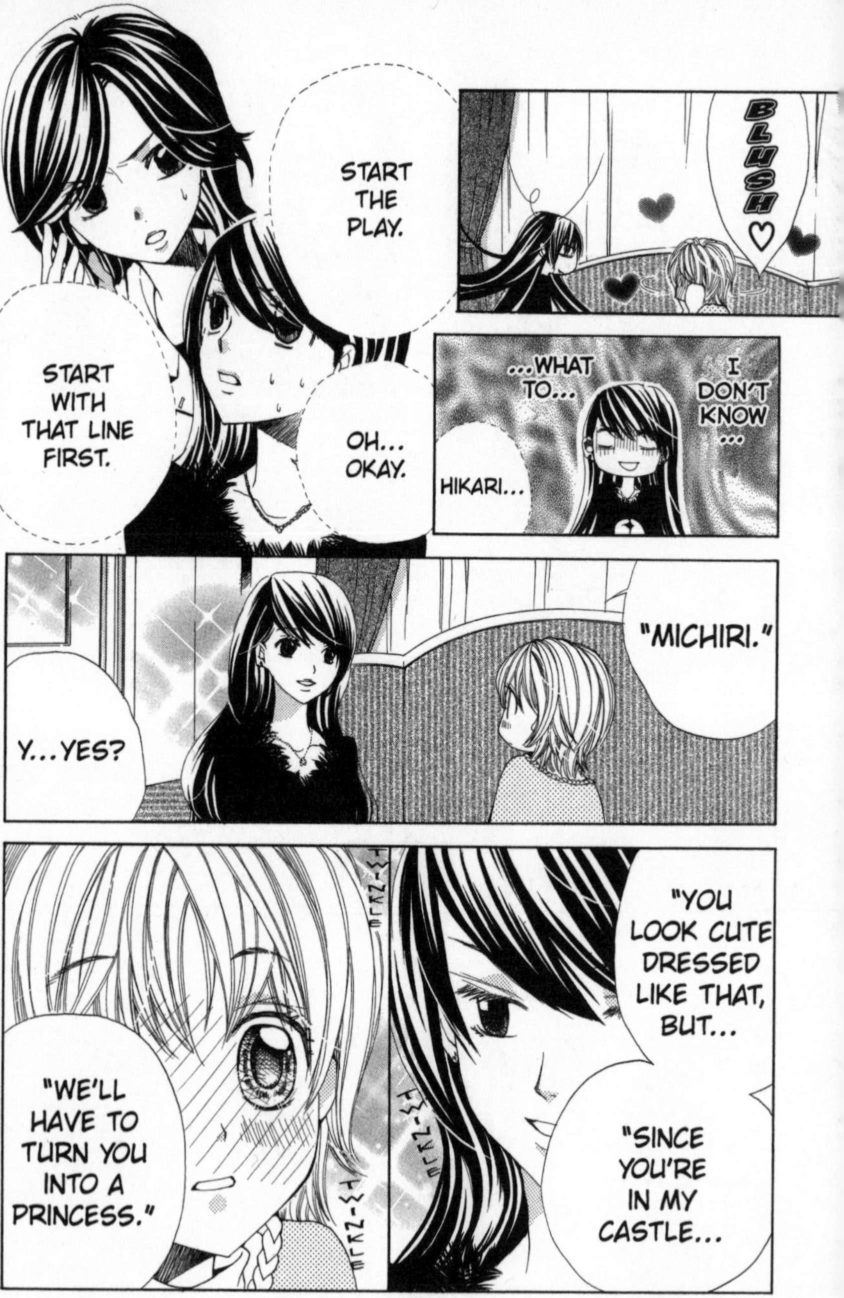
BLUSH ♡
I DON'T KNOW...
...WHAT TO...
HIKARI...
START THE PLAY.
START WITH THAT LINE FIRST.
OH... OKAY.
"MICHIRI."
Y...YES?
"YOU LOOK CUTE DRESSED LIKE THAT, BUT...
"SINCE YOU'RE IN MY CASTLE...
TWINKLE
TWINKLE
TWINKLE
"WE'LL HAVE TO TURN YOU INTO A PRINCESS."

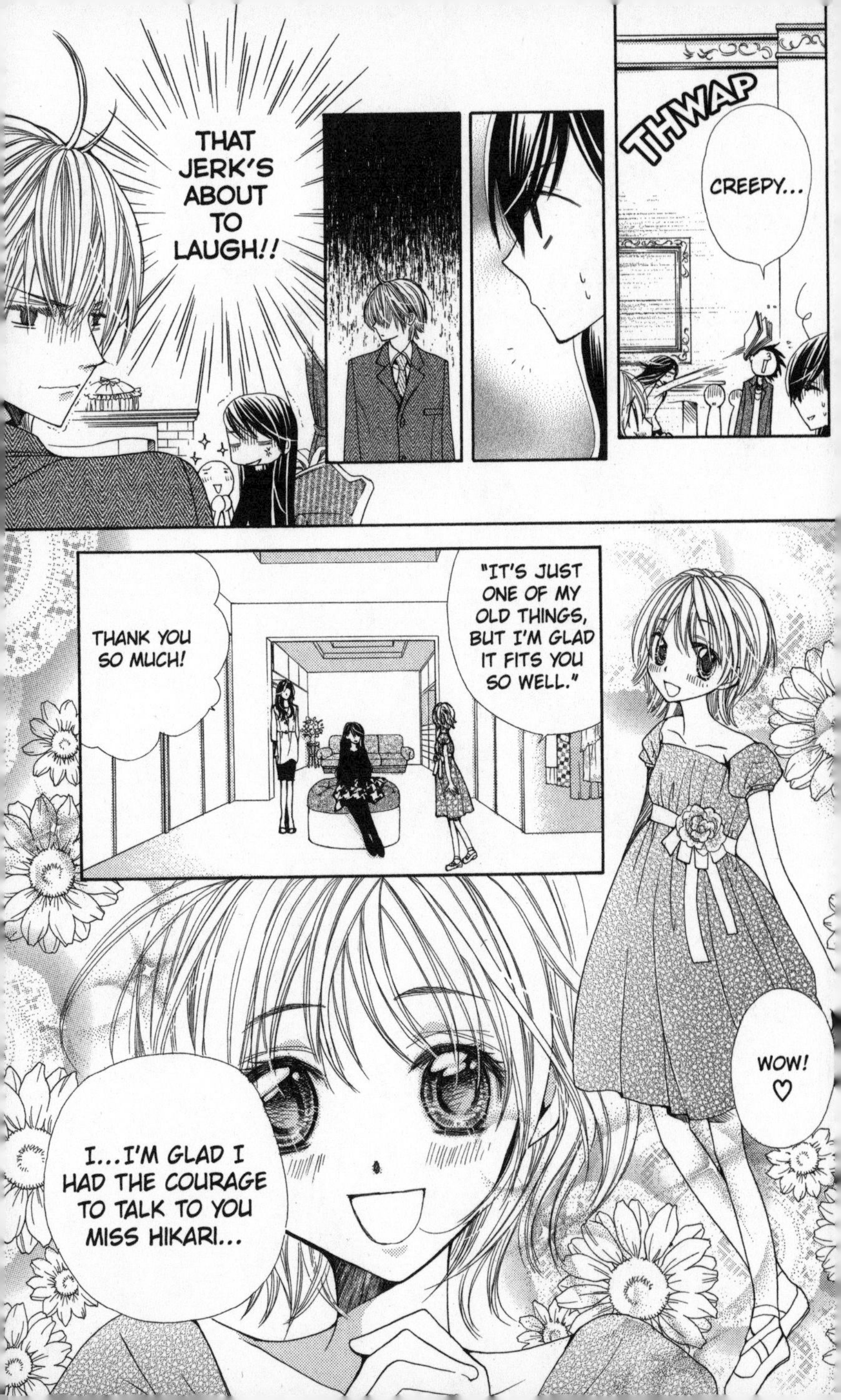
THWAP
CREEPY...
THAT JERK'S ABOUT TO LAUGH!!
"IT'S JUST ONE OF MY OLD THINGS, BUT I'M GLAD IT FITS YOU SO WELL."
THANK YOU SO MUCH!
WOW! ♥
I...I'M GLAD I HAD THE COURAGE TO TALK TO YOU MISS HIKARI...

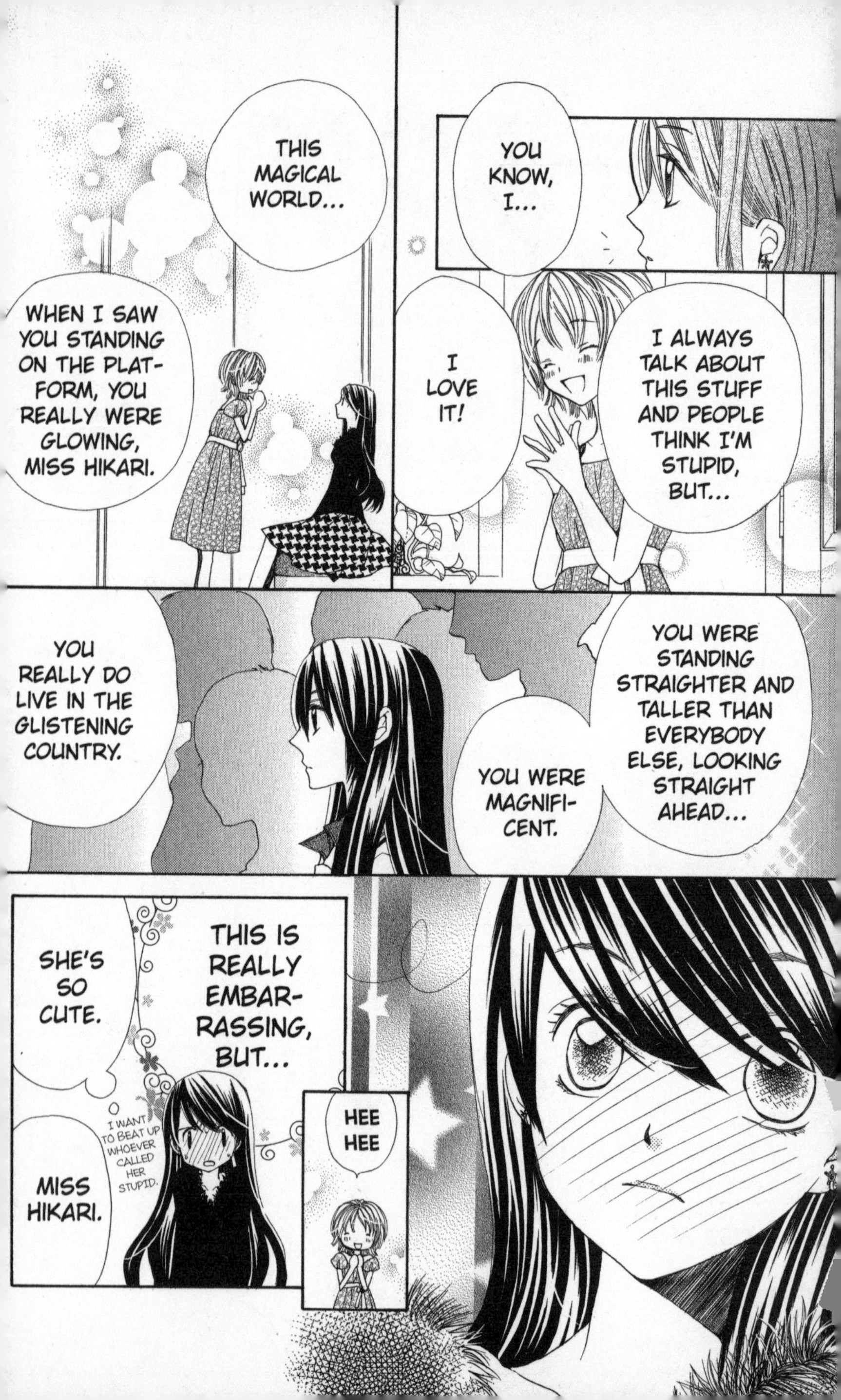
YOU KNOW, I...
I ALWAYS TALK ABOUT THIS STUFF AND PEOPLE THINK I'M STUPID, BUT...
I LOVE IT!
THIS MAGICAL WORLD...
WHEN I SAW YOU STANDING ON THE PLAT-FORM, YOU REALLY WERE GLOWING, MISS HIKARI.
YOU WERE STANDING STRAIGHTER AND TALLER THAN EVERYBODY ELSE, LOOKING STRAIGHT AHEAD...
YOU WERE MAGNIFI-CENT.
YOU REALLY DO LIVE IN THE GLISTENING COUNTRY.
HEE HEE
THIS IS REALLY EMBAR-RASSING, BUT...
SHE'S SO CUTE.
I WANT TO BEAT UP WHOEVER CALLED HER STUPID.
MISS HIKARI.

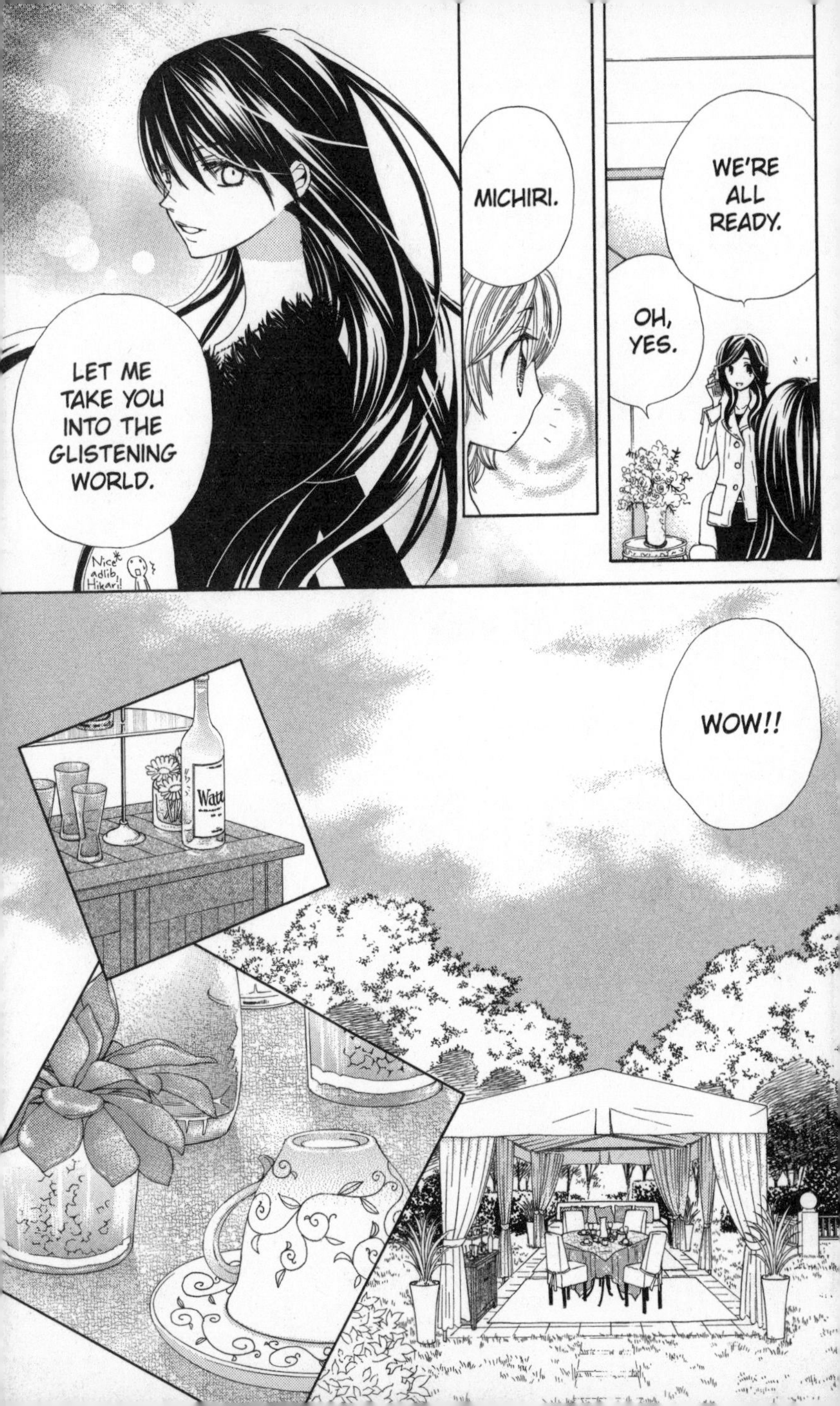
WE'RE ALL READY.
OH, YES.
MICHIRI.
LET ME TAKE YOU INTO THE GLISTENING WORLD.
Nice adlib, Hikari!
WOW!!

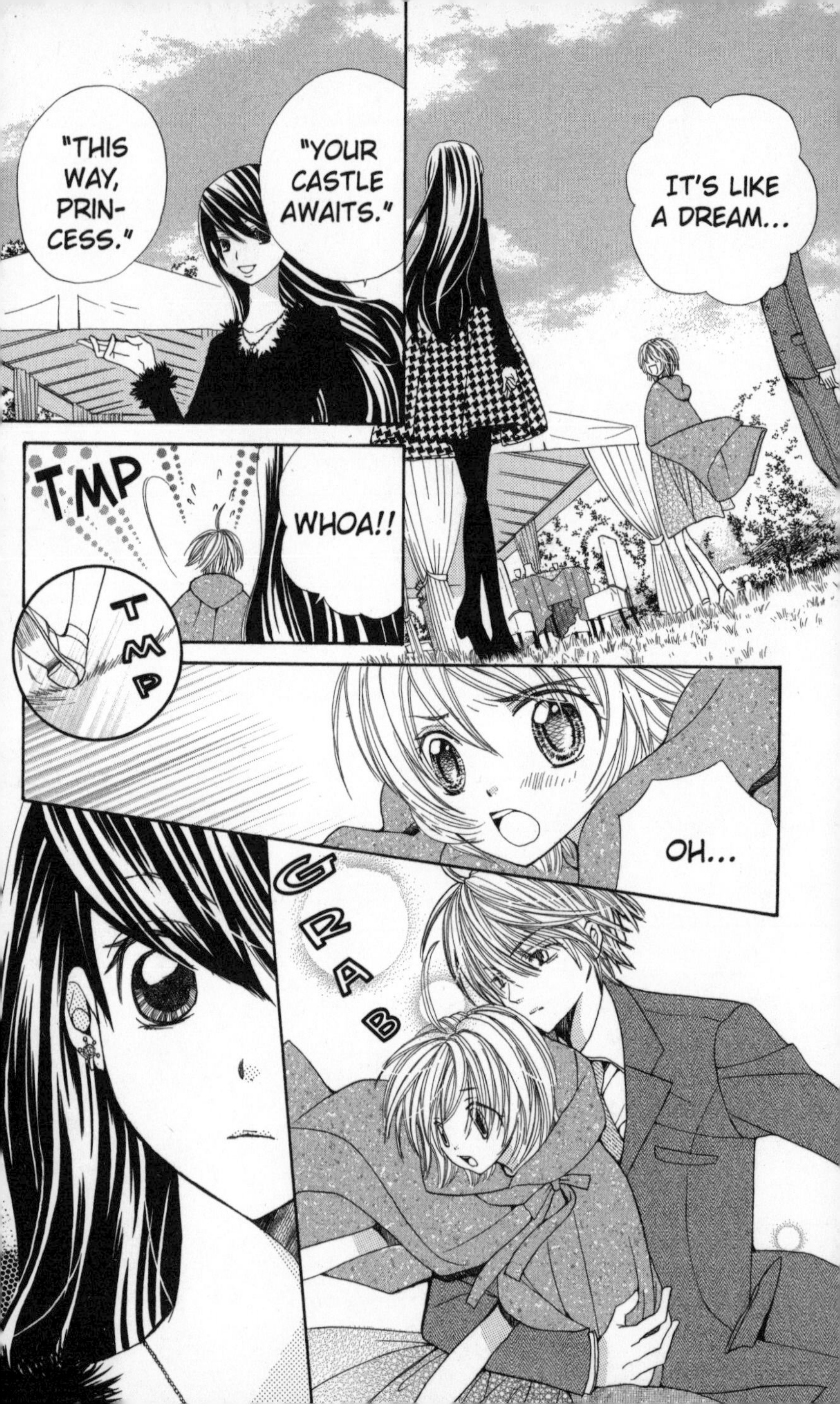
IT'S LIKE A DREAM...
"YOUR CASTLE AWAITS."
"THIS WAY, PRINCESS."
WHOA!!
TMP
TMP
OH...
GRAB

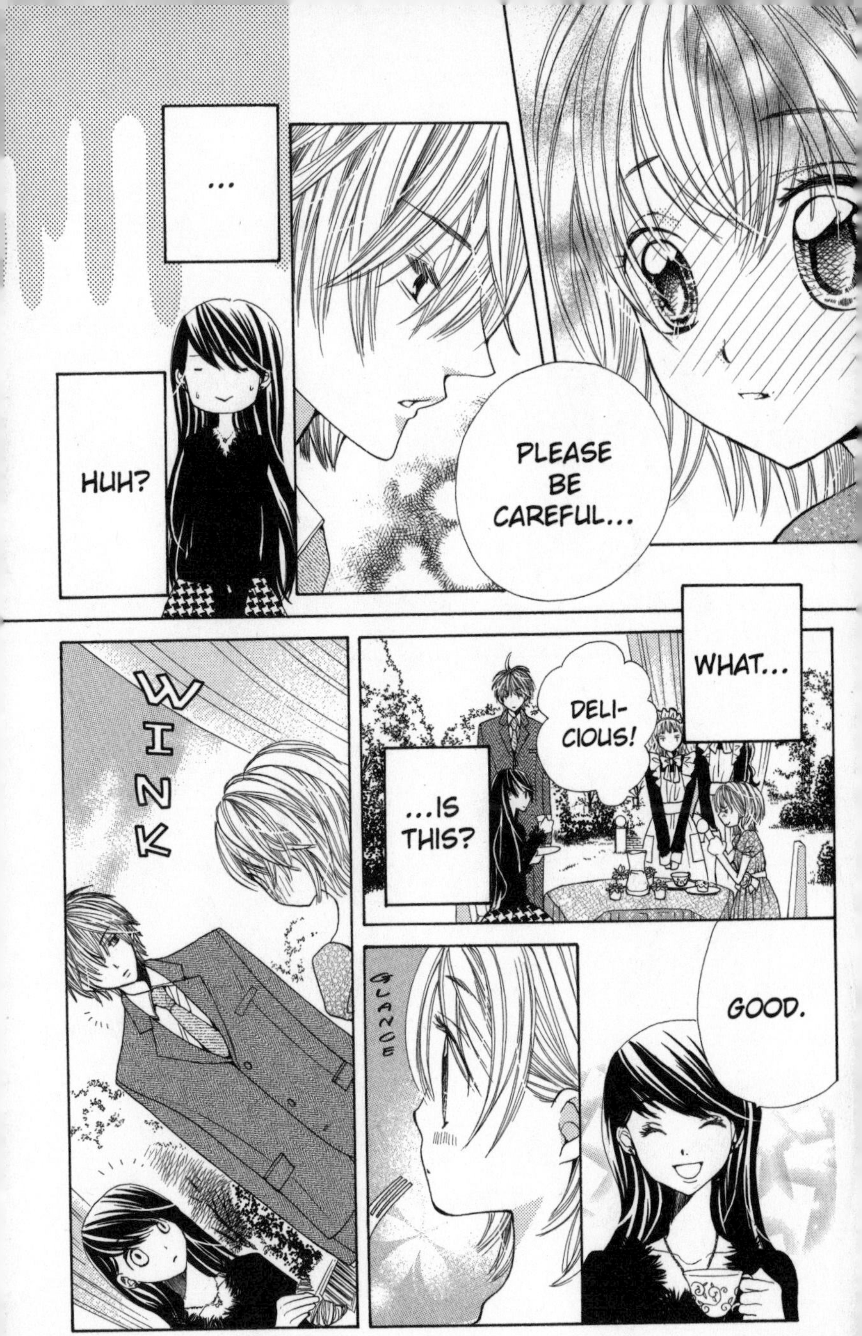
PLEASE BE CAREFUL...
...
HUH?
WHAT...
DELICIOUS!
...IS THIS?
GOOD.
GLANCE
WINK

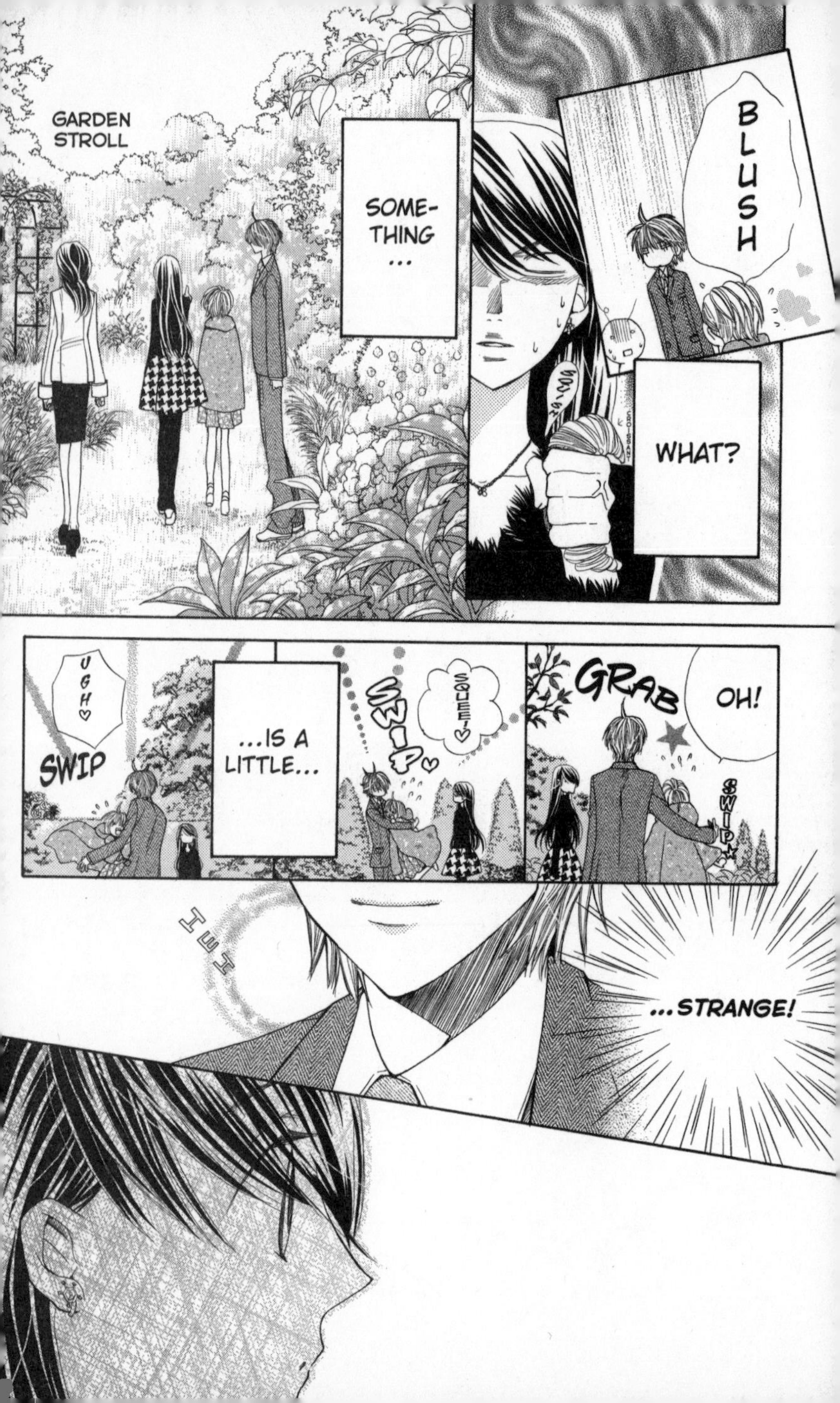
BLUSH
WHAT?
CROISSANT
SOME-THING...
GARDEN STROLL
OH!
GRAB
SWIP
SQUEE!♡
SWIP♡
...IS A LITTLE...
UGH♡
SWIP
...STRANGE!

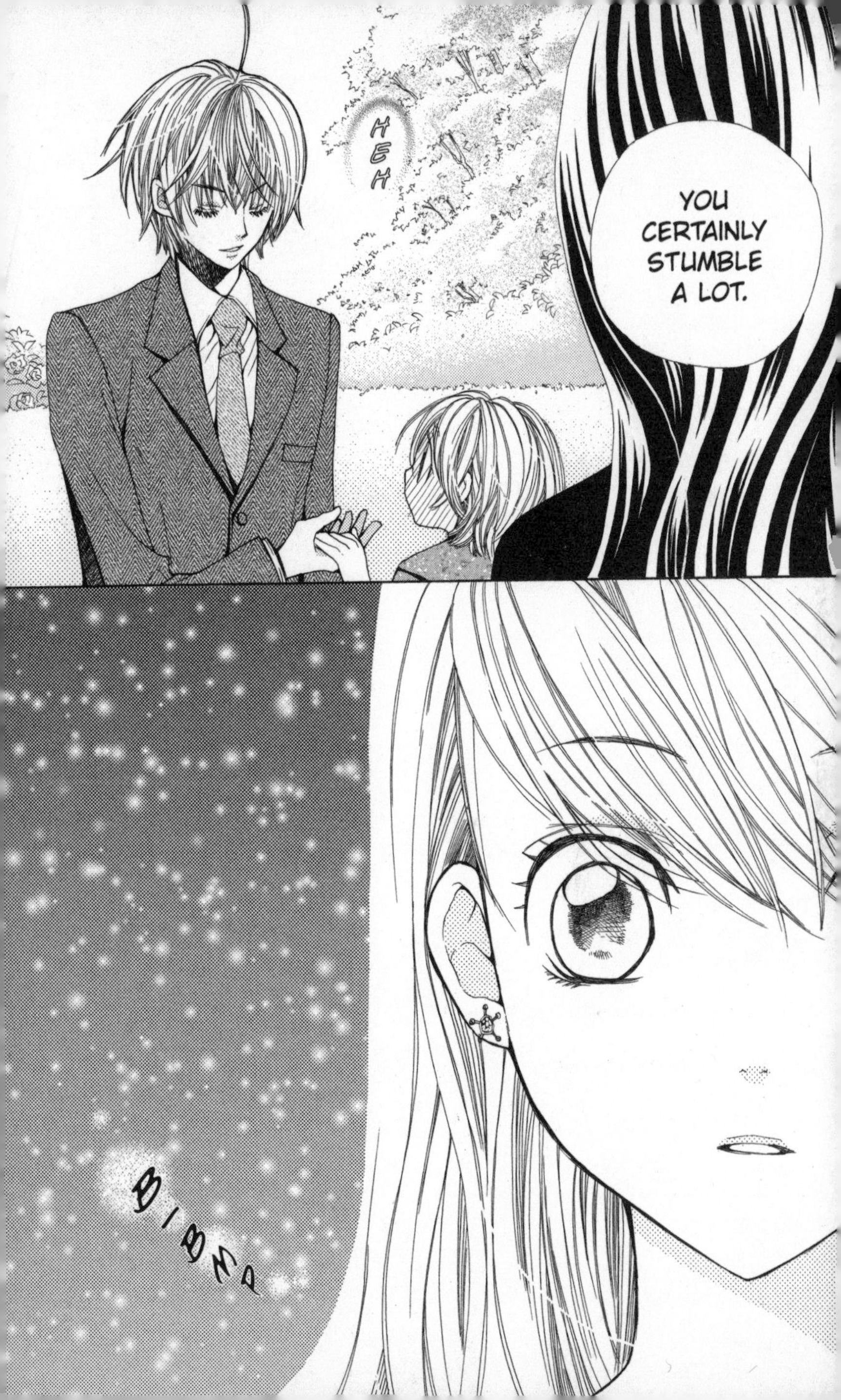
YOU CERTAINLY STUMBLE A LOT.
HEH
BIBAA

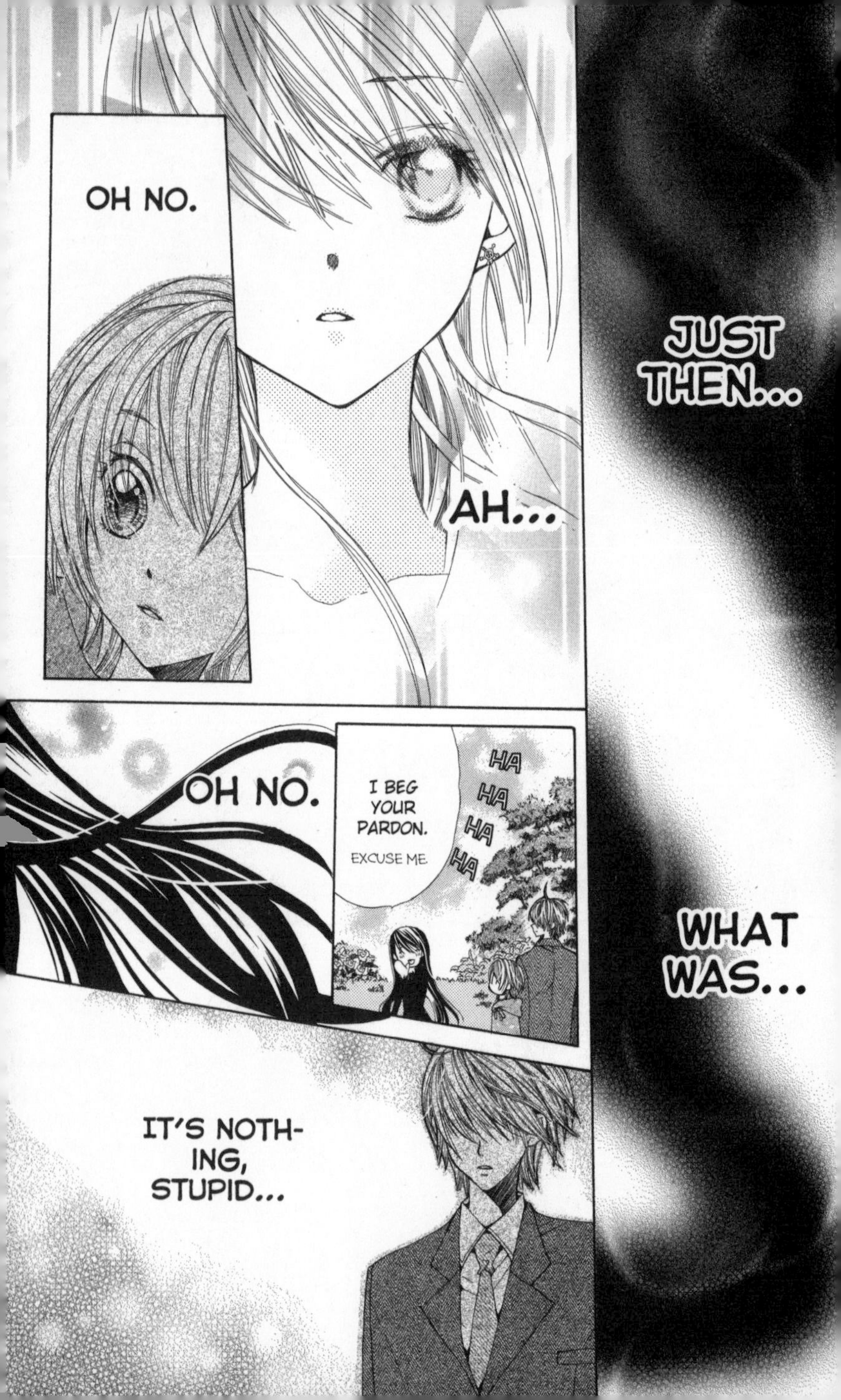
JUST THEN...
WHAT WAS...
OH NO.
AH...
HA HA HA HA
I BEG YOUR PARDON.
EXCUSE ME.
OH NO.
IT'S NOTH-ING, STUPID...

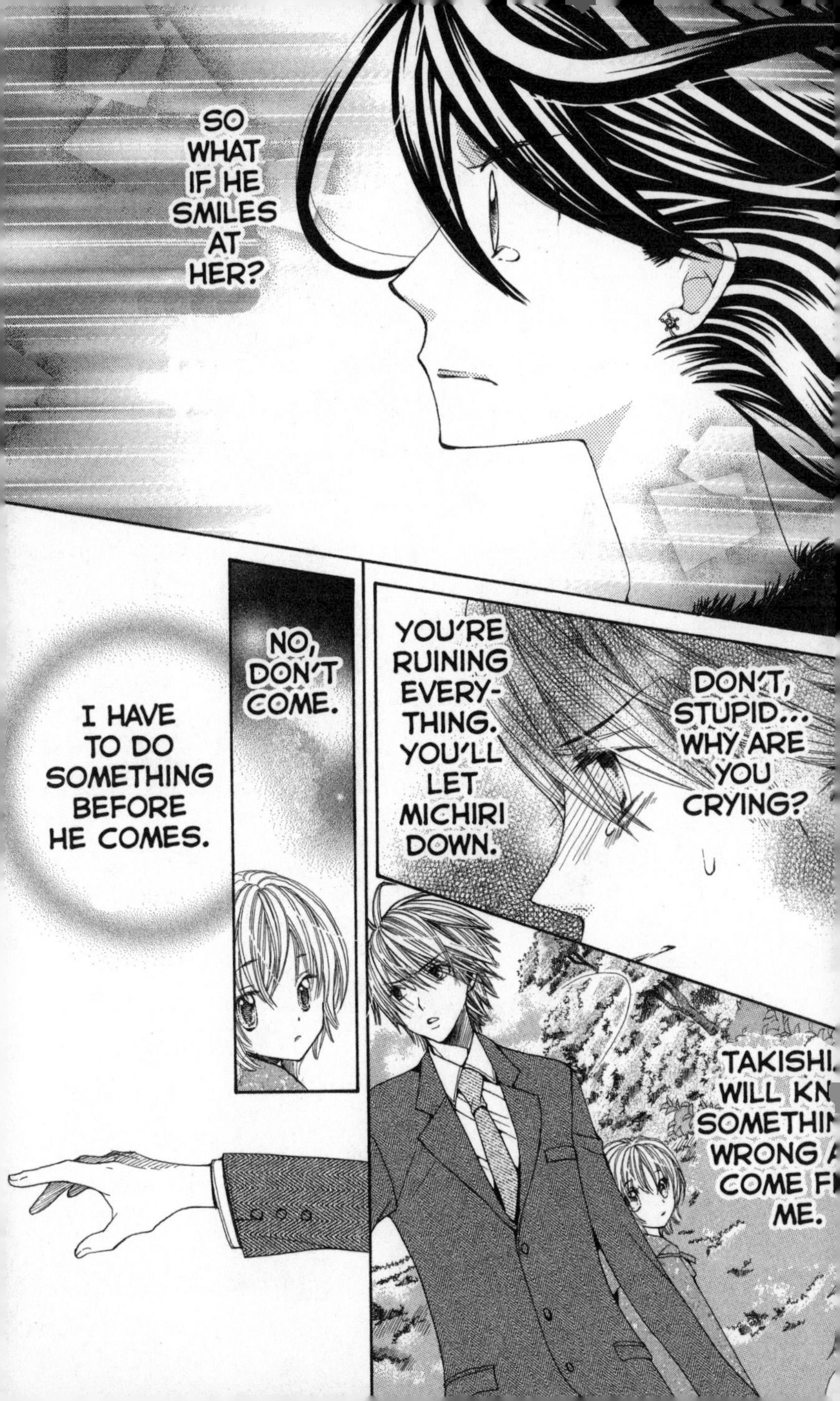
SO WHAT IF HE SMILES AT HER?
DON'T, STUPID... WHY ARE YOU CRYING?
YOU'RE RUINING EVERY-THING. YOU'LL LET MICHIRI DOWN.
TAKISHI. WILL KN SOMETHIN WRONG A COME F ME.
NO, DON'T COME.
I HAVE TO DO SOMETHING BEFORE HE COMES.

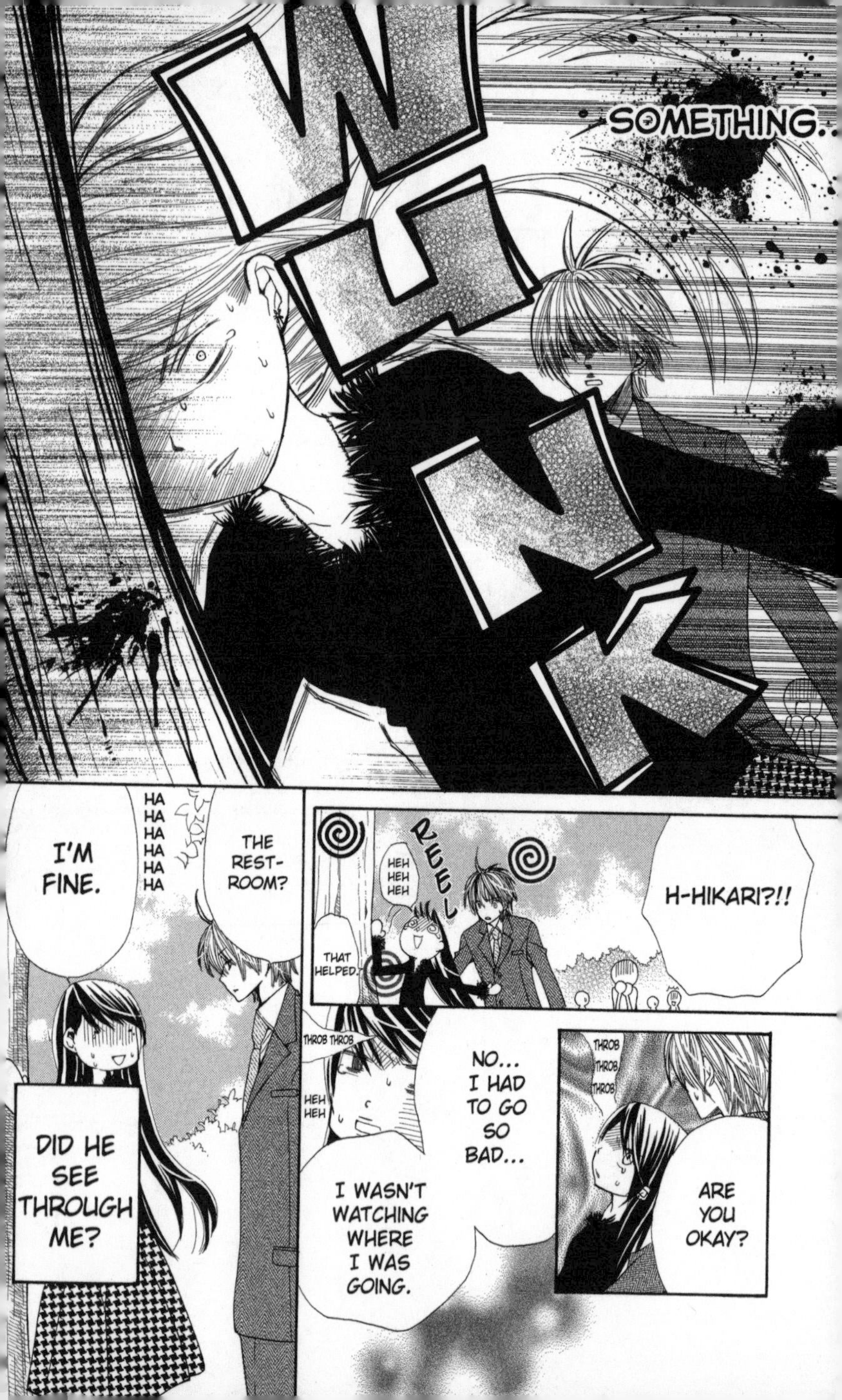
SOMETHING..
WHUNK
H-HIKARI?!!
REEL
HEH HEH HEH
THAT HELPED.
THROB THROB THROB
ARE YOU OKAY?
NO... I HAD TO GO SO BAD...
THROB THROB
HEH HEH
I WASN'T WATCHING WHERE I WAS GOING.
THE REST-ROOM?
HA HA HA HA HA HA
I'M FINE.
DID HE SEE THROUGH ME?

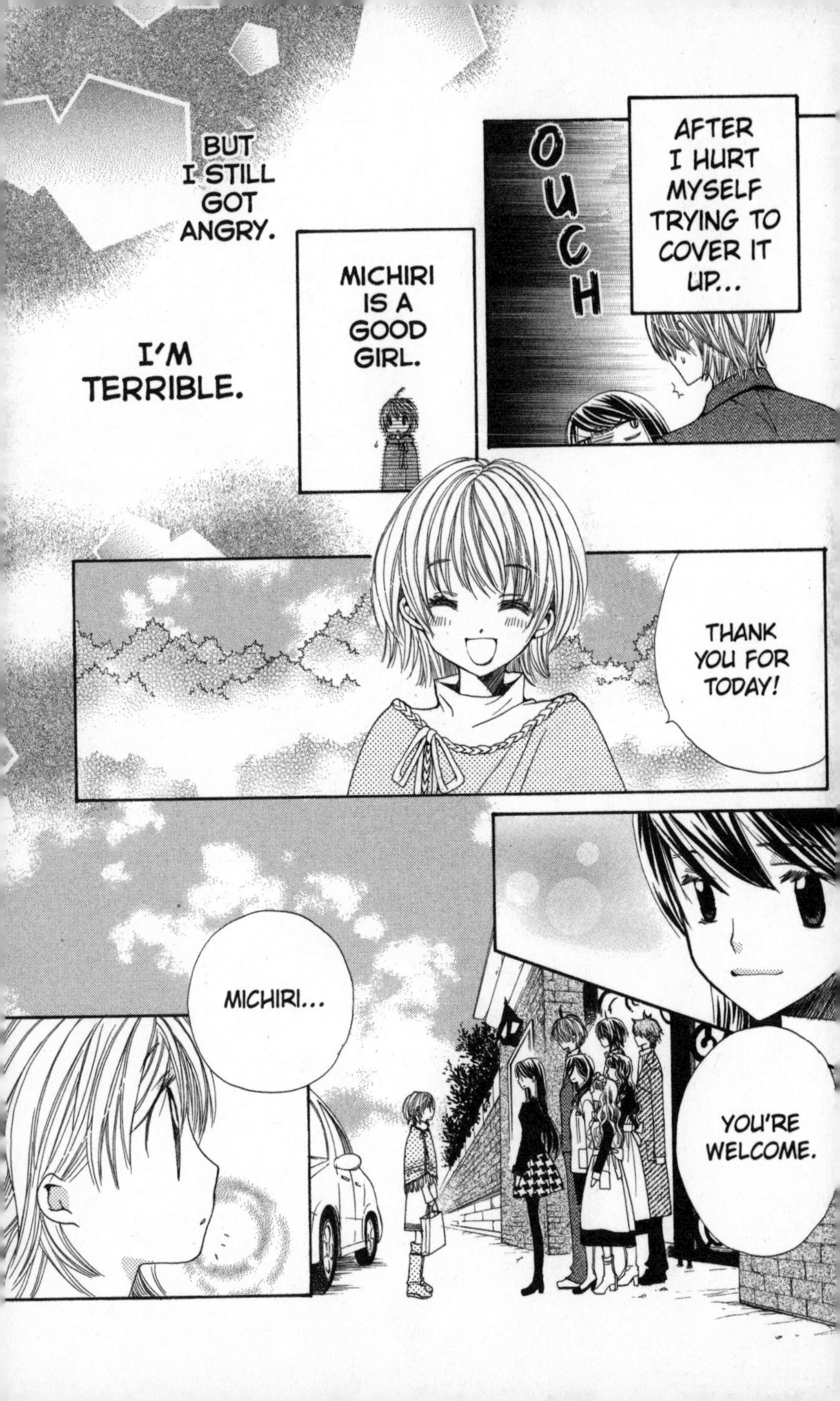
AFTER I HURT MYSELF TRYING TO COVER IT UP...
OUCH
MICHIRI IS A GOOD GIRL.
BUT I STILL GOT ANGRY.
I'M TERRIBLE.
THANK YOU FOR TODAY!
YOU'RE WELCOME.
MICHIRI...

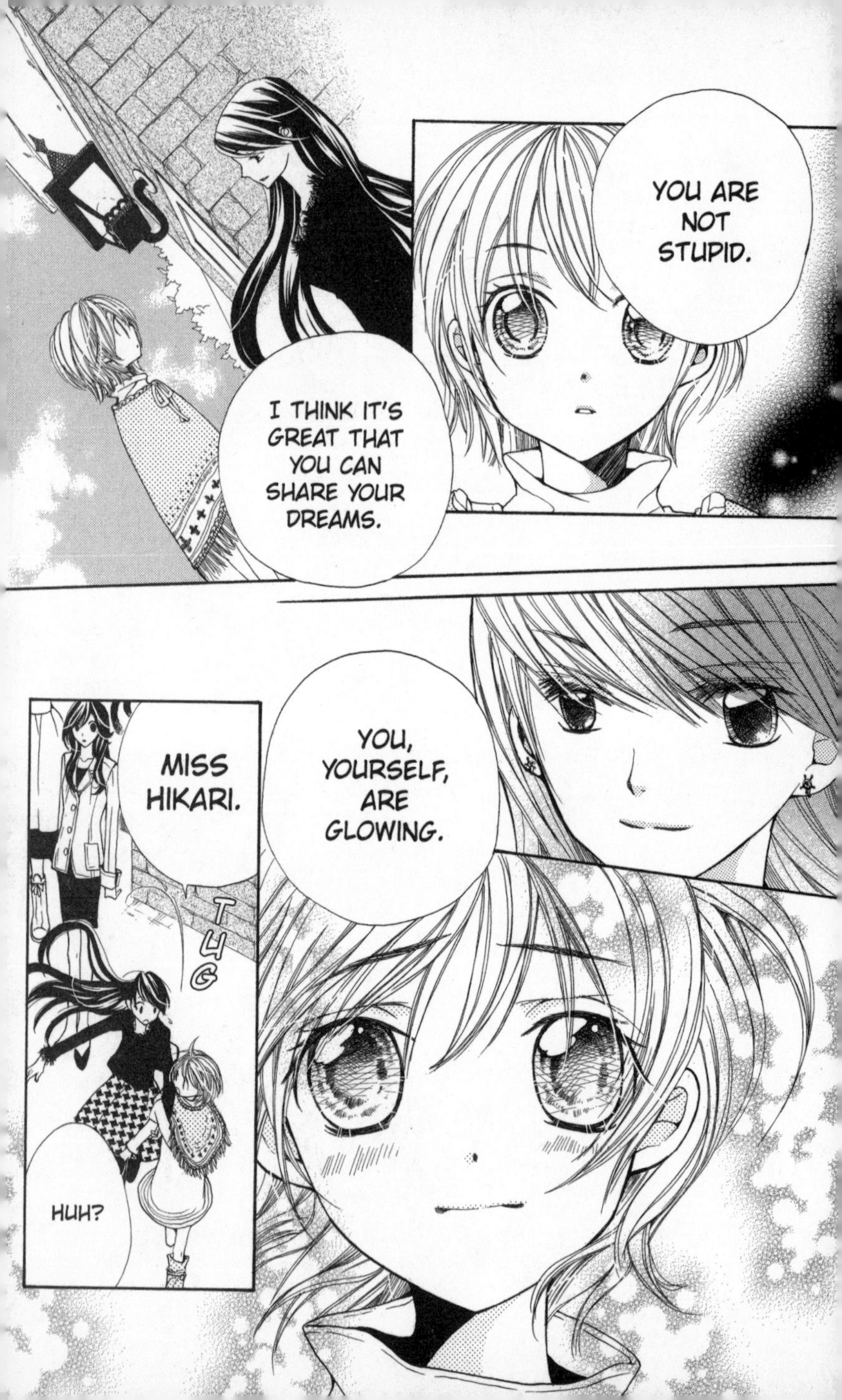
YOU ARE NOT STUPID.
I THINK IT'S GREAT THAT YOU CAN SHARE YOUR DREAMS.
YOU, YOURSELF, ARE GLOWING.
MISS HIKARI.
TUG
HUH?

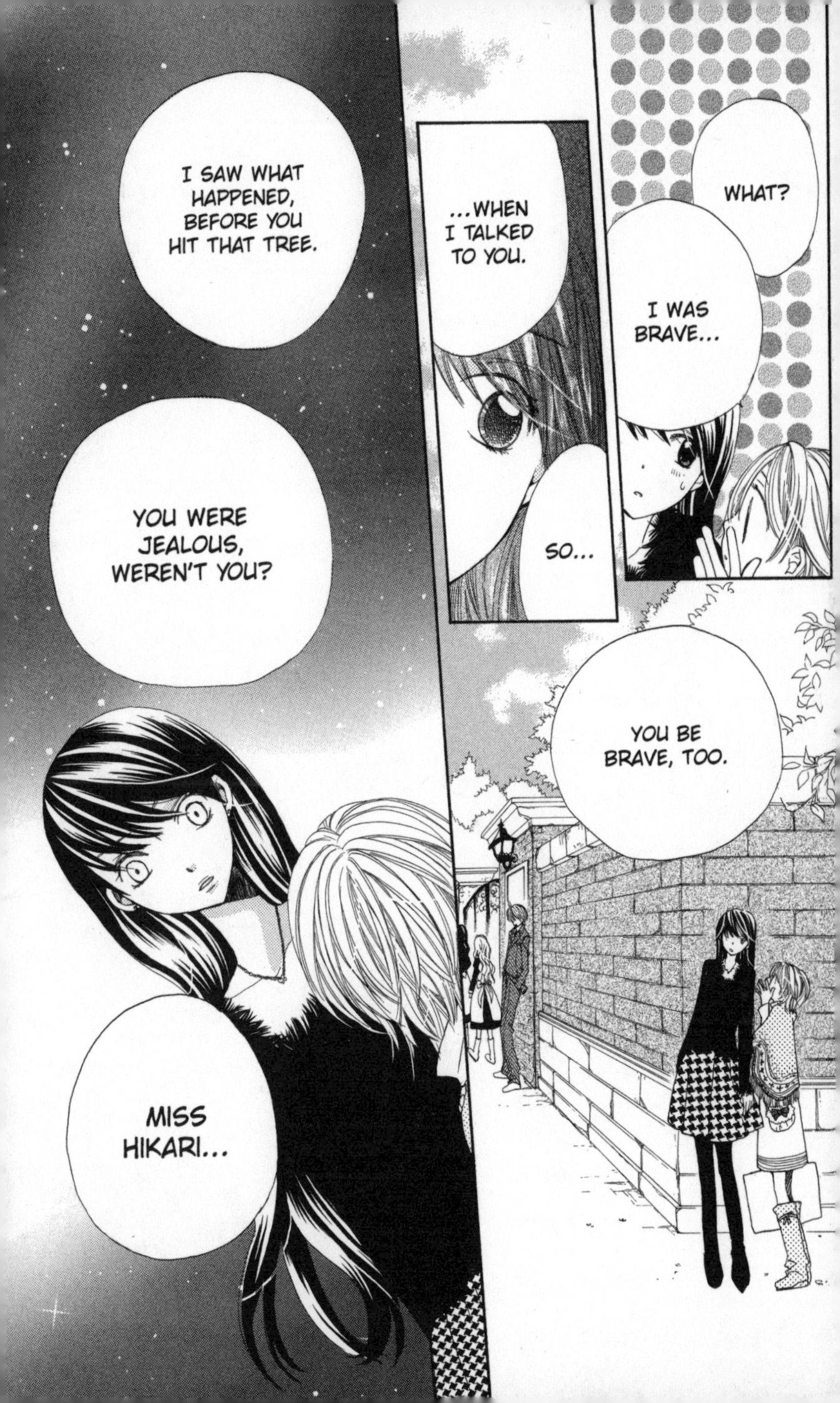
WHAT?
I WAS BRAVE...
...WHEN I TALKED TO YOU.
SO...
YOU BE BRAVE, TOO.
I SAW WHAT HAPPENED, BEFORE YOU HIT THAT TREE.
YOU WERE JEALOUS, WEREN'T YOU?
MISS HIKARI...

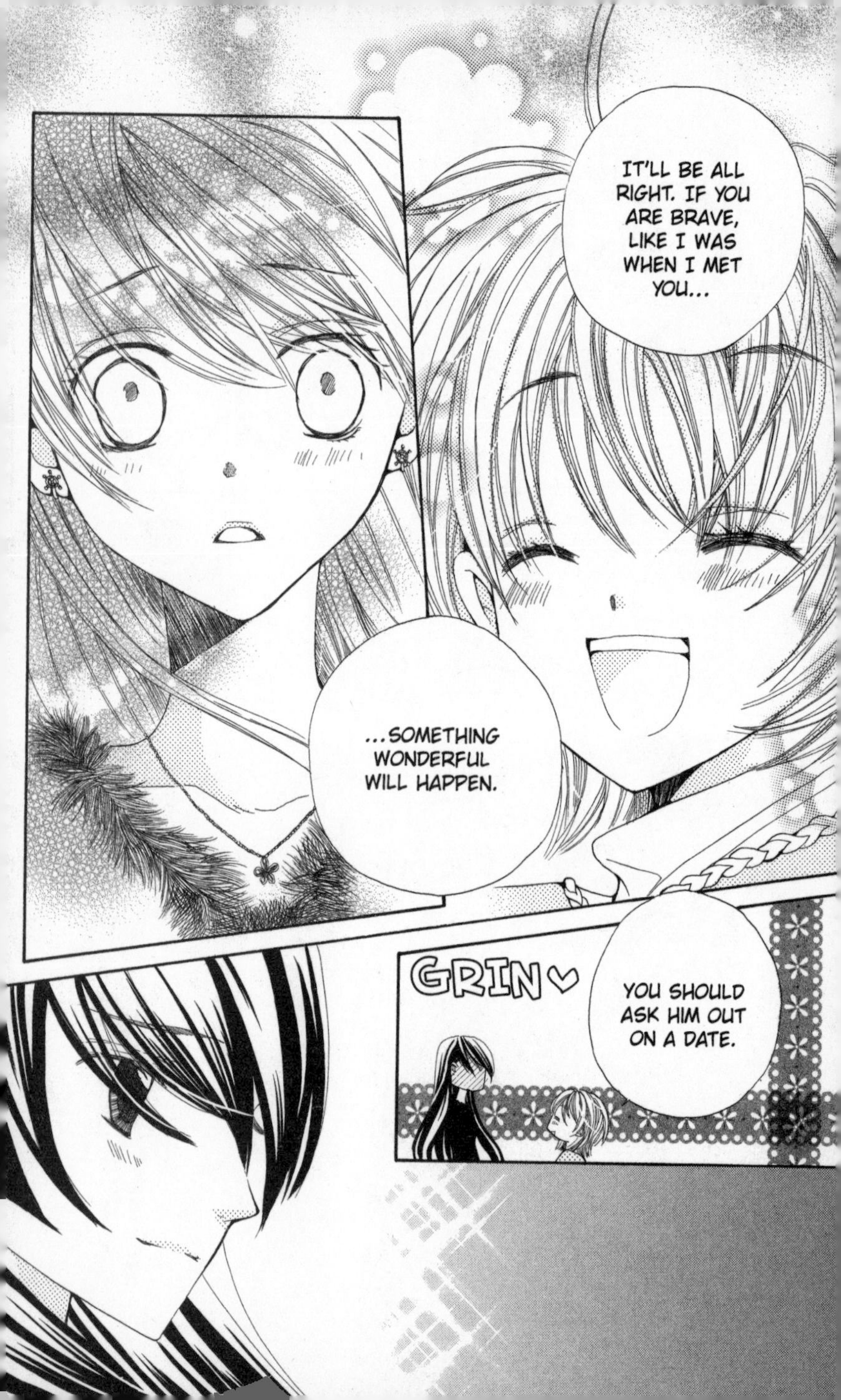
IT'LL BE ALL RIGHT. IF YOU ARE BRAVE, LIKE I WAS WHEN I MET YOU...
...SOMETHING WONDERFUL WILL HAPPEN.
YOU SHOULD ASK HIM OUT ON A DATE.
GRIN♥

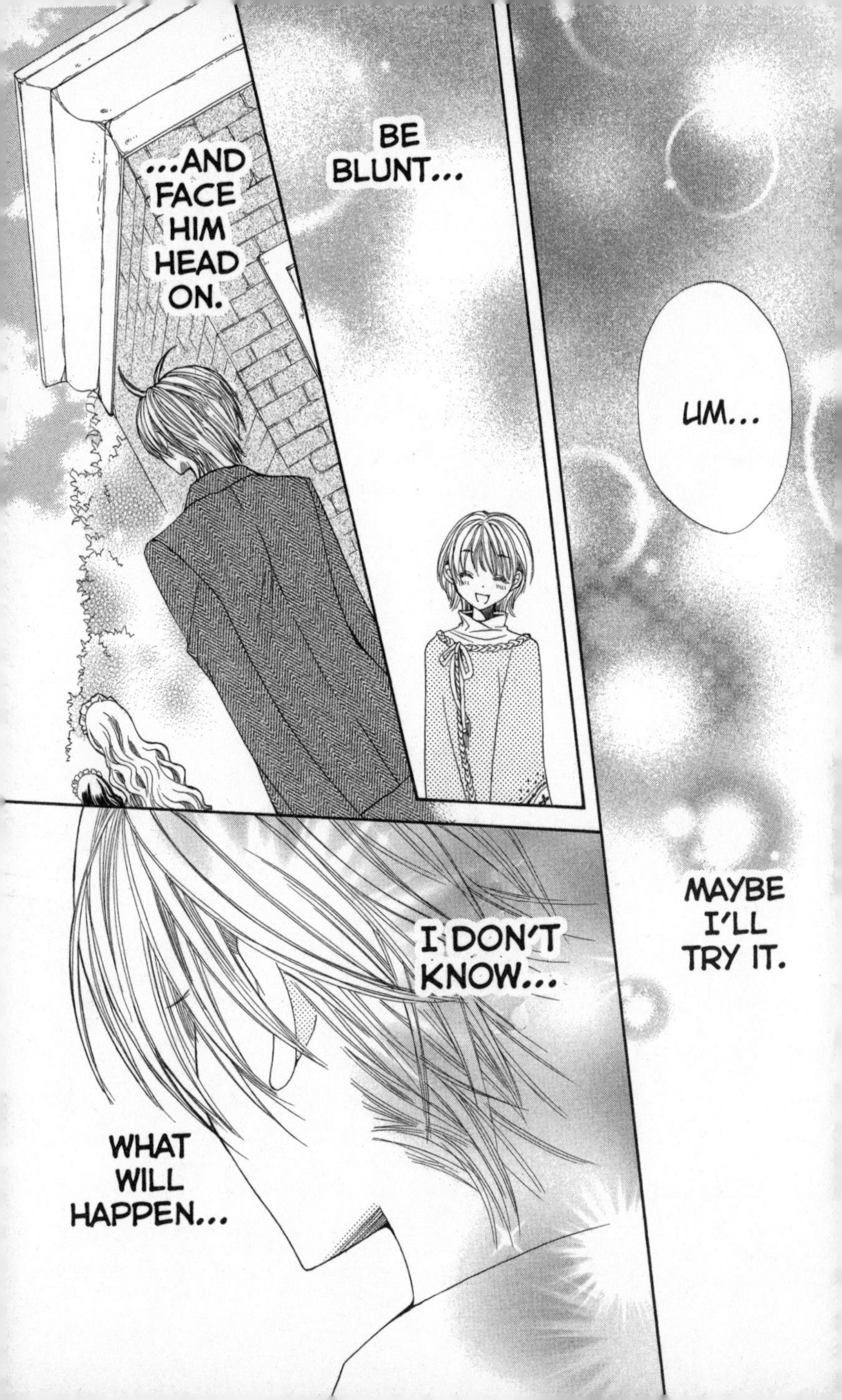
UM...
BE BLUNT...
...AND FACE HIM HEAD ON.
MAYBE I'LL TRY IT.
I DON'T KNOW...
WHAT WILL HAPPEN...

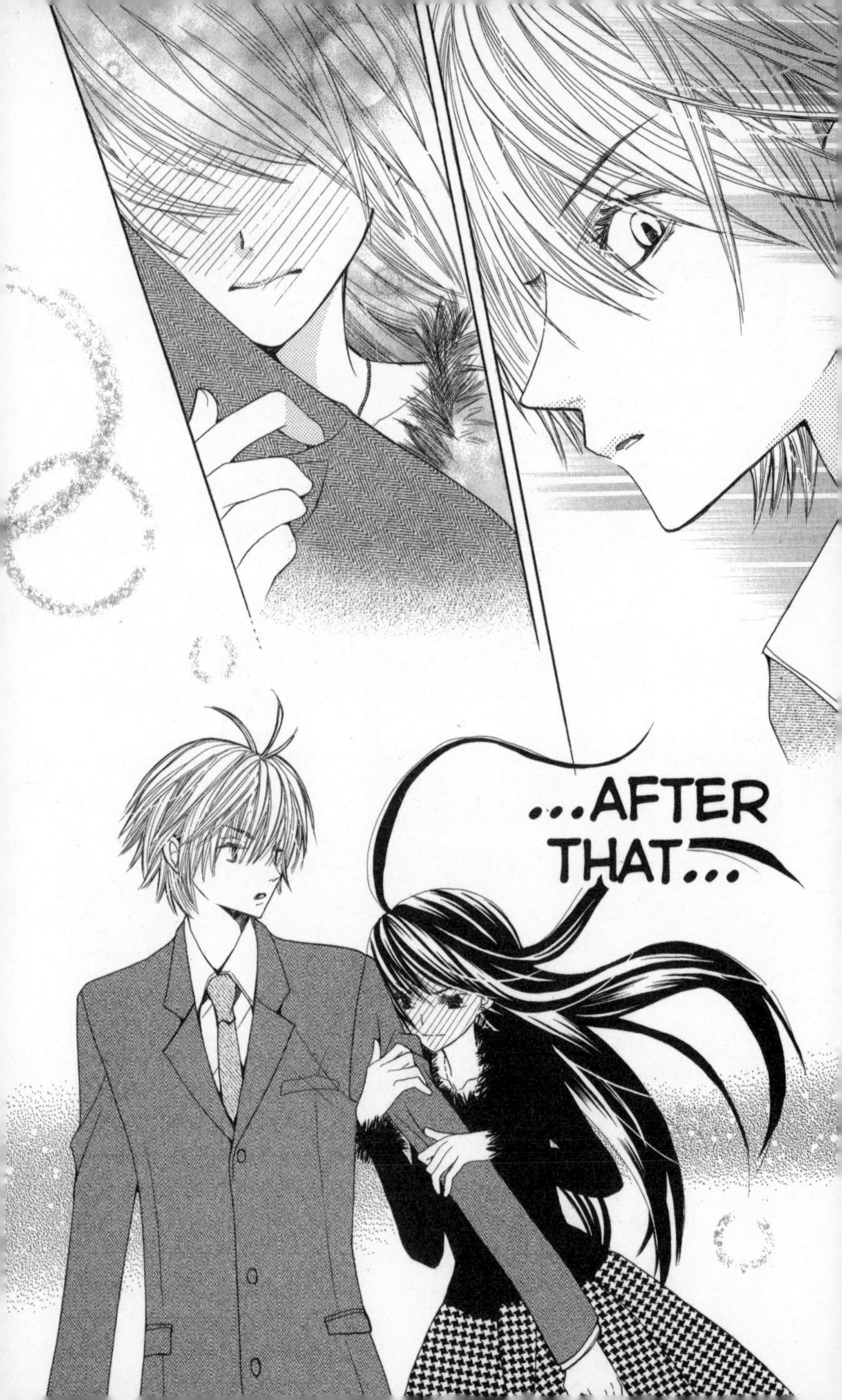
...AFTER THAT...

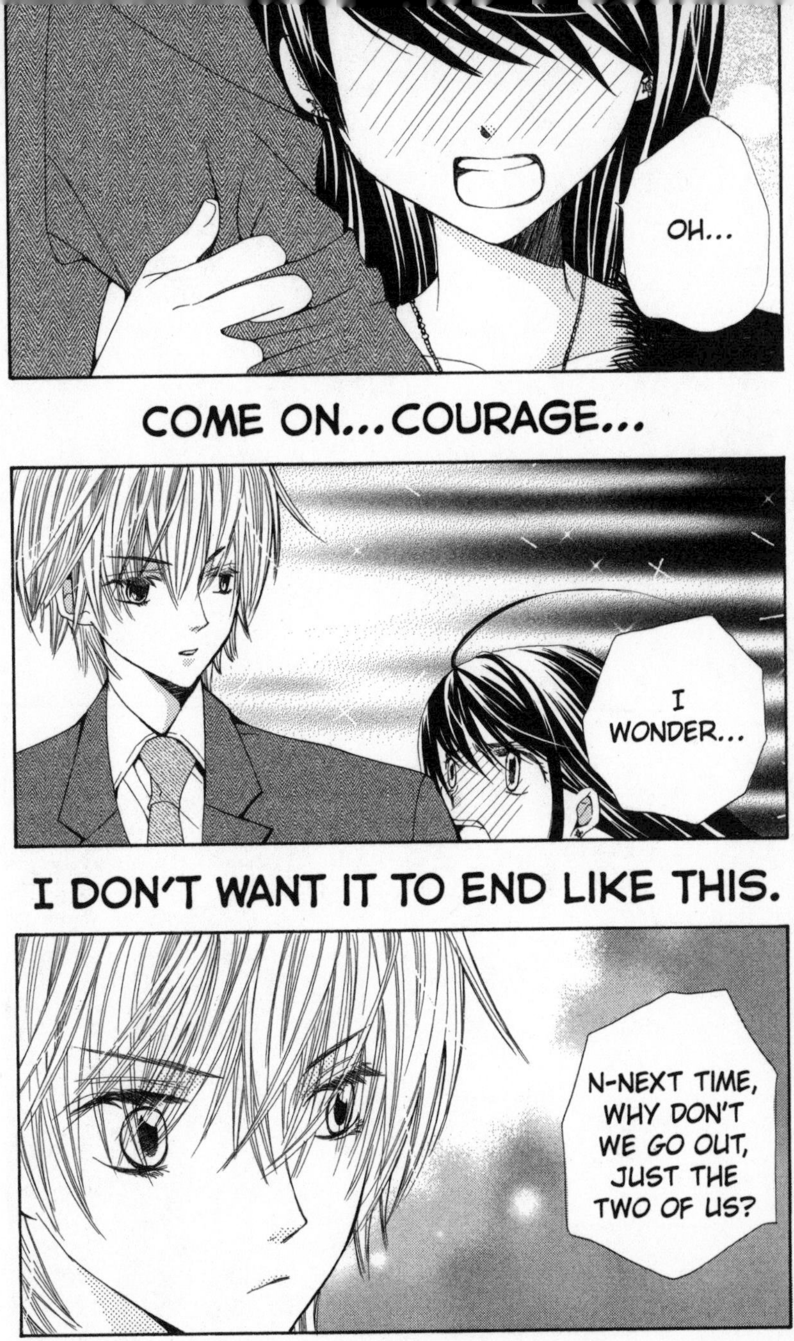
OH...
COME ON...COURAGE...
I WONDER...
I DON'T WANT IT TO END LIKE THIS.
N-NEXT TIME, WHY DON'T WE GO OUT, JUST THE TWO OF US?

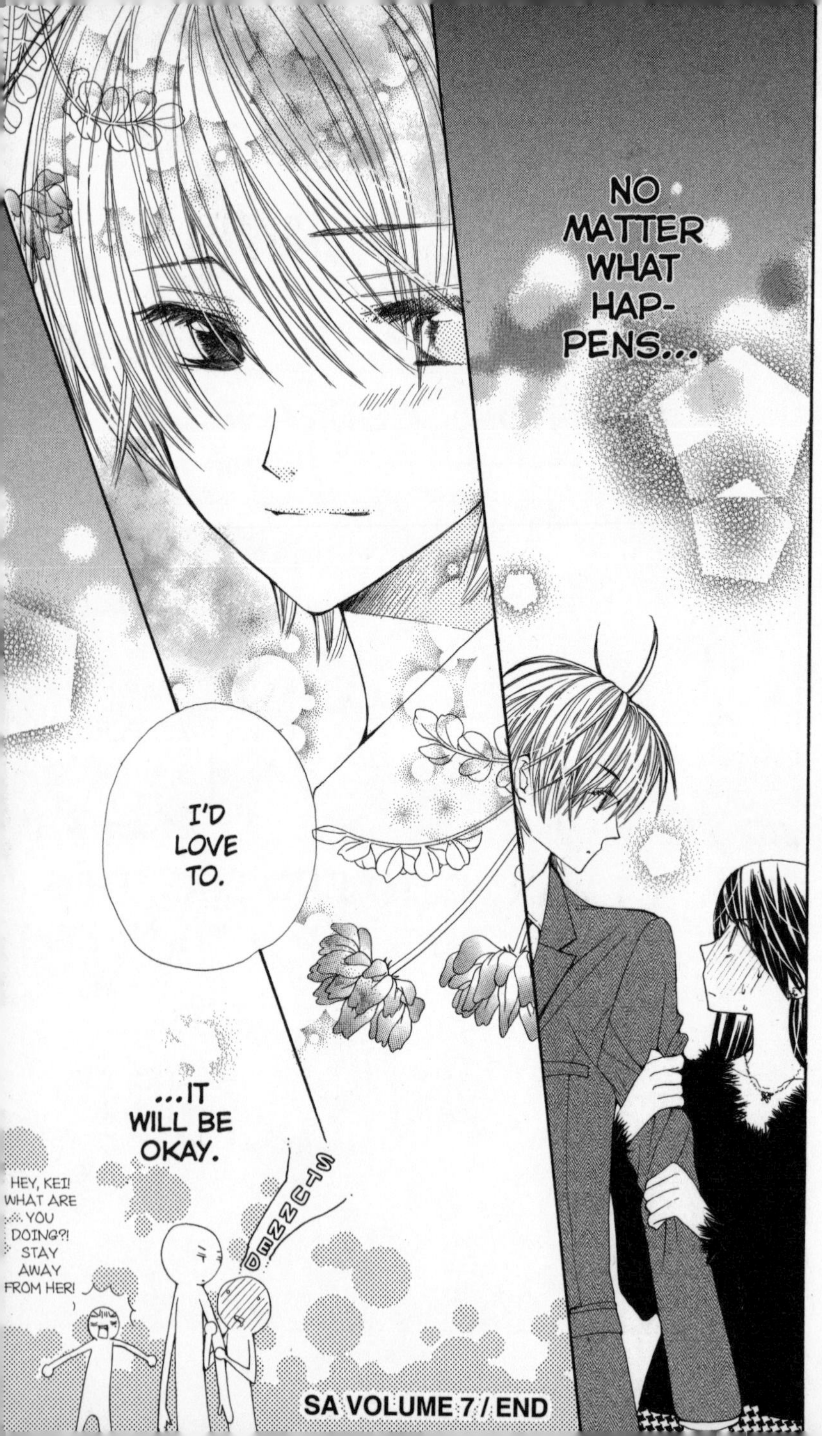

NO MATTER WHAT HAP-PENS...
I'D LOVE TO.
...IT WILL BE OKAY.
HEY, KEI! WHAT ARE YOU DOING?! STAY AWAY FROM HER!
SA VOLUME 7 / END

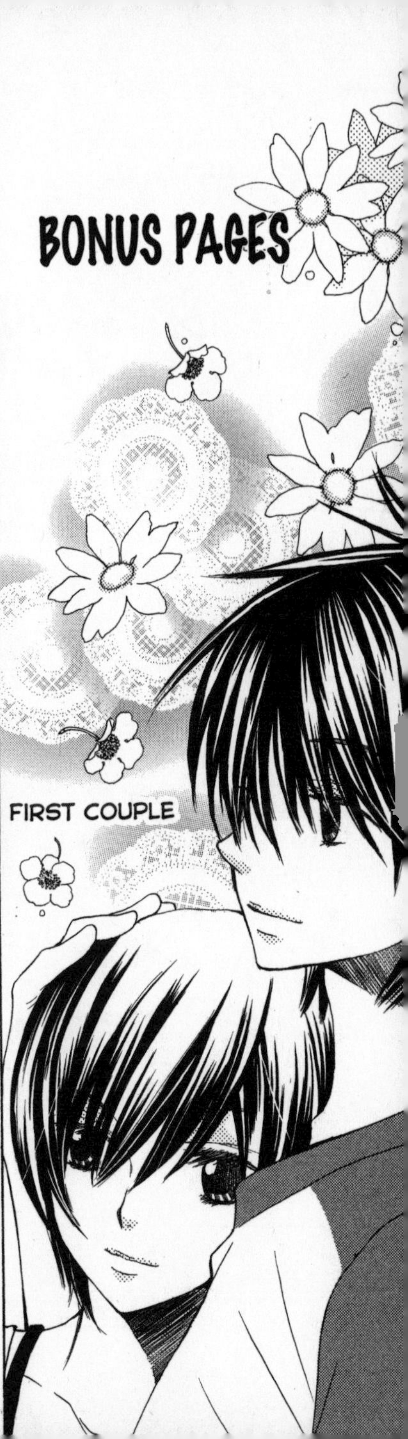
BONUS PAGES
FIRST COUPLE

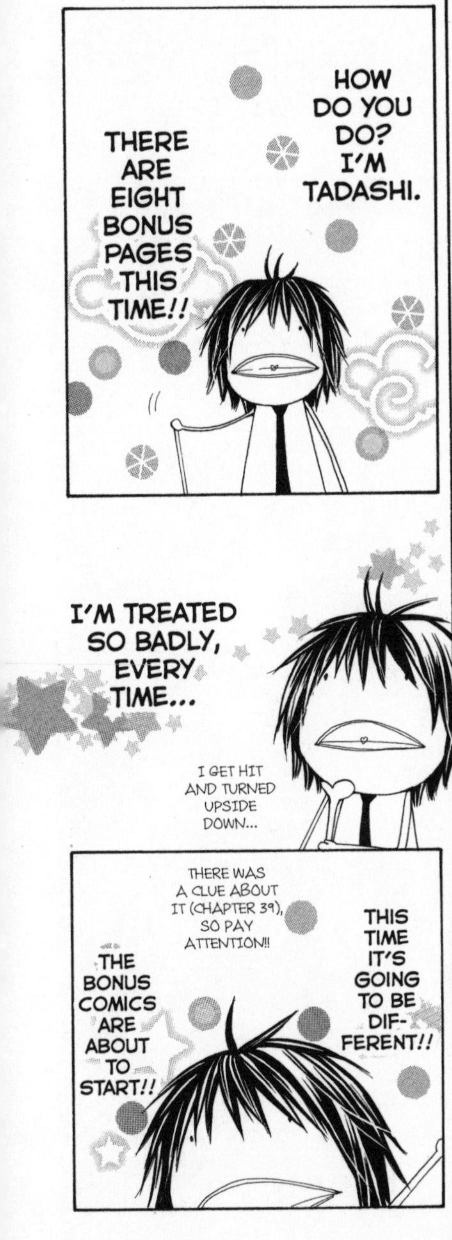
HOW DO YOU DO? I'M TADASHI.
THERE ARE EIGHT BONUS PAGES THIS TIME!!
I'M TREATED SO BADLY, EVERY TIME...
I GET HIT AND TURNED UPSIDE DOWN...
THIS TIME IT'S GOING TO BE DIF-FERENT!!
THERE WAS A CLUE ABOUT IT (CHAPTER 39), SO PAY ATTENTION!!
THE BONUS COMICS ARE ABOUT TO START!!

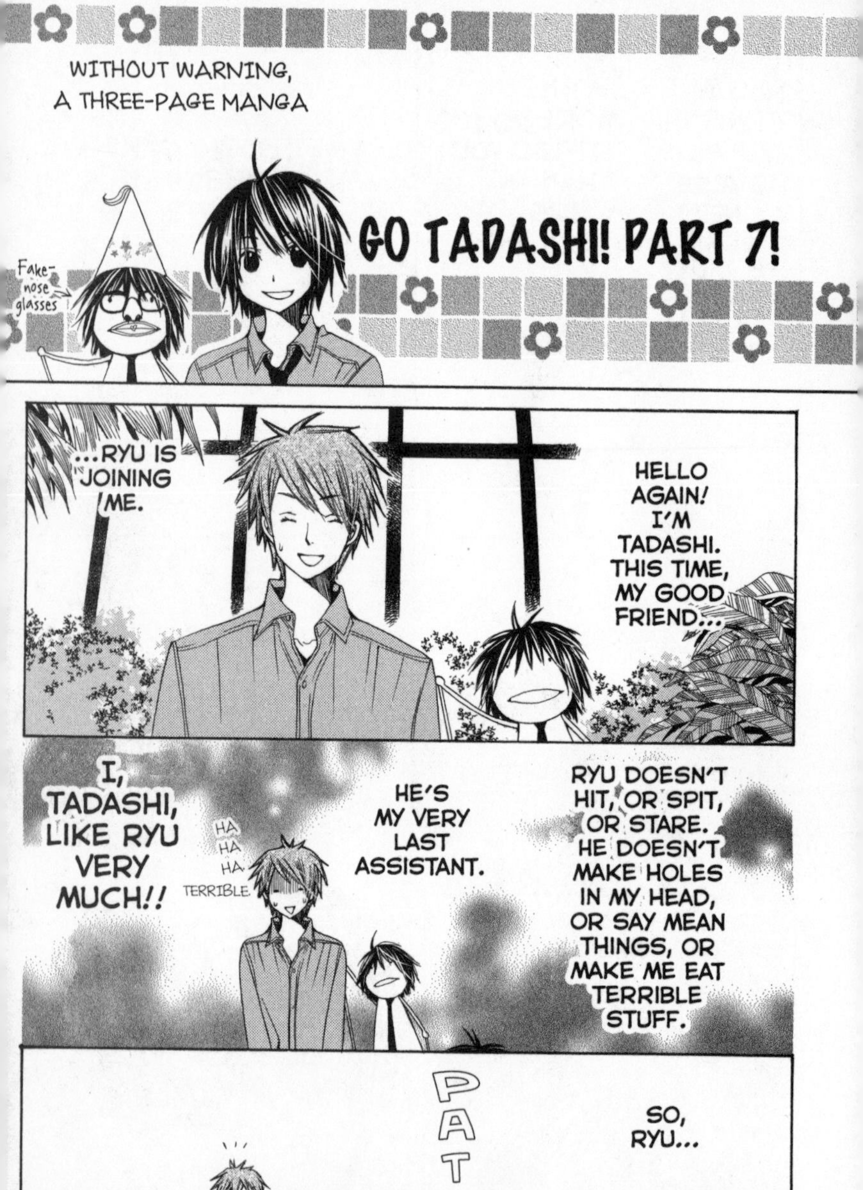
WITHOUT WARNING, A THREE-PAGE MANGA
GO TADASHI! PART 7!
Fake-nose glasses
HELLO AGAIN! I'M TADASHI. THIS TIME, MY GOOD FRIEND...
...RYU IS JOINING ME.
RYU DOESN'T HIT, OR SPIT, OR STARE. HE DOESN'T MAKE HOLES IN MY HEAD, OR SAY MEAN THINGS, OR MAKE ME EAT TERRIBLE STUFF.
HE'S MY VERY LAST ASSISTANT.
HA HA HA
TERRIBLE
I, TADASHI, LIKE RYU VERY MUCH!!
SO, RYU...
PAT

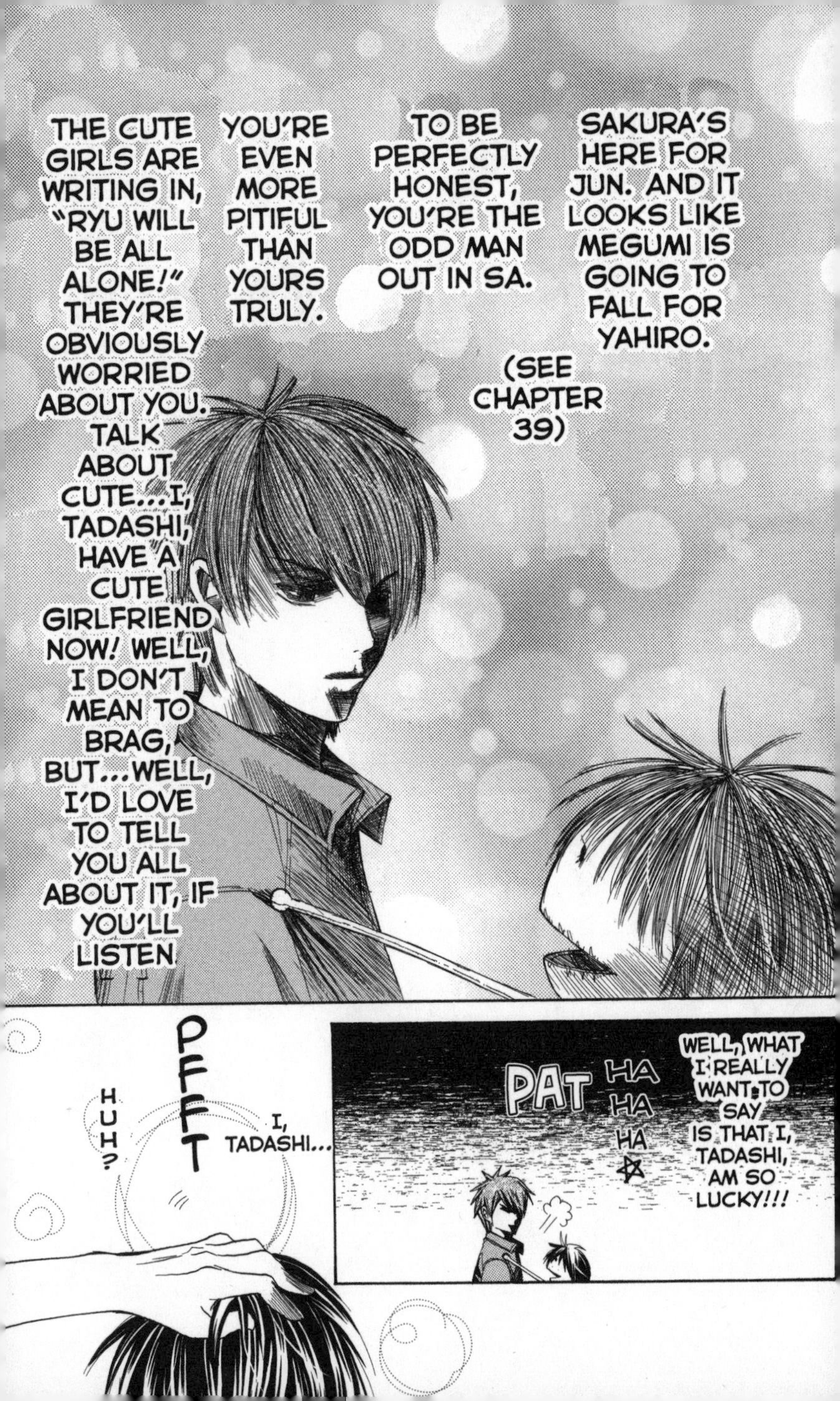
SAKURA'S HERE FOR JUN. AND IT LOOKS LIKE MEGUMI IS GOING TO FALL FOR YAHIRO.
(SEE CHAPTER 39)
TO BE PERFECTLY HONEST, YOU'RE THE ODD MAN OUT IN SA.
YOU'RE EVEN MORE PITIFUL THAN YOURS TRULY.
THE CUTE GIRLS ARE WRITING IN, "RYU WILL BE ALL ALONE!" THEY'RE OBVIOUSLY WORRIED ABOUT YOU. TALK ABOUT CUTE...I, TADASHI, HAVE A CUTE GIRLFRIEND NOW! WELL, I DON'T MEAN TO BRAG, BUT...WELL, I'D LOVE TO TELL YOU ALL ABOUT IT, IF YOU'LL LISTEN
WELL, WHAT I REALLY WANT TO SAY IS THAT I, TADASHI, AM SO LUCKY!!!
PAT
HA HA HA
I, TADASHI...
PFFT
HUH?

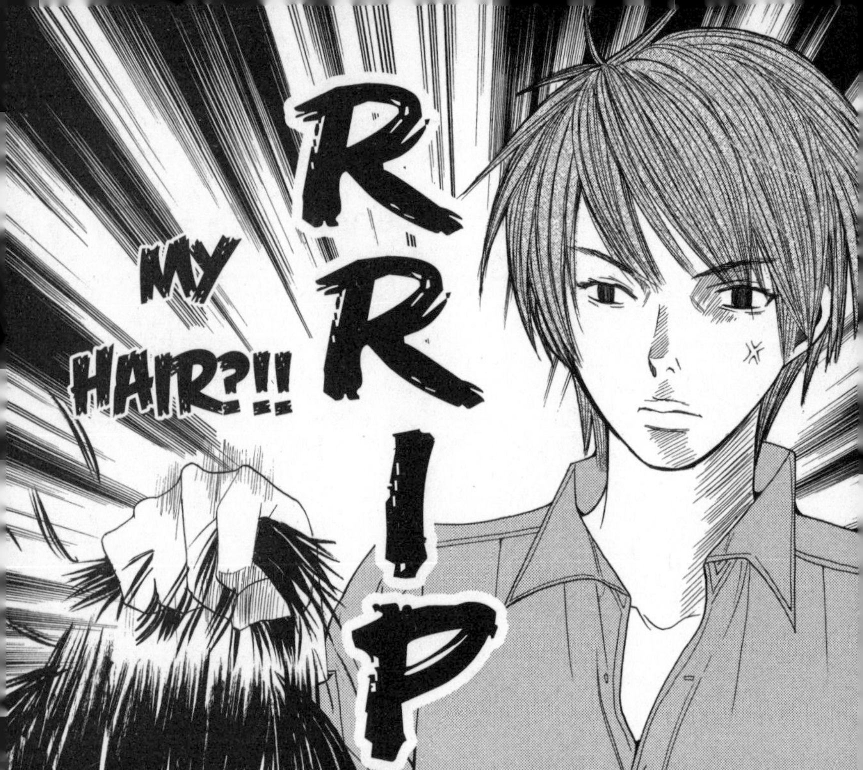
RRIP
MY HAIR?!!

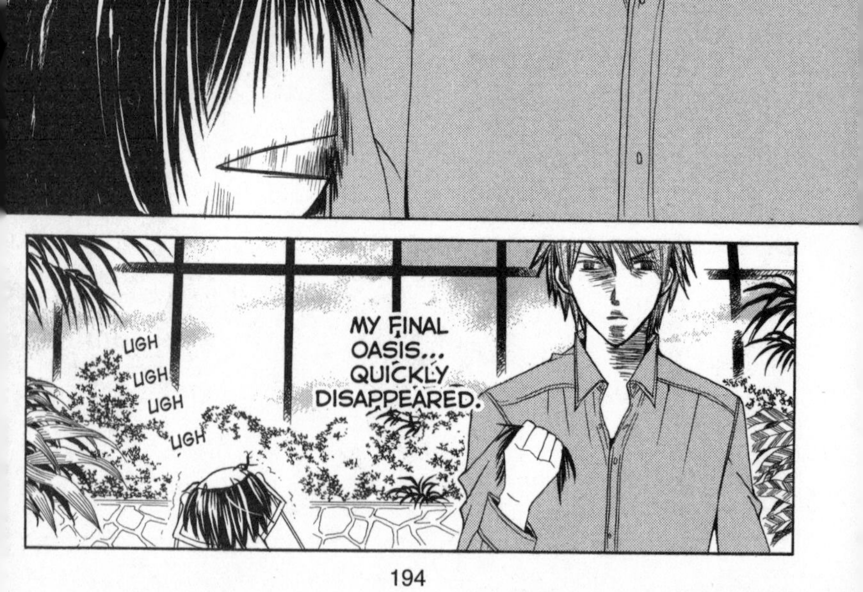
MY FINAL OASIS... QUICKLY DISAPPEARED.
UGH
UGH
UGH
UGH

WITHOUT WARNING, A FOUR-PAGE MANGA

GO, TADASHI! PART 7.5!

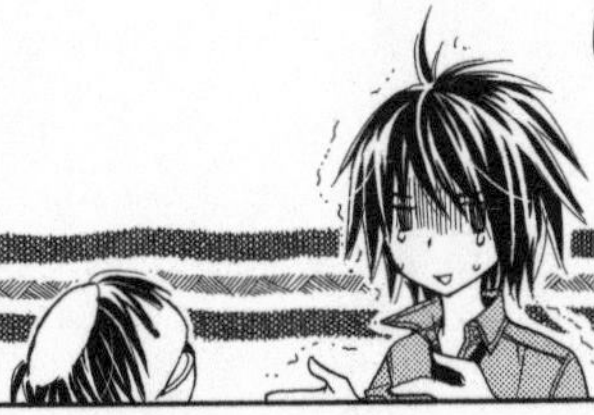

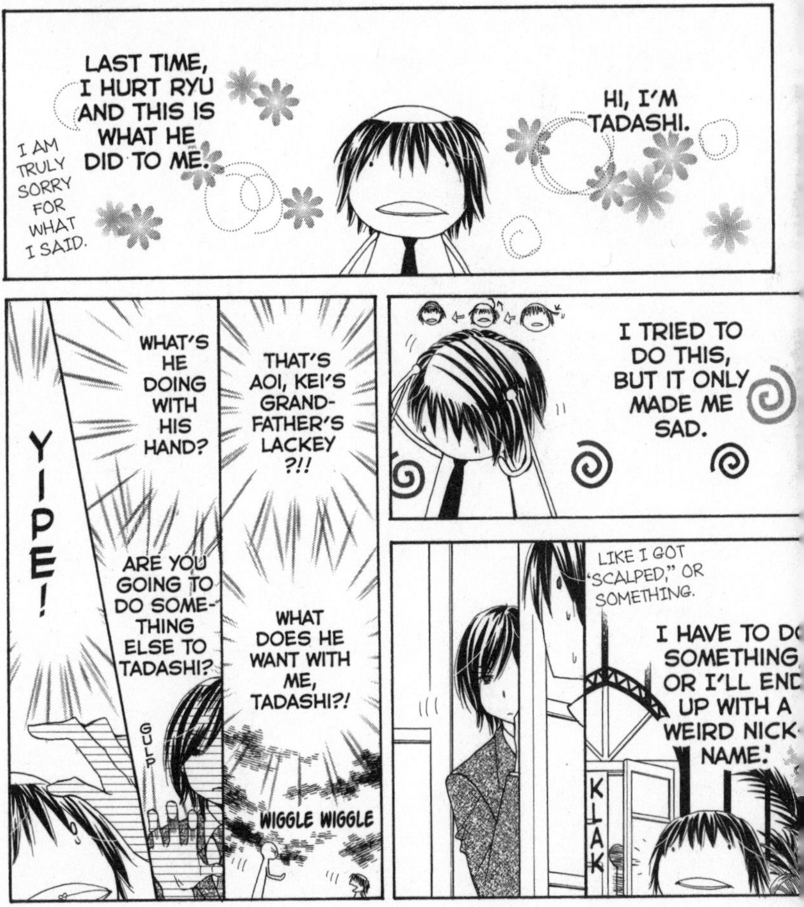
HI, I'M TADASHI.
LAST TIME, I HURT RYU AND THIS IS WHAT HE DID TO ME.
I AM TRULY SORRY FOR WHAT I SAID.
I TRIED TO DO THIS, BUT IT ONLY MADE ME SAD.
I HAVE TO DO SOMETHING, OR I'LL END UP WITH A WEIRD NICK-NAME.
LIKE I GOT "SCALPED," OR SOMETHING.
KLAK
THAT'S AOI, KEI'S GRAND-FATHER'S LACKEY?!!
WHAT DOES HE WANT WITH ME, TADASHI?!
WIGGLE WIGGLE
WHAT'S HE DOING WITH HIS HAND?
YIPE!
ARE YOU GOING TO DO SOME-THING ELSE TO TADASHI?
GULP

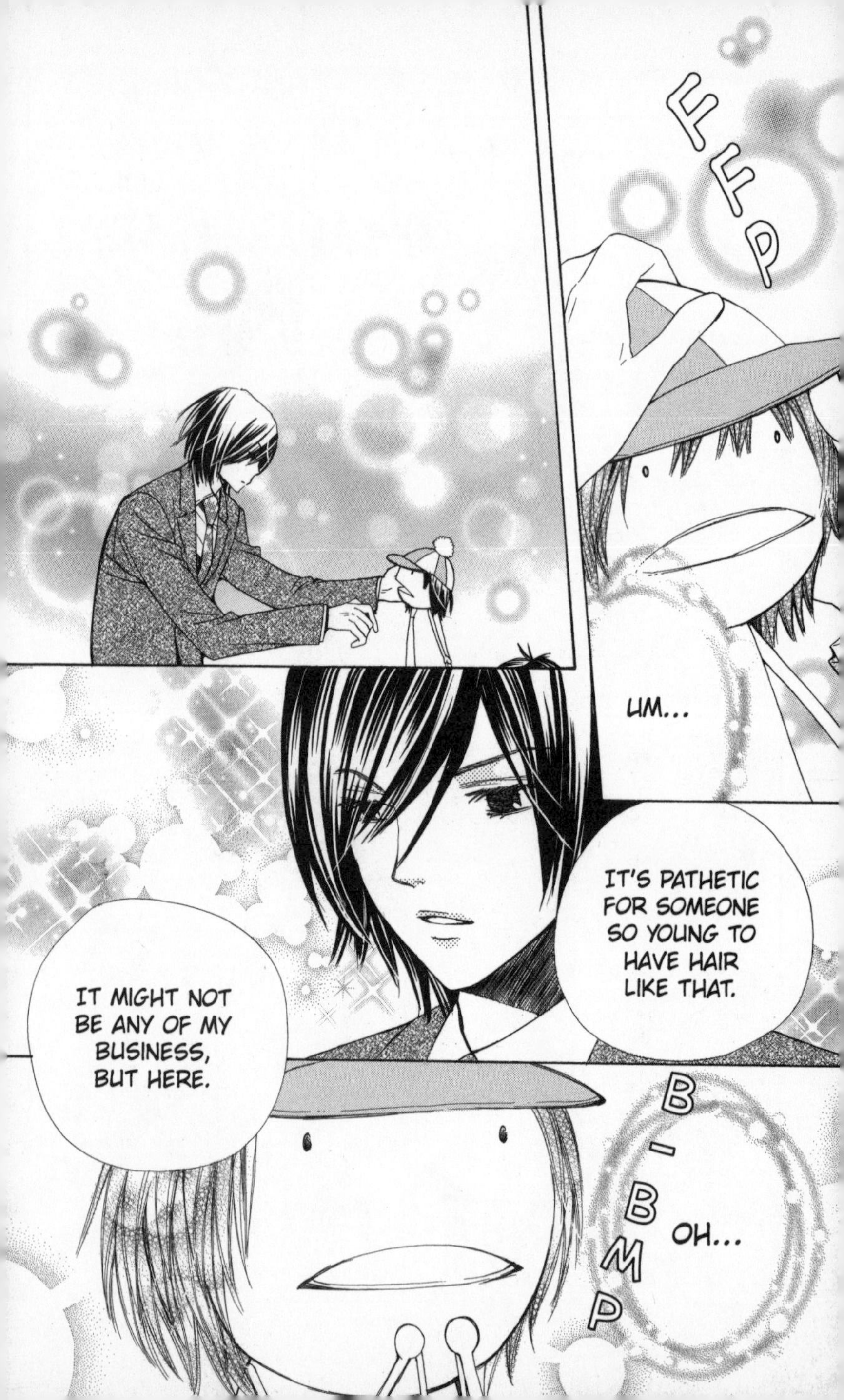
FFFP
UM...
IT'S PATHETIC FOR SOMEONE SO YOUNG TO HAVE HAIR LIKE THAT.
IT MIGHT NOT BE ANY OF MY BUSINESS, BUT HERE.
B-BMP
OH...

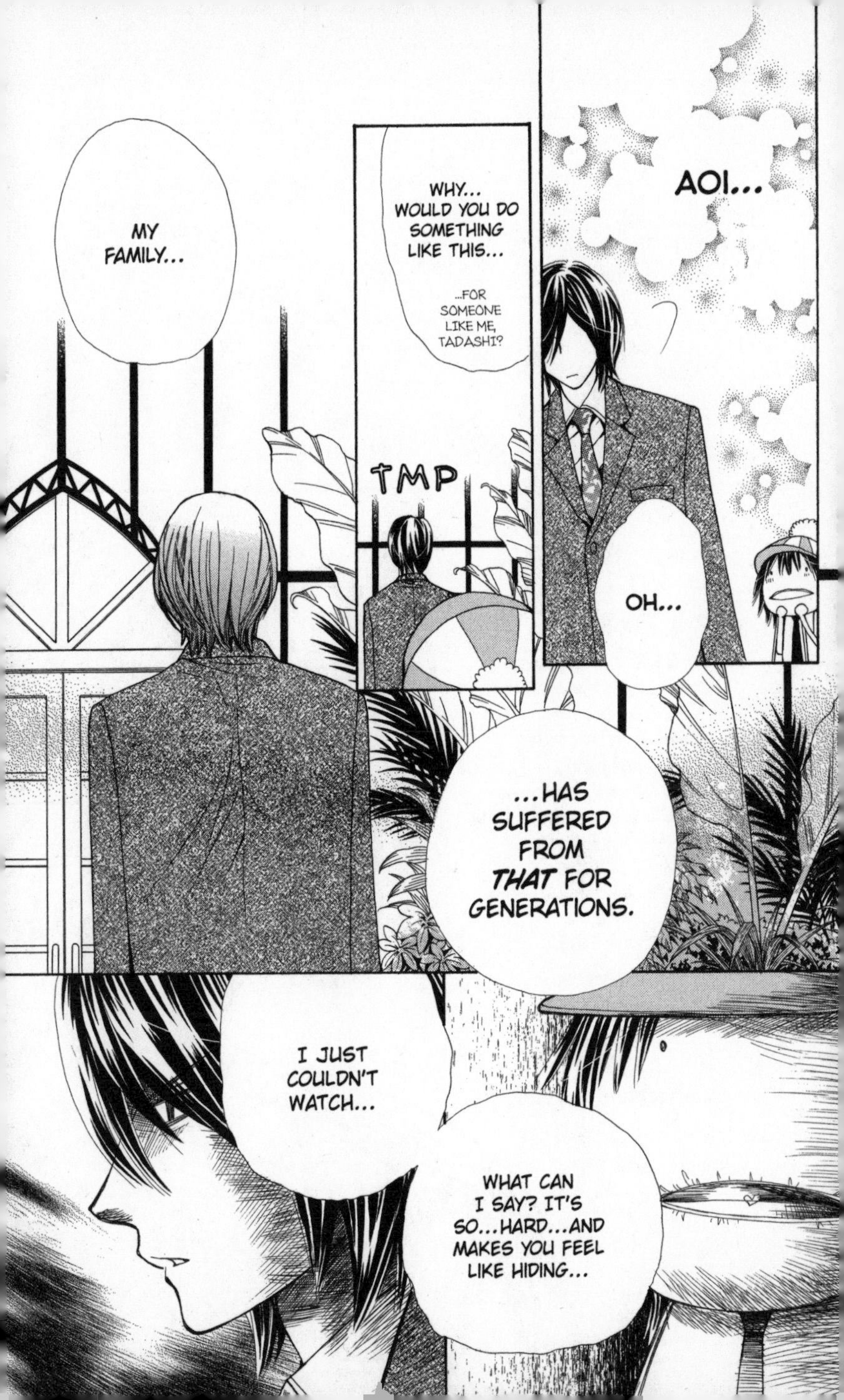
AOI...
OH...
WHY... WOULD YOU DO SOMETHING LIKE THIS...
...FOR SOMEONE LIKE ME, TADASHI?
TMP
MY FAMILY...
...HAS SUFFERED FROM *THAT* FOR GENERATIONS.
I JUST COULDN'T WATCH...
WHAT CAN I SAY? IT'S SO...HARD...AND MAKES YOU FEEL LIKE HIDING...

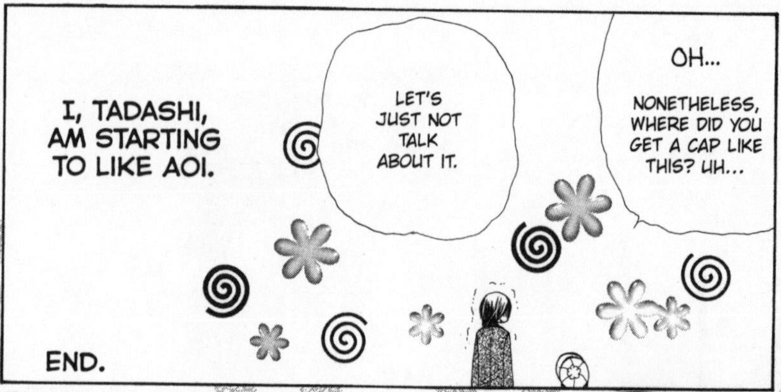
OH...
NONETHELESS, WHERE DID YOU GET A CAP LIKE THIS? UH...
LET'S JUST NOT TALK ABOUT IT.
I, TADASHI, AM STARTING TO LIKE AOI.
END.

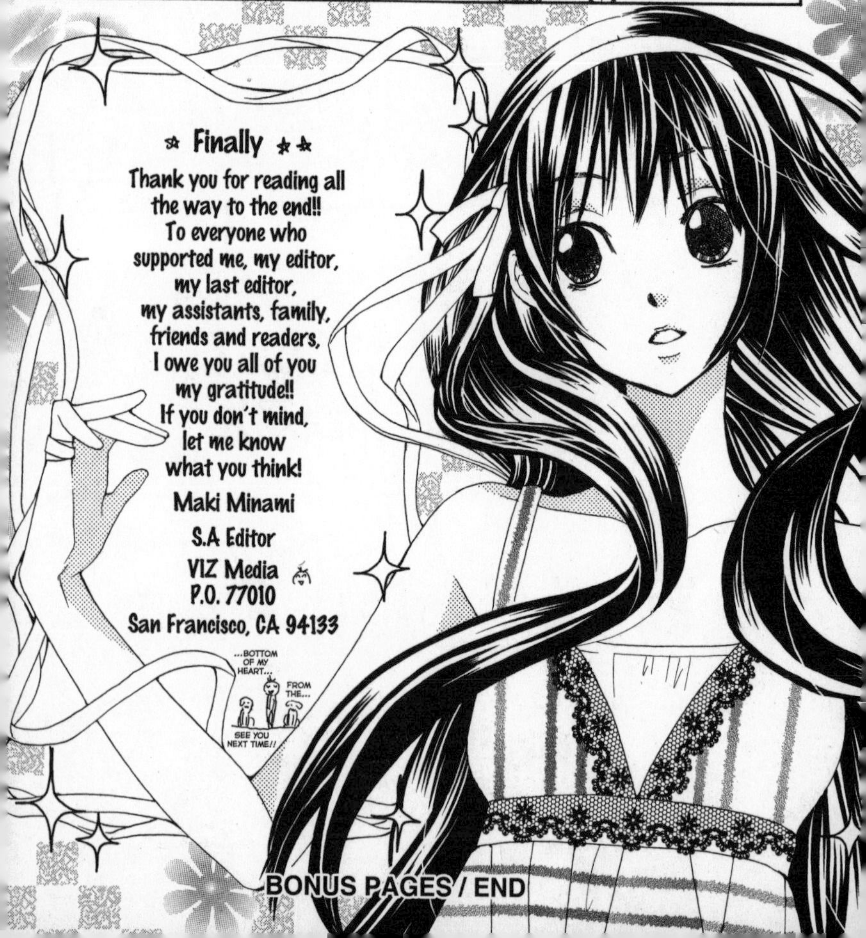
Finally
Thank you for reading all the way to the end!! To everyone who supported me, my editor, my last editor, my assistants, family, friends and readers, I owe you all of you my gratitude!! If you don't mind, let me know what you think!
Maki Minami
S.A Editor
VIZ Media
P.O. 77010
San Francisco, CA 94133
...BOTTOM OF MY HEART...
FROM THE...
SEE YOU NEXT TIME!!
BONUS PAGES / END

Maki Minami is from Saitama
prefecture in Japan. She debuted
in 2001 with *Kanata no Ao*
(Faraway Blue). Her other works
include *Kimi wa Girlfriend*
(You're My Girlfriend), *Mainichi
ga Takaramono* (Every Day Is a
Treasure) and *Yuki Atataka*
(Warm Winter). *S•A* is her current
series in Japan's *Hana to Yume*
magazine.

S•A

Vol. 7

The Shojo Beat Manga Edition

STORY & ART BY

MAKI MINAMI

English Adaptation/Amanda Hubbard
Translation/JN Productions
Touch-up Art & Lettering/HudsonYards
Design/Izumi Hirayama
Interior Design/Deirdre Shiozawa
Editor/Jonathan Tarbox

Editor in Chief, Books/Alvin Lu
Editor in Chief, Magazines/Marc Weidenbaum
VP, Publishing Licensing/Rika Inouye
VP, Sales & Product Marketing/Gonzalo Ferreyra
VP, Creative/Linda Espinosa
Publisher/Hyoe Narita

Printed in Canada

Published by VIZ Media, LLC
P.O. Box 77010
San Francisco, CA 94107

Shojo Beat Manga Edition
10 9 8 7 6 5 4 3 2 1
First printing, November 2008

www.viz.com
store.viz.com

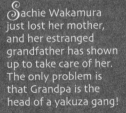

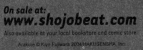

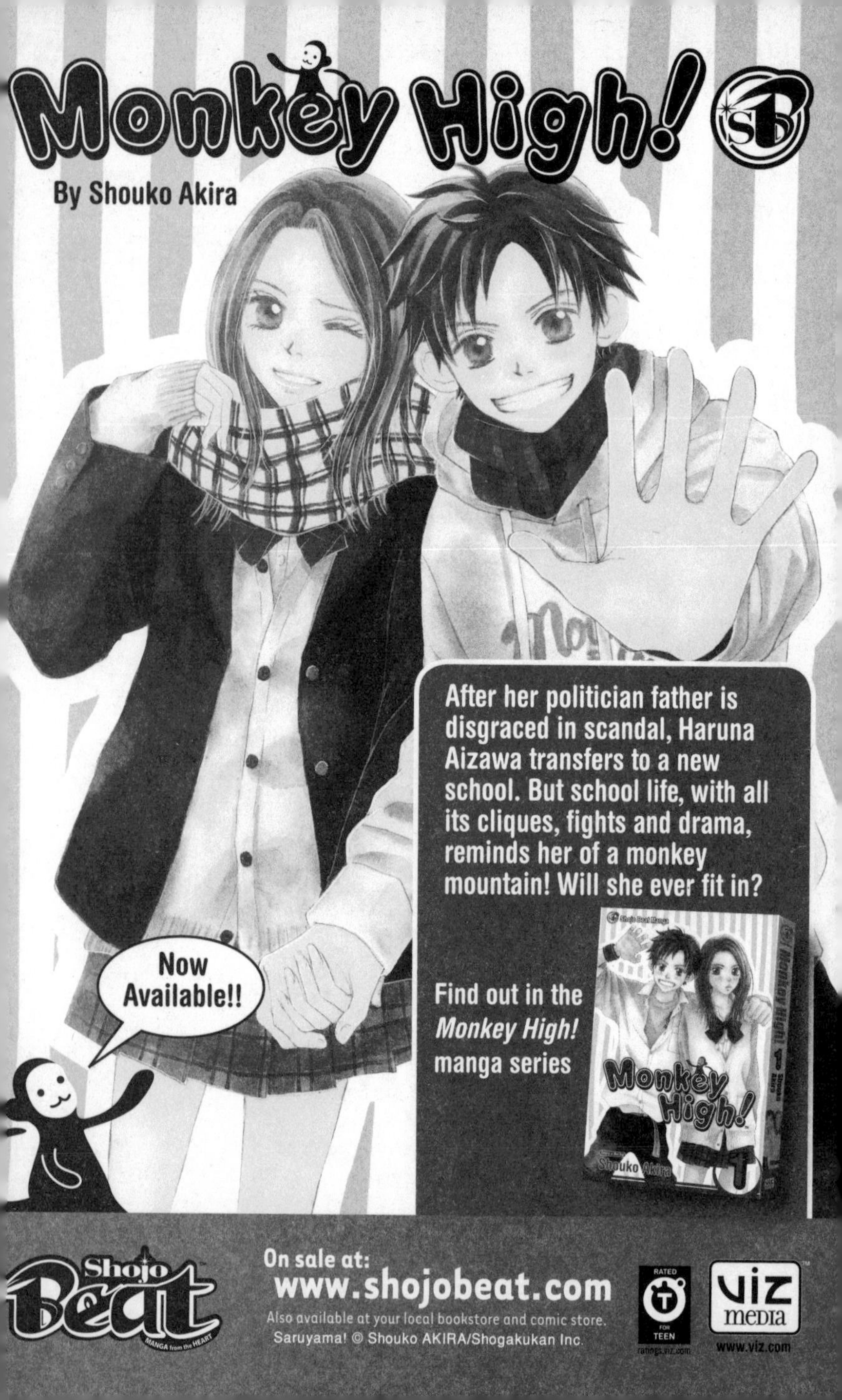
Monkey High!
By Shouko Akira
After her politician father is disgraced in scandal, Haruna Aizawa transfers to a new school. But school life, with all its cliques, fights and drama, reminds her of a monkey mountain! Will she ever fit in?
Now Available!!
Find out in the *Monkey High!* manga series
Monkey High!
Shouko Akira
Shojo Beat
MANGA from the HEART
On sale at:
www.shojobeat.com
Also available at your local bookstore and comic store.
Saruyama! © Shouko AKIRA/Shogakukan Inc.
RATED T FOR TEEN
ratings.viz.com
VIZ media
www.viz.com

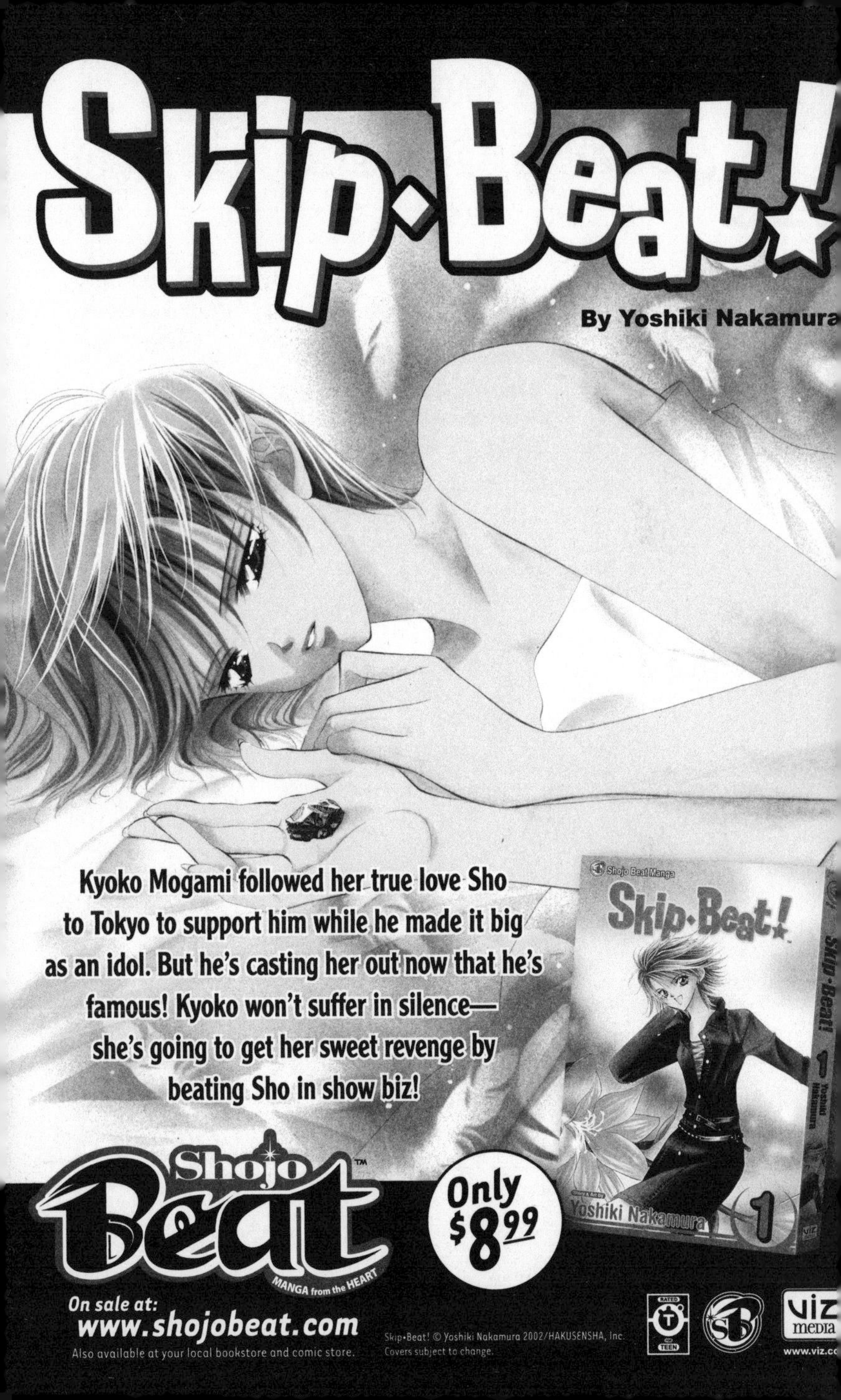
Skip·Beat!
By Yoshiki Nakamura
Kyoko Mogami followed her true love Sho to Tokyo to support him while he made it big as an idol. But he's casting her out now that he's famous! Kyoko won't suffer in silence— she's going to get her sweet revenge by beating Sho in show biz!
Shojo Beat Manga
Skip·Beat!
Skip·Beat!
1
Yoshiki Nakamura
Yoshiki Nakamura
1
Shojo Beat™
MANGA from the HEART
Only $8.99
On sale at:
www.shojobeat.com
Also available at your local bookstore and comic store.
Skip•Beat! © Yoshiki Nakamura 2002/HAKUSENSHA, Inc.
Covers subject to change.
RATED T TEEN
viz media
www.viz.co

Tell us what you think about Shojo Beat Manga!

Our survey is now available online. Go to:

shojobeat.com/mangasurvey

Help us make our product offerings better!